Writing Fiction

Writing Fiction

A GUIDE TO NARRATIVE CRAFT

Third Edition

Janet Burroway

Florida State University

HarperCollins*Publishers*

Sponsoring Editor: Lisa Moore
Project Coordination, Text Design: Editorial Services of New England, Inc.
Cover Design: Hannus Design
Cover Photo: Animals, Animals/Earth Sciences, © Robert Maier
Production Manager: Michael Weinstein
Compositor: Compset, Inc.
Printer and Binder: R.R. Donnelley & Sons Company
Cover Printer: The Lehigh Press, Inc.

HarperCollins has made available an impressive array of high quality video and audiotape productions of literary works to enhance students' experience of literature. For more information, contact your local HarperCollins representative or the Marketing Manager for Literature, College Division, HarperCollins Publishers, 10 East 53rd Street, NY, NY 10022.

For permission to use copyrighted material, grateful acknowledgment is made to the copyright holders on p. 390, which are hereby made part of this copyright page.

Writing Fiction: A Guide to Narrative Craft, Third Edition

Copyright © 1992 by Janet Burroway

Library of Congress Cataloging-in-Publication Data

Burroway, Janet.
    Writing fiction : a guide to narrative craft / Janet Burroway.—
3rd. ed.
        p.   cm.
    Includes bibliographical references and index.
    1. Fiction—Technique.   I. Title.
PN3355.B79   1991
808.3—dc20   91-25654
                                                                    CIP

ISBN 0-673-52119-2

        94 9 8 7 6 5

For David Daiches, mentor and friend

CONTENTS

PREFACE

The student in my desk-side chair has pale hair she drags between thumb and finger. One shin is wrapped around the other under a stonewashed skirt. "I'm ashamed to show it to you," she says. "I can't get it right." Her shame blotches her neck. "I try and try; it just *won't*. . . ." This young woman is talented. She has a quirky command of imagery, wry dialogue at once sexy and sinister; her apathetic characters do credibly violent things. She begins to cry.

The young man has black hair slicked back. He frisbees the manuscript onto my desk. "This is an extra," he says for the third time this week. "Take a look. I think you'll get a kick out of it." His ankles articulate like hinges under the rungs of the chair. His eyes zap my computer screen. His stories are bratpack-slick and turbo-paced and thin. He already self-publishes a magazine on the Macintosh his Dad sent up from Miami. An A in the course matters to him more than sex or money.

This one has vague eyes—grass? madness? mere preoccupation?—and his hair is a congregation of cowlicks. "What I thought; the *doorbell* . . . but I don't know. He comes around to see them, right, it's not clear why. Does he stay? that's the thing. You think?" The tale whereof he speaks is a wildly brilliant mess. Its so-called plot wanders and flails, its surreal personnages leer and galumph in a setting sired by Kafka out of Djuna Barnes; the language flares like an accident in a fireworks factory. "I know, like you said, *form*, but. . . ."

These students will pass into the insurance industry, academia, counseling, husbandry, wifery, public relations, drug-running, state government. Or not. They will continue to write. Or not. For each one of them (and the other dozen in the workshop) I could years hence construct a thumbnail sketch with the message that he or she was recognizably a writer in the making. I know enough not to take any bets on which one I will be asked to write it for. At the end of two or three years in the Writing Program, some who arrived with talent will not have moved on, while some who showed nothing but dedication and cliché will have become writers. Some will have acquired the dedication. Some will make an evolutionary leap. If my students have taught me one thing in twenty years of teaching writing, it is that though I can assess their achievement, I cannot predict it.

If they have taught me two things, the humbling second is that the desire to write in all its modes—ferocity, arrogance, self-doubt, determination, dull despair—bears no relation whatever to ability. We share it all alike.

As a student in the fifties I was, unconsciously, committed to the American notion of a "star system," which is only a vulgar manifestation of a "canon." I was greedy for the creative writing courses that were just beginning to be respectable because I thought they could show me how to be a "great" writer.

When I went on to study in England, I was doubly struck with the unpretentious workaday attitude of writers and actors and with the respect that the professional worlds in those two spheres accorded beginners. (Since that time England has learned a poor lesson from us in this respect, and it now seems to me that there's both a star system and a closed shop.)

But later, on the other side of the podium, I still saw my job as imparting some of the skills of writing to students generally, while I waited for the star student whom I would then help to become a professional and who would provide the *raison d'être* of my teaching.

Now I see it otherwise.

Like most of my colleagues in the writing program boom through the seventies and eighties, I have felt a nagging ambivalence about the teaching of creative writing. Were we giving false hopes to untalented young writers and spawning dozens of little magazines produced by people who couldn't otherwise get published for the entertainment of their amateurish friends? Or were we the monks of the new dark ages, keeping the language alive in our workshop cloisters? Was the truth somewhere in the middle, or at both extremes?

Then at some point I began to hold the "little" magazines in high regard. As telecommunications swallow the custom of writing letters, the least professional of the literary journals are a kind of correspondence; and as the corporate giants swallow the trade publishers, the best magazines provide an alternative place for good writers to get published.

In the classroom, I saw that I could interest writers in reading, and would need to. Literacy is diminishing even as we realize that our ideas of literature are provincial. Literature and creative writing, both, will now have to be taught in universities for the same reason that philosophy is taught—because they are not part of the everyday experience of most people. I observed as a curious paradox, as if it were unconnected, that students with shaky values and small evidence of literary taste could nevertheless, out of their massive television experience, turn a joke, tag a character, shape a plot, produce a recognition scene, or foreshadow, plant, reveal, or betray a truth through a stage lie.

It now seems to me not a curiosity and not merely inexplicable, but a *mystery* that students who have not read nevertheless arrive at university wanting, often passionately, to write. They have some kind of connection with the language that is not satisfied by the passive relationship they have had with it through television. Television is ineluctably seductive. It usurps entirely the escape function of literature, which was always its first lure, and it does so promising that the escape costs no effort.

But by the time these people are eighteen or twenty they have been cheated the way drugs cheat; the effortlessness leaves emptiness. You don't own it if you haven't put any energy into it. And so they come wanting to write. Yes, they want to "express themselves"—there's a therapeutic aspect in all writing—but they also perceive, perhaps dimly, that language has to do with being human, and that they need it at the deepest level, for identity.

In a 1985 survey done for the NEA, it was shown that a quarter of the adults in America believe they write fiction or poetry. *A quarter of the adults in America believe they write fiction or poetry.* This cannot be true. But it argues for more than widespread self-deception. People used to put a lot of effort into writing letters that had an audience of one. Few now think there is much point in writing letters. But in spite of the grim trashy things that are being done with and to the language by all the wielders of pomp, power, and finance, people still want to connect through the written word.

The backlash against creative writing as a university subject is in full flood. Like any backlash it has the substance of the original prejudice in a slightly more sophisticated form. Whereas the fiction courses of the forties were supposed to produce formula adventure for pulp magazines, those of the eighties are charged with producing formula pap for literary magazines.

To Donald Morton and Mas'ud Zavarzadeh, the creative writing workshop fosters only realism, of which minimalism is a subset; for Tom Wolfe the workshop prevents realism, of which minimalism is the antithesis. Joseph Epstein deplores an atmosphere that dictates against genius; the chorus of postmodernists hoots down the notion of genius as hegemony, but agrees that writing stories is too *soft.*

My students don't follow this controversy much—they tend to spend their time on Gustav Flaubert, Eudora Welty, and Margaret Atwood—and when they hear of it, they do not shiver with recognition. I don't either. It is true that on the road to competence, students (and perhaps magazines, decades, media) often pass through a period in which they try each other's strengths and ape each other's successes. It is a kind of learning. Some never get beyond it. But it would be a gross misreading of young writers to suppose that they can't recognize, or don't reward, genuine originality.

One of the things the condemnations of writing programs have in common is a punitive attitude toward those who want to write without having what the critics consider sufficient talent. This is the only-geniuses-need-apply view of fiction and poetry. It is certainly true that many students' desire to write is tainted by false reverence toward writers and artists, a fuzzy notion of genius, and a bedazzlement by celebrity. The students thus fooled attach themselves to writing as to a talisman of magical ascent. But the set of false assumptions they ascribe to is not different from that of the critics who want to scold them for attempting to write. It is the same set. Both sides use the name "Writer" for purposes of name-dropping; they mean to ennoble themselves by knowing it.

Whatever else it argues, the case against creative writing assumes that competence will prevent rather than promote excellence. This seems to me preposterous as a general idea, and it isn't what I see happening in the classroom, which is that competence, excellence, and originality grow together. In Bali everybody's a dancer. It's very good for Bali, and for dance.

Certainly the imaginative activity in the ivory tower has an effect on the world that is commonly referred to as real. The function of the New York and Boston publishers has changed. As the great trade houses knuckle under to their accountants, the university and "little" presses become prestigious places to publish, and the former continue to make writers rich and famous. This they've always done; but they also used to choose who to do it to. Now the nation-wide complex of writing programs, conferences, and literary magazines gently float their best toward the East. Clever New York agents and editors show up at the headwaters and backwaters in Iowa City, Salt Lake, Austin, and Tallahassee.

Basically this pleases and amuses me, though I tell my students that literary success is also a great crapshoot; and in the classroom we don't spend a lot of time talking about it. I used to say, quite blithely, "Of course, you can't teach *talent*," but now I am less sure what talent is, and what its relation is to models and criticism and encouragement. Good writing comes from an ability to connect the interior richness of which all of us are possessed—*all*—with the structure of the language. Creative writing is taught when a teacher helps a student make that connection through verse or story or the stage. This happens only sometimes, but there seems to be no limit to the ways that it can happen.

Sports and literature are the two great surrogates for war, exercising without disaster the impulses toward struggle, competition, the triumph of survival. Business is too tainted with power on the one hand and the possibility of subsistence failure on the other, to operate as a metaphor; the arts outside of literature are not to the same degree dependent on the concepts of struggle and endurance.

We need surrogates for war, and it's good to have a choice. Some people are good at sports and some are good at stories. Writing ought, in my view, to hold a position in our society more or less like playing tennis. A passable amateur tennis player may exercise her skill often, even obsessively, can involve some few others as partners and spectators, can struggle to improve and feel exhilarated by the struggle. It's impressive if she turns pro, but no one despises her for devoting a portion of most days to the game, even if no one will ever pay money to watch her play. Nobody says that because tennis requires innate talent, the buff is an embarrassment.

By the same token, the amateur—that is, lover of—the game does not suppose that because he can catch felt on catgut three returns out of five, he is just a lucky break away from Wimbledon. He does it for the doing. Because although it's hard to get revved up for it, once you start the momentum carries you; because you get better when you work at it; because the effort makes you sweat and it feels good to have done it.

I think we ought to think of writing more like that.

My own expectations as a teacher of writing are quite modest. I only want my students, when they leave me, to write with more accuracy, more eloquence, more originality, and a better sense of the relationship between their language and their truth than the President of the United States. In the twenty years I have been teaching this has not been too much to ask.

For the third edition of *Writing Fiction* I have added a chapter on revision, condensed the references to Aristotle, and expanded the sections on dialogue and action. I have changed most of the short stories, incorporating a couple of classics and some that are very new. I have acknowledged several new classroom techniques and academic perceptions of the writing process, and have tried to update what has staled and clarify what was muddy.

I have many people to thank for help, especially Claudia Johnson, who has shown me that friendship is collaboration, and vice versa; and Marjie Craig, Sheila Taylor, Peter Ruppert, Hilda Raz, and Carole Oles, whose warmth and intelligence sustain me. Bob Shacochis, Steve Bauer, Kevin Murphy, Jerry Stern, and Wendy Bishop had generous good advice. Many others offered excellent reactions, suggestions, insights, and provocations, and I would like to thank Tony Ardizzone, Max Steele, David Johnson, Robin Behn, Robert Love Taylor, Fran Adler, Mary Hazzard, Pery Glasser, Neil Shepard; my editor, Lisa Moore, and my copy editor, Fran Feldman.

Janet Burroway

WHATEVER WORKS
The Writing Process

Get Started
Keep Going

Get Started

What makes you want not to write?

There are a few lucky souls for whom the whole process of writing is easy, for whom the smell of fresh paper is better than air, whose minds chuckle perpetually over their own agility, who forget to eat, and who consider the world at large an intrusion on their good time at the typewriter. But you and I are not among them. Most of us don't like to write at all; we like to have written. We are caught in a guilty paradox in which we grumble over our lack of time, and when we have the time, we sharpen pencils, make phone calls, or clip the hedges. We are in love with words except when we have to face them. Our relationship to writing is uncomfortably like our relationship to dieting, exercise, housework, and charity: We feel better when we have done it, and feel better about ourselves when we have done it, but at any given moment we would rather do something—anything—else.

Of course, all this is overstated, and if there were no pleasure in writing, we wouldn't do it. We write for the satisfaction of having wrestled a sentence to the page, the joy of discovering an image, the excitement of having a character come alive; and even the most successful writers will sincerely say that these pleasures—not money, fame, or glamour—are the real rewards of writing. Nevertheless, we forget what such joy and satisfaction feel like when we confront a blank page.

The narrator of Anita Brookner's novel *Look at Me* records a familiar pattern.

> Sometimes it feels like a physical effort simply to sit down at the desk and pull out the notebook. Sometimes I find myself heaving a sigh when I read through what I have already written. Sometimes the effort of putting pen to paper is so great that I literally feel a pain in my head, as if all the furniture of my mind were being rearranged, as if it were being lined up, being got ready for delivery from the storehouse. And yet when I start to write, all this heaviness vanishes, and I feel charged with a kind of electricity, not unpleasant in itself, but leading, inevitably, to greater restlessness.

It helps to know that most writers share this anomalous reluctance, least wanting to do what we most want to do. It also helps to know some of the reasons for that reluctance.

Novelist Richard Koster offers a blanket absolution for what writers tend to think of as "wasting time"—that hour or two of muddled glaring at the page before a word will allow itself to be placed there. In the process of creating a fiction we must divorce ourselves from the real world, he points out. And that is hard. The real world is insistent not only in its distractions but also in its brute physical presence. To remove ourselves from that sphere and achieve a state in which our mental world is *more* real requires a disciplined effort of displacement.

We may even sense that it is unnatural or dangerous to live in a world of our own creation. People love to read stories about the dreamer who nobody thinks will come to much, and who turns out to be a genius inventor, scientist, artist, or savior. Part of the reason such stories work is that we like to escape from the way the world really works, including the way it works in us. We all feel the pressure of the practical. The writer may sympathize with the dreamer but forget to sympathize with the dreamer-in-himself-or-herself.

There's another impediment to beginning, expressed by a writer character in Lawrence Durrell's *Alexandria Quartet.* Durrell's Pursewarden broods over the illusory significance of what he is about to write, unwilling to begin in case he spoils it. Many of us do this: The idea, whatever it is, seems so luminous, whole, and fragile, that to begin to write about that idea is to commit it to rubble. Knowing in advance that words will never exactly capture what we mean or intend, we must gingerly and gradually work ourselves into a state of accepting what words can do instead. No matter how many times we find out that what words can do is quite all right, we shy again from the next beginning. Against this wasteful impulse I have a motto over my desk that reads: "Don't Dread; Do." It's a fine motto, and I contemplated it for several weeks before I began writing this chapter.

The mundane daily habits of writers are apparently fascinating. No author offers to answer questions at the end of a public reading without being asked: *Do you write in the morning or at night? Do you write every day? Do you compose on the typewriter?* Sometimes such questions show a hagiographic interest in the workings of genius. More often, I think, they are a plea for practical help: *Is there something I can do to make this job less horrific? Is there a trick that will unlock my words?*

The variety of answers suggests that there is no magic to be found in any particular one. Donald Hall will tell you that he spends a dozen hours a day at his desk, moving back and forth between as many projects. Philip Larkin said that he wrote a poem only every eighteen months or so, and never tried to write one that was not a gift. Gail Godwin goes to her workroom every day "because what if the angel came and I wasn't there?" Diane Wakowski thinks that to sit at work against your will is evidence of bourgeois neurosis. Maria Irene Fornes begins her day with a half hour of loosening-up exercises, finding a comfortable "center of gravity" before she sits down to work. Mary Lee Settle advises that writers who teach *must* work in the morning, before the analytical habits of the classroom take over the brain; George Cuomo replies that he solves this problem by taking an afternoon nap. Dickens could not deal with people when he was working: "The mere consciousness of an engagement will worry a whole day." Many writers find a word processor a companionable friend. Hemingway and Thomas Wolfe wrote standing up. Some writers can plop at the kitchen table without clearing the breakfast dishes; some need total seclusion, a beach, a cat, a string quartet.

There is something to be learned from all this, though. It is not an open sesame but a piece of advice older than fairy tales: Know thyself. The bottom line is that if you do not at some point write your story down, it will not get written. Having decided that you *will* write it, the question is not *how do you get it done?* but how do *you* get it done? Any discipline or indulgence that actually helps nudge you into position facing the page is acceptable and productive. If jogging after breakfast energizes your mind, then jog before you sit. If you have to pull an all-nighter on a coffee binge, do that. Some schedule, regularity, pattern in your writing day (or night) will always help, but only you can figure out what pattern is for you.

JOURNAL KEEPING

There are, though, a number of tricks you can teach yourself in order to free the writing self, and the essence of these is to give yourself permission to fail. The best place for permission is a private place, and for that reason a writer's journal is an essential, likely to be the source of originality, ideas, experimentation, and growth.

Keep a journal.

A journal is an intimate, a friend that will accept you as you are. Pick a notebook you like the look of, one you feel comfortable with, as you would pick a friend. I find a bound blank book too elegant to live up to, preferring instead a loose-leaf because I write my journal mainly at the computer and can stick anything in at the flip of a three-hole punch. But you can glue scribbled napkins into a spiral, too.

Keep the journal regularly, at least at first.

It doesn't matter what you write and it doesn't matter very much how much, but it does matter that you make a steady habit of the writing. A major advantage of keeping a journal regularly is that it will put you in the habit of observing in words. If you know at dawn that you are committed to writing so-and-so many words before dusk, you will half-consciously tell the story of your day to yourself as you live it, finding a phrase to catch whatever catches your eye. When that habit is established, you'll begin to find that whatever invites your attention or sympathy, your anger or curiosity, may be the beginning of invention. *Whoever* catches your attention may be the beginning of a character.

But before the habit is developed, you may find that even a blank journal page has the awesome aspect of a void, and you may need some tricks of permission to let yourself start writing there. The playwright Maria Irene Fornes says that there are two of you: one who wants to write and one who doesn't. The one who wants to write had better keep tricking the one who doesn't. Or another way to think of this conflict is between right brain and left brain—the spacial, playful, detail-loving creator, and the linear, cataloging, categorizing critic. The critic is an absolutely essential part of the writing process. The trick is to shut him or her up until there is something to criticize.

FREEWRITING

Freewriting is a technique that allows you to take very literally the notion of getting something down on paper. It can be done whenever you want to write, or just to free up the writing self. The idea is to put

> anything on paper and \i mean anything I , 'm doing it right now I have no idea if I'm going to get the idea acorss but I don' tcareit doesn't matter because if I just keep going, my fingers on the keyboard, makes a little tapdance sound what an awful Hollywoody metaphor I don't think I'll let this get in print but then on the other hand that'd the point, maabbe I can expose it for once just as is is typos and all there I think my two minutes is up but funny i don't want to look at the clock cause now it feels kind of good doesn't it always and that's part of the point too it's like when I get on the—oh, yeah—bike, I think I'll be exhausted by the corner but an hour later I'm just in my stride and wish I didn't have to stop.

That's freewriting. Its point is to keep going, and that is the only point. When the critic intrudes and tells you that what you're doing is awful, tell the critic to take a dive, or acknowledge her/him as you keep writing (*awful Hollywoody metaphor*), and keep writing. If you freewrite often, pretty soon you will be bored with writing about how you don't feel like writing (though that is as good a subject as any; the subject is of no importance whatever and neither is the quality of the writing), and you will find your mind and your phrases running on things that interest you. Fine. It doesn't matter. Freewriting is the literary equivalent of scales at the piano or a short gym workout. All that matters is that you do it. The verbal muscles will develop of their own accord.

Though freewriting is mere technique, it can affect the freedom of the content. Many writers feel themselves to be *an instrument through which,* rather than *a creator of,* and whether you think of this possibility as humble or holy, it is worth finding out what you say when you aren't monitoring it. Fiction is written not so much to inform as to find out, and if you force yourself into a mode of informing when you haven't yet found out, you're likely to end up pontificating, or lying some other way.

In *Becoming a Writer,* a book that only half-facetiously claims to do what teachers of writing claim cannot be done—to teach genius—Dorothea Brande suggests that the way to begin is not with an idea or a form at all, but with an unlocking of your thoughts at the typewriter. She advises that you rise each day and go directly to your desk (if you have to have coffee, put it in a thermos the night before) and begin writing whatever comes to mind, before you are quite awake, before you have read anything or talked to anyone, before reason has begun to take over from the dream-functioning of your brain. Write for twenty or thirty minutes and then put away what you have written without reading it over. After a week or two of this, pick an additional time during the day when you can salvage a half hour or so to write, and when that time arrives, write, even if you "must climb out over the heads of your friends" to do it. It doesn't matter *what* you write: What does matter is that you develop the habit of beginning to write the moment you sit down to do so.

CLUSTERING

Clustering is a technique, described in full by Gabriele Rico in her book *Writing the Natural Way,* that helps you organize on the model of the right brain rather than the left, organically rather than sequentially. Usually when we plan a piece of writing in advance, it is in a linear fashion—topic sentences and subheadings in the case of an essay, usually an outline of the action in the case of fiction. Clustering is a way of quite literally making spatial and visual the organization of your thoughts.

To practice the technique, choose a word that represents your central subject, write it in the center of the page, and circle it. Then for two or three minutes free-associate by jotting down around it any word—image, action, abstraction, or part of speech—that comes to mind. Every now and again, circle the words you have written and draw lines or arrows between words that seem to connect. As with freewriting, it is crucial to keep going, without self-censoring and without worrying about whether you're making sense. What you're doing is *making*; sense will emerge. When you've clustered for two or three minutes, you will have a page that looks like a cobweb with very large dewdrops, and you will probably sense when it is enough. Take a few seconds, no more, to look at what you have done. (*Look at* seems more relevant here than *read over*, because the device does make you see the words as part of a visual composition.) Then start writing. Don't let the critic in yet. This will not be a genuine freewrite because you've chosen the subject, but think of it as a freedraft or focused freewrite, and keep writing.

Here is a sample cluster on the preceding passage.

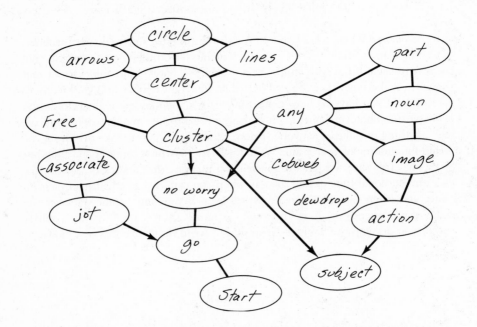

When I first encountered this device, I was aware that it was widely used for freshman English classes and that it had also led to poetry and prose poems, but I was doubtful how much use it would be to a fiction writer. I decided to try it, though, so I sat down to the first exercise offered in Rico's book, which was to cluster on the word "fear." I was not very thrilled with the project, but I wrote the word in the center of my page, and as soon as I circled it, I realized that in the novel I was then writing, there was a lot of fear in the mind of the heroine, a Baltimore Catholic headed for the desert Southwest in 1914. I started free-associating her fear rather than my own, and images erupted out of nowhere, out of her childhood—a cellar, the smell of rotting apples and mice droppings, old newspapers, my heroine as a little girl squatting in the dank dark, the priest upstairs droning on about the catechism. Where had it all come from? Within fifteen minutes I had a two-paragraph memory for my character that revealed her to me, and to my reader, more clearly than anything I had yet written.

Now I cluster any scene, character, narrative passage, or reflection that presents me with the least hint of resistance. When I have a complicated scene with several characters in it, I cluster each character so I have a clear idea at the beginning how each is feeling in that situation. Even if, as is usually the case, the passage is written from the point of view of only one of them, I will know how to make the other characters react, speak, and move if I've been gathering cobwebs in their minds.

Clustering is an excellent technique for journal keeping. It focuses your thoughts, cuts out extraneous material, and reduces writing time. In composing fiction, I recommend frequent clustering, followed by freedrafting and light editing. Then put the passage away for twenty-four hours. Like most recommendations, all this one means is that it seems to work for me.

Something of the same process was my forced habit for many years before I discovered that I could make it work *for* me instead of against. I would sit at my desk from mid-morning to noon paralyzed by the cosmic weight of needing to write something absolutely wonderful. I would lunch at my desk regularly, in despair. By mid-afternoon I would hate myself so thoroughly that I'd decide to splash anything down, any trash at all, just to be free of the blank page and feel justified in fleeing my paper prison. The whole evening would be tainted by the knowledge of having written such garbage. Next morning I would find that although it was mostly orange peels and eggshells, there was a little bit of something salvageable here and there. For a couple of intent hours I would work on that to make it right, feeling better, feeling good. Then I'd be faced with a new passage to begin, which, unlike that mess I'd cleaned up from yesterday, was going to emerge in rough draft as Great Literature. Lunch loomed in gloom.

Now, most days (allow for a few failures, a few relapses into old habits), I write the junk quite happily straight away. Then I begin to tinker—usually with something I did yesterday or last week—which is where I concentrate, lose myself, and am transported into the word world. Often it's two o'clock before I remember to stop for my apple and chunk of cheese.

Cluster, freedraft, lightly edit, put away. I do urge you at least to try this, several times. What you are at this moment reading is no doubt a many-times turned-around, picked at, honed, and buffed version of my paragraphs on clustering. But as I finish the first version, the document on my computer screen runs to three and a half pages, and only seventeen minutes have passed on my desk clock since I sat down to cluster the word "clustering." Moreover, I'm alert and having fun, and I feel like going on to say something about the computer.

THE COMPUTER

A very real and considerable disadvantage of a computer is that unless you have a battery-operated portable (too small for a writer's daily use), you can't take it to the park or the beach. I think it's important for a writer to try a pencil from time to time so as not to lose the knack of it, or the reminder of the cave walls where it all started.

But apart from its cumbersomeness and its need for some energy source other than the writer's mind, a computer is a great boon, and it's a rare idiosyncratic author who will not be wise to invest in one. Freewriting frees more freely on a computer. The knowledge that you can so easily delete makes it easier to quiet the internal critic and put down whatever comes. The "wraparound" feature of the computer means that you need never be aware, visually, through sound, or in the muscles of your carriage-throwing arm, that what you write is chopped into lines of type on the page. You may ignore the screen altogether—look at your fingers if you must (they make a hypnotic sight) or stare out the window, at the wall, into middle space. You can follow the thread of your thought through the labyrinth to the center without a pause.

Enter the critic. The cautionary note that needs to be sounded regarding all the techniques and technology that free you to write is that the critic is absolutely essential afterwards. Because revision, the heart of the writing process, will continue until you finally finish or abandon a piece of work, a chapter on revision is the last in this book. But the revising process is continuous, and begins as soon as you choose to let your critic in. Clustering and freedrafting allow you to create before your criticize, do the essential play before the essential work. Don't forget the essential work. The computer lets you write a lot because you can so easily cut. Don't forget to do so.

CHOOSING A SUBJECT

Some writers, again, are lucky enough never to be faced with the problem of choosing a subject. The world presents itself to them in terms of conflict, crisis, and resolution: Ideas for stories pop into their heads day after day; their only difficulty is choosing among them. In fact, the habit of mind that produces stories is a habit and can be cultivated, so that the more and the longer you write, the less likely you are to run out of ideas.

But sooner if not later you may find yourself faced with the desire (or the deadline necessity) to write a story when your mind is a blank. The sour and untrue impulse crosses your thoughts: Nothing has ever happened to me. The task you face then is to recognize among all the paraphernalia of your mind a situation, idea, perception, or character that you can turn into a story.

Some teachers and critics advise beginning writers to write only from their personal experience, but I feel that this is a misleading and demeaning rule, producing a lot of dead-grandmother stories and tales of dormitory life. It is certainly true that you must draw on your own experience (including your experience of the shape of sentences). But the trick is to identify what is interesting, unique, original in your experience (including your experience of the shape of sentences), which will therefore surprise and attract the reader.

John Gardner, in *The Art of Fiction,* agrees that "nothing can be more limiting to the imagination" than the advice that you write about what you know. He suggests instead that you "write the kind of story you know and like best."

This is a better idea, because the kind of story you know and like best has also taught you something about the way such stories are told, how they are shaped, what kind of surprise, conflict, and change they deal in. Many beginning writers who are not yet avid readers have learned from television more than they realize about structure, the way characters behave and talk, how a joke is arranged, how a lie is revealed, and so forth. The trouble is that if you learn fiction from television, or if the kind of story you know and like best is genre fiction—sci fi, fantasy, romance, mystery—you may have learned about technique without having learned anything about the unique contribution *you* can make to such a story. The result is that you end up writing imitation soap opera or space odyssey, second-rate somebody else instead of first-rate you.

The essential thing is that you write about something you really care about, and the first step is to find out what that is. Playwright Claudia Johnson advises her students to identify their real concerns by making a "menu" of them. Pick the big emotions and make lists in your journal: *What makes you angry? What are you afraid of? What do you want? What hurts?* Or consider the crucial turning points of your life: *What really changed you? Who really changed you?* Those will be the areas to look to for stories, whether or not those stories are autobiographical. Novelist Ron Carlson says, "I always write from my own experiences, whether I've had them or not."

Another journal idea is to jot down the facts of the first seven years of your life under several categories: *Events, People, Your Self, Inner Life, Characteristic Things.* Then underline or highlight the items on your page(s) that you aren't done with yet. What from those first seven years is still unfinished? Those are clues to your concerns, and a possible source of storytelling.

A related device for your journal might be borrowed from the *Pillow Book* of Sei Shonogun. A courtesan in fourteenth-century Japan, she kept a diary of the goings-on at court and concealed it in her wooden pillow—hence *pillow book.* Sei Shonogun made lists under various categories of specific, often quirky *Things.* This device is capable of endless variety and can reveal yourself to you as you find out what sort of thing you want to list. *Things I wish had never been said. Red things. Things more embarrassing than nudity. Things to put off as long as possible. Things to die for. Acid things. Things that last only a day.*

Such devices may be necessary because identifying what we care about is not always easy. We are surrounded by received opinion, a constant barrage of information, drama, ideas, and judgments offered us live, printed, and electronic. It is so much easier to know what we *ought* to think and feel than what we actually do. Worthy authorities constantly exhort us to care about worthy causes, only a few of which really touch us, whereas what we care about at any given moment may seem trivial, self-conscious, or self-serving.

This, I think, is in large part the value of Brande's first exercise, which forces you to write in the intuitively honest period of first light, when the half-sleeping brain is still dealing with its real concerns. Often what seems unworthy is precisely the thing that contains a universal, and by catching it honestly, then stepping back from it, you may achieve the authorial distance that is an essential part of significance. (All you really care about this morning is how you'll look at the dance tonight? This is a trivial obsession that can hit anyone, at any age, anywhere. Write about it as honestly as you can. Now who else might have felt this way? Someone you hate? Someone remote in time from you? Look out: You're on your way to a story.) Sometimes pursuing what you know and feel to its uttermost limits will take you into the realms of fantasy. Sometimes your fantasies will transform themselves into reality.

Brande advises that once you have developed the habit of regular freewriting, you should read your pages over and pick a passage that seems to suggest a simple story. Muse on the idea for a few days, find its shape, and then fill that shape with people, settings, details from your own experience, observation, and imagination. Turn the story over in your mind. Sleep on it—more than once. Finally, pick a time when you are going to write the story, and when that time comes, go to the desk and write a complete first draft as rapidly as possible. Then put it away, at least overnight. When you take it out again, you will have something to work with, and the business of the reason may begin.

Eventually you will learn what sort of experience sparks ideas for your sort of story—and you may be astonished at how such experiences accumulate, as if your life were arranging itself to produce material for you. In the meantime, here are a half dozen suggestions for the kind of idea that may be fruitful.

The dilemma, or catch-22. You find yourself facing, or know someone who is facing, or read about someone who is facing, a situation that offers no solution whatsoever. Any action taken would be painful and costly. You have no chance of solving this dilemma in real life, but you're a writer, and it costs nothing to solve it with imaginary people in an imaginary setting, even if the solution is a tragic one. Some writers use newspaper stories to generate this sort of idea. The situation is there in the bland black and white of this morning's news. But who are these people, and how did they come to be in such a mess? Make it up, think it through.

The incongruity. Something comes to your attention that is interesting precisely because you can't figure it out. It doesn't seem to make sense. Someone is breeding pigs in the backyard of a mansion in the most affluent section of town. Who is it? Why is she doing it? Your inventing mind can find the motives and the meanings. An example from my own experience: Once when my phone was out of order, I went out very late at night to make a call from a public phone at a supermarket plaza. At something like two in the morning all the stores were closed but the plaza was not empty. There were three women there, one of them with a baby in a stroller. *What were they doing there?* It was several years before I figured out a possible answer, and that answer was a short story.

The connection. You notice a striking similarity in two events, people, places, or periods that are fundamentally unlike. The more you explore the similarity, the more striking it becomes. My novel *The Buzzards* came from such a connection: The daughter of a famous politician was murdered, and I found myself in the position of comforting the dead girl's fiancé, at the same time as I was writing lectures on the *Agamemnon* of Aeschylus. Two politicians, two murdered daughters—one in Ancient Greece and one in contemporary America. The connection would not let go of me until I had thought it through and set it down.

The memory. Certain people, places, and events stand out in your memory with an intensity beyond logic. There's no earthly reason you should remember the smell of Aunt K's rouge. It makes no sense that you still flush with shame at the thought of that ball you "borrowed" when you were in fourth grade. But for some reason these things are still vivid in your mind. That vividness can be explored, embellished, given form. Stephen Minot in *Three Genres* wisely advises, though, that if you are going to write from a memory, it should be a memory more than a year old. Otherwise you are likely to be unable to distinguish between what happened and what must happen in the story, or between what is in your mind and what you have conveyed on the page.

The transplant. This is probably writing at its most therapeutic. You find yourself having to deal with a feeling that is either startlingly new to you or else obsessively old. You feel incapable of dealing with it. As a way of distancing yourself from that feeling and gaining some mastery over it, you write about the feeling as precisely as you can, but giving it to an imaginary someone in an imaginary situation. What situation other than your own would produce such a feeling? Who would be caught in that situation? Think it through.

The revenge. An injustice has been done, and you are powerless to do anything about it. But you're not really, because you're a writer. Reproduce the situation with another set of characters, in other circumstances or another setting. Cast the outcome to suit yourself. Punish whomever you choose. Even if the story ends in a similar injustice, you have righted the wrong by enlisting your reader's sympathy on the side of right. (Dante was particularly good at this: He put his enemies in the inferno and his friends in paradise.) Remember too that as human beings we are intensely, sometimes obsessively, interested in our boredom, and you can take revenge against the things that bore you by making them absurd or funny on paper.

Keep Going

A story idea may come from any source at any time. You may not know you have an idea until you spot it in the random jottings of your journal. Once you've identified the idea, the process of thinking it through begins, and doesn't end until you finish (or abandon) the story. Most writing is done between the mind and the hand, not between the hand and the page. It may take a fairly competent typist about three hours to type a twelve-page story. It may take days or months to write it. It follows that, even when you are writing well, most of the time spent writing is not spent putting words on the page. If the story idea grabs hard hold of you, the process of thinking through may be involuntary, a gift. If not, you need to find the inner stillness that will allow you to develop your characters, get to know them, follow their actions in your mind; and it may take an effort of the will to find such stillness.

The metamorphosis of an idea into a story has many aspects, some deliberate and some mysterious. "Inspiration" is a real thing, a gift from the subconscious to the conscious mind. But over and over again, successful writers attest that unless they prepare the conscious mind with the habit of work, the gift does not come. Writing is mind-farming. You have to plow, plant, weed, and hope for growing weather. Why a seed turns into a plant is something you are never going to understand, and the only relevant response to it is gratitude. You may be proud, however, of having plowed.

Many writers besides Dorothea Brande have observed that it is ideal, having turned your story over in your mind, to write the first draft at one sitting, pushing on through the action to the conclusion, no matter how dissatisfied you are with this paragraph, that character, this phrasing, or that incident. There are two advantages to doing this. The first is that you are more likely to produce a coherent draft when you come to the desk in a single frame of mind with a single vision of the whole, than when you write piecemeal, having altered ideas and moods. The second is that fast writing tends to make for fast pace in the story. It is always easier, later, to add and develop than it is to sharpen the pace. If you are the sort of writer who stays on page one for days, shoving commas around and combing the thesaurus for a word with slightly better connotations, then you should probably force yourself to try this method (more than once). A note of caution, though: If you write a draft at one sitting, it will not be the draft you want to show anyone, so schedule the sitting well in advance of whatever deadline you may have.

However, this method does not always work, for a variety of reasons. Obviously it won't work for a novel (though the British author Gabriel Josipovici once startled me by observing that the first draft of a novel could be written in a month: "Ten pages a day for thirty days gives you three hundred—and *then* you rewrite it seventeen times"). Novelist Sheila Taylor recounts how she accomplished her first book: She decided that she would give herself permission to write one bad page a day for a year. At the end of the year she had three hundred and sixty-five pages. She will not show them to anyone, but she had proved that she could write a novel, and her second, third, and fourth novels are in print in several languages.

It may happen—always keeping in mind that a single-sitting draft is the ideal— that as you write, the story takes off of its own accord in some direction totally other than you intended. You thought you knew where you were going and now you don't, and you know that unless you stop for a while and think it through again, you'll go wrong. You may find that although you are doing precisely what you had in mind, it doesn't work, and it needs more imaginative mulching before it will bear fruit. Or you may find, simply, that your stamina gives out, and that though you have done your exercises, been steadfast, loyal, and practiced every writerly virtue known, you're stuck. You have writer's block.

Writer's block is not so popular as it was a few years ago. I suspect people got tired of hearing or even talking about it—sometimes writers can be sensitive even to their own clichés. But it may also be that writers talked so much about the agony of not being able to get on with it, that they began to understand and accept their difficulties. Sometimes the process seems to require working yourself into a muddle and past the muddle to despair; until you have done this, it may be impossible suddenly to see what the shape of a thing ought to be. When you're writing, this feels terrible. You sit spinning your wheels, digging deeper and deeper into the mental muck. You decide you are going to trash the whole thing and walk away from it—only you can't, and you keep coming back to it like a tongue to an aching tooth. Or you decide you are going to sit there until you bludgeon it into shape— and as long as you sit there it remains recalcitrant. W. H. Auden observed that the hardest part of writing is not knowing whether you are procrastinating or you must wait for the words to come.

I know a newspaper editor who says that writer's block always represents a lack of information. I thought this inapplicable to fiction until I noticed that I was mainly frustrated when I didn't know enough about my characters, the scene, or the action; when I had not gone to the imaginative depth where information lies.

So I learned something, but it led to the familiar guilt: *procrastinating again!* Victoria Nelson, in *Writer's Block and How to Use It*, says that if you accuse yourself of procrastinating, you aren't a procrastinator, you're an accuser. I know a psychologist, who lives with a writer, who says she believes that writer's block is writer's guilt.

There is truth in all these perceptions, and probably the best way out of a block is any way that helps you avoid what Natalie Goldberg, in *Writing Down the Bones*, calls "the cycle of guilt, avoidance, and pressure."

I'll tell you a story. I met a woman so adept at asking questions that at the end of three or four of them she had shown me the clue to a character I'd been blocked on for several days.

"You're a therapist, of course," I said. She was. I asked her if she knew any technique to cure a writer of laziness. I complained that I could make the newspaper last till noon and the lunch dishes till two o'clock. I could daydream out the window over the top of my computer for an hour or two without budging myself in its direction.

"You really are lazy, aren't you?" she said.

"Yes, I really am."

She asked if I wanted to try something, and if I would please close my eyes and think of a place where I'd feel extremely comfortable. I was game. After a while, my mind tossed up a memory of a meadow in Cambridge, England, where as an undergraduate I used to go with my bicycle and lie in the buttercups.

"Now, can you see the Lazy Place from there?" she asked.

The Lazy Place presented itself as a Florida sinkhole, behind a scrim of pines. (*Interesting,* my analytical left-brain critic commented; *England is comfortable, but Florida is the Lazy Place.*)

"Now, can you go toward the Lazy Place?"

I must have frowned, because she asked if I was having trouble, and I realized that my bicycle was hard to maneuver over the stones between the pine trees. "My bike's in the way, but I don't want to leave it because I forgot the chain, and somebody will steal it." To my amazement, I began to cry. (*Forgot your chain, did you?* sneered my critic. *Aha!*)

"Well, look around. Maybe you can find a chain."

My new friend pointed out to me later the work-ethic ferocity of my reply: "Well, I'm not going to *find* one, am I!? I'll have to *make* one!"

I figured out that if I undid the lug nut on the wheel, I could shove the wheels together and take the other chain, the one operating the gears, with me. (*Take the chain with you, eh?*—the critic.) That would make the bike uninviting to thieves.

"Are you willing to do that?"

"Yes. It's not absolutely safe, but—yes." And I went on down to the Lazy Place.

In my mind the shore was deep brown silt with mica flecks—all dark and shining. The water was stained with the cypress knees that stuck up out of it, and winking with the sunlight filtered through the pines—all dark and shining. The trees were tall and bounced their branches against each other in the strong sun—all dark and shining. It was beautiful, beautiful!

"Can you think of a phrase to characterize what it's like there?" asked my friend.

"Rich thinking," I immediately replied, and immediately knew the point of the exercise: that I am not a lazy person and that all my best work is done when I seem to be doing nothing—reading the back pages of the newspaper, dragging a wet cloth around a plate, lolling in the armchair farthest from the desk, lazy, no-'count, thinking rich.

For the next week the bicycle appeared to me in various guises, now my shiny new Sears, now a scrofulous, many-coated, flat-tired wreck. By the end of the week I was pretty well satisfied that the bike and its chains represented a whole complex of things I need to get me back from the Lazy Place to where other people are; it's my computer and my discipline, that old work ethic, the craft itself, revision and the dogged doing of it, without which the riches of the Lazy Place would stay secret and never help me make contact with the world.

My wise friend tells me that she does not believe in laziness. Laziness is like money, she says; it doesn't really exist except to represent something else—fear or anger, judgment, or, often in the writer's case, the natural need of the imaginal process. It may be beyond most of us to disbelieve in laziness, but I think it would be wise for writers to try.

The stubborn fact remains that at some point we have to get back on the bicycle and push one pedal after the other into town. There are some guides and techniques to help us on. The poet William Stafford advises his students always to write to their lowest standard. Somebody always corrects him: "You mean your highest standard." No, he means your lowest standard. Victoria Nelson means the same thing when she points out that "there is an almost mathematical ratio between soaring, grandiose ambition . . . and severe creative block." More writers prostitute themselves "up" than "down"; more are false in the determination to write great literature than to throw off a romance. A rough draft is rough; that's its nature. Let it be rough.

Remember: Writing is easy. Not writing is *hard.*

All the later chapters in this book are followed by short stories that operate as examples of the elements of fiction under consideration. What follows here, however, are three excerpts by writers on the writing process from books of exceptional quality, very different from each other in content, tone, and form.

∽

From *One Writer's Beginnings*

EUDORA WELTY

In our house on North Congress Street in Jackson, Mississippi, where I was born, the oldest of three children, in 1909, we grew up to the striking of clocks. There was a mission-style oak grandfather clock standing in the hall, which sent its gong-like strokes through the livingroom, diningroom, kitchen, and pantry, and up the sounding board of the stairwell. Through the night, it could find its way into our ears; sometimes, even on the sleeping porch, midnight could wake us up. My parents' bedroom had a smaller striking clock that answered it. Though the kitchen clock did nothing but show the time, the diningroom clock was a cuckoo clock with weights on long chains, on one of which my baby brother, after climbing on a chair to the top of the china closet, once succeeded in suspending the cat for a moment. I don't know whether or not my father's Ohio family, in having been Swiss back in the 1700s before the first three Welty brothers came to America, had anything to do with this; but we all of us have been time-minded all our lives. This was good at least for a future fiction writer, being able to learn so penetratingly, and almost first of all, about chronology. It was one of a good many things I learned almost without knowing it; it would be there when I needed it.

My father loved all instruments that would instruct and fascinate. His place to keep things was the drawer in the "library table" where lying on top of his folded maps was a telescope with brass extensions, to find the moon and the Big Dipper after supper in our front yard, and to keep appointments with eclipses. There was a folding Kodak that was brought out for Christmas, birthdays, and trips. In the back of the drawer you could find a magnifying glass, a kaleidoscope, and a gyroscope kept in a black buckram box, which he would set dancing for us on a string pulled tight. He had also supplied himself with an assortment of puzzles composed of metal rings and intersecting links and keys chained together, impossible for the rest of us, however patiently shown, to take apart; he had an almost childlike love of the ingenious.

In time, a barometer was added to our diningroom wall; but we didn't really need it. My father had the country boy's accurate knowledge of the weather and its skies. He went out and stood on our front steps first thing in the morning and took a look at it and a sniff. He was a pretty good weather prophet.

"Well, I'm *not*," my mother would say with enormous self-satisfaction.

He told us children what to do if we were lost in a strange country. "Look for where the sky is brightest along the horizon," he said. "That reflects the nearest river. Strike out for a river and you will find habitation." Eventualities were much on his mind. In his care for us children he cautioned us to take measures against such things as being struck by lightning. He drew us all away from the windows during the severe electrical storms that are common where we live. My mother stood apart, scoffing at caution as a character failing. "Why, I always loved a storm! High winds never bothered me in West Virginia! Just listen at that! I wasn't a bit afraid of a little lightning and thunder! I'd go out on the mountain and spread my arms wide and *run* in a good big storm!"

So I developed a strong meteorological sensibility. In years ahead when I wrote stories, atmosphere took its influential role from the start. Commotion in the weather and the inner feelings aroused by such a hovering disturbance emerged connected in dramatic form. (I tried a tornado first, in a story called "The Winds.")

From our earliest Christmas times, Santa Claus brought us toys that instruct boys and girls (separately) how to build things—stone blocks cut to the castle-building style, Tinker Toys, and Erector sets. Daddy made for us himself elaborate kites that needed to be taken miles out of town to a pasture long enough (and my father was not afraid of horses and cows watching) for him to run with and get up on a long cord to which my mother held the spindle, and then we children were given it to hold, tugging like something alive at our hands. They were beautiful, sound, shapely box kites, smelling delicately of office glue for their entire short lives. And of course, as soon as the boys attained anywhere near the right age, there was an electric train, the engine with its pea-sized working headlight, its line of cars, tracks equipped with switches, semaphores, its station, its bridges, and its tunnel, which blocked off all other traffic in the upstairs hall. Even from downstairs, and through the cries of excited children, the elegant rush and click of the train could be heard through the ceiling, running around and around its figure eight.

All of this, but especially the train, represents my father's fondest beliefs—in progress, in the future. With these gifts, he was preparing his children.

And so was my mother with her different gifts.

I learned from the age of two or three that any room in our house, at any time of day, was there to read in, or to be read to. My mother read to me. She'd read to me in the big bedroom in the mornings, when we were in her rocker together, which ticked in rhythm as we rocked, as though we had a cricket accompanying the story. She'd read to me in the diningroom on winter afternoons in front of the coal fire, with our cuckoo clock ending the story with "Cuckoo," and at night when I'd got in my own bed. I must have given her no peace. Sometimes she read to me in the kitchen while she sat churning, and the churning sobbed along with *any* story. It was my ambition to have her read to me while *I* churned; once she granted my wish, but she read off my story before I brought her butter. She was an expressive reader. When she was reading "Puss in Boots," for instance, it was impossible not to know that she distrusted *all* cats.

It had been startling and disappointing to me to find out that story books had been written by *people,* that books were not natural wonders, coming up of themselves like grass. Yet regardless of where they came from, I cannot remember a time when I was not in love with them—with the books themselves, cover and binding and the paper they were printed on, with their smell and their weight and with their possession in my arms, captured and carried off to myself. Still illiterate, I was ready for them, committed to all the reading I could give them.

Neither of my parents had come from homes that could afford to buy many books, but though it must have been something of a strain on his salary, as the youngest officer in a young insurance company, my father was all the while carefully selecting and ordering away for what he and Mother thought we children should grow up with. They bought first for the future.

Besides the bookcase in the livingroom, which was always called "the library," there were the encyclopedia tables and dictionary stand under windows in our diningroom. Here to help us grow up arguing around the diningroom table were the Unabridged Webster, the Columbia Encyclopedia, Compton's Pictured Encyclopedia, the Lincoln Library of Information, and later the Book of Knowledge. And the year we moved into our new house, there was room to celebrate it with the new 1925 edition of the Britannica, which my father, his face always deliberately turned toward the future, was of course disposed to think better than any previous edition.

In "the library," inside the mission-style bookcase with its three diamond-latticed glass doors, with my father's Morris chair and the glass-shaded lamp on its table beside it, were books I could soon begin on—and I did, reading them all alike and as they came, straight down their rows, top shelf to bottom. There was the set of Stoddard's Lectures, in all its late nineteenth-century vocabulary and vignettes of peasant life and quaint beliefs and customs, with matching halftone illustrations: Vesuvius erupting, Venice by moonlight, gypsies glimpsed by their campfires. I didn't know then the clue they were to my father's longing to see the rest of the world. I read straight through his other love-from-afar: the Victrola Book of the Opera, with opera after opera in synopsis, with portraits in costume of Melba, Caruso, Galli-Curci, and Geraldine Farrar, some of whose voices we could listen to on our Red Seal records.

My mother read secondarily for information, she sank as a hedonist into novels. She read Dickens in the spirit in which she would have eloped with him. . . .

My mother always sang to her children. Her voice came out just a little bit in the minor key. "Wee Willie Winkie's" song was wonderfully sad when she sang the lullabies.

"Oh, but now there's a record. She could have her own record to listen to," my father would have said. For there came a Victrola record of "Bobby Shafftoe" and "Rock-a-Bye Baby," all of Mother's lullabies, which could be played to take her place. Soon I was able to play her my own lullabies all day long.

Our Victrola stood in the diningroom. I was allowed to climb onto the seat of a diningroom chair to wind it, start the record turning, and set the needle playing. In a second I'd jumped to the floor, to spin or march around the table as the music called for—now there were all the other records I could play too. I skinned back onto the chair just in time to lift the needle at the end, stop the record and turn it over, then change the needle. That brass receptacle with a hole in the lid gave off a metallic smell like human sweat, from all the hot needles that were fed it. Winding up, dancing, being cocked to start and stop the record, was of course all in one the act of *listening*—to "Overture to *Daughter of the Regiment*," "Selections from *The Fortune Teller*," "Kiss Me Again," "Gypsy Dance from *Carmen*," "Stars and Stripes Forever," "When the Midnight Choo-Choo Leaves for Alabam," or whatever came next. Movement must be at the very heart of listening.

Ever since I was first read to, then started reading to myself, there has never been a line read that I didn't *hear*. As my eyes followed the sentence, a voice was saying it silently to me. It isn't my mother's voice, or the voice of any person I can identify, certainly not my own. It is human, but inward, and it is inwardly that I listen to it. It is to me the voice of the story or the poem itself. The cadence, whatever it is that asks you to believe, the feeling that resides in the printed word, reaches me through the reader-voice. I have supposed, but never found out, that this is the case with all readers—to read as listeners—and with all writers, to write as listeners. It may be part of the desire to write. The sound of what falls on the page begins the process of testing it for truth, for me. Whether I am right to trust so far I don't know.

By now I don't know whether I could do either one, reading or writing, without the other.

My own words, when I am at work on a story, I hear too as they go, in the same voice that I hear when I read in books. When I write and the sound of it comes back to my ears, then I act to make my changes. I have always trusted this voice. . . .

It was my mother who emotionally and imaginatively supported me in my wish to become a writer. It was my father who gave me the first dictionary of my own, a Webster's Collegiate, inscribed on the flyleaf with my full name (he always included Alice, my middle name, after his mother) and the date, 1925. I still consult it. It was also he who expressed his reservations that I wouldn't achieve financial success by becoming a writer, a sensible fear; nevertheless he fitted me out with my first typewriter, my little red Royal Portable, which I carried off to the University of Wisconsin. It was also he who advised me, after I'd told him I still meant to try writing, even though I didn't expect to sell my stories to *The Saturday Evening Post* which paid well, to go ahead and try myself—but to prepare to earn my living some other way. My supportive parents had already very willingly agreed that I go farther from home for my last two years of college and sent me to Wisconsin—my father's choice for its high liberal-arts reputation. Now that I'd been graduated from there, they sent me to my first choice of a place to prepare for a job: New York City, at Columbia University Graduate School of Business. (As certain as I was of wanting to be a writer, I was certain of *not* wanting to be a teacher. I lacked the instructing turn of mind, the selflessness, the patience for teaching, and I had the unreasoning feeling that I'd be trapped. The odd thing is that when I did come to write my stories, the longest list of my characters turns out to be schoolteachers. They are to a great extent my heroines.)

My father did not bring it up, but of course I knew that he had another reason to worry about my decision to write. Though he was a reader, he was not a lover of fiction, because fiction is not true, and for that flaw it was forever inferior to fact. If reading fiction was a waste of time, so was the writing of it. (Why is it, I wonder, that humor didn't count? Wodehouse, for one, whom both of us loved, was a flawless fiction writer.)

But I was not to be in time to show him what I could do, to hear what he thought, on the evidence, of where I was headed. . . .

My first full-time job was rewarding to me in a way I could never have foreseen in those early days of my writing. I went to work for the state office of the Works Progress Administration as junior publicity agent. (This was of course one of President Roosevelt's national measures to combat the Great Depression.) Traveling over the whole of Mississippi, writing news stories for county papers, taking pictures, I saw my home state at close hand, really for the first time.

With the accretion of years, the hundreds of photographs—life as I found it, all unposed—constitute a record of that desolate period; but most of what I learned for myself came right at the time and directly out of the *taking* of the pictures. The camera was a hand-held auxiliary of wanting-to-know.

It had more than information and accuracy to teach me. I learned in the doing how *ready* I had to be. Life doesn't hold still. A good snapshot stopped a moment from running away. Photography taught me that to be able to capture transience, by being ready to click the shutter at the crucial moment, was the greatest need I had. Making pictures of people in all sorts of situations, I learned that every feeling waits upon its gesture; and I had to be prepared to recognize this moment when I saw it. These were things a story writer needed to know. And I felt the need to hold transient life in *words*— there's so much more of life that only words can convey—strongly enough to last me as long as I lived. The direction my mind took was a writer's direction from the start, not a photographer's, or a recorder's.

Along Mississippi roads you'd now and then see bottle trees; you'd see them alone or in crowds in the front yard of remote farmhouses. I photographed one—a bare crape myrtle tree with every branch of it ending in the mouth of a colored glass bottle—a blue Milk of Magnesia or an orange or green pop bottle; reflecting the light, flashing its colors in the sun, it stood as the centerpiece in a little thicket of peach trees in bloom. Later, I wrote a story called "Livvie" about youth and old age: the death of an old, proud, possessive man and the coming into flower, after dormant years, of his young wife—a spring story. Numbered among old Solomon's proud possessions is this bottle tree.

I know that the actual bottle tree, from the time of my actual sight of it, was the origin of my story. I know equally well that the bottle tree appearing in the story is a projection from my imagination; it isn't the real one except in that it is corrected by reality. The fictional eye sees in, through, and around what is really there. In "Livvie," old Solomon's bottle tree stands bright with dramatic significance, it stands vulnerable, ready for invading youth to sail a stone into the bottles and shatter them, as Livvie is claimed by love in the bursting light of spring. This I saw could be brought into being in the form of a story.

I was always my own teacher. The earliest story I kept a copy of was, I had thought, sophisticated, for I'd had the inspiration to lay it in Paris. I wrote it on my new typewriter, and its opening sentence was, "Monsieur Boule inserted a delicate dagger into Mademoiselle's left side and departed with a poised immediacy." I'm afraid it was a perfect example of what my father thought "fiction" mostly was.

From *The Art of Fiction: Notes on Craft for Young Writers*

JOHN GARDNER

Let us look at how the writer works when he plots backward from the climax of a story that is entirely made up. Any event that seems to the given writer startling, curious, or interest-laden can form the climax of a possible story: A roadside vendor's pickup is struck by a transcontinental tractor-trailer; a woman purposely runs over a flagman on the street. Depending on the complexity of the writer's way of seeing the event—depending, that is, on how much background he feels our understanding of the event requires—the climax becomes the high point of a short story, a novella, or a novel. Since plotting is ordinarily no hasty process but something the writer broods and labors over, trying out one approach, then another, carrying the idea around with him, musing on it casually as he drifts off to sleep, writers often find that an idea for a short story may change into an idea for a novella or even a novel. But for convenience here, let us treat the two climaxes I've mentioned—the wreck of the roadside vendor's pickup and the woman's attack on the flagman—as ideas that remain short-story ideas.

A roadside vendor's pickup is hit by a transcontinental tractor-trailer. Let us say the vendor is the story's central character. In any climax in which the central character is in conflict with something else (another character, some animal, or some more or less impersonal force), the climactic encounter may come about either through the knowledge and volition of both parties or by significant accident. (Accident without significance is boring.) The semi driver may hit the pickup on purpose, accidentally, or for some reason we do not know because we lack access to his thoughts. If the semi driver hits the pickup on purpose, the writer working back from the climax is logically required to show dramatically, in earlier scenes, (1) what each of the two focal characters is like; (2) why the semi driver hits the vendor's pickup. (The writer might conceivably get around both 1 and 2, telling us only what the vendor is like; but the introduction of a malevolent semi driver who simply happens into the story, bringing on the climax, has become such a cliché in modern fiction as to be almost unusable.) The story containing 1 and 2 is a relatively easy kind of story to think out and write, which is not to say that it cannot be an excellent story if well done. The value of the standard feud story always depends on the writer's ability to create powerfully convincing characters in irreconcilable conflict, both sides in some measure sympathetic—that is, both sides pursuing real, though mutually exclusive, values. For the climax to be persuasive, we must be shown dramatically why each character believes what he does and why each cannot sympathize with the values of his antagonist; and we must be shown dramatically why the conflicting characters cannot or do not simply avoid each other, as in real life even tigers ordinarily do. For the climax to be not only persuasive but interesting, it must come about in a way that seems both inevitable and surprising. (In a form as standard as the feud story, this last is exceedingly important.) Needless to say, no surprise will be convincing if it rests on chance, however common chance may be in life.

If the semi driver hits the pickup by accident or for some reason we never learn, the construction of an aesthetically valid story is more difficult, since the value conflict that propels the story must be derived entirely from the central character and his situation. In this case the semi driver functions as an impersonal force and can have only such meaning as the roadside vendor projects onto him; in other words, the semi must be, for the vendor, a symbol. Let us say that for the vendor transcontinental trucks represent power and freedom, a symbolic contrast with his own life, which he views as constricted and unsatisfying. The wreck of the pickup, then, will be grimly ironic. Having thought it out this far, we find that the story begins to fall into place. The story's principle of profluence might be a movement from greatest constriction to least constriction—a development abruptly reversed when the semi hits the pickup.

Say the roadside vendor is a redneck bottom-land farmer, a grower of melons, pumpkins, squash, pole beans, yams, and tomatoes in the red-clay country of Kentucky, southern Missouri, or southern Illinois—a man called Pigtoe. (This version of the plot comes from the writer Leigh Wilson.) Constrictions are easy to find for such a man, betrayed by the land, the government, the newly liberalized Baptist Church, perhaps betrayed by life in other ways as well, at least in his own view: His wife, Alice, is worn and haggard, sickly—other men, like his neighbor Pinky Hearns, have healthy, strong wives, good workers. And Pigtoe's children are too numerous (or not numerous enough, choose one) and rebellious.

The writer might lead up to the climax with three relatively short but texturally rich, at least moderately southern gothic scenes. In the first, Pigtoe is at breakfast with his wife, talking, while outside the children load the truck. The writer can quickly and easily establish Pigtoe's feeling of being squeezed by life—his feelings about the church, the school, blacks, his children and neighbors, taxes, and the weather. But whereas his family is pretty much stuck on the farm, as they are grumblingly aware, Pigtoe can at least get away a little, see the larger world, meet strangers, selling produce from the back of his pickup, out by the highway. The scene ends with Pigtoe watching as his children finish their careless loading.

A brief transitional scene might show Pigtoe driving down Lipes Ridge Road (or whatever) toward the junction of the state highway and the interstate. We get some of Pigtoe's thoughts, sharp images of how he drives the truck, and above all a dramatized movement from one world to another. Then the third scene might show Pigtoe with two or three significant customers—a trim suburban housewife, for instance; a university couple—"hippies," to Pigtoe (they might envy his life "close to the land"); perhaps also a well-off family of blacks in a new Chevy wagon. Through all this and, subtly, from the beginning of the story, we get Pigtoe's feelings about the people around him; his contempt and bitterness, and his envy, almost worship, of the people who have escaped his imprisonment, the men who drive the chrome eighteen-wheelers. Now the climax is set up.

How the writer comes out of it (in the denouement), the writer must probably discover as he writes and repeatedly revises the story. Pigtoe may be killed, or he may be left staring at the tipped-over pickup, honeydews and pumpkins rumbling down the highway toward Oklahoma. Again, the semi driver might stop (not at all the supremely free being Pigtoe has imagined him); Pigtoe in his rage might seize the old red gas-can from the pickup and try—successfully or with pitiful ineptitude—to burn the eighteen-wheeler. Or any of a dozen other things might happen. The writer must decide for himself, discovering his ending from within the story.

The risks in this story we've outlined are apparent. The good writer will think them out carefully before he starts. The main one, of course, is that the story's southern gothicism will seem old hat. The fact that the story is of a standard type is no reason not to write it, however. All fiction is derivative, a fact that the good writer turns to his advantage, making the most of the reader's expectations, twisting old conventions, satisfying expectations in unexpected ways. Because his material is so obviously southern gothic, the writer might choose a style not usual in such fiction, a style as far as possible from that of Flannery O'Connor, Eudora Welty, or William Faulkner. Mainly, however, he must see the material with a fresh eye, using his own experience of southern life, choosing details no other writer has noticed or, anyway, emphasized, thus creating a reality as different from that of gothic convention as gothic convention is from reality itself.

Our second story situation, the woman who purposely runs over a flagman, is the opposite of our Pigtoe story, since here the focal character is the aggressor, not (as at the end of the Pigtoe story) the victim. What the writer must figure out, to justify the climax, is (1) what kind of woman would run over a traffic flagman, and (2) why? Either she can know the flagman and have something personal against him, or she may not know him, but sees him as a symbol—a male chauvinist, for instance. I am ignoring, for my convenience, the possibility that the woman might run over the flagman by accident, mainly because in that case we are almost certainly saddled with a victim story. What precedes the climax would necessarily be a set of harassing events that explain the woman's carelessness. At best the story would be, in the abstract, a duplication of our Pigtoe story: The woman believes one thing—that a certain attitude and way of behaving are effective—and is proved wrong by events.

Let us say, arbitrarily (though in fact the given writer's choice would not be arbitrary but guided by his intuition of what would make a good story), that the woman does not know the flagman. What central character shall we choose—for example: a harried, unhappy housewife, a tough female executive, a stripper? Any choice could make a good story, but let's take the stripper, an idea that might appeal to a given writer at least partly because of our present stage of social consciousness: No writer before our own moment would be likely to see the stripper in quite the way we do. What pressure can we put on our stripper that will account for the climactic event?

Let us say that our stripper, Fanny, is thirty-six, well-preserved, even beautiful, but hard put to compete with younger strippers of the new breed. She's an old-style stripper, the kind who teases and scorns her male audience, as if taunting them, asking to be tamed—a classic act (she's been the star for years), but her act, like her body, is slipping. Her act is of the highly polished kind: She unclothes slowly, tormentingly, with artistic style. She has, let us say, trained white doves who fly away with each article of clothing she takes off. The younger strippers, who are beginning to challenge her top billing, are new-style strippers. Nakedness means nothing to them—they take off their clothes as indifferently as trees drop leaves—and their acts, because of their easy and uninhibited sexuality, have no need of high artifice or polish. Whereas Fanny grew up in Texas, of stern, southern Baptist stock, and fled to burlesque in troubled defiance, guiltily but brazenly, the new breed grew up in cities like San Francisco and feels no such inner conflict.

Having worked out this general approach to his story, the writer is ready to start figuring out his scenes. By the rule of elegance and efficiency, he will choose the smallest number of scenes possible—perhaps three. First, the writer might use a scene in which Fanny, fearfully and angrily, watches the rehearsal of a younger stripper's act. She can tell as she watches that, though the act is technically shoddy beside her own, it is being groomed as a starring act and may well push her from her billing. In the next scene, Fanny might confront the manager or director and learn from him that her suspicions are well-founded. She goes into a rage. At the peak of this scene she might slap the director, and he, to her shock and amazement, might slap her back, even fire her. In the third scene, Fanny drives toward the flagman, who unluckily smiles a trifle lewdly at her, bringing on the climax. What happens after this—the story's denouement or pull-away—the writer may know only when he writes it. (Some writers claim they know the last lines of their stories from the beginning. I think this is usually a bad idea, producing fiction that is subtly forced, or mechanical.)

This brief, rough sketch of a possible story raises an extremely important point—a point as fundamental, for the most serious kind of writer, as the concept of the uninterruptible fictional dream. What we have so far, in the sketch we've worked out—and what many quite good writers never go beyond—is a projected piece of fiction that, if well-written, will be no more than a persuasive imitation of reality. It shows how things happen and may imply certain values, but it does not look hard at the meaning of things. It has no real theme. This is a common limitation of second-rate fiction and may sometimes characterize even quite powerful fiction, like Eudora Welty's novel *Losing Battles.* We get an accurate and totally convincing picture of what it feels like to have a death in the family, what it is like to leave one's husband and children for a new "free" life, how it feels to be sued for malpractice or to lose an election; we do not get close examination of some deep-rooted idea. The writer, in other words, has done the first job done in all serious fiction—he has created a convincing and illuminating sequence of events—but he has not done the second, which is to "mine deeper!" as Melville says, dig out the fundamental meaning of events by organizing the imitation of reality around some primary question or theme suggested by the character's concern.

The theme of our story about Fanny the stripper might be, of course, male chauvinism, or it might be Art versus Life (or Nature); or nakedness in all its forms. The writer's choice of theme, partly Fanny's choice, will dictate his selection and organization of details, his style, and so forth. For instance, if what seems to him central in Fanny's struggle has to do with the contrast between Art and Nature, he will focus carefully on the difference between Fanny's act and that of the younger girls, summoning imagery, etc., that subtly underscores his point of focus. He may pay close attention to Fanny's mirror, a beautifully carpentered object with a history and, for Fanny, special meaning. And the flagman's way of doing his job—negligently and artlessly, or officiously and carefully—will have bearing on the climax. If the theme the writer chooses is nakedness, he will choose other details to brood on and develop—the chipping paint on the dressing-room walls, for instance; the psychological nakedness of some character; the manager's unwillingness to disguise or cover over his lack of interest in Fanny's well-being or, if it comes to that, his hatred of all she represents. Given this theme, the writer may find himself introducing a decorous old janitor who clothes his every mood in the most painstaking etiquette and who wears, whatever the weather, two sweaters and a coat. These become the "counters," so to speak, for the writer's thought: They help him find out and express precisely what he means.

Theme, it should be noticed, is not imposed on the story but evoked from within it—initially an intuitive but finally an intellectual act on the part of the writer. The writer muses on the story idea to determine what it is in it that has attracted him, why it seems to him worth telling. Having determined that what interests him—and what chiefly concerns the major character—is the idea of nakedness (physical, psychological, perhaps spiritual), he toys with various ways of telling his story, thinks about what has been said before about nakedness (for instance, in traditional Christianity and pagan myth), broods on every image that occurs to him, turning it over and over, puzzling on it, hunting for connections, trying to figure out—before he writes, while he writes, and in the process of repeated revisions—what it is he really thinks. (How naked should we be or can we be? Is openness, vulnerability, a virtue or a defect? To what extent, with what important qualifications?) He finds himself bringing in black strippers, perhaps an Indian stripper, supported by imagery that recalls primitive nakedness. And so on. Only when he thinks out his story in this way does he achieve not just an alternative reality or, loosely, an imitation of nature, but true, firm art—fiction as serious thought.

From *The Writing Life*

ANNIE DILLARD

When you write, you lay out a line of words. The line of words is a miner's pick, a wood-carver's gouge, a surgeon's probe. You wield it, and it digs a path you follow. Soon you find yourself deep in new territory. Is it a dead end, or have you located the real subject? You will know tomorrow, or this time next year.

You make the path boldly and follow it fearfully. You go where the path leads. At the end of the path, you find a box canyon. You hammer out reports, dispatch bulletins.

The writing has changed, in your hands, and in a twinkling, from an expression of your notions to an epistemological tool. The new place interests you because it is not clear. You attend. In your humility, you lay down the words carefully, watching all the angles. Now the earlier writing looks soft and careless. Process is nothing; erase your tracks. The path is not the work. I hope your tracks have grown over; I hope birds ate the crumbs; I hope you will toss it all and not look back.

The line of words is a hammer. You hammer against the walls of your house. You tap the walls, lightly, everywhere. After giving many years' attention to these things, you know what to listen for. Some of the walls are bearing walls; they have to stay, or everything will fall down. Other walls can go with impunity; you can hear the difference. Unfortunately, it is often a bearing wall that has to go. It cannot be helped. There is only one solution, which appalls you, but there it is. Knock it out. Duck.

Courage utterly opposes the bold hope that this is such fine stuff the work needs it, or the world. Courage, exhausted, stands on bare reality: this writing weakens the work. You must demolish the work and start over. You can save some of the sentences, like bricks. It will be a miracle if you can save some of the paragraphs, no matter how excellent in themselves or hard-won. You can waste a year worrying about it, or you can get it over with now. (Are you a woman, or a mouse?)

The part you must jettison is not only the best-written part; it is also, oddly, that part which was to have been the very point. It is the original key passage, the passage on which the rest was to hang, and from which you yourself drew the courage to begin. Henry James knew it well, and said it best. In his preface to *The Spoils of Poynton,* he pities the writer, in a comical pair of sentences that rises to a howl: "Which is the work in which he hasn't surrendered, under dire difficulty, the best thing he meant to have kept? In which indeed, before the dreadful *done,* doesn't he ask himself what has become of the thing all for the sweet sake of which it was to proceed to that extremity?"

So it is that a writer writes many books. In each book, he intended several urgent and vivid points, many of which he sacrificed as the book's form hardened. "The youth gets together his materials to build a bridge to the moon," Thoreau noted mournfully, "or perchance a palace or temple on the earth, and at length the middle-aged man concludes to build a wood-shed with them." The writer returns to these materials, these passionate subjects, as to unfinished business, for they are his life's work.

It is the beginning of a work that the writer throws away.

A painting covers its tracks. Painters work from the ground up. The latest version of a painting overlays earlier versions, and obliterates them. Writers, on the other hand, work from left to right. The discardable chapters are on the left. The latest version of a literary work begins somewhere in the work's middle, and hardens toward the end. The3 earlier version remains lumpishly on the left; the work's beginning greets the reader with the wrong hand. In those early pages and chapters anyone may find bold leaps to nowhere, read the brave beginnings of dropped themes, hear a tone since abandoned, discover blind alleys, track red herrings, and laboriously learn a setting now false.

Several delusions weaken the writer's resolve to throw away work. If he has read his pages too often, those pages will have a necessary quality, the ring of the inevitable, like poetry known by heart; they will perfectly answer their own familiar rhythms. He will retain them. He may retain those pages if they possess some virtues, such as power in themselves, though they lack the cardinal virtue, which is pertinence to, and unity with, the book's thrust. Sometimes the writer leaves his early chapters in place from gratitude; he cannot contemplate them or read them without feeling again the blessed relief that exalted him when the words first appeared—relief that he was writing anything at all. That beginning served to get him where he was going, after all; surely the reader needs it, too, as groundwork. But no.

Every year the aspiring photographer brought a stack of his best prints to an old, honored photographer, seeking his judgment. Every year the old man studied the prints and painstakingly ordered them into two piles, bad and good. Every year the old man moved a certain landscape print into the bad stack. At length he turned to the young man: "You submit this same landscape every year, and every year I put it on the bad stack. Why do you like it so much?" The young photographer said, "Because I had to climb a mountain to get it."

A cabdriver sang his songs to me, in New York. Some we sang together. He had turned the meter off; he drove around midtown, singing. One long song he sang twice; it was the only dull one. I said, You already sang that one; let's sing something else. And he said, "You don't know how long it took me to get that one together."

How many books do we read from which the writer lacked courage to tie off the umbilical cord? How many gifts do we open from which the writer neglected to remove the price tag? Is it pertinent, is it courteous, for us to learn what it cost the writer personally?

You write it all, discovering it at the end of the line of words. The line of words is a fiber optic, flexible as wire; it illumines the path just before its fragile tip. You probe with it, delicate as a worm. . . .

When you are stuck in a book; when you are well into writing it, and know what comes next, and yet cannot go on; when every morning for a week or a month you enter its room and turn your back on it; then the trouble is either of two things. Either the structure has forked, so the narrative, or the logic, has developed a hairline fracture that will shortly split it up the middle—or you are approaching a fatal mistake. What you had planned will not do. If you pursue your present course, the book will explode or collapse, and you do not know about it yet, quite.

In Bridgeport, Connecticut, one morning in April 1987, a six-story concrete-slab building under construction collapsed, and killed twenty-eight men. Just before it collapsed, a woman across the street leaned from her window and said to a passerby, "That building is starting to shake." "Lady," he said, according to the Hartford *Courant*, "you got rocks in your head."

You notice only this: your worker—your one and only, your prized, coddled, and driven worker—is not going out on that job. Will not budge, not even for you, boss. Has been at it long enough to know when the air smells wrong; can sense a tremor through boot soles. Nonsense, you say; it is perfectly safe. But the worker will not go. Will not even look at the site. Just developed heart trouble. Would rather starve. Sorry.

What do you do? Acknowledge, first, that you cannot do nothing. Lay out the structure you already have, x-ray it for a hairline fracture, find it, and think about it for a week or a year; solve the insoluble problem. Or subject the next part, the part at which the worker balks, to harsh tests. It harbors an unexamined and wrong premise. Something completely necessary is false or fatal. Once you find it, and if you can accept the finding, of course it will mean starting again. This is why many experienced writers urge young men and women to learn a useful trade.

Every morning you climb several flights of stairs, enter your study, open the French doors, and slide your desk and chair out into the middle of the air. The desk and chair float thirty feet from the ground, between the crowns of maple trees. The furniture is in place; you go back for your thermos of coffee. Then, wincing, you step out again through the French doors and sit down on the chair and look over the desktop. You can see clear to the river from here in winter. You pour yourself a cup of coffee.

Birds fly under your chair. In spring, when the leaves open in the maples' crowns, your view stops in the treetops just beyond the desk; yellow warblers hiss and whisper on the high twigs, and catch flies. Get to work. Your work is to keep cranking the flywheel that turns the gears that spin the belt in the engine of belief that keeps you and your desk in midair. . . .

The reason to perfect a piece of prose as it progresses—to secure each sentence before building on it—is that original writing fashions a form. It unrolls out into nothingness. It grows cell to cell, bole to bough to twig to leaf; any careful word may suggest a route, may begin a strand of metaphor or event out of which much, or all, will develop. Perfecting the work inch by inch, writing from the first word toward the last, displays the courage and fear this method induces. The strain, like Giacometti's penciled search for precision and honesty, enlivens the work and impels it toward its truest end. A pile of decent work behind him, no matter how small, fuels the writer's hope, too; his pride emboldens and impels him. One Washington writer—

Charlie Butts—so prizes momentum, and so fears self-consciousness, that he writes fiction in a rush of his own devising. He leaves his house on distracting errands, hurries in the door, and without taking off his coat, sits at a typewriter and retypes in a blur of speed all of the story he has written to date. Impetus propels him to add another sentence or two before he notices he is writing and seizes up. Then he leaves the house and repeats the process; he runs in the door and retypes the entire story, hoping to squeeze out another sentence the way some car engines turn over after the ignition is off, or the way Warner Bros.' Wile E. Coyote continues running for several yards beyond the edge of a cliff, until he notices.

The reason not to perfect a work as it progresses is that, concomitantly, original work fashions a form the true shape of which it discovers only as it proceeds, so the early strokes are useless, however fine their sheen. Only when a paragraph's role in the context of the whole work is clear can the envisioning writer direct its complexity of detail to strengthen the work's ends.

Fiction writers who toss up their arms helplessly because their characters "take over"—powerful rascals, what is a god to do?—refer, I think, to these structural mysteries that seize any serious work, whether or not it possesses fifth-column characters who wreak havoc from within. Sometimes part of a book simply gets up and walks away. The writer cannot force it back in place. It wanders off to die. . . .

You climb a long ladder until you can see over the roof, or over the clouds. You are writing a book. You watch your shod feet step on each round rung, one at a time; you do not hurry and do not rest. Your feet feel the steep ladder's balance; the long muscles in your thighs check its sway. You climb steadily, doing your job in the dark. When you reach the end, there is nothing more to climb. The sun hits you. The bright wideness surprises you; you had forgotten there was an end. You look back at the ladder's two feet on the distant grass, astonished.

The line of words fingers your own heart. It invades arteries, and enters the heart on a flood of breath; it presses the moving rims of thick valves; it palpates the dark muscle strong as horses, feeling for something, it knows not what. A queer picture beds in the muscle like a worm encysted—some film of feeling, some song forgotten, a scene in a dark bedroom, a corner of the woodlot, a terrible dining room, that exalting sidewalk; these fragments are heavy with meaning. The line of words peels them back, dissects them out. Will the bared tissue burn? Do you want to expose these scenes to the light? You may locate them and leave them, or poke the spot hard till the sore bleeds on your finger, and write with that blood. If the sore spot is not fatal, if it does not grow and block something, you can use its power for many years, until the heart resorbs it.

The line of words feels for cracks in the firmament.

The line of words is heading out past Jupiter this morning. Traveling 150 kilometers a second, it makes no sound. The big yellow planet and its white moons spin. The line of words speeds past Jupiter and its cumbrous, dizzying orbit; it looks neither to the right nor to the left. It will be leaving the solar system soon, single-minded, rapt, rushing heaven like a soul. You are in Houston, Texas, watching the monitor. You saw a simulation: the line of words waited still, hushed, pointed with longing. The big yellow planet spun toward it like a pitched ball and passed beside it, low and outside. Jupiter was so large, the arc of its edge at the screen's bottom looked flat. The probe twined on; its wild path passed between white suns small as dots; these stars fell away on either side, like the lights on a tunnel's walls.

Now you watch symbols move on your monitor; you stare at the signals the probe sends back, transmits in your own tongue, numbers. Maybe later you can guess at what they mean—what they might mean about space at the edge of the solar system, or about your instruments. Right now, you are flying. Right now, your job is to hold your breath. . . .

What is this writing life? I was living alone in a house once, and had set up a study on the first floor. A portable green Smith-Corona typewriter sat on the table against the wall. I made the mistake of leaving the room.

I was upstairs when I felt the first tremor. The floor wagged under my feet— what was that?—and the picture frames on the wall stirred. The house shook and made noise. There was a pause; I found my face in the dresser mirror, deadpan. When the floor began again to sway, I walked downstairs, thinking I had better get down while the stairway held.

I saw at once that the typewriter was erupting. The old green Smith-Corona typewriter on the table was exploding with fire and ash. Showers of sparks shot out of its caldera—the dark hollow in which the keys lie. Smoke and cinders poured out, noises exploded and spattered, black dense smoke rose up, and a wild, deep fire lighted the whole thing. It shot sparks.

I pulled down the curtains. When I leaned over the typewriter, sparks burnt round holes in my shirt, and fire singed a sleeve. I dragged the rug away from the sparks. In the kitchen I filled a bucket with water and returned to the erupting typewriter. The typewriter did not seem to be flying apart, only erupting. On my face and hands I felt the heat from the caldera. The yellow fire made a fast, roaring noise. The typewriter itself made a rumbling, grind- .

ing noise; the table pitched. Nothing seemed to require my bucket of water. The table surface was ruined, of course, but not aflame. After twenty minutes or so, the eruption subsided.

That night I heard more rumblings—weak ones, ever farther apart. The next day I cleaned the typewriter, table, floor, wall, and ceiling. I threw away the burnt shirt. The following day I cleaned the typewriter again—a film of lampblack still coated the caldera—and then it was over. I have had no trouble with it since. Of course, now I know it can happen. . . .

The sensation of writing a book is the sensation of spinning, blinded by love and daring. It is the sensation of rearing and peering from the bent tip of a grassblade, looking for a route. At its absurd worst, it feels like what mad Jacob Boehme, the German mystic, described in his first book. He was writing, incoherently as usual, about the source of evil. The passage will serve as well for the source of books.

"The whole Deity has in its innermost or beginning Birth, in the Pith or Kernel, a very tart, terrible *Sharpness*, in which the astringent Quality is very horrible, tart, hard, dark and cold Attraction or Drawing together, like *Winter*, when there is a fierce, bitter cold Frost, when Water is frozen into Ice, and besides is very intolerable."

If you can dissect out the very intolerable, tart, hard, terribly sharp Pith or Kernel, and begin writing the book compressed therein, the sensation changes. Now it feels like alligator wrestling, at the level of the sentence.

This is your life. You are a Seminole alligator wrestler. Half naked, with your two bare hands, you hold and fight a sentence's head while its tail tries to knock you over. Several years ago in Florida, an alligator wrestler lost. He was grappling with an alligator in a lagoon in front of a paying crowd. The crowd watched the young Indian and the alligator twist belly to belly in and out of the water; after one plunge, they failed to rise. A young writer named Lorne Ladner described it. Bubbles came up on the water. Then blood came up, and the water stilled. As the minutes elapsed, the people in the crowd exchanged glances; silent, helpless, they quit the stands. It took the Indians a week to find the man's remains.

At its best, the sensation of writing is that of any unmerited grace. It is handed to you, but only if you look for it. You search, you break your heart, your back, your brain, and then—and only then—it is handed to you. From the corner of your eye you see motion. Something is moving through the air and headed your way. It is a parcel bound in ribbons and bows; it has two white wings. It flies directly at you; you can read your name on it. If it were a baseball, you would hit it out of the park. It is that one pitch in a thousand you see in slow motion; its wings beat slowly as a hawk's.

One line of a poem, the poet said—only one line, but thank God for that one line—drops from the ceiling. Thornton Wilder cited this unnamed writer of sonnets: one line of a sonnet falls from the ceiling, and you tap in the others around it with a jeweler's hammer. Nobody whispers it in your ear. It is like something you memorized once and forgot. Now it comes back and rips away your breath. You find and finger a phrase at a time; you lay it down cautiously, as if with tongs, and wait suspended until the next one finds you: Ah yes, then this; and yes, praise be, then this.

Einstein likened the generation of a new idea to a chicken's laying an egg: "*Kieks—auf einmal ist es da.*" Cheep—and all at once there it is. Of course, Einstein was not above playing to the crowd.

One January day, working alone in that freezing borrowed cabin I used for a study on Puget Sound—heated not at all by the alder I chopped every morning—I wrote one of the final passages of a short, difficult book. It was a wildish passage in which the narrator, I, came upon the baptism of Christ in the water of the bay in front of the house. There was a northeaster on—as I wrote. The stormy salt water I saw from the cabin window looked dark as ink. The parallel rows of breakers made lively, broken lines, closely spaced row on row, moving fast and pulling the eyes; they reproduced the sensation of reading exactly, but without reading's sense. Mostly I shut my eyes. I have never been in so trancelike a state, and in fact I dislike, as romantic, the suggestion that any writer works in any peculiar state. I sat motionless with my eyes shut, like a Greek funerary marble.

The writing was simple yet graceless; it surprised me. It was arrhythmical, nonvisual, clunky. It was halting, as if there were no use trying to invoke beauty or power. It was plain and ugly, urgent, like child's talk. "He led him into the water," it said, without antecedents. It read like a translation from the *Gallic Wars*.

Once when I opened my eyes the page seemed bright. The windows were steamed and the sun had gone behind the firs on the bluff. I must have had my eyes closed long. I had been repeating to myself, for hours, like a song, "It is the grave of Jesus, where he lay." From Wallace Stevens' poem, "Sunday Morning." It was three o'clock then; I heated some soup. By the time I left, I was scarcely alive. The way home was along the beach. The beach was bright and distinct. The storm still blew. I was light, dizzy, barely there. I remembered some legendary lamas, who wear chains to keep from floating away. Walking itself seemed to be a stunt; I could not tell whether I was walking fast or slowly. My thighs felt as if they had been reamed.

And I have remembered it often, later, waking up in that cabin to windows steamed blue and the sun gone around the island; remembered putting down those queer, stark sentences half blind on yellow paper; remembered walking ensorcerized, tethered, down the gray cobble beach like an aisle. Evelyn Underhill describes another life, and a better one, in words that recall to me that day, and many another day, at this queer task: "He goes because he must, as Galahad went towards the Grail: knowing that for those who can live it, this alone is life."

Push it. Examine all things intensely and relentlessly. Probe and search each object in a piece of art. Do not leave it, do not course over it, as if it were understood, but instead follow it down until you see it in the mystery of its own specificity and strength. Giacometti's drawings and paintings show his bewilderment and persistence. If he had not acknowledged his bewilderment, he would not have persisted. A twentieth-century master of drawing, Rico Lebrun, taught that "the draftsman must aggress; only by persistent assault will the live image capitulate and give up its secret to an unrelenting line." Who but an artist fierce to know—not fierce to seem to know—would suppose that a live image possessed a secret? The artist is willing to give all his or her strength and life to probing with blunt instruments those same secrets no one can describe in any way but with those instruments' faint tracks.

Admire the world for never ending on you—as you would admire an opponent, without taking your eyes from him, or walking away.

One of the few things I know about writing is this: spend it all, shoot it, play it, lose it, all, right away, every time. Do not hoard what seems good for a later place in the book, or for another book; give it, give it all, give it now. The impulse to save something good for a better place later is the signal to spend it now. Something more will arise for later, something better. These things fill from behind, from beneath, like well water. Similarly, the impulse to keep to yourself what you have learned is not only shameful, it is destructive. Anything you do not give freely and abundantly becomes lost to you. You open your safe and find ashes.

After Michelangelo died, someone found in his studio a piece of paper on which he had written a note to his apprentice, in the handwriting of his old age: "Draw, Antonio, draw, Antonio, draw and do not waste time. . . ."

Suggestions for Discussion

1. The first of the excerpts is from a memoir, the second from a manual for writers, the third from a collection of essays. What elements of fiction does each employ?

2. Which describes a writing process most congenial to you?

3. Which is written in a form and style most congenial to you?

4. What insights into the writing process surprise you, discourage you, make you want to get to work?

WRITING ASSIGNMENTS

Keep a journal for two weeks. Decide on a comfortable amount to write daily, and then determine not to let a day slide. In addition to the journal suggestions already in this chapter—freewriting, page 4; the Dorothea Brande exercise, page 5; clustering, pages 5–6; a menu of concerns, page 9; a review of your first seven years, page 9; a set of *Pillow Book* lists, page 9—you might try these:

1. Prove to yourself the abundance of your invention by opening this book and pointing at random. Take the noun nearest where your finger falls, cluster it for two or three minutes, and freedraft a paragraph on the subject.

2. Sketch a floor plan of the first house you remember. Place an X on the spots in the plan where significant events happened to you. Write a tour of the house as if you were a guide, pointing out its features and its history.

3. Identify the kernel of a short story from your experience of one of the following:
   first memory
   a dream
   parents
   loss
   unfounded fear
   your body
   yesterday
Cluster the word and freedraft a passage about it. Outline a story based on it. Write the first page of the story.

4. Identify a passage in one of the three excerpts above that seems to parallel or echo your own experience. Cluster, then freedraft, a response to it.

5. Write a short memoir of some moment that has to do with reading or writing—the moment you discovered that you could read, for example, or could write your name; or an early influence that has led you toward writing.

At the end of the two weeks, assess yourself and decide what habit of journal keeping you can develop and stick to. A page a day? A paragraph a day? Three pages a week? Then do it. Probably at least once a day you have a thought worth wording, and sometimes it's better to write one sentence a day than to let the habit slide. Like exercise and piano practice, a journal is most useful when it's kept up regularly and frequently. If you pick an hour during which you write each day, no matter how much or how little, you may find yourself looking forward to, and saving things up for, that time.

WAR GAMES
Story Form and Structure

Conflict, Crisis, and Resolution
Story and Plot
The Short Story and the Novel

What makes you want to write?

It seems likely that the earliest storytellers—in the tent or the harem, around the camp fire or on the Viking ship—told stories out of an impulse to tell stories. They made themselves popular by distracting their listeners from a dull or dangerous evening with heroic exploits and a skill at creating suspense: What happened next? And after that? And then what happened?

Natural storytellers are still around, and a few of them are very rich. Some are on the best-seller list; more are in television and film. But it's probable that your impulse to write has little to do with the desire or the skill to work out a plot. On the contrary, you want to write because you are sensitive. You have something to say that does not answer the question, What happened next? You share with most—and the best—twentieth-century fiction writers a sense of the injustice, the absurdity, and the beauty of the world; and you want to register your protest, your laughter, and your affirmation.

Yet readers still want to wonder what happened next, and unless you make them wonder, they will not turn the page. You must master plot, because no matter how profound or illuminating your vision of the world may be, you cannot convey it to those who do not read you.

E. M. Forster, in *Aspects of the Novel,* mourns the necessity of storytelling.

Let us listen to three voices. If you ask one type of man, "What does a novel do?" he will reply placidly: "Well—I don't know—it seems a funny sort of question to ask—a novel's a novel—well, I don't know—I suppose it kind of tells a story, so to speak." He is quite good-tempered and vague, and probably driving a motor bus at the same time and paying no more attention to literature than it merits. Another man, whom I visualize as on a golf-course, will be aggressive and brisk. He will reply: "What does a novel do? Why, tell a story of course, and I've no use for it if it didn't. I like a story. Very bad taste on my part, no doubt, but I like a story. You can take your art, you can take your literature, you can take your music, but give me a good story. And I like a story to be a story, mind, and my wife's the same." And a third man, he says in a sort of drooping regretful voice, "Yes—oh dear yes—the novel tells a story." I respect and admire the first speaker. I detest and fear the second. And the third is myself. Yes—oh dear yes—the novel tells a story. That is the fundamental aspect without which it could not exist. That is the highest factor common to all novels, and I wish that it was not so, that it could be something different—melody, or perception of the truth, not this low atavistic form.

When editors take the trouble to write a rejection letter to a young author (and they do so only when they think the author talented), the gist of the letter most frequently is: "This piece is sensitive (perceptive, vivid, original, brilliant, funny, moving), but it is not a *story.* "

How do you know when you have written a story? And if you're not a natural-born wandering minstrel, can you go about learning to write one?

It's interesting that we react with such different attitudes to the words "formula" and "form" as they apply to a story. A *formula story* is hackwork, the very lowest "atavistic" form of supplying a demand. To write one, you read three dozen copies of *Cosmopolitan* or *Ellery Queen's Mystery Magazine,* make a list of what kinds of characters and situations the editors buy, shuffle nearly identical characters around in slightly altered situations, and sit back to wait for the check. Whereas *form* is a term of the highest artistic approbation, even reverence, with overtones of *order, harmony, model, archetype.*

And "story" is a "form" of literature. Like a face, it has necessary features in a necessary harmony. We're aware of the infinite variety of human faces, aware of their unique individuality, which is so powerful that you can recognize a face you know even after twenty years of age and fashion have done their work on it. We're aware that minute alterations in the features can express grief, anger, or joy. If you place side by side two photographs of, say, Brooke Shields and Geronimo, you are instantly aware of the fundamental differences of age, race, sex, class, and century; yet these two faces are more like each other than either is like a foot or a fern, both of which have their own distinctive forms. Every face has two eyes, a nose between them, a mouth below, a forehead, two cheeks, two ears, and a jaw. If a face is missing one of these features, you may say, "I love this face in spite of its lacking a nose," but you must acknowledge the *in spite of*. You can't simply say, "This is a wonderful face."

The same is true of a story. You might say, "I love this piece even though there's no crisis action in it." You can't say, "This is a wonderful story."

Conflict, Crisis, and Resolution

Fortunately, the necessary features of the story form are fewer than those of a face. They are *conflict, crisis,* and *resolution*.

Conflict is the first encountered and the fundamental element of fiction, necessary because in literature, only trouble is interesting.

Only trouble is interesting. This is not so in life. Life offers periods of comfortable communication, peaceful pleasure, and productive work, all of which are extremely interesting to those involved. But such passages about such times by themselves make for dull reading; they can be used as lulls in an otherwise tense situation, as a resolution, even as a hint that something awful is about to happen; they cannot be used as a whole plot.

Suppose, for example, you go on a picnic. You find a beautiful deserted meadow with a lake nearby. The weather is splendid and so is the company. The food's delicious, the water's fine, and the insects have taken the day off. Afterward, someone asks you how your picnic was. "Terrific," you reply, "really perfect." No story.

But suppose the next week you go back for a rerun. You set your picnic blanket on an anthill. You all race for the lake to get cold water on the bites, and one of your friends goes too far out on the plastic raft, which deflates. He can't swim and you have to save him. On the way in you gash your foot on a broken bottle. When you get back to the picnic, the ants have taken over the cake, and a possum has demolished the chicken. Just then the sky opens up. When you gather your things to race for the car, you notice an irritated bull has broken through the fence. The others run for it, but because of your bleeding heel the best you can do is hobble. You have two choices: Try to outrun him or stand perfectly still and hope he's interested only in a moving target. At this point, you don't know if your friends can be counted on for help, even the nerd whose life you saved. You don't know if it's true that a bull is attracted by the smell of blood. . . .

A year later, assuming you're around to tell about it, you are still saying, "Let me *tell* you what happened last year. . . ." And your listeners are saying, "What a story!"

If this contrast is true of so trivial a subject as a picnic, it is even more so of the great themes of life: birth, love, sex, work, and death. Here is a very interesting love story to *live*: Jan and Jon meet in college. Both are beautiful, intelligent, talented, popular, and well adjusted. They're of the same race, class, religion, and political persuasion. They are sexually compatible. Their parents become fast friends. They marry on graduating, and both get rewarding work in the same city. They have three children, all of whom are healthy, happy, beautiful, intelligent, and popular; the children love and respect their parents to a degree that is the envy of everyone. All the children succeed in work and marriage. Jan and Jon die peacefully, of natural causes, at the same moment, at the age of eighty-two, and are buried in the same grave.

No doubt this love story is very interesting to Jan and Jon, but you can't make a novel of it. Great love stories involve intense passion and a monumental impediment to that passion's fulfillment. So: They love each other passionately, but their parents are sworn enemies (*Romeo and Juliet*). Or: They love each other passionately, but he's black and she's white, and he has an enemy who wants to punish him (*Othello*). Or: They love each other passionately, but she's married (*Anna Karenina*). Or: He loves her passionately, but she falls in love with him only when she has worn out his passion ("Frankly, my dear, I don't give a damn").

In each of these plots, there is both intense desire and great danger to the achievement of that desire; generally speaking, this shape holds good for all plots. It can be called 3-D: *Drama* equals *desire* plus *danger.* One common fault of talented young writers is to create a main character who is essentially passive. This is an understandable fault; as a writer you are an observer of human nature and activity, and so you identify easily with a character who observes, reflects, and suffers. But such a character's passivity transmits itself to the page, and the story also becomes passive. Aristotle rather startingly claimed that a man *is* his desire. It is true that in fiction, in order to engage our attention and sympathy, the central character must *want,* and want intensely.

The thing that the character wants need not be violent or spectacular; it is the intensity of the wanting that counts. She may want, like *The Suicide's Wife* in David Madden's novel, no more than to get her driver's license, but if so she must feel that her identity and her future depend on her getting a driver's license, while a corrupt highway patrolman tries to manipulate her. He may want, like Samuel Beckett's Murphy, only to tie himself to his rocking chair and rock, but if so he will also want a woman who nags him to get up and get a job. She may want, like the heroine of Margaret Atwood's *Bodily Harm,* only to get away from it all for a rest, but if so she must need rest for her survival, while tourists and terrorists involve her in machinations that begin in discomfort and end in mortal danger.

It's important to realize that the great dangers in life and in literature are not necessarily the most spectacular. Another mistake frequently made by young writers is to think that they can best introduce drama into their stories by way of muggers, murderers, crashes, and monsters, the external stock dangers of pulp and TV. In fact, all of us know that the profoundest impediments to our desire most often lie close to home, in our own bodies, personalities, friends, lovers, and families. Fewer people have cause to panic at the approach of a stranger with a gun than at the approach of mama with the curling iron. More passion is destroyed at the breakfast table than in a time warp.

A frequently used critical tool divides possible conflicts into several basic categories: man against man, man against nature, man against society, man against machine, man against God, man against himself. Most stories fall into these categories, and they can provide a useful way of discussing and comparing works. But the employment of categories can be misleading to someone behind the typewriter, insofar as it suggests that literary conflicts take place in these abstract, cosmic dimensions. A writer needs a specific story to tell, and if you sit down to pit "man" against "nature," you will have less of a story than if you pit seventeen-year-old James Tucker of Weehawken, New Jersey, against a two-and-a-half-foot bigmouth bass in the backwoods of Toomsuba, Mississippi. (The value of specificity is a point to which we will return again and again.)

Once conflict is sharply established and developed in a story, the conflict must end. There must be a crisis and a resolution. This is not like life either, and although it is so obvious a point, it needs to be insisted on. Order is a major value that literature offers us, and order implies that the subject has been brought to closure. In life this never quite happens. Even the natural "happy endings," marriage and birth, leave domesticity and childbearing to be dealt with; the natural "tragic endings," separation and death, leave trauma and bereavement in their wake. Literature absolves us of these nuisances. Whether or not the lives of the characters end, the story does, and leaves us with a satisfying sense of completion. This is one reason we enjoy crying or feeling terrified or even nauseated by fiction; we know in advance that it's going to be *over*, and by contrast with the continual struggle of living, all that ends, ends well.

What I want to do now is to present several ways—they are all essentially metaphors—of seeing this pattern of *conflict-crisis-resolution* in order to make the shape and its many variations clearer, and particularly to indicate what a crisis action is.

The editor and teacher Mel McKee states flatly that "a story is a war. It is sustained and immediate combat." He offers four imperatives for the writing of this "war" story.

> (1) get your fighters fighting, (2) have something—the stake—worth their fighting over, (3) have the fight dive into a series of battles with the last battle in the series the biggest and most dangerous of all, (4) have a walking away from the fight.

The stake over which wars are fought is usually a territory, and it's important that this "territory" in a story be as tangible and specific as the Gaza Strip. For example, in William Carlos Williams's story "The Use of Force," found at the end of this chapter, the war is fought over the territory of the little girl's mouth, and the fight begins narrowing to that territory from the first paragraph. As with warring nations, the story territory itself can come to represent all sorts of serious abstractions—self-determination, domination, freedom, dignity, identity—but the soldiers fight yard by yard over a particular piece of grass or sand.

Just as a "police action" may escalate into a holocaust, story form follows its most natural order of "complications" when each battle is bigger than the last. It begins with a ground skirmish, which does not decide the war. Then one side brings in spies, and the other, guerrillas; these actions do not decide the war. So one side brings in the air force, and the other answers with antiaircraft. One side takes to missiles, and the other answers with rockets. One side has poison gas, and the other has a hand on the nuclear button. Metaphorically, this is what happens in a story. As long as one antagonist can recoup enough power to counterattack, the conflict goes on. But, at some point in the story, one of the antagonists will produce a weapon from which the other cannot recover. *The crisis action is the last battle and occurs when the outcome becomes inevitable;* when, after much doubt, there can no longer be any doubt who wins the particular territory—though there can be much doubt about moral victory.

Notice that although a plot involves desire and a danger to that desire, it does not necessarily end happily if the desire is achieved, nor unhappily if it is not. In *Hamlet*, Hamlet's desire is to kill King Claudius, and he is prevented from doing so for most of the play by other characters, intrigues, and his own mental state. When he finally succeeds, it is at the cost of every significant life in the play, including his own. Although the hero "wins" his particular "territory," the play is a tragedy. In Margaret Atwood's *Bodily Harm,* on the other hand, the heroine ends up in a political prison. Yet the discovery of her own strength and commitment is such that we know she has achieved salvation.

Novelist Michael Shaara describes a story as a power struggle between equal forces. It is imperative, he argues, that each antagonist have sufficient power to leave the reader in doubt about the outcome. We may be wholly in sympathy with one character and even reasonably confident that she or he will triumph. But the antagonist must represent a real and potent danger, and the pattern of the story's complications will be achieved by *shifting the power back and forth from one antagonist to the other.* Finally, an action will occur that will shift the power irretrievably in one direction.

It is also important to understand that "power" takes many forms and that some of them have the external appearance of weakness. Anyone who has ever been tied to the demands of an invalid can understand this: Sickness can be great strength. Weakness, need, passivity, an ostensible desire not to be any trouble to anybody— all these can be used as manipulative tools to prevent the protagonist from achieving his or her desire. Martyrdom is immensely powerful, whether we sympathize with it or not; a dying man absorbs all our energies.

In contrast to this model of narrative as a war or power struggle, some critics of recent years have posited birth as an alternative metaphor. Seeing the world in terms of enemies and warring factions not only limits the possibilities of literature, they argue, but also promulgates an aggressive and antagonistic view of our own lives. Further, the notion of resolution is untrue to life, and holds up perfection, unity, and singularity as goals at the expense of acceptance, nuance, and variety.

Speaking of the "gladiatorial view of fiction," Ursula Le Guin writes:

> People are cross-grained, aggressive, and full of trouble, the storytellers tell us; people fight themselves and one another, and their stories are full of their struggles. But to say that that *is* the story is to use one aspect of existence, conflict, to subsume all other aspects, many of which it does not include and does not comprehend.
>
> *Romeo and Juliet* is a story of the conflict between two families, and its plot involves the conflict of two individuals with those families. Is that all it involves? Isn't *Romeo and Juliet* about something else, and isn't it the something else that makes the otherwise trivial tale of a feud into a tragedy?

Birth presents us with an alternative model in which there is a desired result, drama, struggle, and outcome. But it also represents a process in which the struggle, one toward life and growth, is natural. There is no enemy. The "resolution" suggests continuance rather than finality. It is persuasively argued that the story as power struggle offers a patriarchal view of the world, and that it would improve both stories and world if we would envision human beings as engaged in a struggle toward light.

Still another way of seeing the shape of the story is in terms of situation-action-situation. The story begins by presenting us with a situation. It then recounts an action, and when that action is over, we are left with a situation *that is the opposite* of the opening situation. This formula seems oversimplified, but it is very difficult to find a story it does not describe.

The nineteenth-century German critic Gustav Freitag analyzed five-act dramas and came up with a diagram (page 44) of plot that has come to be known as the Freitag Pyramid. Plot begins, he said, with an exposition, followed by the complication (or *nouement*, the "knotting up" of the situation) leading to a crisis, which is followed by a "falling action" (or anticlimax), resulting in a resolution (or *dénouement*, "unknotting").

The trouble with Freitag's useful diagram is that it visually suggests that a crisis comes in the middle of the "pyramid" shape of a plot, whereas even in a five-act drama the crisis is usually saved for the middle of the fifth act; and in modern fiction, particularly the compact short-story form, the falling action is likely to be very brief or nonexistent. Often the crisis action itself implies the resolution, which is not stated but exists as an idea established in the reader's mind.

For our purposes, it is probably more useful to think of story shape as an inverted check mark. If we take the familiar tale "Cinderella" and look at it in terms of the

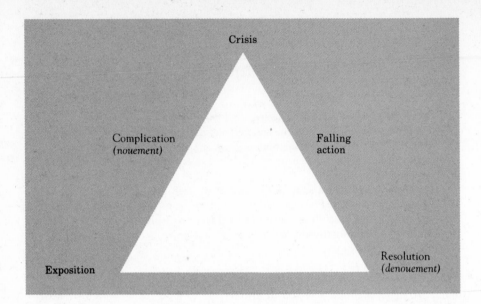

diagram below, we can see how the various elements reveal themselves even in this simple children's story. At the opening of the tale we're given the basic conflict: Cinderella's mother has died, and her father has married a brutal woman with two waspish daughters. Cinderella is made to do all the dirtiest and most menial work, and she weeps among the cinders. The Stepmother has on her side the strength of ugliness and evil (two very powerful qualities in literature as in life). With her daughters she also has the strength of numbers, and she has parental authority.

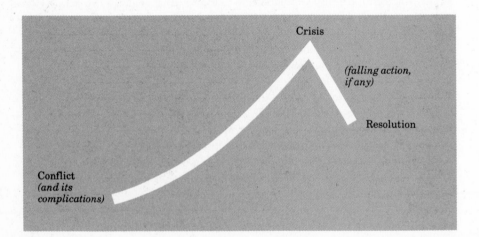

Cinderella has only beauty and goodness, but (in literature and life) these are also very powerful. This is very clearly a tale on the "story as war" model, with a heroine and enemies. (Contrast "The Ugly Duckling," perhaps, for a birth-model fairy tale, where success is achieved through growth and self-realization rather than a fight.)

At the beginning of the struggle in "Cinderella," the power is very clearly on the Stepmother's side. But the first *event* (action, battle) of the story is that an invitation arrives from the Prince, which explicitly states that *all* the ladies of the land are invited to a ball. Notice that Cinderella's desire is not to triumph over her Stepmother (though she eventually will, much to our satisfaction); such a desire would diminish her goodness. She simply wants to be relieved of her mistreatment. She wants equality, so that the Prince's invitation, which specifically gives her a right equal to the Stepmother's and Stepdaughters' rights, shifts the power to her.

The Stepmother takes the power back by blunt force: You may not go; you must get us ready to go. Cinderella does so, and the three leave for the ball.

Then what happens? The Fairy Godmother appears. It is *very* powerful to have magic on your side. The Fairy Godmother offers Cinderella a gown, glass slippers, and a coach with horses and footmen, giving her more force than she has yet had.

But the magic is not all-potent. It has a qualification that portends bad luck. It will last only until midnight (unlike the Stepmother's authority), and Cinderella must leave the ball before the clock strikes twelve or risk exposure and defeat.

What happens next? She goes to the ball and the Prince falls in love with her—and love is an even more powerful weapon than magic in a literary war. In some versions of the tale, the Stepmother and Stepsisters are made to marvel at the beauty of the Princess they don't recognize, pointing to the irony of Cinderella's new power.

And then? The magic quits. The clock strikes twelve, and Cinderella runs down the steps in her rags to her rats and pumpkin, losing a slipper, bereft of her power in every way.

But after that, the Prince sends out a messenger with the glass slipper and a dictum (a dramatic repetition of the original invitation in which all ladies were invited to the ball) that every female in the land is to try on the slipper. Cinderella is given her rights again by royal decree.

What happens then? In most good retellings of the tale, the Stepmother also repeats her assumption of brute authority by hiding Cinderella away, while our expectation of triumph is tantalizingly delayed with grotesque comedy: One sister cuts off a toe, the other a heel, trying to fit into the heroine's rightful slipper.

After that, Cinderella tries on the slipper and it fits. *This is the crisis action.* Magic, love, and royalty join to recognize the heroine's true self; evil, numbers, and authority are powerless against them. At this point, the power struggle has been decided; the outcome is inevitable. When the slipper fits, no further action can occur that will deprive Cinderella of her desire.

The tale has a brief "falling action" or "walking away from the fight": The Prince sweeps Cinderella up on his white horse and gallops away to their wedding. The story comes to closure with the classic resolution of all comedy: They lived happily ever after. Applied to the diagram, the story's pattern looks like the drawing below.

In the *Poetics*, the first extensive work of extant Western literary criticism, Aristotle referred to the crisis action of a tragedy as a *peripeteia*, or reversal of the protagonist's fortunes. Critics and editors agree that a reversal of some sort is necessary to all story structure: Although the protagonist need not lose power, land, or life, he or she must in some significant way be changed or moved by the action. Aristotle specified that this reversal came about because of *hamartia*, which has for centuries been translated as a "tragic flaw" in the protagonist's character, usually assumed to be, or defined as, pride. But more recent critics have defined and translated *hamartia* much more narrowly as a "mistake in identity" whereby the reversal comes about in a "recognition."

It is true that recognition scenes have played a disproportionately large role in the crisis actions of plots both comic and tragic, and that these scenes frequently stretch credibility; it's already been observed that you are unlikely to mistake the face of your mother, son, uncle, or even friend in real life, and yet such mistakes

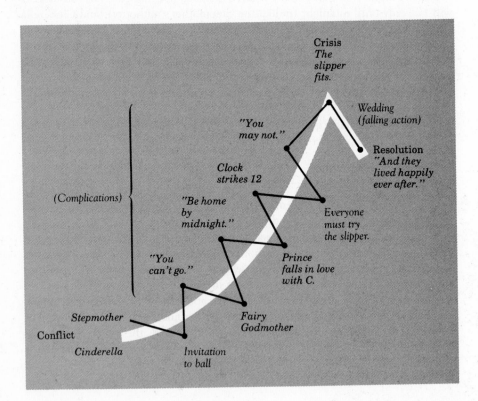

have provided the turning point of many a plot. If, however, the notion of "recognition" is extended to more abstract and subtle realms, it becomes a powerful metaphor for moments of "realization." In other words, the "recognition scene" in literature may stand for that moment in life when we "recognize" that the man we have considered good is evil, the event we have considered insignificant is crucial, the woman we have thought out of touch with reality is a genius, the object we have thought desirable is poison. There is in this symbolic way a recognition in "Cinderella." We knew that she was essentially a princess, but until the Prince recognizes her as one, our knowledge must be frustrated.

James Joyce developed a similar idea when he spoke of, and recorded both in his notebooks and in his stories, moments of what he called *epiphany*. Epiphany as Joyce saw it is a crisis action in the mind, a moment when a person, an event, or a thing is seen in a light so new that it is as if it has never been seen before; at this recognition, the mental landscape of the viewer is permanently changed.

In many of the finest modern short stories and novels, the true territory of struggle is the main character's mind, and so the real crisis action must occur there. Yet it is important to grasp that Joyce chose the word *epiphany* to represent this moment of reversal, and that the word means "*a manifestation* of a supernatural being"; specifically, in Christian doctrine, "the manifestation of Christ to the gentiles." By extension, then, in a short story any mental reversal that takes place in the crisis of a story must be *manifested*; it must be triggered or shown by an action. The slipper must fit. It would not do if the Stepmother just happened to change her mind and give up the struggle; it would not do if the Prince just happened to notice that Cinderella looked like his love. The moment of recognition must be manifested in an action.

This point, that the crisis must be manifested or externalized in an action, is absolutely central, although sometimes difficult to grasp when the struggle of the story takes place in a character's mind.

It is easy to see, for example, how the conflict in a revenge story must end. The common revenge plot, from *Hamlet* to *Beverly Hills Cop*, takes this form: Someone important to the hero (father, sister, lover, friend) is killed, and for some reason the authorities who ought to be in charge of justice can't or won't avenge the death. The hero must do so, then, and the crisis action is manifested in the swing of the dagger, the blast of the gun, the swallowing of the poison, whatever.

But suppose the story is about a struggle between two brothers on a fishing trip, and the change that takes place is that the protagonist, believing for most of the action that he holds his older brother in contempt, discovers at the end of the story that they are deeply bound by love and family history. Clearly this change is an epiphany, a mental reversal. A writer insufficiently aware of the nature of crisis action might signal the change in a paragraph that begins "suddenly Larry remembered their father and realized that Jeff was very much like him." Well, unless that memory and that realization are manifested in an action, the reader is unable to share them, and therefore cannot be moved with the character.

Jeff reached for the old net and neatly bagged the trout, swinging round to offer it with a triumphant, "Got it! We got it, didn't we?" The trout flipped and struggled, giving off a smell of weed and water and fecund mud. Jeff's knuckles were lined with grime. The knuckles and the rich river smell filled him with a memory of their first fishing trip together, the sight of their father's hands on the same scarred net. . . .

Here the epiphany, a memory leading to a realization, has been triggered by an action and sensory details that the reader can share; the reader now has a good chance of also being able to share the epiphany.

Much great fiction, and the preponderance of serious modern fiction, echoes life in its suggestion that there are no clear or permanent solutions, that the conflicts of character, relationship, and the cosmos cannot be permanently resolved. Most of the stories in this volume have the feel of the twentieth century, with its ambiguities and unfinished struggles; none could end "they lived happily ever after" or even "they lived unhappily ever after."

Yet the story form demands a resolution. Is there such a thing as a no-resolution resolution? Yes, and it also has a very specific form. Go back to the metaphor that "a story is a war." After the skirmish, after the guerrillas, after the air strike, after the poison gas and the nuclear holocaust, imagine that the two surviving combatants, one on each side, emerge from their fallout shelters. They crawl, then stumble to the fence that marks the border. Each possessively grasps the barbed wire with a bloodied fist. The "resolution" of this battle is that neither side will ever give up and that no one will ever win; *there will never be a resolution*. This is a distinct reversal (the recognition takes place in the reader's mind) of the opening scene, in which it seemed eminently worthwhile to open a ground skirmish. In the statement of the conflict was an inherent possibility that one side or another could win. Inherent in the resolution is a statement that no one can ever win. That is a distinct reversal and a powerful resolution.

Story and Plot

So far, I have used the words "story" and "plot" interchangeably. The equation of the two terms is so common that they are often comfortably understood as synonyms. When an editor says, "This is not a story," the implication is not that it lacks character, theme, setting, or even incident, but that it has no plot.

Yet there is a distinction frequently drawn between the two terms, a distinction that is simple in itself but that gives rise to manifold subtleties in the craft of narrative and that also represents a vital decision that you as a writer must make: Where does the narrative begin?

The distinction is easily made. A *story* is a series of events recorded in their chronological order. A *plot* is a series of events deliberately arranged so as to reveal their dramatic, thematic, and emotional significance.

Here, for example, is a fairly standard story: A sober, industrious, and rather dull young man meets the woman of his dreams. She is beautiful, brilliant, passionate, and compassionate; more wonderful still, she loves him. They plan to marry, and on the eve of their wedding his friends give him a stag party in the course of which they tease him, ply him with liquor, and drag him off to a whorehouse for a last fling. There he stumbles into a cubicle . . . to find himself facing his bride-to-be.

Where does this story become interesting? Where does the *plot* begin?

You may start, if you like, with the young man's *Mayflower* ancestry. But if you do, it's going to be a very long story, and we're likely to close the book about the middle of the nineteenth century. You may begin with the first time he meets the extraordinary woman, but again you must cover at least weeks, probably months, in a few pages; and that means you must summarize, skip, and generalize, and you'll have a hard time both maintaining your credibility and holding our attention. Begin at the stag party? Better. If you do so, you will somehow have to let us know all that has gone before, either through dialogue or through the young man's memory, but you have only one evening of action to cover, and we'll get to the conflict quickly. Suppose you begin instead the next morning, when the man wakes with a hangover in bed in a brothel with his bride on his wedding day. Is that, perhaps, the best of all? An immediate conflict that must lead to a quick and striking crisis?

Humphry House, in his commentaries on Aristotle, defines *story* as everything the reader needs to know to make coherent sense of the plot, and *plot* as the particular portion of the story the author chooses to present—the "present tense" of the narrative. The story of *Oedipus Rex*, for example, begins before Oedipus's birth with the oracle predicting that he will murder his father and marry his mother. It includes his birth, his abandonment with hobbled ankles, his childhood with his foster parents, his flight from them, his murder of the stranger at the crossroads, his triumph over the Sphinx, his marriage to Jocasta and his reign in Thebes, his fatherhood, the Theban plague, his discovery of the truth, and his self-blinding and self-banishment. When Sophocles set out to plot a play on this story, he began at dawn on the very last day of it. All the information about Oedipus's life is necessary to understand the plot, but the plot begins with the conflict: How can Oedipus get rid of the plague in Thebes? Because the plot is so arranged, it is the revelation of the past that makes up the action of the play, a process of discovery that gives rise to the significant theme: Who am I? Had Sophocles begun with the oracle before Oedipus's birth, no such theme and no such significance could have been explored.

Forster makes substantially the same distinction between plot and story. A story, he says, is:

> the chopped off length of the tape worm of time . . . a narrative of events arranged in their time sequence. A plot is also a narrative of events, the emphasis falling

on causality. "The king died, and then the queen died," is a story. "The king died, and then the queen died of grief," is a plot. The time-sequence is preserved, but the sense of causality overshadows it. Or again: "The queen died, no one knew why, until it was discovered that it was through grief at the death of the king." This is a plot with a mystery in it, a form capable of high development. It suspends the time-sequence, it moves as far away from the story as its limitations will allow. Consider the death of the queen. If it is in a story we say, "and then?" If it is in a plot we ask, "why?"

The human desire to know why is as powerful as the desire to know what happened next, and it is a desire of a higher order. Once we have the facts, we inevitably look for the links between them, and only when we find such links are we satisfied that we "understand." Rote memorization in a science bores almost everyone. Grasp and a sense of discovery begin only when we perceive *why* "a body in motion tends to remain in motion" and what an immense effect this actuality has on the phenomena of our lives.

The same is true of the events of a story. Random incidents neither move nor illuminate; we want to know why one thing leads to another and to feel the inevitability of cause and effect.

Here is a series of uninteresting events chronologically arranged.

> Ariadne had a bad dream.
> She woke up tired and cross.
> She ate breakfast.
> She headed for class.
> She saw Leroy.
> She fell on the steps and broke her ankle.
> Leroy offered to take notes for her.
> She went to a hospital.

This series of events does not constitute a plot, and if you wish to fashion it into a plot, you can do so only by letting us know the meaningful relations among the events. We first assume that Ariadne woke in a temper *because* of her bad dream, and that Leroy offered to take notes for her because she broke her ankle. But why did she fall? Perhaps because she saw Leroy? Does that suggest that her bad dream was about him? Was she, then, thinking about his dream-rejection as she broke her egg irritably on the edge of the frying pan? What is the effect of his offer? Is it a triumph or just another polite form of rejection when, really, he *could* have missed class once to drive her to the x-ray lab? All the emotional and dramatic significance of these ordinary events emerges in the relation of cause to effect, and where such relation can be shown, a possible plot comes into existence.

Ariadne's is a story you might very well choose to tell chronologically: It needs to cover only an hour or two, and that much can be handled in the compressed form of the short story. But such a choice of plot is not inevitable even in this short compass. Might it be more gripping to begin with the wince of pain as she stumbles? Leroy comes to help her up and the yolk yellow of his T-shirt fills her field of vision. In the shock of pain she is immediately back in her dream. . . .

When "nothing happens" in a story, it is because we fail to sense the causal relation between what happens first and what happens next. When something does "happen," it is because the resolution of a short story or a novel describes a change in the character's life, an effect of the events that have gone before. This is why Aristotle insisted with such apparent simplicity on "a beginning, a middle, and an end." A story is capable of many meanings, and it is first of all in the choice of structure, which portion of the story forms the plot, that you offer us the gratifying sense that we "understand."

There are two current terms relating to story structure that it may be well to mention. The first is *minimalism,* which refers to stories that are stylistically spare and structurally flat. They are related to the "slice of life" stories of the fifties in that they do not purport to record a change in the protagonist's life, but rather a revealing photograph or caught passage of time. It would be accurate to describe the form with Forster's definition of story, the "chopped off length of the tape worm of time." Though these stories may contain various conflicts, there is no central conflict, no crisis moment, and no resolution. Ray Carver was considered an important practitioner of minimalism; his story "Cathedral," found later in this volume, is an example of a minimalist story.

Minimalism is one answer to the charge that traditional story structure distorts and lies about life: Implied in the form is the view that people really do not change, and that stories should not show them as changing. Since my own experience is that people do change, are changed, and change themselves, I'm not personally able to subscribe to the idea that minimalism offers a truer look at life than traditional narrative. But I enjoy many minimalist stories.

Metafiction, the second term, refers to a narrative in which the techniques of storytelling and writing become part of the subject matter of the fiction. It is akin to theatricalism in the theater, where the actors acknowledge that they are on a stage, in character, in a play, and that the audience is watching them. In fiction, the author may speak directly to the reader, may ask him or her to supply part of the story, may use the writing of the story itself as metaphor for the struggle—or may invent any way to make the process, history, or techniques of storytelling crucial to the story. John Barth is a prime writer of metafiction, and his stories "Lost in the Funhouse" and "Title" demonstrate the phenomenon well.

The Short Story and the Novel

Many editors and writers insist on an essential disjunction between the form of the short story and that of the novel. It is my belief, however, that, like the distinction between story and plot, the distinction between the two forms is very simple, and the many and profound possibilities of difference proceed from that simple source.

A short story is short, and a novel is long.

Because of this, a short story can waste no words. It can deal with only one or a very few consciousnesses. It may recount only one central action and one major change or effect in the life of the central character or characters. It can afford no digression that does not directly affect the action. A short story strives for a single emotional impact and imparts a single understanding, though both impact and understanding may be complex. The virtue of a short story is its density. If it is tight, sharp, economic, well knit, and charged, then it is a good short story because it has exploited a central attribute of the form—that it is short.

All of these qualities are praiseworthy in a novel, but a novel may also be comprehensive, vast, and panoramic. It may have power, not because of its economy but because of its scope, breadth, and sweep—the virtues of a medium that is long. Therefore, a novel may range through many consciousnesses, cover many years or generations, and travel the world. It may deal with a central line of action and one or several subplots. Many characters may change; many and various effects may constitute our final understanding. Many digressions may be tolerated and will not destroy the balance of the whole as long as they lead, finally, to some nuance of that understanding.

These differences in the possibilities of the novel and short-story forms may directly affect the relationship between story and plot. With the narrative leisure available to a novelist, it may very well be possible to begin with a character's birth, or even ancestry, even though the action culminates in middle or old age.

My own feeling as a writer is that in a novel I may allow myself, and ask the reader to share, an exploration of character, setting, and theme, letting these develop in the course of the narrative. When I am writing a short story, I must reject more, and I must select more rigorously.

One constant principle of artistic effectiveness is that you must discover what a medium cannot do and forget it; and discover what it can do and exploit it. Television is a good medium for domestic drama, but for a battle with a cast of thousands, you need a movie screen twelve feet high. For a woodland scene, watercolor is fine; but for the agony of St. Sebastian, choose oil. If you are writing for radio, the conflict must be expressible in sound; if you are writing a mime, it must be expressible in movement.

This is not to say that one form is superior to another but simply that each is itself and that no medium and no form of that medium can do everything. The greater the limitation in time and space, the greater the necessity for pace, sharpness, and density. For this reason, it is a good idea to learn to write short stories before you attempt the scope of the novel, just as it is good to learn to write a lyric before you attempt an epic or to learn to draw an apple before you paint a god.

Nevertheless, the form of the novel is an expanded story form. It asks for a conflict, a crisis, and a resolution, and no technique described in this book is irrelevant to its effectiveness.

∽

The Use of Force

WILLIAM CARLOS WILLIAMS

They were new patients to me, all I had was the name, Olson. Please come down as soon as you can, my daughter is very sick.

When I arrived I was met by the mother, a big startled looking woman, very clean and apologetic who merely said, Is this the doctor? and let me in. In the back, she added. You must excuse us, doctor, we have her in the kitchen where it is warm. It is very damp here sometimes.

The child was fully dressed and sitting on her father's lap near the kitchen table. He tried to get up, but I motioned for him not to bother, took off my overcoat and started to look things over. I could see that they were all very nervous, eyeing me up and down distrustfully. As often, in such cases, they weren't telling me more than they had to, it was up to me to tell them; that's why they were spending three dollars on me.

The child was fairly eating me up with her cold, steady eyes, and no expression to her face whatever. She did not move and seemed, inwardly, quiet; an unusually attractive little thing, and as strong as a heifer in appearance. But her face was flushed, she was breathing rapidly, and I realized that she had a high fever. She had magnificent blonde hair, in profusion. One of those picture children often reproduced in advertising leaflets and the photogravure sections of the Sunday papers.

She's had a fever for three days, began the father, and we don't know what it comes from. My wife has given her things, you know, like people do, but it don't do no good. And there's been a lot of sickness around. So we tho't you'd better look her over and tell us what is the matter.

As doctors often do I took a trial shot at it as a point of departure. Has she had a sore throat?

Both parents answered me together, No . . . No, she says her throat don't hurt her.

Does your throat hurt you? added the mother to the child. But the little girl's expression didn't change, nor did she move her eyes from my face.

Have you looked?

I tried to, said the mother, but I couldn't see.

As it happens, we had been having a number of cases of diphtheria in the school to which this child went during that month and we were all, quite apparently, thinking of that, though no one had as yet spoken of the thing.

Well, I said, suppose we take a look at the throat first. I smiled in my best professional manner and asking for the child's first name I said, come on, Mathilda, open your mouth and let's take a look at your throat.

Nothing doing.

Aw, come on, I coaxed, just open your mouth wide and let me take a look. Look, I said opening both hands wide, I haven't anything in my hands. Just open up and let me see.

Such a nice man, put in the mother. Look how kind he is to you. Come on, do what he tells you to. He won't hurt you.

At that I ground my teeth in disgust. If only they wouldn't use the word "hurt" I might be able to get somewhere. But I did not allow myself to be hurried or disturbed, but speaking quietly and slowly I approached the child again.

As I moved my chair a little nearer, suddenly with one catlike movement both her hands clawed instinctively for my eyes and she almost reached them too. In fact she knocked my glasses flying and they fell, though unbroken, several feet away from me on the kitchen floor.

Both the mother and father almost turned themselves inside out in embarrassment and apology. You bad girl, said the mother, taking her and shaking her by one arm. Look what you've done. The nice man. . . .

For heaven's sake, I broke in. Don't call me a nice man to her. I'm here to look at her throat on the chance that she might have diphtheria and possibly die of it. But that's nothing to her. Look here, I said to the child, we're going to look at your throat. You're old enough to understand what I'm saying. Will you open it now by yourself or shall we have to open it for you?

Not a move. Even her expression hadn't changed. Her breaths however were coming faster and faster. Then the battle began. I had to do it. I had to have a throat culture for her own protection. But first I told the parents that it was entirely up to them. I explained the danger but said that I would not insist on a throat examination so long as they would take the responsibility.

If you don't do what the doctor says you'll have to go to the hospital, the mother admonished her severely.

Oh yeah? I had to smile to myself. After all, I had already fallen in love with the savage brat, the parents were contemptible to me. In the ensuing struggle they grew more and more abject, crushed, exhausted while she surely rose to magnificent heights of insane fury of effort bred of her terror of me.

The father tried his best, and he was a big man but the fact that she was his daughter, his shame at her behavior and his dread of hurting her made him release her just at the critical moment several times when I had almost achieved success, till I wanted to kill him. But his dread also that she might have diphtheria made him tell me to go on, go on though he himself was almost fainting, while the mother moved back and forth behind us raising and lowering her hands in an agony of apprehension.

Put her in front of you on your lap, I ordered, and hold both her wrists.

But as soon as he did the child let out a scream. Don't, you're hurting me. Let go of my hands. Let them go I tell you. Then she shrieked terrifyingly, hysterically. Stop it! Stop it! You're killing me!

Do you think she can stand it, doctor! said the mother.

You get out, said the husband to his wife. Do you want her to die of diphtheria?

Come on now, hold her, I said.

Then I grasped the child's head with my left hand and tried to get the wooden tongue depressor between her teeth. She fought, with clenched teeth, desperately! But now I also had grown furious—at a child. I tried to hold myself down but I couldn't. I know how to expose a throat for inspection. And I did my best. When finally I got the wooden spatula behind the last teeth and just the point of it into the mouth cavity, she opened up for an instant but before I could see anything she came down again and gripping the wooden blade between her molars she reduced it to splinters before I could get it out again.

Aren't you ashamed, the mother yelled at her. Aren't you ashamed to act like that in front of the doctor?

Get me a smooth-handled spoon of some sort, I told the mother. We're going through with this. The child's mouth was already bleeding. Her tongue was cut and she was screaming in wild hysterical shrieks. Perhaps I should have desisted and come back in an hour or more. No doubt it would have been better. But I have seen at least two children lying dead in bed of neglect in such cases, and feeling that I must get a diagnosis now or never I went at it again. But the worst of it was that I too had got beyond reason. I could have torn the child apart in my own fury and enjoyed it. It was a pleasure to attack her. My face was burning with it.

The damned little brat must be protected against her own idiocy, one says to one's self at such times. Others must be protected against her. It is social necessity. And all these things are true. But a blind fury, a feeling of adult shame, bred of a longing for muscular release are the operatives. One goes on to the end.

In a final unreasoning assault I overpowered the child's neck and jaws. I forced the heavy silver spoon back of her teeth and down her throat till she gagged. And there it was—both tonsils covered with membrane. She had fought valiantly to keep me from knowing her secret. She had been hiding that sore throat for three days at least and lying to her parents in order to escape just such an outcome as this.

Now truly she *was* furious. She had been on the defensive before but now she attacked. Tried to get off her father's lap and fly at me while tears of defeat blinded her eyes.

Suggestions for Discussion

1. Identify the central conflict, the crisis, and the resolution in "The Use of Force."

2. This story has the feel of twentieth-century life, not at all the feel of a tale. Can it be positioned like "Cinderella" on the diagram?

3. How many power struggles are involved in this very short story? Identify the struggles between characters and within each character.

4. The doctor is clearly in a position of power with these poor people. Where and how is that power eroded?

5. How is the situation at the end of the story a reversal of that at the beginning?

❦

Mockingbird

LAURIE BERRY

Peter has just returned from Mexico, where his face turned the chalky pink color of Pepto Bismol. Rachel is at that swooning stage of love, stupid with happiness at his return.

That evening they drink cold vodka and gossip about a child-laden couple they know, who rise at dawn for work and return home at seven to bathe the three-year-old, console the eight-year-old, and struggle through dinner in time to collapse in bed by ten.

"Even so they have a great house," she says. "And nice things. They make a lot of money."

Peter shakes his head and says, offhandedly: "I'd rather inherit it."

They are both shocked by the statement. An island of silence bobs to the surface. Rachel swallows the last of her vodka, and with it the realization that she is in love with a man who has just traveled to a third world nation to play tennis.

"By the way—" He looks up guiltily, making a game of it. "Promise me you'll never tell anyone I said that."

This makes her laugh, freshens her love. They laugh some more. Talk their slow way toward dinner. Spy on the remarkable albino Mexican boy playing in the yard next door. Make love with the windows open and then lie there listening to the mariachi music that pumps through her Houston barrio neighborhood.

Everything is soft, very soft. And luck abundant as Johnson grass. The Mimosa trees' green canopy. And the mockingbirds, not yet vicious, waiting for the fierce end of summer.

❧

The Mayor of the Sister City Speaks to the Chamber of Commerce in Klamath Falls, Oregon

MICHAEL MARTONE

"It was after the raid on Tokyo. We children were told to collect scraps of cloth. Anything we could find. We picked over the countryside; we stripped the scarecrows. I remember this remnant from my sister's obi. Red silk suns bounced like balls. And these patches were quilted together by the women in the prefecture. The seams were waxed as if to make the stitches rainproof. Instead they held air, gasses, and the rags billowed out into balloons, the heavy heads of chrysanthemums. The balloons bobbed as the soldiers attached the bombs. And then they rose up to the high wind, so many, like planets, heading into the rising sun and America. . . ."

I had stopped translating before he reached this point. I let his words fly away. It was a luncheon meeting. I looked down at the tables. The white napkins looked like mountain peaks of a range hung with clouds. We were high above them on the stage. I am *yonsei*, the fourth American generation. Four is an unlucky number in Japan. The old man, the mayor, was trying to say that the world was knit together with threads we could not see, that the wind was a bridge between people. It was a hot day. I told these beat businessmen about children long ago releasing the bright balloons, how they disappeared ages and ages ago. And all of them looked up as if to catch the first sight of the balloons returning to earth, a bright scrap of joy.

Molibi

LEIGH HANCOCK

There is not a spare inch of flesh to Molibi. She presses leather palms into my own, murmuring, "Miss Allen, Miss Allen." All elbows and knees and teeth when she dances, Molibi crooks one arm over her head and wraps her feet around the desk chair when she sits for an exam. Her cheeks are tight drumheads, and her neck as scrawny as the sugar cane she gnaws. Only her eyes and lips are soft, abundant, wet.

Quentin, my British colleague, says Americans are heavy on the hips and adjectives. He kindly excludes me from both judgments, but with Molibi I fall from grace. I want to describe her in flowing sentences, to pad her with adjectives, to protect her against an inevitable life of maize-stamping and child-lugging. I want to convince her that she needn't haul water all her days, nor follow boys out to that narrow strip of sand they call the Metsi-ma-sweu, Once-a-River. These things demand wide hips and square shoulders, a jaw that can clench and a soul that dog-shakes disappointments like water. Molibi has none of these and I worry for her and the place she must find in her country.

Although—Quentin assures me—I shouldn't. The boys, all knees and loose shoes themselves, don't care for the delicate girls, the fine bones and weedy waists. Such etched beauty is lost in the tangle of bony acacia on this desert plain. The boys want to drive themselves into flesh as pliant and welcoming as old, rotting wood. They choose workhorses, sofas and readily furrowed fields as their life's loves.

For a while—Quentin promises and his lips gleam—Molibi is safe.

Suggestions for Discussion

The three short short stories above were winners in different years of the World's Greatest Short Short Story Contest.

1. In each story, describe the central conflict, the crisis, and the resolution.

2. How is the conflict in "Mockingbird" signaled in the first two sentences?

3. "Mockingbird" represents scarcely a single page of double-spaced typing, yet it involves a power struggle in which the power changes sides several times. Show where and how.

4. In "The Mayor of the Sister City . . ." identify three levels of conflict—internal, external, and historical. How does the immediate problem represent the universal and abstract?

5. In "Mobili," consider how the particular conflict in the narrator resonates to her relations with Quentin, those between the boys and girls, male-female relationships generally, and cross-cultural differences.

WRITING ASSIGNMENTS

1. Write a scene placing two characters in this very fundamental conflict: One wants something the other does not want to give. The something may be anything—money, respect, jewelry, sex, information, a match—but be sure to focus on the one desire.

2. A slightly more complicated variation on the same theme: Each of two characters has half of something that is no good without the other half. Neither wants to give up his or her half.

3. Write a short paragraph outlining the conflict between two characters. Then write the crisis scene for this conflict, a scene in which one of the characters "changes his or her mind," that is, realizes something, understands something not understood before, moves from one emotional state to its opposite. Make sure the internal change is shown in, or triggered by, an external action.

4. Write a short story that is a short story in *exactly* one hundred words. Notice that if you're going to manage a conflict, crisis, and resolution in this short compass, you'll have to introduce the conflict immediately.

5. Write a short story of no more than five pages in which the protagonist seems to be weaker than the forces opposing him or her. Give the character one balancing strength. Let him or her triumph.

6. Place a character in conflict with some aspect of nature. The character need not be fighting for survival; the danger may be as small as a mosquito. But balance the forces equally so that the reader is not sure who will "win" until the crisis action happens.

7. Plot an outline (or outline a plot) for a story in which the protagonist does not get what he or she wants—and which nevertheless ends happily.

8. Write a short short story, no longer than one double-spaced page, in which a particular conflict suggests a universal.

SEEING IS BELIEVING
Showing and Telling

Significant Detail
The Active Voice
Prose Rhythm
Mechanics

The purpose of all the arts, including literature, is to quell boredom. People recognize that it feels good to feel and that not to feel is unhealthy. "I don't feel anything" can be said in fear, defiance, or complaint. It is not a boast. The final absence of feeling is death.

But feeling is also dangerous, and it can be deadly. Both the body and the psyche numb themselves in the presence of pain too strong to bear. People often (healthily and unhealthily) avoid good feelings—intimacy, power, speed, drunkenness, possession—having learned that feelings have consequences and that powerful feelings have powerful consequences.

Literature offers feelings for which we do not have to pay. It allows us to love, condemn, condone, hope, dread, and hate without any of the risks those feelings ordinarily involve. Fiction must contain ideas, which give significance to characters and events. If the ideas are shallow or untrue, the fiction will be correspondingly shallow or untrue. But the ideas must be experienced through or with the characters; they must be *felt* or the fiction will fail also.

Much nonfiction writing, including literary criticism, also wants to persuade us to feel one way rather than another, and some—polemics and propaganda, for example—exhort us to feel strongly. But nonfiction works largely by means of reason and reasoning in order to appeal to and produce emotion. Fiction tries to reproduce the emotional impact of experience. And this is a more difficult task, because written words are symbols representing sounds, and the sounds themselves are symbols representing things, actions, qualities, spatial relationships, and so on. Written words are thus at two removes from experience. Unlike the images of film and drama, which directly strike the eye and ear, words are transmitted first to the mind, where they must be translated into images.

In order to move your reader, the standard advice runs, "Show, don't tell." This dictum can be confusing, considering that all a writer has to work with is words. What it means is that your job as as fiction writer is to focus attention not on the words, which are inert, nor on the thoughts these words produce, but through these to felt experience, where the vitality of understanding lies. There are techniques for accomplishing this—for making narrative vivid, moving, and resonant—which can be partly learned and can always be strengthened.

Significant Detail

In *The Elements of Style*, William Strunk, Jr., writes:

> If those who have studied the art of writing are in accord on any one point, it is on this: the surest way to arouse and hold the attention of the reader is by being specific, definite and concrete. The greatest writers . . . are effective largely because they deal in particulars and report the details that matter.

Specific, definite, concrete, particular details—these are the life of fiction. Details (as every good liar knows) are the stuff of persuasiveness. Mary is sure that Ed forgot to go pay the gas bill last Tuesday, but Ed says, "I know I went, because this old guy in a knit vest was in front of me in the line, and went on and on about his twin granddaughters"—and it is hard to refute a knit vest and twins even if the furnace doesn't work. John Gardner in *The Art of Fiction* speaks of details as "proofs," rather like those in a geometric theorem or a statistical argument. The novelist, he says, "gives us such details about the streets, stores, weather, politics, and concerns of Cleveland (or wherever the setting is) and such details about the looks, gestures, and experiences of his characters that we cannot help believing that the story he tells us is true."

A detail is "definite" and "concrete" when it appeals to the senses. It should be seen, heard, smelled, tasted, or touched. The most superficial survey of any bookshelf of published fiction will turn up dozens of examples of this principle. Here is a fairly obvious one.

It was a narrow room, with a rather high ceiling, and crowded from floor to ceiling with goodies. There were rows and rows of hams and sausages of all shapes and colors—white, yellow, red and black; fat and lean and round and long—rows of canned preserves, cocoa and tea, bright translucent glass bottles of honey, marmalade and jam. . . .

I stood enchanted, straining my ears and breathing in the delightful atmosphere and the mixed fragrance of chocolate and smoked fish and earthy truffles. . . . I spoke into the silence, saying: "Good day" in quite a loud voice; I can still remember how my strained, unnatural tones died away in the stillness. No one answered. And my mouth literally began to water like a spring. One quick, noiseless step and I was beside one of the laden tables. I made one rapturous grab into the nearest glass urn, filled as it chanced with chocolate creams, slipped a fistful into my coat pocket, then reached the door, and in the next second was safely round the corner.

THOMAS MANN, *Confessions of Felix Krull, Confidence Man*

The shape of this passage is a tour through the five senses. Mann lets us see: *narrow room, high ceiling, hams, sausages, preserves, cocoa, tea, glass bottles, honey, marmalade, jam.* He lets us smell: *fragrance of chocolate, smoked fish, earthy truffles.* He lets us hear: *"Good day," unnatural tones, stillness.* He lets us taste: *mouth, water like a spring.* He lets us touch: *grab, chocolate creams, slipped, fistful into my coat pocket.* The writing is alive because we do in fact live through our sense perceptions, and Mann takes us past words and through thought to let us perceive the scene in this way.

In this process, a number of ideas *not* stated reverberate off the sense images, so that we are also aware of a number of generalizations the author might have made but does not need to make: We will make them ourselves. Mann could have had his character "tell" us: *I was quite poor, and I was not used to seeing such a profusion of food, so that although I was very afraid there might be someone in the room and that I might be caught stealing, I couldn't resist taking the risk.*

This version would be very flat, and none of it is necessary. The character's relative poverty is inherent in the tumble of images of sight and smell; if he were used to such displays, his eyes and nose would not dart about as they do. His fear is inherent in the "strained, unnatural tones" and their dying away in the stillness. His desire is in his watering mouth, his fear in the furtive speed of "quick" and "grab" and "slipped."

The points to be made here are two, and they are both important. The first is that the writer must deal in sense detail. The second is that these must be details "that matter." As a writer of fiction you are at constant pains not simply to say what you mean, but to mean more than you say. Much of what you mean will be an abstraction or a judgment. But if you write in abstractions or judgments, you are writing an essay, whereas if you let us use our senses and do our own generalizing and interpreting, we will be involved as participants in a real way. Much of the pleasure of reading comes from the egotistical sense that we are clever enough to understand. When the author explains to us or interprets for us, we suspect that he or she doesn't think us bright enough to do it for ourselves.

A detail is *concrete* if it appeals to one of the five senses; it is *significant* if it also conveys an idea or a judgment or both. *The windowsill was green* is concrete, because we can see it. *The windowsill was shedding flakes of fungus-green paint* is concrete, and also conveys the idea that the paint is old and suggests the judgment that the color is ugly. The second version can also be seen more vividly.

Here is a passage from a young writer, which fails through lack of appeal to the senses.

> Debbie was a very stubborn and completely independent person, and was always doing things her way despite her parents' efforts to get her to conform. Her father was an executive in a dress manufacturing company, and was able to afford his family all the luxuries and comforts of life. But Debbie was completely indifferent to her family's affluence.

This passage contains a number of judgments we might or might not share with the author, and she has not convinced us that we do. What constitutes stubbornness? Independence? Indifference? Affluence? Further, since the judgments are supported by generalizations, we have no sense of the individuality of the characters, which alone would bring them to life on the page. What things was she always doing? What efforts did her parents make to get her to conform? What level of executive? What dress manufacturing company? What luxuries and comforts?

> Debbie would wear a tank top to a tea party if she pleased, with fluorescent earrings and ankle-strap sandals.
>
> "Oh, sweetheart," Mrs. Chiddister would stand in the doorway wringing her hands. "It's not *nice.*"
>
> "Not who?" Debbie would say, and add a fringed belt.
>
> Mr. Chiddister was Artistic Director of the Boston branch of Cardin, and had a high respect for what he called "elegant textures," which ranged from handwoven tweed to gold filigree, and which he willingly offered his daughter. Debbie preferred her laminated wrist bangles.

We have not passed a final judgment on the merits of these characters, but we know a good deal more about them, and we have drawn certain interim conclusions that are our own and not forced on us by the author. Debbie is independent of her parents' values, rather careless of their feelings, energetic, and possibly a tart. Mrs. Chiddister is quite ineffectual. Mr. Chiddister is a snob, though perhaps Debbie's taste is so bad we'll end up on his side.

But maybe that isn't at all what the author had in mind. The point is that we weren't allowed to know what the author did have in mind. Perhaps it was more like this version.

One day Debbie brought home a copy of *Ulysses*. Mrs. Strum called it "filth" and threw it across the sunporch. Debbie knelt on the parquet and retrieved her bookmark, which she replaced. "No, it's not," she said.

"You're not so old I can't take a strap to you!" Mr. Strum reminded her.

Mr. Strum was controlling stockholder of Readywear Conglomerates, and was proud of treating his family, not only on his salary, but also on his expense account. The summer before he had justified their company on a trip to Belgium, where they toured the American Cemetery and the torture chambers of Ghent Castle. Entirely ungrateful, Debbie had spent the rest of the trip curled up in the hotel with a shabby copy of some poet.

Now we have a much clearer understanding of *stubbornness, independence, indifference,* and *affluence,* both their natures and the value we are to place on them. This time our judgment is heavily weighed in Debbie's favor—partly because people who read books have a sentimental sympathy with people who read books— but also because we hear hysteria in "filth" and "take a strap to you," whereas Debbie's resistance is quiet and strong. Mr. Strum's attitude toward his expense account suggests that he's corrupt, and his choice of "luxuries" is morbid. The passage does contain two overt judgments, the first being that Debbie was "entirely ungrateful." Notice that by the time we get to this, we're aware that the judgment is Mr. Strum's and that Debbie has little enough to be grateful for. We understand not only what the author says but also that she means the opposite of what she says, and we feel doubly clever to get it; that is the pleasure of irony. Likewise, the judgment that the poet's book is "shabby" shows Mr. Strum's crass materialism toward what *we* know to be the finer things. At the very end of the passage, we are denied a detail that we might very well be given: *What* poet did Debbie curl up with? Again, by this time we understand that we are being given Mr. Strum's view of the situation and that it's Mr. Strum (not Debbie, not the author, and certainly not us) who wouldn't notice the difference between John Keats and Stanley Kunitz.

It may be objected that both rewrites of the passage are longer than the original. Doesn't "adding" so much detail make for long writing? The answer is yes and no. *No* because in the rewrites we know so much more about the values, activities, life-styles, attitudes, and personalities of the characters that it would take many times the length of the original to "tell" it all in generalizations. *Yes* in the sense that detail requires words, and if you are to realize your characters through detail, then you must be careful to select the details that convey the characteristics essential to our understanding. You can't convey a whole person, or a whole action, or everything there is to be conveyed about a single moment of a single day. You must select the significant.

No amount of concrete detail will move us unless it also implicitly suggests meaning and value. Following is a passage that fails, not through lack of appeal to the senses, but through lack of significance.

Terry Landon, a handsome young man of twenty-two, was six foot four and broad shouldered. He had medium-length thick blond hair and a natural tan, which set off the blue of his intense and friendly long-lashed eyes.

Here we have a good deal of sense information, but we still know very little about Terry. There are so many broad-shouldered twenty-two-year-olds in the world, so many blonds, and so on. This sort of cataloguing of characteristics suggest an all-points bulletin: *Male Caucasian, medium height, dark hair, last seen wearing gray raincoat.* Such a description may help the police locate a suspect in a crowd, but the assumption is that the identity of the person is not known. As an author you want us to know the character individually and immediately.

The fact is that all our ideas and judgments are formed through our sense perceptions, and daily, moment by moment, we receive information that is not merely sensuous in this way. Four people at a cocktail party may *do* nothing but stand and nibble canapes and may *talk* nothing but politics and the latest films. But you feel perfectly certain that X is furious at Y, who is flirting with Z, who is wounding Q, who is trying to comfort X. You have only your senses to observe with. How do you reach these conclusions? By what gestures, glances, tones, touches, choices of words?

It may be that this constant emphasis on judgment makes the author, and the reader, seem opinionated or self-righteous. "I want to present my characters objectively/neutrally. I'm not making any value judgments. I want the reader to make up his or her own mind." This can be a legitimate position, and the whole school of the *nouveau roman* strives, in fiction, to be wholly objective and to eschew the judgmental. But this is a highly sophisticated experimental form, and it entails a difficulty and a danger. The difficulty is that human beings *are* constantly judging: *How was the film? He seemed friendly. What a boring class! Do you like it here? What did you think of them? That's kind of you. Which do you want? I'm not convinced. She's very thin. That's fascinating. I'm so clumsy. You're gorgeous tonight. Life is crazy, isn't it?*

The danger is that when we are not passing such judgments, it's because we aren't much interested. We are indifferent. Although you may not want to sanctify or damn your characters, you do want us to care about them, and if you refuse to direct our judgment, you may be inviting our indifference. Usually, when you "don't want us to judge," you mean that you want our feelings to be mixed, paradoxical, complex. *She's horribly irritating, but it's not her fault. He's sexy, but there's something cold about it underneath.* If this is what you mean, then you must direct our judgment in both or several directions, not in no direction.

Even a character who doesn't exist except as a type or function will come to life if presented through significant detail, as in this example from *The Right Stuff* by Tom Wolfe.

The matter mustn't be bungled!—that's the idea. No, a man should bring the news when the time comes, a man with some official or moral authority, a clergyman or a comrade of the newly deceased. Furthermore, he should bring the bad news in person. He should turn up at the front door and ring the bell and be standing there like a pillar of coolness and competence, bearing the bad news on ice, like a fish.

For a character who is just "a man," we have a remarkably clear image of this personage! Notice how Wolfe moves us from generalization toward sharpness of image, gradually bringing the nonexistent character into focus. First he has only a gender, then a certain abstract quality, "authority"; then a distinct role, "a clergy-man or a comrade." Then he appears "in person" at the front door, then acts, ringing the doorbell. Finally, his quality is presented to us in the sharp focus of similes that also suggest his deadly message: *pillar, ice, fish.*

John Gardner, in *The Art of Fiction*, points out that in addition to the two faults of insufficient detail and the use of abstraction, there's a third failure.

> . . . to run straight at the image; that is, the needless filtering of the image through some observing consciousness. The amateur writes: "Turning, she noticed two snakes fighting in among the rocks." Compare: "She turned. In among the rocks, two snakes were fighting." (The improvement can of course be further improved. The phrase "two snakes were fighting" is more abstract than, say, "two snakes whipped and lashed, striking at each other"; and verbs with auxiliaries ["were fighting"] are never as sharp in focus as verbs without auxiliaries, since the former indicate indefinite time, whereas the latter [e.g., "fought"] suggest a given instant.) Generally speaking—though no laws are absolute in fiction—vividness urges that almost every occurrence of such phrases as "she noticed" and "she saw" be suppressed in favor of direct presentation of the thing seen.

In the following paragraph from Virginia Woolf's *Mrs. Dalloway,* we are introduced to an anonymous crowd and four other characters, none of whom we ever see again. Notice that although we observe the scene through the consciousness of the character, it is presented directly. We watch *with* her rather than watching her watch.

> The crush was terrific for the time of day. Lords, Ascot, Hurlingham, what was it? she wondered, for the street was blocked. The British middle classes sitting sideways on the tops of omnibuses with parcels and umbrellas, yes, even furs on a day like this, were, she thought, more ridiculous, more unlike anything there has ever been than one could conceive; and the Queen herself held up; the Queen herself unable to pass. Clarissa was suspended on one side of Brook Street; Sir John Buckhurst, the old Judge on the other, with the car between them (Sir John had laid down the law for years and liked a well-dressed woman) when the chauf-

feur, leaning ever so slightly, said or showed something to the policeman, who saluted and raised his arm and jerked his head and moved the omnibus to the side and the car passed through.

The whole range of British class and class consciousness is conveyed in this brief passage through the use of significant detail. Clarissa's wry attitude toward the British middle classes is given credence by the fussiness of "parcels ands umbrellas" and the pretension of "furs on a day like this." The judge's aristocratic hauteur is carried in the clichés he would use, "laid down the law" and "liked a well-dressed woman." That the Queen's chauffeur is described as leaning "ever so slightly" shows his consciousness of his own position's superiority to that of the policeman, who "saluted" him but then exercises his own brand of authority as he "jerked his head" to order the traffic about. Only the Queen is characterized by no detail of object or action, and that she is not emphasizes her royal remoteness: "the Queen herself . . . the Queen herself."

The point is not that an author must never express an idea, quality, or judgment. In the foregoing passages from Mann, Wolfe, and Woolf, each author uses several generalizations: *I stood enchanted, delightful atmosphere; the matter mustn't be bungled, coolness and competence; the crush was terrific, more unlike anything there has ever been than one could conceive.* The point is that in order to carry the felt weight of fiction, these abstractions must be realized through an appeal to the senses. It is in the details that they live.

Exciting discoveries in brain research, particularly the work done in brain evolution by Dr. Paul MacLean at the University of Washington, suggest that there may be a biological justification for the old literary rule "Show, don't tell." Scientists conclude that the brain has evolved in three layers, from reptile to mammal to primate, each layer adapting to its successor but not being entirely replaced by it. Human beings therefore have a "triune brain," each layer operating with a separate purpose and in a different way.

The reptilian brain, or *R-complex*, operates ritualistically and repetitiously, always in the service of preservation of the individual or the species. At least twenty-eight separate functions for this brain have been identified, having to do with choosing the nest, preparing the nest, defending the nest, choosing a mate, displaying for the mate, and so forth.

The mammalian brain, or *limbic system*, apparently developed in such a way as to give mammals a greater range of choice in reacting to situations that threatened the individual or the species. This brain takes in information through the five senses and then produces a wide variety of sense responses within the body.

The primatial brain, or *neocortex*, also takes in information through the five senses, but it has a much more complex system of categorization, comparison, and connection, does not produce bodily responses, and is not particularly concerned with preservation. The human brain can therefore store and compare information in such a way as to remember, conclude, and predict. The capacity for empathy and altruism is made possible by these workings, since the human brain can compare without constantly referring itself to its own interest.

Here is an example of how the limbic system and the neocortex would react to the same situation: You break an egg on the edge of the skillet; the egg stinks and spreads. Your human brain takes this information in through the senses of sight and smell, and then rapidly concludes, remembers, and predicts: "That egg is rotten. That's the third time I've bought rotten eggs from Pearson's Market; I won't buy them there again. This afternoon I'll be able to get back there between class and supper, and I'm sure the clerk will give me my money back because he was so embarrassed about that bad chicken last month, poor guy." Meanwhile, the same information of sight and smell is being taken in by the mammalian brain, which reacts physically: Your stomach surges, a spasm grips the back of your throat, your tongue jerks forward, and you gasp, "Gyaagh!" This may be a particularly literal example of a "gut reaction," but the slang contains a scientific truth: The physical reaction of the body to sense information *is what emotion is*.

Clearly, language and literature belong primarily to the human brain, with its computerlike possibilities of comparison and symbolic meaning. Yet if as a fiction writer you deal in abstraction and comparison only, if you name qualities rather than provide sense images, you will not penetrate to the layer of the brain where emotion lies. If, however, you provide concrete details that appeal to the senses, both the human and the mammalian brain will be electrically excited, and your reader will both think *and* feel.

The Active Voice

If your prose is to be vigorous as well as vivid, if your characters are to be people who *do* rather than people to whom things are done, if your descriptions are to "come to life," you must make use of the active voice.

The active voice occurs when the subject of a sentence performs the action described by the verb of that sentence: *She spilled the milk.* When the passive voice is used, the object of the active verb becomes the subject of the passive verb: *The milk was spilled by her.* The passive voice is more indirect than the active; the subject is acted upon rather than acting, and the effect is to weaken the prose and to distance the reader from the action.

The passive voice does have an important place in fiction, precisely because it expresses a sense that the character is being acted upon. If a prison guard is kicking the hero, then *I was slammed into the wall; I was struck blindingly from behind and forced to the floor* appropriately carries the sense of his helplessness.

In general, you should seek the active voice in all prose and use the passive only when the actor is unknown or insignificant or when you want to achieve special stylistic effects like the one above.

But there is one other common grammatical construction that is *effectively passive* in fiction and can distance the reader from a sense of immediate experience. All the verbs that we learn in school to call *linking verbs* are effectively passive because they invite complements that tend to be generalized or judgmental: *Her hair was beautiful. He was very happy. The room seemed expensively furnished. They became morose.* Let her hair bounce, tumble, cascade, or swing; we'll see better. Let him laugh, leap, cry, or hug a tree; we'll experience his joy.

Compare the first passage about Debbie on page 63 with the rewrite at the top of page 64. In the generalized original we have *was stubborn, was doing things, was executive, was able, was indifferent.* Apart from the compound verb *was doing,* all these are linking verbs. In the rewrite the characters *brought, called, threw, knelt, retrieved, replaced, said, reminded, justified, toured, spent,* and *curled up.* What energetic people! The rewrite contains two linking verbs: Mr. Strum *was stockholder* and *was proud;* these properly represent static states, a position and an attitude.

One beneficial side effect of active verbs is that they tend to call forth significant details. If you say "she was shocked," you are telling us; but if you are to show us that she was shocked through an action, you are likely to have to search for an image as well. "She clenched the arm of the chair so hard that her knuckles whitened." *Clenched* and *whitened* actively suggest shock, and at the same time we see her knuckles on the arm of the chair.

To be is the most common of the linking verbs and also the most overused, but all the linking verbs invite generalization and distance. *To feel, to seem, to look, to appear, to experience, to express, to show, to demonstrate, to convey, to display*—all these suggest in fiction that the character is being acted upon or observed by someone rather than doing something. *She felt happy/sad/amused/mortified* does not convince us. We want to see her and infer her emotion for ourselves. *He very clearly conveyed his displeasure.* It isn't clear to us. How did he convey it? To whom?

Most linking verbs have active as well as effectively passive forms, and it is important to distinguish between them. *She felt sad* is effectively passive, but *she felt his forehead* is an action. If *the magician appeared,* he is acting; but if *he appeared annoyed,* then the verb is a linking verb, and the only action implied is that of the observer who perceives this.

Linking verbs, like the passive voice, can appropriately convey a sense of passivity or helplessness when that is the desired effect. Notice that in the passage by Mann quoted earlier in this chapter, where Felix Krull is momentarily stunned by the sight of the food before him, linking verbs are used: *It was a narrow room, there were rows and rows,* while all the colors and shapes buffet his senses. Only as he gradually recovers can he *stand, breathe, speak,* and eventually *grab.*

In the following excerpt from Lawrence Durrell's *Justine,* Melissa is trapped into a ride she doesn't want, and we feel her passivity with her while the car and the headlights take all the power.

Melissa was afraid now. . . . . She was aghast at what she had done. . . . . There was no way of refusing the invitation. She dressed in her shabby best and carrying her fatigue like a heavy pack followed Selim to the great car which stood in deep shadow. She was helped in beside Nessim. They moved off slowly into the dense crepuscular evening of an Alexandria which, in her panic, she no longer recognized. They scouted a sea turned to sapphire and turned inland, folding up the slum, toward Mareotis and the bituminous slag-heaps of Mex where the pressure of the headlights now peeled off layer after layer of the darkness.

Was afraid, was aghast, was no way, was helped in—all imply Melissa's impotence. The active verbs that apply specifically to her either express weakness (*she followed*) or are negated (*no longer recognized*); the most active thing she can manage is to dress. In contrast, the "great car" *stands*, and it is inside and under the power of the car that they *move off, scout, turn,* and *fold up;* it is the headlights that *peel off.*

I don't mean to suggest either that Durrell is deliberately using a linking verb here, the passive or the active voice there, or that as an author you should analyze your grammar as you go along. Most word choice is instinctive, and instinct is often the best guide. I do mean to suggest that you should be aware of the vigor and variety of available verbs and that if a passage lacks energy, it may be because your instinct has let you down. How often *are* things or are they acted *upon*, when they could more forcefully *do?*

A note of caution about active verbs: Make sparing use of what John Ruskin called the "pathetic fallacy"—the attributing of human emotions to natural and man-made objects. Even a description of a static scene can be invigorated if the houses *stand*, the streets *wander*, and the trees *bend*. But if the houses *frown*, the streets *stagger drunkenly*, and the trees *weep*, we will feel more strain than energy in the writing.

Prose Rhythm

Novelists and short-story writers are not under the same obligation as poets to reinforce sense with sound. In prose, on the whole, the rhythm is all right if it isn't clearly wrong. But it can be wrong if, for example, the cadence contradicts the meaning; on the other hand, rhythm can greatly enhance the meaning if it is sensitively used.

The river moved slowly. It seemed sluggish. The surface lay flat. Birds circled lazily overhead. Jon's boat slipped forward.

In this extreme example, the short, clipped sentences and their parallel structures—subject, verb, adverb—work against the sense of slow, flowing movement.

The rhythm could be effective if the character whose eyes we're using is not appreciating or sharing the calm; otherwise it needs recasting.

> The surface lay flat on the sluggish, slow-moving river, and the birds circled lazily overhead as Jon's boat slipped forward.

There is nothing very striking about the rhythm of this version, but at least it moves forward without obstructing the flow of the river.

> The first impression I had as I stopped in the doorway of the immense City Room was of extreme rush and bustle, with the reporters moving rapidly back and forth in the long aisles in order to shove their copy at each other, or making frantic gestures as they shouted into their many telephones.

This long and leisurely sentence cannot possibly provide a sense of rush and bustle. The phrases need to move as fast as the reporters; the verbiage must be pared down because it slows them down.

> I stopped in the doorway. The City Room was immense, reporters rushing down the aisles, shoving copy at each other, bustling back again, flinging gestures, shouting into telephones.

The poet Rolfe Humphries remarked that "*very* is the least *very* word in the language." It is frequently true that adverbs expressing emphasis or suddenness—*extremely, rapidly, suddenly, phenomenally, quickly, immediately, instantly, definitely, terribly, awfully*—slow the sentence down so as to dilute the force of the intended meaning. "'It's a very nice day,'" said Humphries, "is not as nice a day as 'It's a day!'" Likewise, "They stopped very abruptly" is not as abrupt as "They stopped."

The rhythm of an action can be imitated by the rhythm of a sentence in a rich variety of ways. In the example above, simplifying the clauses helped create a sense of rush. James Joyce, in the short story "The Dead," structures a long sentence with a number of prepositional phrases so that it carries us headlong.

> Lily, the caretaker's daughter, was literally run off her feet. Hardly had she brought one gentleman into the little pantry behind the office on the ground floor and helped him off with his overcoat than the wheezy hall-door bell clanged and she had to scamper along the bare hallway to let in another guest.

Lily's haste is largely created by beginning the sentence, "Hardly had she brought . . . ," so that we anticipate the clause that will finish the meaning, "than the bell clanged. . . ." Our anticipation forces us to scamper like Lily through the intervening actions.

Not only action but also character can be revealed and reinforced by sensitive use of rhythm. In Tillie Olsen's "Tell Me a Riddle," half a dozen grown children of a couple who have been married for forty-seven years ask each other what, after all this time, could be tearing their parents apart. The narrative answers:

> Something tangible enough.
> Arthritic hands, and such work as he got, occasional. Poverty all his life, and there was little breath left for running. He could not, could not turn away from this desire: to have the troubling of responsibility, the fretting with money, over and done with; to be free, to be *carefree* where success was not measured by accumulation, and there was use for the vitality still in him.

The old man's anguished irritability is conveyed by syncopation, the syntax wrenched, clauses and qualifiers erupting out of what would be their natural place in the sentence, just as they would erupt in the man's mind. Repetition conveys his frustration: "He could not, could not . . ." and "to be free, to be *carefree*. . . ."

Just as action and character can find an echo in prose rhythm, so it is possible to help us experience a character's emotions and attitudes through control of the starts and stops of prose tempo. In the following passage from *Persuasion*, Jane Austen combines generalization, passive verbs, and a staccato speech pattern to produce a kind of breathless blindness in the heroine.

> . . . a thousand feelings rushed on Anne, of which this was the most consoling, that it would soon be over. And it was soon over. In two minutes after Charles's preparation, the others appeared; they were in the drawing room. Her eye half met Captain Wentworth's, a bow, a courtesy passed; she heard his voice; he talked to Mary, said all that was right, said something to the Miss Musgroves, enough to mark an easy footing; the room seemed full, full of persons and voices, but a few minutes ended it.

Sometimes a contrast in rhythm can help reinforce a contrast in characters, actions, attitudes, and emotions. In this passage from Frederick Busch's short story "Company," a woman whose movements are relatively confined watches her husband move, stop, and move again.

> Every day did not start with Vince awake that early, dressing in the dark, moving with whispery sounds down the stairs and through the kitchen, out into the autumn morning while groundfog lay on the milkweed burst open and on the stumps of harvested corn. But enough of them did.
> I went to the bedroom window to watch him hunt in a business suit.
> He moved with his feet in the slowly stirring fog, moving slowly himself with the rifle held across his body and his shoulders stiff. Then he stopped in a frozen watch for woodchucks. His stillness made the fog look faster as it blew across our field behind the barn. Vince stood. He waited for something to shoot. I went back to bed and lay between our covers again. I heard the bolt click. I heard the unem-

phatic shot, and then the second one, and after a while his feet on the porch, and soon the rush of water, the rattle of the pots on top of the stove, and later his feet again, and the car starting up as he left for work an hour before he had to.

The long opening sentence is arranged in a series of short phrases to move Vince forward. By contrast, "But enough of them did" comes abruptly, its abruptness as well as the sense of the words suggesting the woman's alienation. When Vince starts off again more slowly, the repetition of "moved . . . slowly stirring . . . moving slowly" slows down the sentence to match his strides. "Vince stood" again stills him, but the author also needs to convey that Vince stands for a long time, waiting, so we have the repetitions, "he stopped . . . his stillness . . . Vince stood. He waited. . . ." As his activity speeds up again, the tempo of the prose speeds up with another series of short phrases, of which only the last is drawn out with a dependent clause, "as he left for work an hour before he had to," so that we feel the retreat of the car in the distance. Notice that Busch chooses the phrase "the rush of water," not the flow or splash of water, as the sentence and Vince begin to rush. Here, meaning reinforces a tempo that, in turn, reinforces meaning.

Mechanics

Significant detail, the active voice, and prose rhythm are techniques for achieving the sensuous in fiction, means of taking the reader past the words and the thought to feeling and experience. None is of much use if the reader's eye is wrenched back to the surface; for that reason a word or two ought to be said here about the mechanics of the written language.

Spelling, grammar, and punctuation are a kind of magic; their purpose is to be invisible. If the sleight of hand works, we will not notice a comma or a quotation mark but will translate each instantly into a pause or an awareness of voice; we will not focus on the individual letters of a word but extract its sense whole. When the mechanics are incorrectly used, the trick is revealed and the magic fails; the reader's focus is shifted from the story to its surface. The reader is irritated at the author, and of all the emotions she or he was willing to experience, irritation at the author is not one.

There is no intrinsic virtue in standardized mechanics, and you can depart from them whenever you produce an effect that adequately compensates for the attention called to the surface. But only then. Unlike the techniques of narrative, the rules of spelling, grammar, and punctuation can be coldly learned anywhere in the English-speaking world—and they should be learned by anyone who aspires to write. Poor mechanics read instant amateurism to an editor. Perhaps a demonstrated genius can get away with sloppy mechanics, but in that case some other person must be hired to fill in. Since ghostwriters and editors are likely to be paid more per hour for their work than the author, this would constitute a heavy drain on the available resources of those who publish fiction.

The Things They Carried

TIM O'BRIEN

First Lieutenant Jimmy Cross carried letters from a girl named Martha, a junior at Mount Sebastian College in New Jersey. They were not love letters, but Lieutenant Cross was hoping, so he kept them folded in plastic at the bottom of his rucksack. In the late afternoon, after a day's march, he would dig his foxhole, wash his hands under a canteen, unwrap the letters, hold them with the tips of his fingers, and spend the last hour of light pretending. He would imagine romantic camping trips into the White Mountains in New Hampshire. He would sometimes taste the envelope flaps, knowing her tongue had been there. More than anything, he wanted Martha to love him as he loved her, but the letters were mostly chatty, elusive on the matter of love. She was a virgin, he was almost sure. She was an English major at Mount Sebastian, and she wrote beautifully about her professors and room-mates and midterm exams, about her respect for Chaucer and her great af- fection for Virginia Woolf. She often quoted lines of poetry; she never men- tioned the war, except to say, Jimmy, take care of yourself. The letters weighed 10 ounces. They were signed Love, Martha, but Lieutenant Cross understood that Love was only a way of signing and did not mean what he sometimes pretended it meant. At dusk, he would carefully return the letters to his rucksack. Slowly, a bit distracted, he would get up and move among his men, checking the perimeter, then at full dark he would return to his hole and watch the night and wonder if Martha was a virgin.

The things they carried were largely determined by necessity. Among the necessities or near-necessities were P-38 can openers, pocket knives, heat tabs, wristwatches, dog tags, mosquito repellent, chewing gum, candy, ciga- rettes, salt tablets, packets of Kool-Aid, lighters, matches, sewing kits, Mil- itary Payment Certificates, C rations, and two or three canteens of water. Together, these items weighed between 15 and 20 pounds, depending upon a man's habits or rate of metabolism. Henry Dobbins, who was a big man, carried extra rations; he was especially fond of canned peaches in heavy syrup over pound cake. Dave Jensen, who practiced field hygiene, carried a toothbrush, dental floss, and several hotel-sized bars of soap he'd stolen on R&R in Sydney, Australia. Ted Lavender, who was scared, carried tranquilizers until he was shot in the head outside the village of Than Khe in mid-April. By necessity, and because it was SOP, they all carried steel helmets that weighed 5 pounds including the liner and camouflage cover. They carried the standard fatigue jackets and trousers. Very few carried underwear. On their feet they carried jungle boots—2.1 pounds—and Dave Jensen carried three pairs of socks and a can of Dr. Scholl's foot powder as a precaution against trench foot. Until he was shot, Ted Lavender carried six or seven ounces of premium dope, which for him was a necessity. Mitchell Sanders, the RTO, carried condoms. Norman Bowker carried a diary. Rat Kiley carried comic books. Kiowa, a devout Baptist, carried an illustrated New Testament that had been presented to him by his father, who taught Sunday school in Oklahoma City, Oklahoma. As a hedge against bad times, however, Kiowa also carried his grandmother's distrust of the white man, his grandfather's old hunting hatchet. Necessity dictated. Because the land was mined and booby-trapped, it was SOP for each man to carry a steel-centered, nylon-covered flak jacket, which weighed 6.7 pounds, but which on hot days seemed much heavier. Because you could die so quickly, each man carried at least one large compress bandage, usually in the helmet band for easy access. Because the nights were cold, and because the monsoons were wet, each carried a green plastic poncho that could be used as a raincoat or groundsheet or makeshift tent. With its quilted liner, the poncho weighed almost two pounds, but it was worth every ounce. In April, for instance, when Ted Lavender was shot, they used his poncho to wrap him up, then to carry him across the paddy, then to lift him into the chopper that took him away.

They were called legs or grunts.

To carry something was to hump it, as when Lieutenant Jimmy Cross humped his love for Martha up the hills and through the swamps. In its intransitive form, to hump meant to walk, or to march, but it implied burdens far beyond the intransitive.

Almost everyone humped photographs. In his wallet, Lieutenant Cross carried two photographs of Martha. The first was a Kodacolor snapshot signed Love, though he knew better. She stood against a brick wall. Her eyes were gray and neutral, her lips slightly open as she stared straight-on at the camera. At night, sometimes, Lieutenant Cross wondered who had taken the picture, because he knew she had boyfriends, because he loved her so much, and because he could see the shadow of the picture-taker spreading out against the brick wall. The second photograph had been clipped from the 1968 Mount Sebastian yearbook. It was an action shot—women's volleyball—and Martha was bent horizontal to the floor, reaching, the palms of her hands in sharp focus, the tongue taut, the expression frank and competitive. There was no visible sweat. She wore white gym shorts. Her legs, he thought, were almost certainly the legs of a virgin, dry and without hair, the left knee cocked and carrying her entire weight, which was just over one hundred pounds. Lieutenant Cross remembered touching that left knee. A dark theater, he remembered, and the movie was *Bonnie and Clyde,* and Martha wore a tweed skirt, and during the final scene, when he touched her knee, she turned and looked at him in a sad, sober way that made him pull his hand back, but he would always remember the feel of the tweed skirt and the knee beneath it and the sound of the gunfire that killed Bonnie and Clyde, how embarrassing it was, how slow and oppressive. He remembered kissing her good night at the dorm door. Right then, he thought, he should've done something brave. He should've carried her up the stairs to her room and tied her to the bed and touched that left knee all night long. He should've risked it. Whenever he looked at the photographs, he thought of new things he should've done.

What they carried was partly a function of rank, partly of field specialty.

As a first lieutenant and platoon leader, Jimmy Cross carried a compass, maps, code books, binoculars, and a .45-caliber pistol that weighed 2.9 pounds fully loaded. He carried a strobe light and the responsibility for the lives of his men.

As an RTO, Mitchell Sanders carried the PRC-25 radio, a killer, 26 pounds with its battery.

As a medic, Rat Kiley carried a canvas satchel filled with morphine and plasma and malaria tablets and surgical tape and comic books and all the things a medic must carry, including M&M's for especially bad wounds, for a total weight of nearly 20 pounds.

As a big man, therefore a machine gunner, Henry Dobbins carried the M-60, which weighed 23 pounds unloaded, but which was almost always loaded. In addition, Dobbins carried between 10 and 15 pounds of ammunition draped in belts across his chest and shoulders.

As PFCs or Spec 4s, most of them were common grunts and carried the standard M-16 gas-operated assault rifle. The weapon weighed 7.5 pounds unloaded, 8.2 pounds with its full 20-round magazine. Depending on numerous factors, such as topography and psychology, the riflemen carried anywhere from 12 to 20 magazines, usually in cloth bandoliers, adding on another 8.4 pounds at minimum, 14 pounds at maximum. When it was available, they also carried M-16 maintenance gear—rods and steel brushes and swabs and tubes of LSA oil—all of which weighed about a pound. Among the grunts, some carried the M-79 grenade launcher, 5.9 pounds unloaded, a reasonably light weapon except for the ammunition, which was heavy. A single round weighed 10 ounces. The typical load was 25 rounds. But Ted Lavender, who was scared, carried 34 rounds when he was shot and killed outside Than Khe, and he went down under an exceptional burden, more than 20 pounds of ammunition, plus the flak jacket and helmet and rations and water and toilet paper and tranquilizers and all the rest, plus the un-weighed fear. He was dead weight. There was no twitching or flopping. Kiowa, who saw it happen, said it was like watching a rock fall, or a big sandbag or something—just boom, then down—not like the movies where the dead guy rolls around and does fancy spins and goes ass over teakettle—not like that, Kiowa said, the poor bastard just flat-fuck fell. Boom. Down. Nothing else. It was a bright morning in mid-April. Lieutenant Cross felt the pain. He blamed himself. They stripped off Lavender's canteens and ammo, all the heavy things, and Rat Kiley said the obvious, the guy's dead, and Mitchell Sanders used his radio to report one U.S. KIA and to request a chopper. Then they wrapped Lavender in his poncho. They carried him out to a dry paddy, established security, and sat smoking the dead man's dope until the chopper came. Lieutenant Cross kept to himself. He pictured Martha's smooth young face, thinking he loved her more than anything, more than his men, and now Ted Lavender was dead because he loved her so much and could not stop thinking about her. When the dustoff arrived, they carried Lavender aboard. Afterward they burned Than Khe. They marched until dusk, then dug their holes, and that night Kiowa kept explaining how you had to be there, how fast it was, how the poor guy just dropped like so much concrete. Boom-down, he said. Like cement.

In addition to the three standard weapons—the M-60, M-16, and M-79—they carried whatever presented itself, or whatever seemed appropriate as a means of killing or staying alive. They carried catch-as-catch-can. At various times, in various situations, they carried M-14s and CAR-15s and Swedish Ks and grease guns and captured AK-47s and Chi-Coms and RPGs and Simonov carbines and black market Uzis and .38-caliber Smith & Wesson handguns and 66 mm LAWs and shotguns and silencers and blackjacks and bayonets and C-4 plastic explosives. Lee Strunk carried a slingshot; a weapon of last resort, he called it. Mitchell Sanders carried brass knuckles. Kiowa carried his grandfather's feathered hatchet. Every third or fourth man carried a Claymore antipersonnel mine—3.5 pounds with its firing device. They all carried fragmentation grenades—14 ounces each. They all carried at least one M-18 colored smoke grenade—24 ounces. Some carried CS or tear gas grenades. Some carried white phosphorus grenades. They carried all they could bear, and then some, including a silent awe for the terrible power of the things they carried.

In the first week of April, before Lavender died, Lieutenant Jimmy Cross received a good-luck charm from Martha. It was a simple pebble, an ounce at most. Smooth to the touch, it was a milky white color with flecks of orange and violet, oval-shaped, like a miniature egg. In the accompanying letter, Martha wrote that she had found the pebble on the Jersey's shoreline, precisely where the land touched water at high tide, where things came together but also separated. It was this separate-but-together quality, she wrote, that had inspired her to pick up the pebble and to carry it in her breast pocket for several days, where it seemed weightless, and then to send it through the mail, by air, as a token of her truest feelings for him. Lieutenant Cross found this romantic. But he wondered what her truest feelings were, exactly, and what she meant by separate-but-together. He wondered how the tides and waves had come into play on that afternoon along the Jersey shoreline when Martha saw the pebble and bent down to rescue it from geology. He imagined bare feet. Martha was a poet, with the poet's sensibilities, and her feet would be brown and bare, the toenails unpainted, the eyes chilly and somber like the ocean in March, and though it was painful, he wondered who had been with her that afternoon. He imagined a pair of shadows moving along the strip of sand where things came together but also separated. It was phantom jealousy, he knew, but he couldn't help himself. He loved her so much. On the march, through the hot days of early April, he carried the pebble in his mouth, turning it with his tongue, tasting sea salt and moisture. His mind wandered. He had difficulty keeping his attention on the war. On occasion he would yell at his men to spread out the column, to keep their eyes open, but then he would slip away into daydreams, just pretending, walking barefoot along the Jersey shore, with Martha, carrying nothing. He would feel himself rising. Sun and waves and gentle winds, all love and lightness.

What they carried varied by mission.

When a mission took them to the mountains, they carried mosquito netting, machetes, canvas tarps, and extra bug juice.

If a mission seemed especially hazardous, or if it involved a place they knew to be bad, they carried everything they could. In certain heavily mined AOs, where the land was dense with Toe Poppers and Bouncing Betties, they took turns humping a 28-pound mine detector. With its headphones and big sensing plate, the equipment was a stress on the lower back and shoulders, awkward to handle, often useless because of the shrapnel in the earth, but they carried it anyway, partly for safety, partly for the illusion of safety.

On ambush, or other night missions, they carried peculiar little odds and ends. Kiowa always took along his New Testament and a pair of moccasins for silence. Dave Jensen carried night-sight vitamins high in carotene. Lee Strunk carried his slingshot; ammo, he claimed, would never be a problem. Rat Kiley carried brandy and M&M's candy. Until he was shot, Ted Lavender carried the starlight scope, which weighed 6.3 pounds with its aluminum carrying case. Henry Dobbins carried his girlfriend's pantyhose wrapped around his neck as a comforter. They all carried ghosts. When dark came, they would move out single file across the meadows and paddies to their ambush coordinates, where they would quietly set up the Claymores and lie down and spend the night waiting.

Other missions were more complicated and required special equipment. In mid-April, it was their mission to search out and destroy the elaborate tunnel complexes in the Than Khe area south of Chu Lai. To blow the tunnels, they carried one-pound blocks of pentrite high explosives, four blocks to a man, 68 pounds in all. They carried wiring, detonators, and battery-powered clackers. Dave Jensen carried earplugs. Most often, before blowing the tunnels, they were ordered by higher command to search them, which was considered bad news, but by and large they just shrugged and carried out orders. Because he was a big man, Henry Dobbins was excused from tunnel duty. The others would draw numbers. Before Lavender died there were 17 men in the platoon, and whoever drew the number 17 would strip off his gear and crawl in headfirst with a flashlight and Lieutenant Cross's .45-caliber pistol. The rest of them would fan out as security. They would sit down or kneel, not facing the hole, listening to the ground beneath them, imagining cobwebs and ghosts, whatever was down there—the tunnel walls squeezing in—how the flashlight seemed impossibly heavy in the hand and how it was tunnel vision in the very strictest sense, compression in all ways, even time, and how you had to wiggle in—ass and elbows—a swallowed-up feeling—and how you found yourself worrying about odd things: Will your flashlight go dead? Do rats carry rabies? If you screamed, how far would the sound carry? Would your buddies hear it? Would they have the courage to drag you out? In some respects, though not many, the waiting was worse than the tunnel itself. Imagination was a killer.

On April 16, when Lee Strunk drew the number 17, he laughed and muttered something and went down quickly. The morning was hot and very still. Not good, Kiowa said. He looked at the tunnel opening, then out across a dry paddy toward the village of Than Khe. Nothing moved. No clouds or birds or people. As they waited, the men smoked and drank Kool-Aid, not talking much, feeling sympathy for Lee Strunk but also feeling the luck of the draw. You win some, you lose some, said Mitchell Sanders, and sometimes you settle for a rain check. It was a tired line and no one laughed.

Henry Dobbins ate a tropical chocolate bar. Ted Lavender popped a tranquilizer and went off to pee.

After five minutes, Lieutenant Jimmy Cross moved to the tunnel, leaned down, and examined the darkness. Trouble, he thought—a cave-in maybe. And then suddenly, without willing it, he was thinking about Martha. The stresses and fractures, the quick collapse, the two of them buried alive under all that weight. Dense, crushing love. Kneeling, watching the hole, he tried to concentrate on Lee Strunk and the war, all the dangers, but his love was too much for him, he felt paralyzed, he wanted to sleep inside her lungs and breathe her blood and be smothered. He wanted her to be a virgin and not a virgin, all at once. He wanted to know her. Intimate secrets: Why poetry? Why so sad? Why that grayness in her eyes? Why so alone? Not lonely, just alone—riding her bike across campus or sitting off by herself in the cafeteria—even dancing, she danced alone—and it was the aloneness that filled him with love. He remembered telling her that one evening. How she nodded and looked away. And how, later, when he kissed her, she received the kiss without returning it, her eyes wide open, not afraid, not a virgin's eyes, just flat and uninvolved.

Lieutenant Cross gazed at the tunnel. But he was not there. He was buried with Martha under the white sand at the Jersey shore. They were pressed together, and the pebble in his mouth was her tongue. He was smiling. Vaguely, he was aware of how quiet the day was, the sullen paddies, yet he could not bring himself to worry about matters of security. He was beyond that. He was just a kid at war, in love. He was twenty-four years old. He couldn't help it.

A few moments later Lee Strunk crawled out of the tunnel. He came up grinning, filthy but alive. Lieutenant Cross nodded and closed his eyes while the others clapped Strunk on the back and made jokes about rising from the dead.

Worms, Rat Kiley said. Right out of the grave. Fuckin' zombie.

The men laughed. They all felt great relief.

Spook city, said Mitchell Sanders.

Lee Strunk made a funny ghost sound, a kind of moaning, yet very happy, and right then, when Strunk made that high happy moaning sound, when he went *Ahhooooo*, right then Ted Lavender was shot in the head on his way back from peeing. He lay with his mouth open. The teeth were broken. There was a swollen black bruise under his left eye. The cheekbone was gone. Oh shit, Rat Kiley said, the guy's dead. The guy's dead, he kept saying, which seemed profound—the guy's dead. I mean really.

The things they carried were determined to some extent by superstition. Lieutenant Cross carried his good-luck pebble. Dave Jensen carried a rabbit's foot. Norman Bowker, otherwise a very gentle person, carried a thumb that had been presented to him as as gift by Mitchell Sanders. The thumb was dark brown, rubbery to the touch, and weighed four ounces at most. It had been cut from a VC corpse, a boy of fifteen or sixteen. They'd found him at the bottom of an irrigation ditch, badly burned, flies in his mouth and eyes. The boy wore black shorts and sandals. At the time of his death he had been carrying a pouch of rice, a rifle, and three magazines of ammunition.

You want my opinion, Mitchell Sanders said, there's a definite moral here.

He put his hand on the dead boy's wrist. He was quiet for a time, as if counting a pulse, then he patted the stomach, almost affectionately, and used Kiowa's hunting hatchet to remove the thumb.

Henry Dobbins asked what the moral was.

Moral?

You know. *Moral.*

Sanders wrapped the thumb in toilet paper and handed it across to Norman Bowker. There was no blood. Smiling, he kicked the boy's head, watched the flies scatter, and said, It's like what that old TV show—Paladin. Have gun, will travel.

Henry Dobbins thought about it.

Yeah, well, he finally said. I don't see no moral.

There it *is,* man.

Fuck off.

They carried USO stationery and pencils and pens. They carried Sterno, safety pins, trip flares, signal flares, spools of wire, razor blades, chewing to-bacco, liberated joss sticks and statuettes of the smiling Buddha, candles, grease pencils, *The Stars and Stripes,* fingernail clippers, Psy Ops leaflets, bush hats, bolos, and much more. Twice a week, when the resupply choppers came in, they carried hot chow in green mermite cans and large canvas bags filled with iced beer and soda pop. They carried plastic water containers, each with a two-gallon capacity. Mitchell Sanders carried a set of starched tiger fatigues for special occasions. Henry Dobbins carried Black Flag insecticide. Dave Jensen carried empty sandbags that could be filled at night for added protec-tion. Lee Strunk carried tanning lotion. Some things they carried in com-mon. Taking turns, they carried the big PRC-77 scrambler radio, which weighed 30 pounds with its battery. They shared the weight of memory. They took up what others could no longer bear. Often, they carried each other, the wounded or weak. They carried infections. They carried chess sets, basketballs, Vietnamese-English dictionaries, insignia of rank, Bronze Stars and Purple Hearts, plastic cards imprinted with the Code of Conduct. They carried diseases, among them malaria and dysentery. They carried lice and ringworm and leeches and paddy algae and various rots and molds. They carried the land itself—Vietnam, the place, the soil—a powdery orange-red dust that covered their boots and fatigues and faces. They carried the sky. The whole atmosphere, they carried it, the humidity, the monsoons, the stink of fungus and decay, all of it, they carried gravity. They moved like mules. By daylight they took sniper fire, at night they were mortared, but it was not battle, it was just the endless march, village to village, without purpose, nothing won or lost. They marched for the sake of the march. They plodded along slowly, dumbly, leaning forward against the heat, unthinking, all blood and bone, simple grunts, soldiering with their legs, toiling up the hills and down into the paddies and across the rivers and up again and down, just humping, one step and then the next and then another, but no volition, no will, because it was automatic, it was anatomy, and the war was entirely a matter of posture and carriage, the hump was everything, a kind of inertia, a kind of emptiness, a dullness of desire and intellect and conscience and hope and human sensibility. Their principles were in their feet. Their calculations were biological. They had no sense of strategy or mission. They searched the villages without knowing what to look for, not caring, kicking over jars of rice, frisking children and old men, blowing tunnels, sometimes setting fires and sometimes not, then forming up and moving on to the next village, then other villages, where it would always be the same. They carried their own lives. The pressures were enormous. In the heat of early afternoon, they would remove their helmets and flak jackets, walking bare, which was dangerous but which helped ease the strain. They would often discard things along the route of march. Purely for comfort, they would throw away rations, blow their Claymores and grenades, no matter, because by nightfall the re-supply choppers would arrive with more of the same, then a day or two later still more, fresh watermelons and crates of ammunition and sunglasses and woolen sweaters—the resources were stunning—sparklers for the Fourth of July, colored eggs for Easter—it was the great American war chest—the fruits of science, the smokestacks, the canneries, the arsenals at Hartford, the Minnesota forests, the machine shops, the vast fields of corn and wheat—they carried like freight trains; they carried it on their backs and shoulders—and for all the ambiguities of Vietnam, all the mysteries and unknowns, there was at least the single abiding certainty that they would never be at a loss for things to carry.

After the chopper took Lavender away, Lieutenant Jimmy Cross led his men into the village of Than Khe. They burned everything. They shot chickens and dogs, they trashed the village well, they called in artillery and watched the wreckage, then they marched for several hours through the hot afternoon, and then at dusk, while Kiowa explained how Lavender died, Lieutenant Cross found himself trembling.

He tried not to cry. With his entrenching tool, which weighed five pounds, he began digging a hole in the earth.

He felt shame. He hated himself. He had loved Martha more than his men, and as a consequence Lavender was now dead, and this was something he would have to carry like a stone in his stomach for the rest of the war.

All he could do was dig. He used his entrenching tool like an ax, slashing, feeling both love and hate, and then later, when it was full dark, he sat at the bottom of his foxhole and wept. It went on for a long while. In part, he was grieving for Ted Lavender, but mostly it was for Martha, and for himself, because she belonged to another world, which was not quite real, and because she was a junior at Mount Sebastian College in New Jersey, a poet and a virgin and uninvolved, and because he realized she did not love him and never would.

Like cement, Kiowa whispered in the dark. I swear to God—boom, down. Not a word.

I've heard this, said Norman Bowker.

A pisser, you know? Still zipping himself up. Zapped while zipping.

All right, fine. That's enough.

Yeah, but you had to see it, the guy just—

I *heard*, man. Cement. So why not shut the fuck *up?*

Kiowa shook his head sadly and glanced over at the hole where Lieutenant Jimmy Cross sat watching the night. The air was thick and wet. A warm dense fog had settled over the paddies and there was the stillness that precedes rain.

After a time Kiowa sighed.

One thing for sure, he said. The lieutenant's in some deep hurt. I mean that crying jag—the way he was carrying on—it wasn't fake or anything, it was real heavy-duty hurt. The man cares.

Sure, Norman Bowker said.

Say what you want, the man does care.

We all got problems.

Not Lavender.

No, I guess not, Bowker said. Do me a favor, though.

Shut up?

That's a smart Indian. Shut up.

Shrugging, Kiowa pulled off his boots. He wanted to say more, just to lighten up his sleep, but instead he opened his New Testament and arranged it beneath his head as a pillow. The fog made things seem hollow and unattached. He tried not to think about Ted Lavender, but then he was thinking how fast it was, no drama, down and dead, and how it was hard to feel anything except surprise. It seemed unchristian. He wished he could find some great sadness, or even anger, but the emotion wasn't there and he couldn't make it happen. Mostly he felt pleased to be alive. He liked the smell of the New Testament under his cheek, the leather and ink and paper and glue, whatever the chemicals were. He liked hearing the sounds of night. Even his fatigue, it felt fine, the stiff muscles and the prickly awareness of his own body, a floating feeling. He enjoyed not being dead. Lying there, Kiowa admired Lieutenant Jimmy Cross's capacity for grief. He wanted to share the man's pain, he wanted to care as Jimmy Cross cared. And yet when he closed his eyes, all he could think was Boom-down, and all he could feel was the pleasure of having his boots off and the fog curling in around him and the damp soil and the Bible smells and the plush comfort of night.

After a moment Norman Bowker sat up in the dark.

What the hell, he said. You want to talk, *talk*. Tell it to me.

Forget it.

No, man, go on. One thing I hate, it's a silent Indian.

For the most part they carried themselves with poise, a kind of dignity. Now and then, however, there were times of panic, when they squealed or wanted to squeal but couldn't, when they twitched and made moaning sounds and covered their heads and said Dear Jesus and flopped around on the earth and fired their weapons blindly and cringed and sobbed and begged for the noise to stop and went wild and made stupid promises to themselves and to God and to their mothers and fathers, hoping not to die. In different ways, it happened to all of them. Afterward, when the firing ended, they would blink and peek up. They would touch their bodies, feeling shame, then quickly hiding it. They would force themselves to stand. As if in slow motion, frame by frame, the world would take on the old logic—absolute silence, then the wind, then sunlight, then voices. It was the burden of being alive. Awkwardly, the men would reassemble themselves, first in private, then in groups, becoming soldiers again. They would repair the leaks in their eyes. They would check for casualties, call in dustoffs, light cigarettes, try to smile, clear their throats and spit and begin cleaning their weapons. After a time someone would shake his head and say, No lie, I almost shit my pants, and someone else would laugh, which meant it was bad, yes, but the guy had obviously not shit his pants, it wasn't that bad, and in any case nobody would ever do such a thing and then go ahead and talk about it. They would squint into the dense, oppressive sunlight. For a few moments, perhaps, they would fall silent, lighting a joint and tracking its passage from man to man, inhaling, holding in the humiliation. Scary stuff, one of them might say. But then someone else would grin or flick his eyebrows and say, Roger-dodger, almost cut me a new asshole, *almost*.

There were numerous such poses. Some carried themselves with a sort of wistful resignation, others with pride or stiff soldierly discipline or good humor or macho zeal. They were afraid of dying but they were even more afraid to show it.

They found jokes to tell.

They used a hard vocabulary to contain the terrible softness. *Greased* they'd say. *Offed, lit up, zapped while zipping.* It wasn't cruelty, just stage presence. They were actors. When someone died, it wasn't quite dying, because in a curious way it seemed scripted, and because they had their lines mostly memorized, irony mixed with tragedy, and because they called it by other names, as if to encyst and destroy the reality of death itself. They kicked corpses. They cut off thumbs. They talked grunt lingo. They told stories about Ted Lavender's supply of tranquilizers, how the poor guy didn't feel a thing, how incredibly tranquil he was.

There's a moral here, said Mitchell Sanders.

They were waiting for Lavender's chopper, smoking the dead man's dope.

The moral's pretty obvious, Sanders said, and winked. Stay away from drugs. No joke, they'll ruin your day every time.

Cute, said Henry Dobbins.

Mind blower, get it? Talk about wiggy. Nothing left, just blood and brains.

They made themselves laugh.

There it is, they'd say. Over and over—there it is, my friend, there it is—as if the repetition itself were an act of poise, a balance between crazy and almost crazy, knowing without going, there it is, which meant be cool, let it ride, because Oh yeah, man, you can't change what can't be changed, there it is, there it absolutely and positively and fucking well *is*.

They were tough.

They carried all the emotional baggage of men who might die. Grief, terror, love, longing—these were intangibles, but the intangibles had their own mass and specific gravity, they had tangible weight. They carried shameful memories. They carried the common secret of cowardice barely restrained, the instinct to run or freeze or hide, and in many respects this was the heaviest burden of all, for it could never be put down, it required perfect balance and perfect posture. They carried their reputations. They carried the soldier's greatest fear, which was the fear of blushing. Men killed, and died, because they were embarrassed not to. It was what had brought them to the war in the first place, nothing positive, no dreams of glory or honor, just to avoid the blush of dishonor. They died so as not to die of embarrassment. They crawled into tunnels and walked point and advanced under fire. Each morning, despite the unknowns, they made their legs move. They endured. They kept humping. they did not submit to the obvious alternative, which was simply to close the eyes and fall. So easy, really. Go limp and tumble to the ground and let the muscles unwind and not speak and not budge until your buddies picked you up and lifted you into the chopper that would roar and dip its nose and carry you off to the world. A mere matter of falling, yet no one ever fell. It was not courage, exactly; the object was not valor. Rather, they were too frightened to be cowards.

By and large they carried these things inside, maintaining the masks of composure. They sneered at sick call. They spoke bitterly about guys who had found release by shooting off their own toes or fingers. Pussies, they'd say. Candy-asses. It was fierce, mocking talk, with only a trace of envy or awe, but even so the image played itself out behind their eyes.

They imagined the muzzle against flesh. So easy: squeeze the trigger and blow away a toe. They imagined it. They imagined the quick, sweet pain, then the evacuation to Japan, then a hospital with warm beds and cute geisha nurses.

And they dreamed of freedom birds.

At night, on guard, staring into the dark, they were carried away by jumbo jets. They felt the rush of takeoff. *Gone!* they yelled. And then velocity—wings and engines—a smiling stewardess—but it was more than a plane, it was a real bird, a big sleek silver bird with feathers and talons and high screeching. They were flying. The weights fell off; there was nothing to bear. They laughed and held on tight, feeling the cold slap of wind and altitude, soaring, thinking *It's over, I'm gone!*—they were naked, they were light and free—it was all lightness, bright and fast and buoyant, light as light, a helium buzz in the brain, a giddy bubbling in the lungs as they were taken up over the clouds and the war, beyond duty, beyond gravity and mortification and global entanglements—*Sin loi!* they yelled. *I'm sorry, motherfuckers, but I'm out of it, I'm goofed, I'm on a space cruise, I'm gone!*—and it was a restful, unencumbered sensation, just riding the light waves, sailing that big silver freedom bird over the mountains and oceans, over America, over the farms and great sleeping cities and cemeteries and highways and the golden arches of McDonald's, it was flight, a kind of fleeing, a kind of falling, falling higher and higher, spinning off the edge of the earth and beyond the sun and through the vast, silent vacuum where there were no burdens and where everything weighed exactly nothing—*Gone!* they screamed. *I'm sorry but I'm gone!*—and so at night, not quite dreaming, they gave themselves over to lightness, they were carried, they were purely borne.

On the morning after Ted Lavender died, First Lieutenant Jimmy Cross crouched at the bottom of his foxhole and burned Martha's letters. Then he burned the two photographs. There was a steady rain falling, which made it difficult, but he used heat tabs and Sterno to build a small fire, screening it with his body, holding the photographs over the tight blue flame with the tips of his fingers.

He realized it was only a gesture. Stupid, he thought. Sentimental, too, but mostly just stupid.

Lavender was dead. You couldn't burn the blame.

Besides, the letters were in his head. And even now, without photographs, Lieutenant Cross could see Martha playing volleyball in her white gym shorts and yellow T-shirt. He could see her moving in the rain.

When the fire died out, Lieutenant Cross pulled his poncho over his shoulders and ate breakfast from a can.

There was no great mystery, he decided.

In those burned letters Martha had never mentioned the war, except to say, Jimmy, take care of yourself. She wasn't involved. She signed the letters Love, but it wasn't love, and all the fine lines and technicalities did not matter. Virginity was no longer an issue. He hated her. Yes, he did. He hated her. Love, too, but it was a hard, hating kind of love.

The morning came up wet and blurry. Everything seemed part of everything else, the fog and Martha and the deepening rain.

He was a soldier, after all.

Half smiling, Lieutenant Jimmy Cross took out his maps. He shook his head hard, as if to clear it, then bent forward and began planning the day's march. In ten minutes, or maybe twenty, he would rouse the men and they would pack up and head west, where the maps showed the country to be green and inviting. They would do what they had always done. The rain might add some weight, but otherwise it would be one more day layered upon all the other days.

He was realistic about it. There was that new hardness in his stomach. He loved her but he hated her.

No more fantasies, he told himself.

Henceforth, when he thought about Martha, it would be only to think that she belonged elsewhere. He would shut down the daydreams. This was not Mount Sebastian, it was another world, where there were no pretty poems or mid-term exams, a place where men died because of carelessness and gross stupidity. Kiowa was right. Boom-down, and you were dead, never partly dead.

Briefly, in the rain, Lieutenant Cross saw Martha's gray eyes gazing back at him.

He understood.

It was very sad, he thought. The things men carried inside. The things men did or felt they had to do.

He almost nodded at her, but didn't.

Instead he went back to his maps. He was now determined to perform his duties firmly and without negligence. It wouldn't help Lavender, he knew that, but from this point on he would comport himself as an officer. He would dispose of his good-luck pebble. Swallow it, maybe, or use Lee Strunk's slingshot, or just drop it along the trail. On the march he would impose strict field discipline. He would be careful to send out flank security, to prevent straggling or bunching up, to keep his troops moving at the proper pace and at the proper interval. He would insist on clean weapons. He would confiscate the remainder of Lavender's dope. Later in the day, perhaps, he would call the men together and speak to them plainly. He would accept the blame for what had happened to Ted Lavender. He would be a man about it. He would look them in the eyes, keeping his chin level, and he would issue the new SOPs in a calm, impersonal tone of voice, a lieutenant's voice, leaving no room for argument or discussion. Commencing immediately, he'd tell them, they would no longer abandon equipment along the route of march. They would police up their acts. They would get their shit together, and keep it together, and maintain it neatly and in good working order.

He would not tolerate laxity. He would show strength, distancing himself.

Among the men there would be grumbling, of course, and maybe worse, because their days would seem longer and their loads heavier, but Lieutenant Jimmy Cross reminded himself that his obligation was not to be loved but to lead. He would dispense with love; it was not now a factor. And if anyone quarreled or complained, he would simply tighten his lips and arrange his shoulders in the correct command posture. He might give a curt little nod. Or he might not. He might just shrug and say, Carry on, then they would saddle up and form into a column and move out toward the villages west of Than Khe.

Suggestions for Discussion

1. For the most part, "The Things They Carried" uses a matter-of-fact tone listing an accumulation of concrete details. How do these details create the atmosphere of the Vietnam War and the feelings of the soldiers there?

2. What is the effect of insisting on the exact weight of things?

3. Lavender's death is reiterated several times as an incidental illustration of the worth or necessity of things—poncho, ammo, flashlight. What effect is achieved by this?

4. The story is structured around the verb "to carry." Note the frequency and variety of other active verbs.

5. How would you describe the overall rhythm of the story? How is it achieved?

6. At several points the soldiers carry, in addition to their gear, abstracts like *distrust of the white man, all they could bear, infections, grief, terror, love, fear*. How does O'Brien get away with using so many grand abstractions?

7. On page 80 we have a detailed description of Lavender after his death, and immediately thereafter a description of the thumb of a dead VC and of that corpse. What abstractions and judgments result from the juxtaposition?

8. How is Jimmy Cross's situation at the end of the story the opposite of that at the beginning? Why?

Rape Fantasies

MARGARET ATWOOD

The way they're going on about it in the magazines you'd think it was just invented, and not only that but it's something terrific, like a vaccine for cancer. They put it in capital letters on the front cover, and inside they have these questionnaires like the ones they used to have about whether you were a good enough wife or an endomorph or an ectomorph, remember that? with the scoring upside down on page 73, and then these numbered do-it-yourself dealies, you know? RAPE, TEN THINGS TO DO ABOUT IT, like it was ten new hairdos or something. I mean, what's so new about it?

So at work they all have to talk about it because no matter what magazine you open, there it is, staring you right between the eyes, and they're beginning to have it on the television, too. Personally I'd prefer a June Allyson movie anytime but they don't make them any more and they don't even have them that much on the Late Show. For instance, day before yesterday, that would be Wednesday, thank god it's Friday as they say, we were sitting around in the women's lunch room—the *lunch* room, I mean you'd think you could get some peace and quiet in there—and Chrissy closes up the magazine she's been reading and says, "How about it, girls, do you have rape fantasies?"

The four of us were having our game of bridge the way we always do, and I had a bare twelve points counting the singleton with not that much of a bid in anything. So I said one club, hoping Sondra would remember about the one club convention, because the time before when I used that she thought I really meant clubs and she bid us up to three, and all I had was four little ones with nothing higher than a six, and we went down two and on top of that we were vulnerable. She is not the world's best bridge player. I mean, neither am I but there's a limit.

Darlene passed but the damage was done. Sondra's head went round like it was on ball bearings and she said, "*What* fantasies?"

"Rape fantasies," Chrissy said. She's a receptionist and she looks like one; she's pretty but cool as a cucumber, like she's been painted all over with nail polish, if you know what I mean. Varnished. "It says here all women have rape fantasies."

"For Chrissake, I'm eating an egg sandwich," I said, "and I bid one club and Darlene passed."

"You mean, like some guy jumping you in an alley or something," Sondra said. She was eating her lunch, we all eat our lunches during the game, and she bit into a piece of that celery she always brings and started to chew away on it with this thoughtful expression in her eyes and I knew we might as well pack it in as far as the game was concerned.

"Yeah, sort of like that," Chrissy said. She was blushing a little, you could see it even under her makeup.

"I don't think you should go out alone at night," Darlene said, "you put yourself in a position," and I may have been mistaken but she was looking at me. She's the oldest, she's forty-one though you wouldn't know it and neither does she, but I looked it up in the employees' file. I like to guess a person's age and then look it up to see if I'm right. I let myself have an extra pack of cigarettes if I am, though I'm trying to cut down. I figure it's harmless as long as you don't tell. I mean, not everyone has access to that file, it's more or less confidential. But it's all right if I tell you. I don't expect you'll ever meet her, though you never know, it's a small world. Anyway.

"For *heaven's* sake, it's only *Toronto*," Greta said. She worked in Detroit for three years and she never lets you forget it, it's like she thinks she's a war hero or something, we should all admire her just for the fact that she's still walking this earth, though she was really living in Windsor the whole time, she just worked in Detroit. Which for me doesn't really count. It's where you sleep, right?

"Well, do you?" Chrissy said. She was obviously trying to tell us about hers but she wasn't about to go first, she's cautious, that one.

"I certainly don't," Darlene said, and she wrinkled up her nose, like this, and I had to laugh. "I think it's disgusting." She's divorced, I read that in the file too, she never talks about it. It must've been years ago anyway. She got up and went over to the coffee machine and turned her back on us as though she wasn't going to have anything more to do with it.

"Well," Greta said. I could see it was going to be between her and Chrissy. They're both blondes, I don't mean that in a bitchy way but they do try to outdress each other. Greta would like to get out of Filing, she'd like to be a receptionist too so she could meet more people. You don't meet much of anyone in Filing except other people in Filing. Me, I don't mind it so much, I have outside interests.

"Well," Greta said, "I sometimes think about, you know my apartment? It's got this little balcony, I like to sit out there in the summer and I have a few plants out there. I never bother that much about locking the door to the balcony, it's one of those sliding glass ones, I'm on the eighteenth floor for heaven's sake, I've got a good view of the lake and the CN Tower and all. But I'm sitting around one night in my housecoat, watching TV with my shoes off, you know how you do, and I see this guy's feet, coming down past the window, and the next thing you know he's standing on the balcony, he's let himself down by a rope with a hook on the end of it from the floor above, that's the nineteenth, and before I can even get up off the chesterfield he's inside the apartment. He's all dressed in black with black gloves on"—I knew right away what show she got the black gloves off because I saw the same one—"and then he, well, you know."

"You know what?" Chrissy said, but Greta said, "And afterwards he tells me that he goes all over the outside of the apartment building like that, from one floor to another, with his rope and his hook . . . and then he goes out to the balcony and tosses his rope, and he climbs up it and disappears."

"Just like Tarzan," I said, but nobody laughed.

"Is that all?" Chrissy said. "Don't you ever think about, well, I think about being in the bathtub, with no clothes on . . ."

"So who takes a bath in their clothes?" I said, you have to admit it's stupid when you come to think of it, but she just went on, ". . . with lots of bubbles, what I use is Vitabath, it's more expensive but it's so relaxing, and my hair pinned up, and the door opens and this fellow's standing there. . . ."

"How'd he get in?" Greta said.

"Oh, I don't know, through a window or something. Well, I can't very well get out of the bathtub, the bathroom's too small and besides he's blocking the doorway, so I just *lie* there, and he starts to very slowly take his own clothes off, and then he gets into the bathtub with me."

"Don't you scream or anything?" said Darlene. She'd come back with her cup of coffee, she was getting really interested. "I'd scream like bloody murder."

"Who'd hear me?" Chrissy said. "Besides, all the articles say it's better not to resist, that way you don't get hurt."

"Anyway you might get bubbles up your nose," I said, "from the deep breathing," and I swear all four of them looked at me like I was in bad taste, like I'd insulted the Virgin Mary or something. I mean, I don't see what's wrong with a little joke now and then. Life's too short, right?

"Listen," I said, "those aren't *rape* fantasies. I mean, you aren't getting *raped*, it's just some guy you haven't met formally who happens to be more attractive than Derek Cummins"—he's the Assistant Manager, he wears elevator shoes or at any rate they have these thick soles and he has this funny way of talking, we call him Derek Duck—"and you have a good time. Rape is when they've got a knife or something and you don't want to."

"So what about you, Estelle," Chrissy said, she was miffed because I laughed at her fantasy, she thought I was putting her down. Sondra was miffed too, by this time she'd finished her celery and she wanted to tell about hers, but she hadn't got in fast enough.

"All right, let me tell you one," I said. "I'm walking down this dark street at night and this fellow comes up and grabs my arm. Now it so happens that I have a plastic lemon in my purse, you know how it always says you should carry a plastic lemon in your purse? I don't really do it, I tried it once but the darn thing leaked all over my chequebook, but in this fantasy I have one, and I say to him, "You're intending to rape me, right?" and he nods, so I open my purse to get the plastic lemon, and I can't find it! My purse is full of all this junk, Kleenex and cigarettes and my change purse and my lipstick and my driver's licence, you know the kind of stuff; so I ask him to hold out his hands, like this, and I pile all this junk into them and down at the bottom there's the plastic lemon, and I can't get the top off. So I hand it to him and he's very obliging, he twists the top off and hands it back to me, and I squirt him in the eye."

I hope you don't think that's too vicious. Come to think of it, it is a bit mean, especially when he was so polite and all.

"*That's* your rape fantasy?" Chrissy says. "I don't believe it."

"She's a card," Darlene says, she and I are the ones that've been here the longest and she never will forget the time I got drunk at the office party and insisted I was going to dance under the table instead of on top of it, I did a sort of Cossack number but then I hit my head on the bottom of the table— actually it was a desk—when I went to get up, and I knocked myself out cold. She's decided that's the mark of an original mind and she tells everyone new about it and I'm not sure that's fair. Though I did do it.

"I'm being totally honest," I say. I always am and they know it. There's no point in being anything else, is the way I look at it, and sooner or later the truth will out so you might as well not waste the time, right? "You should hear the one about the Easy-Off Oven Cleaner."

But that was the end of the lunch hour, with one bridge game shot to hell, and the next day we spent most of the time arguing over whether to start a new game or play out the hands we had left over from the day before, so Sondra never did get a chance to tell about her rape fantasy.

It started me thinking though, about my own rape fantasies. Maybe I'm abnormal or something. I mean I have fantasies about handsome strangers coming in through the window too, like Mr. Clean, I wish one would, please god somebody without flat feet and big sweat marks on his shirt, and over five feet five, believe me being tall is a handicap though it's getting better, tall guys are starting to like someone whose nose reaches higher than their belly button. But if you're being totally honest you can't count those as rape fantasies. In a real rape fantasy, what you should feel is this anxiety, like when you think about your apartment building catching on fire and whether you should use the elevator or the stairs or maybe just stick your head under a wet towel, and you try to remember everything you've read about what to do but you can't decide.

For instance, I'm walking along this dark street at night and this short, ugly fellow comes up and grabs my arm, and not only is he ugly, you know, with a sort of puffy nothing face, like those fellows you have to talk to in the bank when your account's overdrawn—of course I don't mean they're all like that—but he's absolutely covered in pimples. So he gets me pinned against the wall, he's short but he's heavy, and he starts to undo himself and the zipper gets stuck. I mean, one of the most significant moments in a girl's life, it's almost like getting married or having a baby or something, and he sticks the zipper.

So I say, kind of disgusted, "Oh for Chrissake," and he starts to cry. He tells me he's never been able to get anything right in his entire life, and this is the last straw, he's going to go jump off a bridge.

"Look," I say, I feel so sorry for him, in my rape fantasies I always end up feeling sorry for the guy, I mean there has to be something *wrong* with them, if it was Clint Eastwood it'd be different but worse luck it never is. I was the kind of little girl who buried dead robins, know what I mean? It used to drive my mother nuts, she didn't like me touching them, because of the germs I guess. So I say, "Listen, I know how you feel. You really should do something about those pimples, if you got rid of them you'd be quite good looking, honest; then you wouldn't have to go around doing stuff like this. I had them myself once," I say, to comfort him, but in fact I did, and it ends up I give him the name of my old dermatologist, the one I had in high school, that was back in Leamington, except I used to go to St. Catharine's for the dermatologist. I'm telling you, I was really lonely when I first came here; I thought it was going to be such a big adventure and all, but it's a lot harder to meet people in a city. But I guess it's different for a guy.

Or I'm lying in bed with this terrible cold, my face is all swollen up, my eyes are red and my nose is dripping like a leaky tap, and this fellow comes in through the window and *he* has a terrible cold too, it's a new kind of flu that's been going around. So he says, "I'b goig do rabe you"—I hope you don't mind me holding my nose like this but that's the way I imagine it— and he lets out this terrific sneeze, which slows him down a bit, also I'm no object of beauty myself, you'd have to be some kind of pervert to want to rape someone with a cold like mine, it'd be like raping a bottle of LePages mucilage the way my nose is running. He's looking wildly around the room, and I realize it's because he doesn't have a piece of Kleenex! "Id's ride here,"

I say, and I pass him the Kleenex, god knows why he even bothered to get out of bed, you'd think if you were going to go around climbing in windows you'd wait till you were healthier, right? I mean, that takes a certain amount of energy. So I ask him why doesn't he let me fix him a NeoCitran and scotch, that's what I always take, you still have the cold but you don't feel it, so I do and we end up watching the Late Show together. I mean, they aren't all sex maniacs, the rest of the time they must lead a normal life. I figure they enjoy watching the Late Show just like anybody else.

I do have a scarier one though . . . where the fellow says he's hearing angel voices that're telling him he's got to kill me, you know, you read about things like that all the time in the papers. In this one I'm not in the apartment where I live now, I'm back in my mother's house in Leamington and the fellow's been hiding in the cellar, he grabs my arm when I go downstairs to get a jar of jam and he's got hold of the axe too, out of the garage, that one is really scary. I mean, what do you say to a nut like that?

So I start to shake but after a minute I get control of myself and I say, is he sure the angel voices have got the right person, because I hear the same angel voices and they've been telling me for some time that I'm going to give birth to the reincarnation of St. Anne who in turn has the Virgin Mary and right after that comes Jesus Christ and the end of the world, and he wouldn't want to interfere with that, would he? So he gets confused and listens some more, and then he asks for a sign and I show him my vaccination mark, you can see it's sort of an odd-shaped one, it got infected because I scratched the top off, and that does it, he apologizes and climbs out the coal chute again, which is how he got in in the first place, and I say to myself there's some advantage in having been brought up a Catholic even though I haven't been to church since they changed the service into English, it just isn't the same, you might as well be a Protestant. I must write to Mother and tell her to nail up that coal chute, it always has bothered me. Funny, I couldn't tell you at all what this man looks like but I know exactly what kind of shoes he's wearing, because that's the last I see of him, his shoes going up the coal chute, and they're the old-fashioned kind that lace up the ankles, even though he's a young fellow. That's strange, isn't it?

Let me tell you though I really sweat until I see him safely out of there and I go upstairs right away and make myself a cup of tea. I don't think about that one much. My mother always said you shouldn't dwell on unpleasant things and I generally agree with that, I mean, dwelling on them doesn't make them go away. Though not dwelling on them doesn't make them go away either, when you come to think of it.

Sometimes I have these short ones where the fellow grabs my arm but I'm really a Kung-Fu expert, can you believe it, in real life I'm sure it would just be a conk on the head and that's that, like getting your tonsils out, you'd wake up and it would be all over except for the sore places, and you'd be lucky if your neck wasn't broken or something, I could never even hit the volleyball in gym and a volleyball is fairly large, you know?—and I just go *zap* with my fingers into his eyes and that's it, he falls over, or I flip him against a wall or something. But I could never really stick my fingers in anyone's eyes, could you? It would feel like hot jello and I don't even like cold jello, just thinking about it gives me the creeps. I feel a bit guilty about that one, I mean how would you like walking around knowing someone's been blinded for life because of you?

But maybe it's different for a guy.

The most touching one I have is when the fellow grabs my arm and I say, sad and kind of dignified, "You'd be raping a corpse." That pulls him up short and I explain that I've just found out I have leukaemia and the doctors have only given me a few months to live. That's why I'm out pacing the streets alone at night, I need to think, you know, come to terms with myself. I don't really have leukaemia but in the fantasy I do, I guess I chose that particular disease because a girl in my grade four class died of it, the whole class sent her flowers when she was in the hospital. I didn't understand then that she was going to die and I wanted to have leukaemia too so I could get flowers. Kids are funny, aren't they? Well, it turns out that he has leukaemia himself, and *he* only has a few months to live, that's why he's going around raping people, he's very bitter because he's so young and his life is being taken from him before he's really lived it. So we walk along gently under the street lights, it's spring and sort of misty, and we end up going for coffee, we're happy we've found the only other person in the world who can understand what we're going through, it's almost like fate, and after a while we just sort of look at each other and our hands touch, and he comes back with me and moves into my apartment and we spend our last months together before we die, we just sort of don't wake up in the morning, though I've never decided which one of us gets to die first. If it's him I have to go on and fantasize about the funeral, if it's me I don't have to worry about that, so it just about depends on how tired I am at the time. You may not believe this but sometimes I even start crying. I cry at the ends of movies, even the ones that aren't all that sad, so I guess it's the same thing. My mother's like that too.

The funny thing about these fantasies is that the man is always someone I don't know, and the statistics in the magazines, well, most of them anyway, they say it's often someone you do know, at least a little bit, like your boss or something—I mean, it wouldn't be *my* boss, he's over sixty and I'm sure he couldn't rape his way out of a paper bag, poor old thing, but it might be someone like Derek Duck, in his elevator shoes, perish the thought—or someone you just met, who invites you up for a drink, it's getting so you can hardly be sociable any more, and how are you supposed to meet people if you can't trust them even that basic amount? You can't spend your whole life in the Filing Department or cooped up in your own apartment with all the doors and windows locked and the shades down. I'm not what you would call a drinker but I like to go out now and then for a drink or two in a nice place, even if I am by myself, I'm with Women's Lib on that even though I can't agree with a lot of the other things they say. Like here for instance, the waiters all know me and if anyone, you know, bothers me . . . I don't know why I'm telling you all this, except I think it helps you get to know a person, especially at first, hearing some of the things they think about. At work they call me the office worry wart, but it isn't so much like worrying, it's more like figuring out what you should do in an emergency, like I said before.

Anyway, another thing about it is that there's a lot of conversation, in fact I spend most of my time, in the fantasy that is, wondering what I'm going to say and what he's going to say, I think it would be better if you could get a conversation going. Like, how could a fellow do that to a person he's just had a long conversation with, once you let them know you're human, you have a life too, I don't see how they could go ahead with it, right? I mean, I know it happens but I just don't understand it, that's the part I really don't understand.

Suggestions for Discussion

1. How do the concrete details of "Rape Fantasies" orient you to the character, class, and values of the narrator? How do details evoke the story's setting?

2. What is the effect of using brand names in this story?

3. Describe the rhythm. How does it help to characterize the narrator?

4. Each of the narrator's "rape fantasies" tends to throw out an incongruous detail—a plastic lemon, Kleenex, dead robins. How do these details contribute to the comic effect?

5. There are no rape fantasies in "Rape Fantasies." What is the story about? What is its conflict?

RETROSPECT

1. Examine the first page of the excerpt from Annie Dillard's The Writing Life on page 27 to see how she uses active verbs to describe the writing process.

2. Look at the three short short stories on pages 56–58 and note the density of concrete details that are used to make story vivid in such short compass.

WRITING ASSIGNMENTS

1. In your journal, cluster the word "concrete." Write a passage about it. When you're finished, check whether you have used any abstractions or generalizations that could be effectively replaced by concrete details.

2. Paint a self-portrait in words. Prop a mirror in front of you and describe, in the most focused sight details you can manage, twenty or thirty things that you see. Then try to distance yourself from your portrait and choose the two or three details that most vividly and concisely convey the image you want to present. What attitude do you want the reader to have? Should we find you funny, intense, pitiable, vain, dedicated? Add a detail of sound, touch, smell, or taste that will help convey the image.

3. Make a list of four qualities that describe a character real or imagined. Then place that character in a scene and write the scene so that the qualities are conveyed through significant detail. Use no generalizations and no judgments. No word on your list will appear in the scene.

4. Write a description of a rural landscape, a city street, or a room. Use only active verbs to describe inanimate as well as animate things. Avoid the pathetic fallacy.

5. Write about a boring situation. Convince us that the situation is boring and that your characters are bored or boring or both. Fascinate us. Or make us laugh. Use no generalizations, no judgments, and no verbs in the passive voice.

6. Write about one of the following and suggest the rhythm of the subject in your prose: a machine, a vehicle, a piece of music, sex, something that goes in a circle, an avalanche.

7. Write about a character who begins at a standstill; works up to great speed (in a vehicle or on foot, pursued or pursuing, competing in a sport—or let the rush be purely emotional); and comes to a halt again, either gradually or abruptly. Let the prose rhythm reflect the changes.

4

BOOK PEOPLE
Characterization, Part I

Individual, Typical, and Universal Characters
Round and Flat Characters
The Aristotelian Hero
The Indirect Method of Character Presentation
The Direct Methods of Character Presentation

Human character is in the foreground of all fiction, however the humanity might be disguised. Anthropomorphism may be a scientific sin, but it is a literary necessity. Bugs Bunny isn't a rabbit; he's a plucky youth in ears. Peter Rabbit is a mischievous boy. Brer Rabbit is a sassy rebel. The romantic heroes of *Watership Down* are out of the Arthurian tradition, not out of the hutch. And that doesn't cover fictional *rabbits*.

Henri Bergson, in his essay "On Laughter," observes:

> . . . the comic does not exist outside the pale of what is strictly human. A landscape may be beautiful, charming or sublime, or insignificant and ugly; it will never be laughable.

Bergson is right, but it is just as true that only the human is tragic. We may describe a landscape as "tragic" because nature has been devastated by industry, but the tragedy lies in the cupidity of those who wrought the havoc, in the dreariness, poverty, or disease of those who must live there. A conservationist or ecologist (or a novelist) may care passionately about nature and dislike people because of it;

then we say he or she "identifies" with nature (a wholly human capacity) or "respects the natural unity" (of which humanity is a part) or wants to keep the earth "habitable" (for whom?) or "values nature for its own sake" (using standards of value that nature does not share). By all available evidence, the universe is indifferent to the destruction of trees, property, peoples, and planets. Only people care.

If this is so, then your fiction can be only as successful as the characters who move it and move within it. Whether they are "drawn from life" or are "pure fantasy"—and all fictional characters lie somewhere between the two—we must find them interesting, we must find them believable, and we must care about what happens to them.

Individual, Typical, and Universal Characters

Characters, we're told, should be *individual, typical,* and *universal.* I don't think this truism is very helpful to a practicing writer. For example, I don't think you can *set out to be* "universal" in your writing.

It is true, I believe, that if literature has any social justification or use it is that readers can identify the common humanity in, and can therefore identify with, characters vastly different from themselves in century, geography, gender, culture, and beliefs; and that this enhances the scope of the reader's sympathy. It is also true that if the fiction does not have this universal quality—if a middle-class American male author creates as protagonist a middle-class American male with whom only middle-class American male readers can sympathize—then the fiction is thin and small. William Sloane voices the "frightening" demand of the reader in his book *The Craft of Writing:* "Tell me about me. I want to be more alive. Give me *me.* " But unfortunately, the capacity for universality, like talent, is a trick of the genes or a miracle of the soul, and if you aim for the universal, you're likely to achieve the pompous.

If you're determined to create a "typical" character, you're likely to produce a caricature, because people are typical only in the generalized qualities that lump them together. *Typical* is the most provincial adjective in a writer's vocabulary, signaling that you're writing only for those who share your assumptions. A "typical schoolgirl" in Dar es Salaam is a very different type from one in San Francisco. Furthermore, every person is typical of many things successively or simultaneously. She may be in turn a "typical" schoolgirl, bride, divorcée, and feminist. He may be at one and the same time a "typical" New Yorker, math professor, doting father, and adulterer. It is in the confrontation and convolution of types that much of our individuality is produced.

Writing in generalities and typicalities is akin to bigotry—we only see what's alike about people, not what's unique. When effective, a description of type blames the character for the failure to individualize, and if an author sets out deliberately to produce types rather than individuals, then that author invariably wants to condemn or ridicule those types. Joyce Carol Oates illustrates the technique in "How I Contemplated the World from the Detroit House of Correction and Began My Life Over Again."

> George, Clyde G. 240 Sioux. A manufacturer's representative; children, a dog, a wife. Georgian with the usual columns. You think of the White House, then of Thomas Jefferson, then your mind goes blank on the white pillars and you think of nothing.

Mark Helprin, in "The Schreuderspitze," takes the ridicule of type to comic extreme.

> In Munich are many men who look like weasels. Whether by genetic accident, meticulous crossbreeding, an early and puzzling migration, coincidence, or a reason that we do not know, they exist in great numbers. Remarkably, they accentuate this unfortunate tendency by wearing mustaches, Alpine hats, and tweed. A man who resembles a rodent should never wear tweed.

Typicality invites judgment. We can identify only with characters who come alive to us through their individuality.

It may clarify the distinctions among the universal, the typical, and the individual if you imagine this scene: The child chases a ball into the street. The tires screech, the bumper thuds, the blood geysers into the air, the pulp of the small body lies inert on the asphalt. How would a bystander react? (Is it universal?) How would a passing doctor react? (Is it typical?) How would Dr. Henry Lowes, just coming from the maternity ward of his own hospital, where his wife has had her fourth miscarriage, react? (Is it individual?) Each question narrows the range of convincing reaction, and as a writer you want to convince in each range. If you succeed in the third, you are likely to have succeeded in the other two.

Except where you want us to find your characters ridiculous or heinous or both, then, the rule of thumb is to aim for the individual (which means the specific, concrete, definite, and particular). The typical will take care of itself. The universal can't be forced.

Round and Flat Characters

We're also told that characters should be *round* rather than *flat*. A flat character is one who has only one distinctive characteristic, exists only to exhibit that characteristic, and is incapable of varying from that characteristic. A round character is many faceted and is capable of change. Several critics have, however, persuasively defended flat characters. Eric Bentley suggests in *The Life of the Drama* that if a messenger's function in a play is to deliver his message, it would be very tedious to stop and learn about his psychology. The same is true in fiction; the Queen's chauffeur in the passage from *Mrs. Dalloway* (see chapter 3) exists for no purpose but leaning "ever so slightly," and we do not want to hear about his children or his hernia. Nevertheless, onstage even a flat character has a face and a costume, and in fiction detail can give even a flat character a few angles and contours. The servant classes in the novels of Henry James are notoriously absent as individuals because they exist only in their functions (*that excellent creature had already assembled the baggage,* etc.), whereas Charles Dickens, who peoples his novels with dozens of flat characters, brings even these alive in detail.

> And Mrs. Miff, the wheezy little pew opener—a mighty dry old lady, sparely dressed, with not an inch of fullness anywhere about her—is also here.
>
> *Dombey and Son*

To borrow a notion from George Orwell's *Animal Farm,* all good characters are created round, but some are created rounder than others.

But the central characters in your story or novel need to be not merely round, but spherical. They should contain enough conflict and contradiction so that we can recognize them as belonging to the contradictory human race; and they should be, as we are or hope we are, capable of change.

The Aristotelian Hero

Aristotle, in the *Poetics,* listed four requirements of a successful hero—he should be "*good, appropriate, like,* and *consistent*"—and although literature has changed a great deal in the twenty-three intervening centuries, these four qualities throw light on the critical notions of universal, typical, individual, flat and round.

GOOD

"There will be an element of character," Aristotle says, "if . . . what a person says or does reveals a certain moral purpose; and a good element of character, if the purpose so revealed is good." It might seem that the antiheroes, brutes, hoods, whores, perverts, and bums who people modern literature do very little in the way of revealing good moral purpose. The history of Western literature shows a movement downward and inward: downward through society from royalty to gentry to the middle classes to the lower classes to the dropouts; inward from heroic action to social drama to individual consciousness to the subconscious to the unconscious. What has remained consistent is that, for the time spent in an author's world, we understand and identify with the protagonist or protagonists, we "see their point of view," and the fiction succeeds largely because we are willing to grant them a goodness that we would not grant them in life. Aristotle goes on to explain that "such goodness is possible in every type of personage, even in a woman or a slave, though the one is perhaps an inferior, and the other a wholly worthless being"— and the sentence strikes us as both offensive and funny. But in Aristotle's society, women and slaves were legally designated inferior and worthless, and what Aristotle is saying is precisely what Ken Kesey acknowledges when he picks the inmates of an "Institute of Psychology" as his heroes: that the external status granted by society is not an accurate measure of good moral purpose.

> This new redheaded admission, McMurphy, knows right away he's not a Chronic . . . The Acutes look spooked and uneasy when he laughs, the way kids look in a schoolroom when one ornery kid is raising too much hell. . . .
> . . . "Which one of you claims to be the craziest? Which one is the biggest looney? Who runs these card games? It's my first day, and what I like to do is make a good impression straight off on the right man if he can prove to me he is the right man. Who's the bull goose looney here?"
>
> *One Flew Over the Cuckoo's Nest*

If you met McMurphy in real life, you'd probably say he was crazy and you'd hope he would be locked up. If you encountered the Neanderthals of William Golding's *The Inheritors* on your evening walk, you'd run. If you were forced to live with the visionaries of Doris Lessing's *Four-Gated City* or the prisoners of Jean Genet's *Our Lady of the Flowers*, you would live in skepticism and fear. But while you read you expand your mental scope by identifying with, temporarily "becoming," a character who convinces you that the inmates of the asylum are saner than the staff, that the apemen are more human than *Homo sapiens*, that mental breakdown is mental breakthrough, that perversion is purer than the sexual code by which you live. For the drama audiences of fourth-century B.C. Athens, it was easier to see human nobility embodied in the heroic external actions of those designated by class as noble. It is largely because literature has moved inward, within the mind, that it is possible to move downward in social status—even to women and slaves!—and maintain this sympathy. In our own minds each of us is fundamentally justified, however conscious we are of our flaws—indeed, the more conscious of our flaws, the more commendable we are. As readers we are allowed to borrow a different mind. Fiction, as critic Laurence Gonzales said of rock music, "lets you wander around in someone else's hell for a while and see how similar it is to your own."

APPROPRIATE

Aristotle offends again when he explains what he means by "appropriate." "The character before us may be, say, manly; but it is not appropriate in a female character to be manly." Again, he offends because our ideas of *female* and *manly* have changed, not because we have outgrown a sense of what is appropriate. We are dealing here again with the idea of the "typical," which includes all the biological and environmental influences that form us. A Baptist Texan behaves differently from an Italian nun; a rural schoolboy behaves differently from a professor emeritus at Harvard. If you are to succeed in creating an individual character, particular and alive, you will also inevitably know what is appropriate to that sort of person and will let us know as much as we need to know to feel the appropriateness of the behavior.

We need to know soon, for instance, preferably in the first paragraph, the character's gender, age, and race or nationality. We need to know something of his or her class, period, and region. A profession (or the clear lack of it) and a marital status help, too. Almost any reader can identify with almost any character; what no reader can identify with is confusion. When some or several of the fundamentals of type are withheld from us—when we don't know whether we're dealing with a man or a woman, an adult or a child—the process of identifying cannot begin, and the story is slow to move us.

None of the information need come as information; it can be implied by appearance, tone, action, or detail. In the next example William Melvin Kelley pitches his protagonist straight into the conflict. Only the character's gender is given us directly, but by the end of the story's opening paragraph, we know a lot about his life and type.

> To find this Cooley, the Black baby's father, he knew he would have to contact Opal Simmons. After dressing, he began to search for her address and number. Tam, very organized for a woman, saved everything. Among the envelopes containing the sports-clothes receipts, a letter from her dressmaker asking for payment, old airline tickets, the nursery school bill, the canceled checks and deposit slips, he finally found Opal's address.
>
> *Passing*

We know from the apparently "irrelevant" collection of bills that the protagonist is middle class, married, a father, affluent, and perhaps (that letter from the dressmaker) living at the edge of his income. Because he specifies a "Black baby," we know that he is white. We also know something about his attitudes toward both blacks ("this Cooley") and women ("very organized for a woman"). With an absolute minimum of exposition, letting us share the search for the address, Kelley has drawn clear boundaries of what we may expect from a character whose name we don't yet know.

Students of writing are sometimes daunted by the need to give so much information immediately. Once again, the trick is to find telling details that will convey the information indirectly while our attention remains on the desire or emotion of the character. Nobody wants to read a story that begins:

> She was a twenty-eight-year-old suburban American woman, relatively affluent, who was extremely distressed when her husband Peter left her.

But most of that, and much more besides, could be contained in a few details.

> After Peter left with the VCR, the microwave, and the key to the garage, she went down to the kitchen and ate three jars of peanut butter without tasting a single spoonful.

I don't mean to imply that it is necessarily easy to signal the essentials of type immediately. It would be truer to say that it is necessary and hard. The opening paragraph of a story is its second strongest statement (the final paragraph is the strongest) and sets the tone for all that follows. If the right words don't come to you as a gift, you may have to sit sifting and discarding the inadequate ones for a long time before you achieve both clarity and interest.

LIKE

There is a critical controversy over what Aristotle meant by "likeness." The first interpretation is that by "like" Aristotle meant "natural"—that we should find the character credibly human, that her or his reactions should ring true. The second comes from Aristotle's comparison of the writer and the portrait painter, in which he said that each tries to capture the best possible "likeness" of the model. If we update the painting analogy, the important question is, Is the camera in focus? If the image is sharp, it will be a better likeness than if it's blurred.

Here is an example of a quickly drawn, tightly focused character sketch in which attention to detail provides both sharpness of focus and naturalness.

> Larry Landers looked more like a bass player than ole Mingus himself. Got these long arms that drape down over the bass like they were grown special for that purpose. Fine, strong hands with long fingers and muscular knuckles, the dimples deep black at the joints. His calluses so other-colored and hard, looked like Larry had swiped his grandmother's tarnished thimbles to play with. He'd move in on that bass like he was going to hump it or something, slide up behind it as he lifted it from the rug, all slinky. He'd become one with the wood. Head dipped down

sideways bobbing out the rhythm, feet tapping, legs jiggling, he'd look good. Thing about it, though, ole Larry couldn't play for shit.

TONI CADE BAMBARA, Medley

As a writer you may have the lucky, facile sort of imagination to which characters spring full-blown, complete with gestures, histories, and passions. Or it may be that you need to explore in order to exploit, to draw your characters out gradually and coax them into being. That can be lucky, too.

For either kind of writer, but especially the latter, the journal is an invaluable help. A journal lets you coax and explore without committing yourself to anything or anyone. It allows you to know everything about your character whether you use it or not. Before you put a character in a story, know how well that character sleeps. Know what the character eats for lunch and how much it matters, what he or she buys and how the bills get paid, how he or she spends what we call working hours. Know how your character would prefer to spend evenings and weekends and why such plans get thwarted. Know what memories the character has of pets and parents, cities, snow, or school. You may use none of this information in the brief segment of your character's life that is your plot, but knowing it may teach you how your bookperson taps a pencil or twists a lock of hair, and when and why. When you know these things, you will have taken a step past invention toward the moment of imagination in which you become your character, live in his or her skin, and produce an action that, for the reader, rings universally true.

Use the journal to note your observations of people. Try clustering your impressions of the library assistant who annoys you or the loner at the bar who intrigues you. Try to capture a gesture or the messages that features and clothing send. Invent a reason for that harshness or that loneliness; invent a past. Then try taking the character out of context and setting him or her in another. Get your character in trouble, and you may be on your way to a short story.

It is interesting and relevant that actors schooled in what is called the Stanislavski Method write biographies of the characters they must play. Adherents of "The Method" believe that in the process of inventing a dramatic character's past the actor will find points of emotional contact with that role and so know how to make the motives and actions prescribed by the script natural and genuine. As a writer you can also use "The Method," imagining much that you will not bring specifically to "the script" but that will enrich your sense of that character until you know with absolute certainty how he or she will move, act, react, and speak.

CONSISTENT

Aristotle says that an author should make characters "consistent and the same throughout"—that is, again, that their actions should be plausible in light of what we know about them—for "even if inconsistency should be part of the man . . .

he should still be consistently inconsistent." It is with this last injunction that we leave the area of plausibility and acknowledge the complexity of character. "Consistently inconsistent" does not mean that a character should be continually behaving unnaturally or acting against type. On the contrary, Aristotle here acknowledges the continuing conflict *within* character that is the source of most human trouble and most literature.

Conflict is at the core of character as it is of plot. If plot begins with trouble, then character begins with a person in trouble; and trouble most dramatically occurs because we all have traits, tendencies, and desires that are at war, not simply with the world and other people, but with other of our own traits, tendencies, and desires. All of us probably know a woman of the strong, striding, independent sort, attractive only to men who like a strong and striding woman. And when she falls in love? She becomes a clinging sentimentalist. All of us know a father who is generous, patient, and dependable. And when the children cross the line? He smashes crockery and wields a strap. All of us are gentle, violent; logical, schmaltzy; tough, squeamish; lusty, prudish; sloppy, meticulous; energetic, apathetic; manic, depressive. Perhaps you don't fit that particular list of contradictions, but you are sufficiently in conflict with yourself that as an author you have characters enough in your own psyche to people the work of a lifetime if you will identify, heighten, and dramatize these consistent inconsistencies.

If you think of the great characters of literature, you can see how consistent inconsistency brings each to a crucial dilemma. Hamlet is a strong and decisive man who procrastinates. Dorothea Brooke of *Middlemarch* is an idealistic and intellectual young woman, a total fool in matters of the heart. Ernest Hemingway's Francis Macomber wants to test his manhood against a lion and cannot face the test. Here, in a moment of crisis from *Mom Kills Self and Kids*, Alan Saperstein reveals with great economy the consistent inconsistency of his protagonist, a man who hadn't much time for his family until their absence makes clear how dependent he has been on them.

> When I arrived home from work I found my wife had killed our two sons and taken her own life.
>
> I uncovered a blast of foul, black steam from the pot on the stove and said, "Hi, hon, what's for dinner?" But she did not laugh. She did not bounce to her feet and pirouette into the kitchen to greet me. My little one didn't race into my legs and ask what I brought him. The seven-year-old didn't automatically beg me to play a game knowing my answer would be a tired, "Maybe later."

It is, of course, impossible to know to what degree Shakespeare, Eliot, Hemingway, or Saperstein used consistent inconsistencies of which they were aware in themselves to build and dramatize their characters. An author works not only from his or her own personality but also from observation and imagination, and I fully believe that you are working at full stretch only when all three are involved. The question of autobiography is a complicated one, and as writer you frequently won't know yourself how much you have experienced, how much you have observed, and how much you have invented. Actress Mildred Dunnock once observed that "drama is possible because people can feel what they haven't experienced"; if this is true of audiences and readers, I see no reason the capacity should be denied to writers. A vast proportion of our experience is mental, and it is safe to say that all your writing is autobiographical in the sense that it must have passed through your mind.

The Indirect Method of Character Presentation: Authorial Interpretation

In the writing itself, there are five basic *methods of presentation,* of which the indirect method, *authorial interpretation,* and one of the four direct methods, *appearance,* will be discussed in this chapter. Three further direct methods, *speech, action,* and *thought,* will be discussed in chapter 5. Employing a variety of these methods can help you draw a full character. If you produce a conflict among the methods, it can also help you create a three-dimensional character.

The indirect method of presenting a character is *authorial interpretation*—"telling" us the character's background, motives, values, virtues, and the like. The advantages of the indirect method are enormous, for its use leaves you free to move in time and space; to know anything you choose to know whether the character knows it or not; and godlike, to tell us what we are to feel. The indirect method allows you to convey a great deal of information in a short time.

> The most excellent Marquis of Lumbria lived with his two daughters, Caroline, the elder, and Luisa; and his second wife, Doña Vicenta, a woman with a dull brain, who, when she was not sleeping, was complaining of everything, especially the noise. : . .
>
> The Marquis of Lumbria had no male children, and this was the most painful thorn in his existence. Shortly after having become a widower, he had married Doña Vicenta, his present wife, in order to have a son, but she proved sterile.
>
> The Marquis' life was as monotonous and as quotidian, as unchanging and regular, as the murmur of the river below the cliff or as the liturgic services in the cathedral.
>
> MIGUEL DE UNAMUNO, *The Marquis of Lumbria*

The disadvantages of this indirect method are outlined in chapter 3. Indeed, in the passage above, it may well be part of Unamuno's purpose to convey the "monotonous and . . . quotidian" quality of the Marquis's life by this summarized and distanced rehearsal of facts, motives, and judgments. Nearly every author will use the indirect method occasionally, and you may find it useful when you want to cover the exposition quickly. Occasionally you may convince us that you are so much more knowledgeable about a character than we can be, and so much more subtle at analyzing him or her, that we will accept your explanations. Very occasionally an author will get away with explaining the characters as much as, or more than, they are presented. Henry James is such an author; he is not an author I would advise anyone to imitate.

> Mrs. Touchett was certainly a person of many oddities, of which her behavior on returning to her husband's house after many months was a noticeable specimen. She had her own way of doing all that she did, and this is the simplest description of a character which, although it was by no means without benevolence, rarely succeeded in giving an impression of softness. Mrs. Touchett might do a great deal of good, but she never pleased.
>
> *Portrait of a Lady*

The very clear presence of the author in this passage, commenting, guiding our reactions, is the hallmark of James's prose, and (although it is by no means without benevolence) the technique is a difficult one to sustain. Direct presentation of the characters is much more likely to please the modern reader.

The Direct Methods of Character Presentation

The four methods of direct presentation are *appearance, speech, action,* and *thought.* A character may also be presented through the opinions of other characters, which may be considered a second indirect method. When this method is employed, however, the second character must give his or her opinions in speech, action, or thought. In the process, the character is inevitably also characterized. Whether we accept the opinion depends on what we think of that character as he or she is thus directly characterized. In this scene from Jane Austen's *Mansfield Park,* for example, the busybody Mrs. Norris gives her opinion of the heroine.

> ". . . there is something about Fanny, I have often observed it before,—she likes to go her own way to work; she does not like to be dictated to; she takes her own independent walk whenever she can; she certainly has a little spirit of secrecy, and independence, and nonsense, about her, which I would advise her to get the better of."
>
> As a general reflection on Fanny, Sir Thomas thought nothing could be more unjust, though he had been so lately expressing the same sentiments himself, and he tried to turn the conversation, tried repeatedly before he could succeed.

Here Mrs. Norris's opinion is directly presented in her speech and Sir Thomas's in his thoughts, each of them being characterized in the process. It is left to the reader to decide (without much difficulty) whose view of Fanny is the more reliable.

APPEARANCE

Of the four methods of direct presentation, appearance is especially important because our eyes are our most highly developed means of perception, and we receive more non-sensuous information by sight than by any other sense. Beauty is only skin deep, but people are embodied, and whatever beauty—or ugliness—there is in them must somehow surface in order for us to perceive it. Such surfacing involves speech and action as well as appearance, but it is appearance that prompts our first reaction to people, and everything they wear and own bodies forth some aspect of their inner selves.

Writers are sometimes inclined to neglect or even deny this. The choice of writing as a profession or avocation usually contains an implicit rejection of materialism (an English degree won't get you a job; your folks wish you'd major in business; starving in a gloomy basement is a likely option), and writers are concerned to see beyond mere appearances.

In fact, much of the tension and conflict in character does proceed from the truth that appearance is not reality. But in order to know this, we must see the appearance, and it is often in the contradiction between appearances that the truth comes out. Features, shape, style, clothing, and objects can make statements of internal values that are political, religious, social, intellectual, and essential. The woman in the Ultrasuede jacket with the cigarette holder is making a different statement from the one in the holey sweatshirt with the palmed joint. Even a person who has forsaken our materialistic society altogether, sworn off supermarkets, and gone to the country to grow organic potatoes has a special relationship with his or her hoe. However indifferent we may be to our looks, that indifference is the result of experiences with our bodies. A twenty-two-year-old Apollo who has been handsome since he was six is a very different person from the man who spent his childhood cocooned in fat and burst the chrysalis at age sixteen.

Following are four very brief portraits of women in which each is mainly characterized by such trivialities as fabric, hairdo, and cosmetics. It would nevertheless be impossible to mistake the essential nature of any one of them for that of any of the others.

> Mrs. Withers, the dietician, marched in through the back door, drew up, and scanned the room. She wore her usual Betty Grable hairdo and open-toed pumps, and her shoulders had an aura of shoulder pads even in a sleeveless dress.
>
> MARGARET ATWOOD, *The Edible Woman*

My grandmother had on not just one skirt, but four, one over the other. It should not be supposed that she wore one skirt and three petticoats; no, she wore four skirts; one supported the next, and she wore the lot of them in accordance with a definite system, that is, the order of the skirts was changed from day to day. . . . The one that was closest to her yesterday clearly disclosed its pattern today, or rather its lack of pattern: all my grandmother Anna Bronski's skirts favored the same potato color. It must have been becoming to her.

GÜNTER GRASS, The Tin Drum

How beautiful Helen is, how elegant, how timeless: how she charms Esther Songford and how she flirts with Edwin, laying a scarlet fingernail on his dusty lapel, mesmerizing.

She comes in a chauffered car. She is all cream and roses. Her stockings are purest silk; her underskirt, just briefly showing, is lined with lace.

FAY WELDON, Female Friends

As soon as I entered the room, a pungent odor of phosphorus told me she'd taken rat poison. She lay groaning between the quilts. The tatami by the bed was splashed with blood, her waved hair was matted like rope waste, and a bandage tied round her throat showed up unnaturally white. . . . The painted mouth in her waxen face created a ghastly effect, as though her lips were a gash open to the ears.

MASUJI IBUSE, "Tajinko Village"

Vividness and richness of character are created in these four passages, which use nothing more than appearance to characterize.

Girl

JAMAICA KINCAID

Wash the white clothes on Monday and put them on the stone heap; wash the color clothes on Tuesday and put them on the clothesline to dry; don't walk barehead in the hot sun; cook pumpkin fritters in very hot sweet oil; soak your little cloths right after you take them off; when buying cotton to make yourself a nice blouse, be sure that it doesn't have gum on it, because that way it won't hold up well after a wash; soak salt fish overnight before you cook it; is it true that you sing benna in Sunday school?; always eat your food in such a way that it won't turn someone else's stomach; on Sundays try to walk like a lady and not like the slut you are so bent on becoming; don't sing benna in Sunday school; you mustn't speak to wharf-rat boys, not even to give directions; don't eat fruits on the street—flies will follow you; *but I don't sing benna on Sundays at all and never in Sunday school;* this is how to sew on a button; this is how to make a buttonhole for the button you have just sewed on; this is how to hem a dress when you see the hem coming down and so to prevent yourself from looking like the slut I know you are so bent on becoming; this is how you iron your father's khaki shirt so that it doesn't have a crease; this is how you iron your father's khaki pants so that they don't have a crease; this is how you grow okra—far from the house, because okra tree harbors red ants; when you are growing dasheen, make sure it gets plenty of water or else it makes your throat itch when you are eating it; this is how you sweep a corner; this is how you sweep a whole house; this is how you sweep a yard; this is how you smile to someone you don't like too much; this is how you smile to someone you don't like at all; this is how you smile to someone you like completely; this is how you set a table for tea; this is how you set a table for dinner; this is how you set a table for dinner with an important guest; this is how you set a table for lunch; this is how you set a table for breakfast; this is how to behave in the presence of men who don't know you very well, and this way they won't recognize immediately the slut I have warned you against becoming; be sure to wash every day, even if it is with your own spit; don't squat down to play marbles—you are not a boy, you know; don't pick people's flowers—you might catch something; don't throw stones at blackbirds, because it might not be a blackbird at all; this is how to make a bread pudding; this is how to make doukona; this is how to make pepper pot; this is how to make a good medicine for a cold; this is how to make a good medicine to throw away a child before it even becomes a child; this is how to catch a fish; this is how to throw back a fish you don't like, and that way something bad won't fall on you; this is how to bully a man; this is how a man bullies you; this is how to love a man, and if this doesn't work there are other ways, and if they don't work don't feel too bad about giving up; this is how to spit up in the air if you feel like it, and this is how to move quick so that it doesn't fall on you; this is how to make ends meet; always squeeze bread to make sure it's fresh; *but what if the baker won't let me feel the bread?;* you mean to say that after all you are really going to be the kind of woman who the baker won't let near the bread?

Suggestions for Discussion

1. This very short story is written in the form of a single ongoing sentence. How does it nevertheless have the form of a story? What are the conflict, crisis, and resolution?

2. How, without any description as such, does Kincaid manage to make you see the characters?

3. What details signal the essentials of type in the girl and her mother—age, gender, race, nationality, class (period, profession, marital status)?

4. How would you describe the "universals" of character that are achieved in "Girl"?

5. What "flat" characters are included? To what extent are they characterized?

6. The story contains several details that, if you live in the continental United States, are likely to be obscure to you: *benna, dasheen, doukona*. It's also possible that you can't exactly see pumpkin fritters, wharf-rat boys, an okra tree, a pepper pot. How much does it matter? How much do sound, tone, and approximate meaning add to your understanding?

7. The story is full of moral admonitions and certainly in Aristotle's terms "reveals a certain moral purpose." Is the moral purpose of the speaker identical to the moral purpose of the story? Who in the story is "good"? In what way? Where does your sympathy lie? Why?

8. Even in this short compass, Kincaid manages to create the character of the daughter in such a way that we see her consistent inconsistency. Identify it.

⤨

Orbiting

BHARATI MUKHERJEE

On Thanksgiving morning I'm still in my night-gown thinking of Vic when Dad raps on my apartment door. Who's he rolling joints for, who's he initiating now into the wonders of his inner space? What got me on Vic is remembering last Thanksgiving and his famous cranberry sauce with Grand Marnier, which Dad had interpreted as a sign of permanence in my life. A man who cooks like Vic is ready for other commitments. Dad cannot imagine cooking as self-expression. You cook *for* someone. Vic's sauce was a sign of his permanent isolation, if you really want to know.

Dad's come to drop off the turkey. It's a seventeen-pounder. Mr. Vitelli knows to reserve a biggish one for us every Thanksgiving and Christmas. But this November what with Danny in the Marines, Uncle Carmine having to be very careful after the bypass, and Vic taking off for outer space as well, we might as well have made do with one of those turkey rolls you pick out of the freezer. And in other years, Mr. Vitelli would not have given us a frozen bird. We were proud of that, our birds were fresh killed. I don't bring this up to Dad.

"Your mama took care of the thawing," Dad says. "She said you wouldn't have room in your Frigidaire."

"You mean Mom said Rindy shouldn't be living in a dump, right?" Mom has the simple, immigrant faith that children should do better than their parents, and her definition of better is comfortingly rigid. Fair enough—I believed it, too. But the fact is all I can afford is this third-floor studio with an art deco shower. The fridge fits under the kitchenette counter. The room has potential. I'm content with that. And I *like* my job even though it's selling, not designing, jewelry made out of seashells and semiprecious stones out of a boutique in Bellevue Plaza.

Dad shrugs. "You're an adult, Renata." He doesn't try to lower himself into one of my two deck chairs. He was a minor league catcher for a while and his knees went. The fake zebra-skin cushions piled as seats on the rug are out of the question for him. My futon bed folds up into a sofa, but the satin sheets are still lasciviously tangled. My father stands in a slat of sunlight, trying not to look embarrassed.

"Dad, I'd have come to the house and picked it up. You didn't have to make the extra trip out from Verona." A sixty-five-year-old man in wingtips and a Borsalino hugging a wet, heavy bird is so poignant I have to laugh.

"You wouldn't have gotten out of bed until noon, Renata." But Dad smiles. I know what he's saying. He's saying *he's* retired and *he* should be able to stay in bed till noon if he wants to, but he can't and he'd rather drive twenty miles with a soggy bird than read the *Ledger* one more time.

Grumbling and scolding are how we deMarcos express love. It's the North Italian way, Dad used to tell Cindi, Danny, and me when we were kids. Sicilians and Calabrians are emotional; we're contained. Actually, *he's* contained, the way Vic was contained for the most part. Mom's a Calabrian and she was born and raised there. Dad's very American, so Italy's a safe source of pride for him. I once figured it out: *his* father, Arturo deMarco, was a fifteen-week-old fetus when his mother planted her feet on Ellis Island. Dad, a proud son of North Italy had one big adventure in his life, besides fighting in the Pacific, and that was marrying a Calabrian peasant. He made it sound as though Mom was a Korean or something, and their marriage was a kind of taming of the West, and that everything about her could be explained as a cultural deficiency. Actually, Vic could talk beautifully about his feelings. He'd brew espresso, pour it into tiny blue pottery cups and analyze our relationship. I should have listened. I mean really listened. I thought he was talking about us, but I know now he was only talking incessantly about himself. I put too much faith in mail-order night-gowns and bras.

"Your mama wanted me out of the house," Dad goes on. "She didn't used to be like this, Renata."

Renata and Carla are what we were christened. We changed to Rindy and Cindi in junior high. Danny didn't have to make such leaps, unless you count dropping out of Montclair State and joining the Marines. He was always Danny, or Junior.

I lug the turkey to the kitchen sink where it can drip away at a crazy angle until I have time to deal with it.

"Your mama must have told you girls I've been acting funny since I retired."

"No, Dad, she hasn't said anything about you acting funny," What she *has* said is do we think she ought to call Doc Brunetti and have a chat about Dad? Dad wouldn't have to know. He and Doc Brunetti are, or were, on the same church league bowling team. So is, or was, Vic's dad, Vinny Riccio.

"Your mama thinks a man should have an office to drive to every day. I sat at a desk for thirty-eight years and what did I get? Ask Doc, I'm too embarrassed to say." Dad told me once Doc—his real name was Frankie, though no one ever called him that—had been called Doc since he was six years old and growing up with Dad in Little Italy. There was never a time in his life when Doc wasn't Doc, which made his professional decision very easy. Dad used to say, no one ever called me Adjuster when I was a kid. Why didn't they call me something like Sarge or Teach? Then I would have known better.

I wish I had something breakfasty in my kitchen cupboard to offer him. He wants to stay and talk about Mom, which is the way old married people have. Let's talk about me means: What do you think of Mom? I'll take the turkey over means: When will Rindy settle down? I wish this morning I had bought the Goodwill sofa for ten dollars instead of letting Vic haul off the fancy deck chairs from Fortunoff's. Vic had flash. He'd left Jersey a long time before he actually took off.

"I can make you tea."

"None of that herbal stuff."

We don't talk about Mom, but I know what he's going through. She's just started to find herself. He's not burned out, he's merely stuck. I remember when Mom refused to learn to drive, wouldn't leave the house even to mail a letter. Her litany those days was: when you've spent the first fifteen years of your life in a mountain village, when you remember candles and gaslight and carrying water from a well, not to mention holding in your water at night because of wolves and the unlit outdoor privy, you *like* being housebound. She used those wolves for all they were worth, as though imaginary wolves still nipped her heels in the Clifton Mall.

Before Mom began to find herself and signed up for a class at Paterson, she used to nag Cindi and me about finding the right men. "Men," she said; she wasn't coy, never. Unembarrassed, she'd tell me about her wedding night, about her first sighting of Dad's "thing" ("Land Ho!" Cindi giggled. "Thar she blows!" I chipped in.) and she'd giggle at our word for it, the common word, and she'd use it around us, never around Dad. Mom's peasant, she's earthy but never coarse. If I could get that across to Dad, how I admire it in men or in women, I would feel somehow redeemed of all my little mistakes with them, with men, with myself. Cindi and Brent were married on a cruise ship by the ship's captain. Tony, Vic's older brother, made a play for me my senior year. Tony's solid now. He manages a funeral home but he's invested in crayfish ponds on the side.

"You don't even own a dining table." Dad sounds petulant. He uses "even" a lot around me. Not just a judgment, but a comparative judgment. Other people have dining tables. *Lots* of dining tables. He softens it a bit, not wanting to hurt me, wanting more for me to judge him a failure. "We've always had a sit-down dinner, hon."

Okay, so traditions change. This year dinner's potluck. So I don't have real furniture. I eat off stack-up plastic tables as I watch the evening news. I drink red wine and heat a pita bread on the gas burner and wrap it around alfalfa sprouts or green linguine. The Swedish knockdown dresser keeps popping its sides because Vic didn't glue it properly. Swedish engineering, he said, doesn't need glue. Think of Volvos, he said, and Ingmar Bergman. He isn't good with directions that come in four languages. At least he wasn't.

"Trust me, Dad." This isn't the time to spring new lovers on him. "A friend made me a table. It's in the basement."

"How about chairs?" Ah, my good father. He could have said, friend? What friend?

Marge, my landlady, has all kinds of junky stuff in the basement. "Jorge and I'll bring up what we need. You'd strain your back, Dad." Shot knees, bad back: daily pain but nothing fatal. Not like Carmine.

"Jorge? Is that the new boyfriend?"

Shocking him makes me feel good. It would serve him right if Jorge were my new boyfriend. But Jorge is Marge's other roomer. He gives Marge Spanish lessons, and does the heavy cleaning and the yard work. Jorge has family in El Salvador he's hoping to bring up. I haven't met Marge's husband yet. He works on an offshore oil rig in some emirate with a funny name.

"No, Dad." I explain about Jorge.

"El Salvador!" he repeats. "That means 'the Savior.' " He passes on the information with a kind of awe. It makes Jorge's homeland, which he's shown me pretty pictures of, seem messy and exotic, at the very rim of human comprehension.

After Dad leaves, I call Cindi, who lives fifteen minutes away on Upper Mountainside Road. She's eleven months younger and almost a natural blond, but we're close. Brent wasn't easy for me to take, not at first. He owns a discount camera and electronics store on Fifty-fourth in Manhattan. Cindi met him through Club Med. They sat on a gorgeous Caribbean beach and talked of hogs. His father is an Amish farmer in Kalona, Iowa. Brent, in spite of the obvious hairpiece and the gold chain, is a rebel. He was born Schwartzendruber, but changed his name to Schwartz. Now no one believes the Brent, either. They call him Bernie on the street and it makes everyone more comfortable. His father's never taken their buggy out of the county.

The first time Vic asked me out, he talked of feminism and holism and macrobiotics. Then he opened up on cinema and literature, and I was very impressed, as who wouldn't be? Ro, my current lover, is very different. He picked me up in an uptown singles bar that I and sometimes Cindi go to. He bought me a Cinzano and touched my breast in the dark. He was direct, and at the same time weirdly courtly. I took him home though usually I don't, at first. I learned in bed that night that the tall brown drink with the lemon twist he'd been drinking was Tab.

I went back on the singles circuit even though the break with Vic should have made me cautious. Cindi thinks Vic's a romantic. I've told her how it ended. One Sunday morning in March he kissed me awake as usual. He'd brought in the *Times* from the porch and was reading it. I made us some cinnamon rose tea. We had a ritual, starting with the real estate pages, passing remarks on the latest tacky towers. Not for us, we'd say, the view is terrible! No room for the servants, things like that. And our imaginary children's imaginary nanny. "Hi, gorgeous," I said. He is gorgeous, not strong, but showy. He said, "I'm leaving, babe. New Jersey doesn't do it for me anymore." I said, "Okay, so where're we going?" I had an awful job at the time, taking orders for MCI. Vic said, "I didn't say we, babe." So I asked, "You mean it's over? Just like that?" And he said, "Isn't that the best way? No fuss, no hang-ups." Then I got a little whiny. "But *why?*" I wanted to know. But he was macrobiotic in lots of things, including relationships. Yin and yang, hot and sour, green and yellow. "You know, Rindy, there are *places*. You don't fall off the earth when you leave Jersey, you know. Places you see pictures of and read about. Different weathers, different trees, different everything. Places that get the Cubs on cable instead of the Mets." He was into that. For all the sophisticated things he liked to talk about, he was a very local boy. "Vic," I pleaded, "you're crazy. You need help." "I need help because I want to get out of Jersey? You gotta be kidding!" He stood up and for a moment I thought he would do something crazy, like destroy something, or hurt me. "Don't ever call me crazy, got that? And give me the keys to the van."

He took the van. Danny had sold it to me when the Marines sent him overseas. I'd have given it to him anyway, even if he hadn't asked.

"Cindi, I need a turkey roaster," I tell my sister on the phone.
"I'll be right over," she says. "The brat's driving me crazy."
"Isn't Franny's visit working out?"
"I could kill her. I think up ways. How does that sound?"

"Why not send her home?" I'm joking. Franny is Brent's twelve-year-old and he's shelled out a lot of dough to lawyers in New Jersey and Florida to work out visitation rights.

"Poor Brent, He feels so *divided*," Cindi says. "He shouldn't have to take sides."

I want her to ask who my date is for this afternoon, but she doesn't. It's important to me that she like Ro, that Mom and Dad more than tolerate him.

All over the country, I tell myself, women are towing new lovers home to meet their families. Vic is simmering cranberries in somebody's kitchen and explaining yin and yang. I check out the stuffing recipe. The gravy calls for cream and freshly grated nutmeg. Ro brought me six whole nutmegs in a Ziplock bag from his friend, a Pakistani, who runs a spice store in SoHo. The nuts look hard and ugly. I take one out of the bag and sniff it. The aroma's so exotic my head swims. On an impulse I call Ro.

The phone rings and rings. He doesn't have his own place yet. He has to crash with friends. He's been in the States three months, maybe less. I let it ring fifteen, sixteen, seventeen times.

Finally someone answers. "Yes?" The voice is guarded, the accent obviously foreign even though all I'm hearing is a one-syllable word. Ro has fled here from Kabul. He wants to take classes at NJIT and become an electrical engineer. He says he's lucky his father got him out. A friend of Ro's father, a man called Mumtaz, runs a fried chicken restaurant in Brooklyn in a neighborhood Ro calls "Little Kabul," though probably no one else has ever noticed. Mr. Mumtaz puts the legal immigrants to work as waiters out front. The illegals hide in a backroom as pluckers and gutters.

"Ro? I miss you. We're eating at three, remember?"

"Who is speaking, please?"

So I fell for the accent, but it isn't a malicious error. I *can* tell one Afghan tribe from another now, even by looking at them or by their names. I can make out some Pashto words. "Tell Ro it's Rindy. Please? I'm a friend. He wanted me to call this number."

"Not knowing any Ro."

"Hey, wait. Tell him it's Rindy deMarco."

The guy hangs up on me.

I'm crumbling cornbread into a bowl for the stuffing when Cindi honks half of "King Cotton" from the parking apron in the back. Brent bought her the BMW on the gray market and saved a bundle—once discount, always discount—then spent three hundred dollars to put in a horn that beeps a Sousa march. I wave a potato masher at her from the back window. She doesn't get out of the car. Instead she points to the pan in the back seat. I come down, wiping my hands on a dish towel.

"I should stay and help." Cindi sounds ready to cry. But I don't want her with me when Ro calls back.

"You're doing too much already, kiddo." My voice at least sounds comforting. "You promised one veg and the salad."

"I ought to come up and help. That or get drunk." She shifts the stick. When Brent bought her the car, the dealer threw in driving gloves to match the upholstery.

"Get Franny to shred the greens," I call as Cindi backs up the car. "Get her involved."

The phone is ringing in my apartment. I can hear it ring from the second-floor landing.

"Ro?"

"You're taking a chance, my treasure. It could have been any other admirer, then where would you be?"

"I don't have any other admirers." Ro is not a conventionally jealous man, not like the types I have known. He's totally unlike any man I have ever known. He wants men to come on to me. Lately when we go to a bar he makes me sit far enough from him so some poor lonely guy thinks I'm looking for action. Ro likes to swagger out of a dark booth as soon as someone buys me a drink. I go along. He comes from a macho culture.

"How else will I know you are as beautiful as I think you are? I would not want an unprized woman," he says. He is asking me for time, I know. In a few more months he'll know I'm something of a catch in my culture, or at least I've never had trouble finding boys. Even Brent Schwartzendruber has begged me to see him alone.

"I'm going to be a little late," Ro says. "I told you about my cousin, Abdul, no?"

Ro has three or four cousins that I know of in Manhattan. They're all named Abdul something. When I think of Abdul, I think of a giant black man with goggles on, running down a court. Abdul is the teenage cousin whom immigration officials nabbed as he was gutting chickens in Mumtaz's backroom. Abdul doesn't have the right papers to live and work in this country, and now he's been locked up in a detention center on Varick Street. Ro's afraid Abdul will be deported back to Afghanistan. If that happens, he'll be tortured.

"I have to visit him before I take the DeCamp bus. He's talking nonsense. He's talking of starting a hunger fast."

"A hunger strike! God!" When I'm with Ro I feel I am looking at America through the wrong end of a telescope. He makes it sound like a police state, with sudden raids, papers, detention centers, deportations, and torture and death waiting in the wings. I'm not a political person. Last fall I wore the Ferraro button because she's a woman and Italian.

"Rindy, all night I've been up and awake. All night I think of your splendid breasts. Like clusters of grapes, I think. I am stroking and fondling your grapes this very minute. My talk gets you excited?"

I tell him to test me, please get here before three. I remind him he can't buy his ticket on the bus.

"We got here too early, didn't we?" Dad stands just outside the door to my apartment, looking embarrassed. He's in his best dark suit, the one he wears every Thanksgiving and Christmas. This year he can't do up the top button on his jacket.

"Don't be so formal, Dad." I give him a showy hug and pull him indoors so Mom can come in.

"As if your papa ever listens to me!" Mom laughs. But she sits primly on the sofa bed in her velvet cloak, with her tote bag and evening purse on her lap. Before Dad started courting her, she worked as a seamstress. Dad rescued her from a sweatshop. He married down, she married well. That's the family story.

"She told me to rush."

Mom isn't in a mood to squabble. I think she's reached the point of knowing she won't have him forever. There was Carmine, at death's door just a month ago. Anything could happen to Dad. She says, "Renata, look what I made! Crostolis." She lifts a cake tin out of her tote bag. The pan still feels warm. And for dessert, I know, there'll be a jar of super-thick, super-rich Death by Chocolate.

The story about Grandma deMarco, Dad's mama, is that every Thanksgiving she served two full dinners, one American with the roast turkey, candied yams, pumpkin pie, the works, and another with Grandpa's favorite pastas.

Dad relaxes. He appoints himself bartender. "Don't you have more ice cubes, sweetheart?"

I tell him it's good Glenlivet. He shouldn't ruin it with ice, just a touch of water if he must. Dad pours sherry in Vic's pottery espresso cups for his women. Vic made them himself, and I used to think they were perfect blue jewels. Now I see they're lumpy, uneven in color.

"Go change into something pretty before Carla and Brent come." Mom believes in dressing up. Beaded dresses lift her spirits. She's wearing a beaded dress today.

I take the sherry and vanish behind a four-panel screen, the kind long-legged showgirls change behind in black and white movies while their moustached lovers keep talking. My head barely shows above the screen's top, since I'm no long-legged showgirl. My best points, as Ro has said, are my clusters of grapes. Vic found the screen at a country auction in the Adirondacks. It had filled the van. Now I use the panels as a bulletin board and I'm worried Dad'll spot the notice for the next meeting of Amnesty International, which will bother him. He will think the two words stand for draft dodger and communist. I was going to drop my membership, a legacy of Vic, when Ro saw it and approved. Dad goes to the Sons of Italy Anti-Defamation dinners. He met Frank Sinatra at one. He voted for Reagan last time because the Democrats ran an Italian woman.

Instead of a thirties lover, it's my moustached papa talking to me from the other side of the screen. "So where's this dining table?"

"Ro's got the parts in the basement. He'll bring it up, Dad."

I hear them whispering. "Bo? Now she's messing with a Southerner?" and "Shh, it's her business."

I'm just smoothing on my pantyhose when Mom screams for the cops. Dad shouts too, at Mom for her to shut up. It's my fault, I should have warned Ro not to use his key this afternoon.

I peek over the screen's top and see my lover the way my parents see him. He's a slight, pretty man with hazel eyes and a tufty moustache, so whom can he intimidate? I've seen Jews and Greeks, not to mention Sons of Italy, darker-skinned than Ro. Poor Ro resorts to his Kabuli prep-school manners.

"How do you do, Madam! Sir! My name is Roashan."

Dad moves closer to Ro but doesn't hold out his hand. I can almost read his mind: *he speaks*. "Come again?" he says, baffled.

I cringe as he spells his name. My parents are so parochial. With each letter he does a graceful dip and bow. "Try it syllable by syllable, sir. Then it is not so hard."

Mom stares past him at me. The screen doesn't hide me because I've strayed too far in to watch the farce. "Renata, you're wearing only your camisole."

I pull my crew neck over my head, then kiss him. I make the kiss really sexy so they'll know I've slept with this man. Many times. And if he asks me, I will marry him. I had not known that till now. I think my mother guesses.

He's brought flowers: four long-stemmed, stylish purple blossoms in a florist's paper cone. "For you, madam." He glides over the dirty broadloom to Mom who fills up more than half the sofa bed. "This is my first Thanksgiving dinner, for which I have much to give thanks, no?"

"He was born in Afghanistan," I explain. But Dad gets continents wrong. He says, "We saw your famine camps on TV. Well, you won't starve this afternoon."

"They smell good," Mom says. "Thank you very much but you shouldn't spend a fortune."

"No, no, madam. What you smell good is my cologne. Flowers in New York have no fragrance."

"His father had a garden estate outside Kabul." I don't want Mom to think he's putting down American flowers, though in fact he is. Along with American fruits, meats, and vegetables. "The Russians bulldozed it," I add.

Dad doesn't want to talk politics. He senses, looking at Ro, this is not the face of Ethiopian starvation. "Well, what'll it be, Roy? Scotch and soda?" I wince. It's not going well.

"Thank you but no. I do not imbibe alcoholic spirits, though I have no objection for you, sir." My lover goes to the fridge and reaches down. He knows just where to find his Tab. My father is quietly livid, staring down at his drink.

In my father's world, grown men bowl in leagues and drink the best whiskey they can afford. Dad whistles "My Way." He must be under stress. That's his usual self-therapy: how would Francis Albert handle this?

"Muslims have taboos, Dad." Cindi didn't marry a Catholic, so he has no right to be upset about Ro, about us.

"Jews," Dad mutters. "So do Jews." He knows because catty-corner from Vitelli's is a kosher butcher. This isn't the time to parade new words before him, like *halal*, the Muslim kosher. An Italian-American man should be able to live sixty-five years never having heard the word, I can go along with that. Ro, fortunately, is cosmopolitan. Outside of pork and booze, he eats anything else I fix.

Brent and Cindi take forever to come. But finally we hear his MG squeal in the driveway. Ro glides to the front window; he seems to blend with the ficus tree and hanging ferns. Dad and I wait by the door.

"Party time!" Brent shouts as he maneuvers Cindi and Franny ahead of him up three flights of stairs. He looks very much the head of the family, a rich man steeply in debt to keep up appearances, to compete, to head off middle age. He's at that age—and Cindi's nowhere near that age—when people notice the difference and quietly judge it. I know these things from Cindi—I'd never guess it from looking at Brent. If he feels divided, as Cindi says he does, it doesn't show. Misery, anxiety, whatever, show on Cindi though; they bring her cheekbones out. When I'm depressed, my hair looks rough, my skin breaks out. Right now, I'm lustrous.

Brent does a lot of whooping and hugging at the door. He even hugs Dad who looks grave and funereal like an old-world Italian gentleman because of his outdated, pinched dark suit. Cindi makes straight for the fridge with her casserole of squash and browned marshmallow. Franny just stands in the middle of the room holding two biggish Baggies of salad greens and vinaigrette in an old Dijon mustard jar. Brent actually bought the mustard in Dijon, a story that Ro is bound to hear and not appreciate. Vic was mean enough last year to tell him that he could have gotten it for more or less the same price at the Italian specialty foods store down on Watchung Plaza. Franny doesn't seem to have her own winter clothes. She's wearing Cindi's car coat over a Dolphins sweatshirt. Her mother moved down to Florida the very day the divorce became final. She's got a Walkman tucked into the pocket of her cords.

"You could have trusted me to make the salad dressing at least," I scold my sister.

Franny gives up the Baggies and the jar of dressing to me. She scrutinizes us—Mom, Dad, me and Ro, especially Ro, as though she can detect something strange about him—but doesn't take off her earphones. A smirk starts twitching her tanned, feral features. I see what she is seeing. Asian men carry their bodies differently, even these famed warriors from the Khyber Pass. Ro doesn't stand like Brent or Dad. His hands hang kind of stiffly from the shoulder joints, and when he moves, his palms are tucked tight against his thighs, his stomach sticks out like a slightly pregnant woman's. Each culture establishes its own manly posture, different ways of claiming space. Ro, hiding among my plants, holds himself in a way that seems both too effeminate and too macho. I hate Franny for what she's doing to me. I am twenty-seven years old, I should be more mature. But I see now how wrong Ro's clothes are. He shows too much white collar and cuff. His shirt and his wool-blend flare leg pants were made to measure in Kabul. The jacket comes from a discount store on Canal Street, part of a discontinued line of two-trousered suits. I ought to know, I took him there. I want to shake Franny or smash the earphones.

Cindi catches my exasperated look. "Don't pay any attention to her. She's unsociable this weekend. We can't compete with the Depeche Mode."

I intend to compete.

Franny, her eyes very green and very hostile, turns on Brent. "How come she never gets it right, Dad?"

Brent hi-fives his daughter, which embarrasses her more than anyone else in the room. "It's a Howard Jones, hon," Brent tells Cindi.

Franny, close to tears, runs to the front window where Ro's been hanging back. She has an ungainly walk for a child whose support payments specify weekly ballet lessons. She bores in on Ro's hidey hole like Russian artillery. Ro moves back to the perimeter of family intimacy. I have no way of helping yet. I have to set out the dips and Tostitos. Brent and Dad are talking sports, Mom and Cindi are watching the turkey. Dad's going on about the Knicks. He's in despair, so early in the season. He's on his second Scotch. I see Brent try. "What do you think, Roy?" He's doing his best to get my lover involved. "Maybe we'll get lucky, huh? We can always hope for a top draft pick. End up with Patrick Ewing!" Dad brightens. "That guy'll change the game. Just wait and see. He'll fill the lane better than Russell." Brent gets angry, since for some strange Amish reason he's a Celtics fan. So was Vic. "Bird'll make a monkey out of him." He looks to Ro for support.

Ro nods. Even his headshake is foreign. "You are undoubtedly correct, Brent," he says "I am deferring to your judgment because currently I have not familiarized myself with these practices."

Ro loves squash, but none of my relatives have ever picked up a racket. I want to tell Brent that Ro's skied in St. Moritz, lost a thousand dollars in a casino in Beirut, knows where to buy Havana cigars without getting hijacked. He's sophisticated, he could make monkeys out of us all, but they think he's a retard.

Brent drinks three Scotches to Dad's two; then all three men go down to the basement. Ro and Brent do the carrying, negotiating sharp turns in the stairwell. Dad supervises. There are two trestles and a wide, splintery plywood top. "Try not to take the wall down!" Dad yells.

When they make it back in, the men take off their jackets to assemble the table. Brent's wearing a red lamb's wool turtleneck under his camel hair blazer. Ro unfastens his cuff links—they are 24-karat gold and his father's told him to sell them if funds run low—and pushes up his very white shirt sleeves. There are scars on both arms, scars that bubble against his dark skin, scars like lightning flashes under his thick black hair. Scar tissue on Ro is the color of freshwater pearls. I want to kiss it.

Cindi checks the turkey one more time. "You guys better hurry. We'll be ready to eat in fifteen minutes."

Ro, the future engineer, adjusts the trestles. He's at his best now. He's become quite chatty. From under the plywood top, he's holding forth on the Soviet menace in Kabul. Brent may actually have an idea where Afghanistan is, in a general way, but Dad is lost. He's talking of being arrested for handing out pro-American pamphlets on his campus. Dad stiffens at "arrest" and blanks out the rest. He talks of this "so-called leader," this "criminal" named Babrak Karmal and I hear other buzz-words like Kandahār and Pamir, words that might have been Polish to me a month ago, and I can see even Brent is slightly embarrassed. It's his first exposure to Third World passion. He thought only Americans had informed political opinion—other people staged coups out of spite and misery. It's an unwelcome revelation to him that a reasonably educated and rational man like Ro would die for things that he, Brent, has never heard of and would rather laugh about. Ro was tortured in jail. Franny has taken off her earphones. Electrodes, canes, freezing tanks. He leaves nothing out. Something's gotten into Ro.

Dad looks sick. The meaning of Thanksgiving should not be so explicit. But Ro's in a daze. He goes on about how—inshallah—his father, once a rich landlord, had stashed away enough to bribe a guard, sneak him out of this cell and hide him for four months in a tunnel dug under a servant's adobe hut until a forged American visa could be bought. Franny's eyes are wide, Dad joins Mom on the sofa bed, shaking his head. Jail, bribes, forged, what is this? I can read his mind. "For six days I must orbit one international airport to another," Ro is saying. "The main trick is having a valid ticket, that way the airline has to carry you even if the country won't take you in. Colombo, Seoul, Bombay, Geneva, Frankfurt, I know too too well the transit lounges of many airports. We travel the world with our gym bags and prayer rugs, unrolling them in the transit lounges. The better airports have special rooms."

Brent tries to ease Dad's pain. "Say, buddy," he jokes, "you wouldn't be ripping us off, would you?"

Ro snakes his slender body from under the make-shift table. He hasn't been watching the effect of his monologue. "I am a working man," he says stiffly. I have seen his special permit. He's one of the lucky ones, though it might not last. He's saving for NJIT. Meantime he's gutting chickens to pay for room and board in Little Kabul. He describes the gutting process. His face is transformed as he sticks his fist into imaginary roasters and grabs for gizzards, pulls out the squishy stuff. He takes an Afghan dagger out of the pocket of his pants. You'd never guess, he looks like such a victim. "This," he says, eyes glinting. "This is all I need."

"Cool," Franny says.

"Time to eat," Mom shouts. "I made the gravy with the nutmeg as you said, Renata."

I lead Dad to the head of the table. "Everyone else sit where you want to."

Franny picks out the chair next to Ro before I can put Cindi there. I want Cindi to know him, I want her as an ally.

Dad tests the blade of the carving knife. Mom put the knife where Dad always sits when she set the table. He takes his thumb off the blade and pushes the switch. "That noise makes me feel good."

But I carry in the platter with the turkey and place it in front of Ro. "I want you to carve," I say.

He brings out his dagger all over again. Franny is practically licking his fingers. "You mean this is a professional job?"

We stare fascinated as my lover slashes and slices, swiftly, confidently, at the huge browned juicy breast. The dagger scoops out flesh.

Now I am the one in a daze. I am seeing Ro's naked body as though for the first time, his nicked, scarred, burned body. In his body, the blemishes seem embedded, more beautiful, like wood. I am seeing character made manifest. I am seeing Brent and Dad for the first time too. They have their little scars, things they're proud of, football injuries and bowling elbows they brag about. Our scars are so innocent; they are invisible and come to us from rough-housing gone too far. Ro hates to talk about his scars. If I trace the puckered tissue on his left thigh and ask "How, Ro?" he becomes shy, dismissive: a pack of dogs attacked him when he was a boy. The skin on his back is speckled and lumpy from burns, but when I ask he laughs. A crazy villager whacked him with a burning stick for cheekiness, he explains. He's ashamed that he comes from a culture of pain.

The turkey is reduced to a drying, whitened skeleton. On our plates, the slices are symmetrical, elegant. I realize all in a rush how much I love this man with his blemished, tortured body. I will give him citizenship if he asks. Vic was beautiful, but Vic was self-sufficient. Ro's my chance to heal the world.

I shall teach him how to walk like an American, how to dress like Brent but better, how to fill up a room as Dad does instead of melting and blending but sticking out in the Afghan way. In spite of the funny way he holds himself and the funny way he moves his head from side to side when he wants to say yes, Ro is Clint Eastwood, scarred hero and survivor. Dad and Brent are children. I realize Ro's the only circumcised man I've slept with.

Mom asks, "Why are you grinning like that, Renata?"

Suggestions for Discussion

1. How does Mukherjee use idiosyncratic details to suggest the typical in gender, generation, nationality?

2. On page 113 there is a kind of catalog of national characteristics and contrasts. To what extent are these contradicted by the characters of the story?

3. How do food, drink, fads, and life-style characterize Vic?

4. When Brent and Cindi arrive for Thanksgiving (page 121), there's a very large cast of characters for the reader to keep straight. How do details of appearance help? How does Ro's appearance signal his essential contrast to the family?

5. Identify Ro's consistent inconsistency.

6. On pages 123–124, what details of Ro's life focus the conflict of the story?

RETROSPECT

1. How are Eudora Welty's parents characterized as individuals in the excerpt from *One Writer's Beginnings*? What elements of type are suggested?

2. What is the value of the "flat" characters in "The Things They Carried"?

3. How much do you know about the narrator of "Rape Fantasies"? How much do you know that you aren't told? How?

WRITING ASSIGNMENTS

1. Each day for two weeks, cluster and write a paragraph in your journal about a character drawn from memory, observation, or invention. Each day, also go back and add to a former characterization. Focus on details. Try to invent a past, motives, memories, and situations for the characters that interest you the most.

2. Below is a list of familiar "types," each of them comic or unsympathetic to the degree that they have become clichés. Write a short character sketch of one or two of them, but individualizing the character through particular details that will make us sympathize and/or identify with him or her.

an absent-minded professor
a lazy laborer
a rock band groupie
an aging film star
a domineering wife
her timid husband
a tyrannical boss
a staggering drunk

3. In the sociological science of "garbology," human habits are assessed by studying what people throw away. Write a character sketch by describing the contents of a wastebasket or garbage can.

4. For an exercise (only), try writing a character sketch without any of the elements of type. We shouldn't be able to tell the age, race, gender, nationality, or class of your character. Can you do it? Is it satisfying?

5. Briefly describe a character who is as unlike yourself as you can imagine. Then get inside this character's head; give him or her one mental habit, desire, fear, love or longing that you have. Make us see the character as "good."

6. Pick two contrasting or contradictory qualities of your own personality (consistent inconsistencies). Create a character that embodies each, and set them in conflict with each other. Since you are not writing about yourself but aiming at heightening and dramatizing these qualities, make each character radically different from yourself in at least one fundamental aspect of type: age, race, gender, nationality, or class.

5

THE FLESH MADE WORD
Characterization, Part II

The Direct Methods of Character Presentation (Cont'd)
Character: A Summary

Appearance reveals, which is one of the things that is meant by *showing* rather than telling in fiction. But characters also reveal themselves in the way they speak, act, and think, and the revelation is more profound when they are also shown in one or more of these ways.

Note that sense impressions other than sight are still a part of the way a character "appears." A limp handshake or a soft cheek; an odor of Chanel, oregano, or decay—if we are allowed to taste, smell, or touch a character through the narrative, then these sense impressions characterize the way looks do.

The sound and associations of a character's name, too, can give a clue to personality: The affluent Mr. Chiddister in chapter 3 is automatically a more elegant sort than the affluent Mr. Strum; Huck Finn must have a different life from that of the Marquis of Lumbria. Although names with a blatant meaning—Joseph Surface, Billy Pilgrim, Martha Quest—tend to stylize a character and should be used sparingly, if at all, ordinary names can hint at traits you mean to heighten, and it is worth combining any list of names, including the telephone book, to find suggestive sounds. My own telephone book yields, at a glance this morning, Linda Holladay, Marvin Entzminger, and Melba Peebles, any one of which might set me to speculating on a character.

Sound also characterizes as a part of "appearance" insofar as sound represents timbre, tenor, or quality or noise and speech, the characterizing reediness or gruffness of a voice, the lift of laughter or stiffness of delivery.

SPEECH

Speech, however, characterizes in a way that is different from appearance, because speech represents an effort, mainly voluntary, to externalize the internal and to manifest not merely taste or preference but also deliberated thought. Like fiction itself, human dialogue attempts to marry logic to emotion.

We have many means of communicating that are direct expressions of emotion: laughing, leering, shaking hands, screaming, shouting, shooting, making love. We have many means of communicating that are symbolic and emotionless: mathematical equations, maps, checkbooks, credit cards, and chemical formulas. Between body language and pure math lies language, in which judgments and feelings take the form of structured logic: in vows, laws, news, notes, essays, letters, and talk; and the greatest of these is talk.

I am going to claim that dialogue is important to fiction, so it's probably worth hearing the other argument from a first-rate author, Bob Shacochis.

> Some fine writers have flat ears—they are smart enough to ignore the impulse to have characters "speak." Almost any story can be successfully told without dialogue, so it seems to me that although it can be a rich accompaniment, dialogue is fundamentally one of the most minor elements to be concerned with in storytelling. It should be seen first and foremost as a device that *interrupts*—I mean a pacer, a rhythm-making device. If a writer learns to use it that way first, then the writer has a chance of using dialogue successfully to develop character. But, I think, it's close to being a dispensable item.

There is sense and comfort in this view, and any author who knows his or her ear is flat might do well to listen to Shacochis. Most, if not all, stories *can* be told without the characters' voices. But the peculiar tension between emotion and logic in human speech also makes it a rich storytelling device, and as a beginning author I would not scrap the skill before I'd worked at developing it.

Because speech has this dual nature, the purpose of dialogue in fiction is never merely to convey information. Dialogue may do that, but it must also simultaneously characterize, provide exposition, set the scene, advance the action, and foreshadow and/or remind. William Sloane, in *The Craft of Writing*, says:

> There is . . . . a tentative rule that pertains to all fiction dialogue. It must do more than one thing at a time or it is too inert for the purposes of fiction. This may sound harsh, but I consider it an essential discipline.

In considering Sloane's "tentative rule," I place the emphasis on *rule*. With dialogue as with significant detail, when you write you are constantly at pains to mean more than you say. If a significant detail must both call up a sense image and *mean*, then the character's words, which presumably mean something, should simultaneously suggest image, personality, or emotion. Even rote exchanges can call up images. A character who says, "It is indeed a pleasure to meet you," carries his back at a different angle, dresses differently, from a character who says, "Hey, man, what it is?"

In the three very brief speeches that follow are three fictional men, sharply differentiated from each other not only by what they say, but also by how they say it. How much do you know about each? How does each look?

"I had a female cousin one time—a Rockefeller, as it happened—" said the Senator, "and she confessed to me that she spent the fifteenth, sixteenth and seventeenth years of her life saying nothing but, 'No, thank you.' Which is all very well for a girl of that age and station. But it would have been a damned unattractive trait in a *male* Rockefeller."

KURT VONNEGUT, *God Bless You, Mr. Rosewater*

"Hey, that's nice, Grandma," says Phantom as he motions me to come in the circle with him. "I'll tell you what. You can have a contest too. Sure. I got a special one for you. A sweater contest. You get all the grannies out on the porch some night when you could catch a death a chill, and see which one can wear the most sweaters. I got an aunt who can wear fourteen. You top that?"

ROBERT WARD, *Shedding Skin*

The Knight looked surprised at the question. "What does it matter where my body happens to be?" he said. "My mind goes on working all the same. In fact, the more head downward I am, the more I keep inventing new things.

"Now, the cleverest thing of the sort that I ever did," he went on after a pause, "was inventing a new pudding during the meat course."

LEWIS CARROLL, *Through the Looking-Glass*

There are forms of insanity that condemn people to hear voices against their will, but as writers we invite ourselves to hear voices without relinquishing our hold on reality or our right to control. The trick to writing good dialogue is hearing voice. The question is, What would he or she say? The answer is entirely in language. The choice of language reveals content, character, and conflict, as well as type.

It's logical that if you must develop voices in order to develop dialogue, you'd do well to start with monologue and develop voices one by one. Use your journal to experiment with speech patterns that will characterize. Some people speak in telegraphically short sentences missing various parts of speech. Some speak in convoluted eloquence or rhythms tedious with qualifying phrases. Some rush head-long without a pause for breath until they're breathless; others are measured or terse or begrudge even forming a sentence. Trust your "inner ear" and use your journal to practice catching voices. Freewriting is invaluable to dialogue writing because it is the manner of composition closest to speech without time to mull or edit, making qualifications, corrections, and disavowels part of the process and the text.

When you hear a passage of speech that interests you, next time you sit down at your journal freedraft a monologue passage of that speech. Don't look for words that seem right; just listen to the voice and let it flow. The principle is the same as keeping your eye on the ball. If you feel you're going wrong, let yourself go wrong, and keep going. You're allowed to fail. And the process has two productive outcomes in any case: You begin to develop your own range of voices whether you catch a particular voice or not, and you develop your ear by the very process of "hearing" it go wrong.

Here is a freedrafted passage from a conversation I heard this morning.

> Really I must say, what's been happening these past few years is absolutely ap-palling, all these takeovers—naturally just another one of those dreadful imports from America, like plastic bags and McDonald's. Now the publishers are all in a muddle, editors changing right and left, accountants on top of the heap, and they don't have the time of day for the booksellers, who are after all the ones who know what sells, aren't they?

I'm not thrilled with this; the voice sounds false to me, straining to be British. But the freedrafting loosened me up, and a couple of specifics not in the actual con-versation—those plastic bags and McDonald's—are the bright spots. Next, I'll try putting the same sentiments in the mouth of someone quite different, to play at hearing voices.

> These money men don't know squat. Who makes the decisions? Some candyass with dollar signs in his gold teeth. Foo-Co who? We oughtta take off for some, I dunno—nah, no point setting up a press on a desert island, is there? But I get sick of this diddly—blockbuster, high concept, you scratch my oil well and I'll scratch yours. Whole continent of illiterates, give it back to the Navahos.

Well, I don't know this character well enough to use him (hmmm, her?) in a short story, and probably never will. But the second scribble is more fun, so at least I'm limber.

You can also limber up in your journal by setting yourself deliberate exercises in making dialogue—or monologue—do more than one thing at a time. In addition to revealing character, dialogue can set the scene.

"We didn't know no one was here. We thought hit a summer camp all closed up. Curtains all closed up. Nothing here. No cars or gear nor nothing. Looks closed to me, don't hit to you, J.J.?"

JOY WILLIAMS, *Woods*

It can set the mood.

"I have a lousy trip to Philadelphia, lousy flight back, I watch my own plane blow a tire on closed-circuit TV, I go to my office, I find Suzy in tears because Warren's camped in her one-room apartment, I come home and I find my wife hasn't gotten *dressed* in two days. . . ."

JOAN DIDION, *Book of Common Prayer*

It can reveal the theme because, as William Sloane says, the characters talk about what the story is about.

"In my view you might just as well go for a bearded old man in the sky. Then there are physicists who find it convenient to describe time as a kind of substance, an efflorescence of undetectable particles. There are dozens of other theories, equally potty. They set out to smooth a few wrinkles in one corner of quantum theory. The mathematics are reasonable enough in a local sort of way, but the rest, the grand theorising, is whistling in the dark. . . ."

IAN MCEWAN, *The Child in Time*

Dialogue is also one of the simplest ways of revealing the past (a fundamental playwrighting device is to have a character who knows tells a character who doesn't know); and it is also one of the most effective, because we get both the drama of the memory and the drama of the telling. Here is a passage from Toni Morrison's *The Bluest Eye* in which the past is evoked, the speaker characterized, the scene and mood set, and the theme revealed, all at the same time and in less than a dozen lines.

"The onliest time I be happy seem like was when I was in the picture show. Every time I got, I went. I'd go early, before the show started. They'd cut off the lights, and everything be black. Then the screen would light up, and I'd move right on in them pictures. White men taking such good care of they women, and they all dressed up in big clean houses with the bathtubs right in the same room with the toilet. Them pictures gave me a lot of pleasure, but it made coming home hard, and looking at Cholly hard. I don't know."

If the telling of a memory *changes the relationship* between the teller and the listener (what is in theater called an emotional recall), then you have a scene of high drama, and the dialogue has become an action.

Listen to the patterns of speech you hear and try to catch differences of character through syntax—the arrangement of words within a sentence. Then put two or more of these characters in a scene and see how much their differing voices can have to do with conflict.

Here is an exchange among three members of a Chinese-American family in which the subject of the talk is political but in which much more than politics is conveyed.

> In fact, he hardly ever stopped talking, and we kids watched the spit foam at the corners of his mouth. . . . It was more like a lecture than a conversation. . . .
>
> "Actually these aren't dreams or plans," Uncle Bun said. "I'm making predictions about ineluctabilities. This Beautiful Nation, this Gold Mountain, this America will end as we know it. There will be one nation, and it will be a world nation. A united planet. Not just Russian Communism. Not just Chinese Communism. World Communism."
>
> He said, "When we don't need to break our bodies earning our daily living any more, and we have time to think, we'll write poems, sing songs, develop religions, invest customs, build statues, plant gardens and make a perfect world." He paused to contemplate the wonders.
>
> "Isn't that great?" I said after he left.
>
> "Don't get brainwashed," said my mother. "He's going to get in trouble for talking like that."
>
> MAXINE HONG KINGSTON, *China Men*

Uncle Bun is richly characterized by his idealistic eloquence, but so are the narrator and her mother in their brief reactions. The contrast between Uncle Bun's "predictions about ineluctabilities" and the narrator's "Isn't that great?" makes her both a teenager and Americanized, whereas the mother's hostile practicality comes out in her blunt imperative.

This passage also illustrates an essential element of conflict in dialogue: tension and drama are heightened when characters are constantly (in one form or another) saying no to each other. Here the mother is saying a distinct no to both Uncle Bun and her daughter. In the following exchange from Ernest Hemingway's *The Old Man and the Sea*, the old man feels only love for his young protégé, and their conversation is a pledge of affection. Nevertheless, it is the old man's steady denial that lends the scene tension.

> "Can I go out and get sardines for you tomorrow?"
>
> "No. Go and play baseball. I can still row and Rogelio will throw the net."
>
> "I would like to go. If I cannot fish with you, I would like to serve in some way."
>
> "You brought me a beer," the old man said. "You are already a man."
>
> "How old was I when you first took me in a boat?"
>
> "Five and you were nearly killed when I brought the fish in too green and he nearly tore the boat to pieces. Can you remember?"

"I can remember the tail slapping and banging and the thwart breaking and the noise of the clubbing. I can remember you throwing me into the bow where the wet coiled lines were and feeling the whole boat shiver and the noise of you club-bing him like chopping a tree down and the sweet blood smell all over me."

"Can you really remember that or did I just tell it to you?"

"I remember everything from when we first went together."

The old man looked at him with his sunburned, confident loving eyes.

"If you were my boy I'd take you out and gamble," he said. "But you are your father's and mother's and you are in a lucky boat."

Neither of these characters is consciously eloquent, and the dialogue is extremely simple. But look how much more it does than "one thing at a time"! It provides exposition on the beginning of the relationship, and it conveys the mutual affec-tion of the two and the conflict within the old man between his love for the boy and his loyalty to the parents. It conveys the boy's eagerness to persuade and carries him into the emotion he had as a small child while the fish was clubbed. The dialogue represents a constant shift of power back and forth between the boy and the old man, as the boy, whatever else he is saying, continues to say *please,* and the old man, whatever else he is saying, continues to say *no.*

It's interesting that the same law of plausibility operates in dialogue as in nar-rative. We will tend to believe a character who speaks in concrete details and to be skeptical of one who generalizes or who delivers judgments unsupported by ex-ample. Uncle Bun is eloquent and attractive, but he hardly convinces us he has the formula for a perfect world. When the boy in the Hemingway passage protests, "I remember everything," however, we believe him because of the vivid details in his memory of the fish. If one character says, "It's perfectly clear from all his actions that he adores me and would do anything for me," and another says, "I had my hands all covered with the clay slick, and he just reached over to lift a lock of hair out of my eyes and tuck it behind my ear," which character do you believe is the more loved?

It's interesting to observe that, whereas in narrative you will demonstrate control if you state the facts and let the emotional value rise off of them, in dialogue you will convey information more naturally if the emphasis is on the speaker's feelings. "My brother is due to arrive at mid-afternoon and is bringing his four children with him" reads as bald exposition; whereas, "That idiot brother of mine thinks he can walk in in the middle of the afternoon and plunk his four kids in my lap!" or, "I can't wait till my brother gets here at three! You'll see—those are the four sweetest kids this side of the planet."—will sound like talk and will slip us the information sideways.

Often the most forceful dialogue can be achieved by *not* having the characters say what they mean. People in extreme emotional states—whether of fear, pain, anger, or love—are at their least articulate. There is more narrative tension in a love scene where the lovers make anxious small talk, terrified of revealing their feelings, than in one where they hop into bed. A character who is able to say "I hate you!" hates less than one who bottles the fury and pretends to submit, unwilling to expose the truth. Dialogue often fails if it is too eloquent; the characters debate ideas with great accuracy or are able to define their feelings precisely and honestly. But often the purpose of human exchange is to conceal as well as to reveal; to impress, hurt, protect, seduce, or reject.

In this rather extreme example from Kazuo Ishiguro's *The Remains of the Day*, a British lord and his butler, early in the Second World War, discuss a staff matter. How much concealed emotion can you identify? What information is given without being stated? What are the political sympathies of each character? What lies are told?

> 'I've been doing a great deal of thinking, Stevens. A great deal of thinking. And I've reached my conclusion. We cannot have Jews on the staff here at Darlington Hall.'
> 'Sir?'
> 'It's for the good of this house, Stevens. In the interests of the guests we have staying here. I've looked into this carefully, Stevens, and I'm letting you know my conclusion.'
> 'Very well, sir.'
> 'Tell me, Stevens, we have a few on the staff at the moment, don't we? Jews, I mean.'
> 'I believe two of the present staff members would fall into that category, sir.'
> 'Ah.' His lordship paused for a moment, staring out of his window. 'Of course, you'll have to let them go.'
> 'I beg your pardon, sir?'
> 'It's regrettable, Stevens, but we have no choice. There's the safety and well-being of my guests to consider. Let me assure you, I've looked into this matter and thought it through thoroughly. It's in all our best interests.'

Examine your dialogue to see if it does more than one thing at a time. Do the sound and syntax characterize by region, education, attitude? Do the choice of words and their syntax reveal that he or she is stiff, outgoing, stifling anger, ignorant of the facts, perceptive, bigoted, afraid? Is the conflict advanced by "*no-dialogue*," in which the characters say no to each other? Is the drama heightened by the characters' inability or unwillingness to tell the whole truth?

Once you are comfortable with the voice of your character, it is well to acknowledge that everyone has many voices and that what that character says will be, within his or her verbal range, determined by the character *to whom* it is said. All of us have one sort of speech for the vicar and another for the man who pumps the gas. Huck Finn, whose voice is idiosyncratically his own says, "Yes, sir," to the judge, and "Maybe I am, maybe I ain't," to his degenerate dad.

Dialect is a tempting, and can be an excellent, means of characterizing, but it is difficult to do well and easy to overdo. Dialect should always be achieved by word choice and syntax, and misspellings kept to a minimum. They distract and slow the reader, and worse, they tend to make the character seem stupid rather than regional. There is no point in spelling phonetically any word as it is ordinarily pronounced: almost all of us say things like "fur" for *for*, "uv" for *of*, "wuz" for *was*, "an" for *and*, "sez" for *says*. Nearly everyone drops the g in words ending in *ing*, at least now and then. When you misspell these words in dialogue, you indicate that the speaker is ignorant enough to spell them that way when he or she writes. Even if you want to indicate ignorance, you may alienate the reader by the means you choose to do so.

These "rules" for dialect have changed in the past fifty years or so, largely for political reasons. Nineteenth-century authors felt free to misspell the dialogue of foreigners, the lower classes, and racial, regional, and ethnic groups. This literary habit persisted into the first decades of the twentieth century. But the world is considerably smaller now, and its consciousness has been raised. Dialect, after all, is entirely relative, and an author who seems unaware of this may sound like a bigot. The word "bath" pronounced by an Englishman may sound like *bahth* to an American, and pronounced by an American may sound like *banth* to an Englishman, but both know how the word is spelled and resent the implied mockery. Liverpudlians have been knighted; the White House has been inhabited by two Texans, a Georgian, and a Californian; and we resent the implication that regionality is ignorance. Ignorance itself is a charged issue. If you misspell a foreign accent or black English, the reader is likely to have a political rather than a literary reaction. A line of dialogue that runs "Doan rush me nun, Ah be gwine" reads as caricature, whereas, "Don't rush me none, I be going" makes legitimate use of black English syntax and lets us concentrate on the meaning and emotion.

In dialect or standard English, the bottom-line rule is that dialogue must be speakable; conversely, if it isn't speakable, it isn't dialogue.

> "Certainly I had had a fright I wouldn't soon forget," Reese would say later, "and as I slipped into bed fully dressed except for my shoes, which I flung God-knows-where, I wondered why I had subjected myself to a danger only a fool would fail to foresee for the dubious pleasure of spending one evening in the company of a somewhat less than brilliant coed."

Nobody would say this because it can't be said. It is not only convoluted beyond reason but also stumbles over its alliteration, "only a fool would fail to foresee for," and takes more breath than the human lungs can hold. Read your dialogue aloud and make sure it is comfortable to the mouth, the breath, and the ear. If not, then it won't ring true as talk.

Identifying dialogue sometimes presents more of a problem than it needs to. The purpose of a *dialogue tag* is to make clear who is speaking, and it usually needs to do nothing else. *Said* is quite adequate to the purpose. People also *ask* and *reply* and occasionally *add, recall, remember,* or *remind.* But sometimes an unsure writer will strain for emphatic synonyms: *She gasped, he whined, they chorused, John snarled, Mary spat.* This is unnecessary and obtrusive, because although unintentional repetition usually makes for awkward style, the word "said" is as invisible as punctuation. When reading we're scarcely aware of it, whereas we are forced to be aware of *she wailed*. If it's clear who is speaking without any dialogue tag at all, don't use one. Usually an identification at the beginning of a dialogue passage and an occasional reminder are sufficient. If the speaker is inherently identified in the speech pattern, so much the better.

Similarly, tonal dialogue tags should be used sparingly: *he said with relish; she added limply*. Such phrases are blatant "telling," and the chances are that good dialogue will convey its own tone. *"Get off my case!" she said angrily.* We do not need to be told that she said this angrily. If she said it sweetly, then we would probably need to be told. If the dialogue does not give us a clue to the manner in which it is said, an action will often do so better than an adverb. *"I'll have a word with Mr. Ritter about it," he said with finality* is weaker than *"I'll have a word with Mr. Ritter about it," he said, and picked up his hat.*

If human character is the center of fiction, it follows inevitably that you must master dialogue. People speak; they confront each other with speech; they change through speech. It is by hearing your characters speak that we experience them. There may be times when a summary of speech is justified—when, for example, one character has to inform another of events that we already know, or when the emotional point of a conversation is that it has become tedious.

> Carefully, playing down the danger, Len filled her in on the events of the long night.

> After that, Samantha told us everything we had never wanted to know about the lost art of ormolu, and Marlene gave us a play-by-play account of her last bridge game.

But nothing is more frustrating to a reader than to be told that significant events are taking place in talk and to be denied the drama of the dialogue.

> They whispered to each other all night long, and as he told her all about his past, she began to realize that she was falling in love with him.

Such a summary—it's *telling*—is a stingy way of treating the reader, who wants the chance to fall in love, too: Give me *me*!

ACTION

The significant characters of a fiction must be both capable of causing an action and capable of being changed by it.

It is important to understand the difference between action and movement, terms that are not synonymous. Physical movement is generally necessary to the action, but it is not adequate to ensure that there will be an action. Much movement in a story—the way he crosses his legs, the way she charges down the hall—is actually part of appearance and characterizes without necessarily moving the plot forward. When a book or film is advertised as "action-packed," it is also likely that what is being touted is movement rather than action—lots of sword fights, karate chops, or bombs away—but not necessarily that meaningful arrangement of events in which a character is convincingly compelled to pursue a goal, to make decisions along the way, and to find himself or herself subtly or dramatically altered in the process. It's particularly important to keep this in mind when writing dialogue because talk is not action unless it contains the possibility of change. *To discuss* is not of itself a dramatic action; *to realize* is. The words "motive," "motion," and "emotion" have the same root, and this is neither accidental nor irrelevant to the way the human drama unfolds.

Playwrights are good people to ask about action, since plays depend on the externalized, rather than on interior thought. Sam Smiley, in *Playwrighting: The Structure of Action*, defines action simply as "human change." Change occurs with a dramatic event, an event that makes a difference. Smiley recognizes four dramatic events: decision, discovery, deed, and accident.

Claudia Johnson agrees. Each drama (or for our purposes each story), she says, is *a pattern of change*. Scenes are built around dramatic events, Johnson says, and she thinks of the scene as an oyster, the dramatic event as the pearl. Building a story is stringing the pearls. She finds that *decision* and *discovery* are the agents of real change—and goes so far as to say that all human turning points are moments of either discovery or decision. Deeds and accidents are necessary to both drama and fiction, but the moment of change for the characters involved is the moment at which she decides to do something, or he discovers that the accident has occurred. (No doubt this is why, when the hero is hit, he so often calls attention to the fact. Once he is dead no further action can occur that will change him, and the drama shifts to the friend who discovers him.) Likewise, revelation is a stunning moment of drama, but the change in the characters occurs when one decides to reveal and the other discovers whatever has been revealed.

Thus it turns out that the internal or mental moment of change is where the action lies. Much movement in a story is mere event, and this is why descriptions of actions, like stage directions in a dull play, sometimes add little or nothing. When the wife picks up a cup of coffee, that is mere *event*. If she finds that the lipstick on the cup is not her shade, that is a dramatic event, a *discovery*; it makes a difference. She makes a *decision* to fling it at the woman wearing the Cherry Ice mouth. Flinging it is a *deed*, but this changes nothing of itself until the second character's realization that she has been hit. Or suppose instead the first woman has an *accident*, hitting her wrist against the mantelpiece as she raises the cup to fling it. No change has been made in the character until her *discovery* that the coffee is spreading across her white skirt—and so on.

Every story is a pattern of change (events connected, as Forster observed, primarily by cause and effect) in which small and large changes are made through decision and discovery. Here is a passage in which mere events are followed by a moment of discovery that changes the character's mood and situation—and involves us in immediate suspense.

> I turned on a light in the living room and looked at Rachel's books. I chose one by an author named Lin Yutang and sat down on a sofa under a lamp. Our living room is comfortable. The book seemed interesting. I was in a neighborhood where most of the front doors were unlocked, and on a street that is very quiet on a summer night. All the animals are domesticated, and the only night birds that I've ever heard are some owls way down by the railroad track. So it was very quiet. I heard the Barstows' dog bark, briefly, as if he had been waked by a nightmare, and then the barking stopped. Everything was quiet again. Then I heard, very close to me, a footstep and a cough.
>   I felt my flesh get hard—you know that feeling—but I didn't look up from my book, although I felt that I was being watched.
>
>   JOHN CHEEVER, *The Cure*

Here is another passage, where the character's insistence that there is no discovery to be made—the disease is no mystery, she knows how a virus works—throws into dramatic relief her discovery that her perception has changed.

> I wonder if it is possible to prepare yourself for anything. Of course I lay there, saying, This is the flu, it isn't supposed to last more than two or three days, I should find the Tylenol. In the moment I didn't feel bad, really, a little queasy, a degree feverish. The disease wasn't a mystery to me. I know what a virus looks like, how it works. I could imagine the invasion and the resistance. In fact, imagining the invasion and the resistance took my attention off the queasiness and the feverishness. But when I opened my eyes and my gaze fell upon the bookcases looming above me in the half-light, I shuddered reflexively, because the books seemed to swell outward from the wall and threaten to drop on me, and my thoughts about the next few days had exactly that quality as well. I did not see how we would endure, how I would endure.
>
>   JANE SMILEY, *The Age of Grief*

You don't want your technique to show, and once you're sure of your structure, you need to bury it. In the next example, from Raymond Carver's "Neighbors," the pattern of change—Bill Miller's gradual intrusion into his neighbor's house—is based on a series of decisions that Carver does not explicitly state. The passage ends with a turning point, a moment of discovery.

> When he returned to the kitchen the cat was scratching in her box. She looked at him steadily for a minute before she turned back to the litter. He opened all

the cupboards and examined the canned goods, the cereals, the packaged foods, the cocktail and wine glasses, the china, the pots and pans. He opened the refrigerator. He sniffed some celery, took two bites of cheddar cheese, and chewed on an apple as he walked into the bedroom. The bed seemed enormous, with a fluffy white bedspread draped to the floor. He pulled out a nightstand drawer, found a half-empty package of cigarettes and stuffed them into his pocket. Then he stepped to the closet and was opening it when the knock sounded at the front door.

There is hardly grand larceny being committed here, but the actions build toward tension through two distinct techniques. The first is that they do actually "build": At first Bill only "examines." The celery he only sniffs, whereas he takes two bites of the cheese, then a whole apple, then half a pack of cigarettes. He moves from the kitchen to the bedroom, which is a clearer invasion of privacy, and from cupboard to refrigerator to nightstand to closet, each a more intimate intrusion than the last.

The second technique is that the narrative subtly hints at Bill's own sense of stealth. It would be easy to imagine a vandal who performed the same actions with complete indifference. But Bill thinks the cat looks "steadily" at him, which is hardly of any importance except that he feels it to be. His awareness of the enormous white bed hints at sexual guilt. When the knock at the front door sounds, we start, as he must, in a clear sense of getting caught.

THOUGHT

Aristotle is helpful at clarifying the relationship among desire, thought, and action. Aristotle says, as we have seen, that a man "is his desire," that is, his character is defined by his ultimate purpose, good or bad. *Thought*, says Aristotle, is the process by which a person works backward in his mind from his goal to determine what *action* he can take toward that goal at a given moment.

It is not, for example, your ultimate desire to read this book. Very likely you don't even "want" to read it; you'd rather be asleep or jogging or making love. But your ultimate goal is, say, to be a rich, respected, and famous writer. In order to attain this goal, you reason, you must know as much about the craft as you can learn. To do this, you would like to take a graduate degree at the Writer's Workshop in Iowa. To do that, you must take an undergraduate degree in _____, where you now find yourself, and must get an A in Ms. or Mr. _____'s creative writing course. To do that, you must produce a character sketch from one of the assignments at the end of this chapter by a week from Tuesday. To do so, you must sit here reading this chapter now instead of sleeping, jogging, or making love. Your ultimate motive has led you logically backward to a deliberate "moral" decision on the action you can take at this minor crossroads. In fact, it turns out that you want to be reading after all.

The pattern that Aristotle perceives in this relation among desire, thought, and action seems to me a very fruitful one for an author both in the structuring of plot and in the creation of character. What does this protagonist want to happen in the last paragraph of this story? What is the particular thought process by which this person works backward to determine what he or she will do now, in the situation that presents itself in the first paragraph on page one?

The action, of course, may be the wrong one. Thought thwarts us, because the thought process itself is mistaken (if only you'd gone to sleep, you would now be having a dream that would give you the most brilliant idea for a short story you've ever had), or because thought is full of conflicting desires and consistent inconsistencies (actually you *are* no longer reading this paragraph; someone knocked on your door and suggested a pizza and you couldn't resist), or because there is enormous human tension between suppressed thought and expressed thought (you didn't want a pizza, and certainly not in the company of that bore, but you'd turned him down twice this week already).

At the opening of Flannery O'Connor's "Everything That Rises Must Converge," which follows this chapter, Julian wants to be free of his mother's tedious demands, but he is also financially dependent upon her, so he wants to meet those demands as minimally as possible. He will take her to the Y, then, but he'll do it in bad grace. At the end of the story he is free of her; but it turns out that his thought processes were faulty, his desire unattainable, and his "dependency" is deeper than he understood.

A person, a character, can't do much about what he or she wants; it just is (which is another way of saying that character is desire). What we can deliberately choose is our behavior, the action we take in a given situation. Achievement of our desire would be easy if the thought process between desire and act were not so faulty and so wayward, or if there were not such an abyss between the thoughts we think and those which we are willing and able to express.

CONFLICT BETWEEN METHODS OF PRESENTATION

The conflict that is the essence of character can be effectively (and, if it doesn't come automatically, quite consciously) achieved in fiction by producing a conflict between methods of presentation. A character can be directly revealed to us through *appearance, speech, action,* and *thought.* If you set one of these methods (in narrative practice most frequently *thought*) at odds with the others, then dramatic tension will be produced. Imagine, for example, a character who is impeccably and expensively dressed, who speaks eloquently, who acts decisively, and whose mind is revealed to us as full of order and determination. He is inevitably a flat character. But suppose that he is impeccable, eloquent, decisive, and that his mind is a *mess* of wounds and panic. He is at once interesting.

Here is the opening passage of Saul Bellow's *Seize the Day*, in which appearance and action are blatantly at odds with thought. Notice that it is the tension between suppressed thought and what is expressed through appearance and action that produces the rich character conflict.

> When it came to concealing his troubles, Tommy Wilhelm was not less capable than the next fellow. So at least he thought, and there was a certain amount of evidence to back him up. He had once been an actor—no, not quite, an extra— and he knew what acting should be. Also, he was smoking a cigar, and when a man is smoking a cigar, wearing a hat, he has an advantage: it is harder to find out how he feels. He came from the twenty-third floor down to the lobby on the mezzanine to collect his mail before breakfast, and he believed—he hoped—he looked passably well: doing all right.

Tommy Wilhelm is externally composed but mentally anxious, mainly anxious about looking externally composed. By contrast, in the next passage, from Samuel Beckett's *Murphy*, the landlady, Miss Carridge, who has just discovered a suicide in one of her rooms, is anxious in speech and action but is mentally composed.

> She came speeding down the stairs one step at a time, her feet going so fast that she seemed on little caterpillar wheels, her forefinger sawing horribly at her craw for Celia's benefit. She slithered to a stop on the steps of the house and screeched for the police. She capered in the street like a consternated ostrich, with strangled distracted rushes towards the York and Caledonian Roads in turn, embarrassingly equidistant from the tragedy, tossing up her arms, undoing the good work of the samples, screeching for police aid. Her mind was so collected that she saw clearly the impropriety of letting it appear so.

I have said that thought is most frequently at odds with one or more of the other three methods of direct presentation—reflecting the difficulty we have expressing ourselves openly or accurately—but this is by no means always the case. A character may be successfully, calmly, even eloquently expressing fine opinions while betraying himself by pulling at his ear, or herself by crushing her skirt. Captain Queeg of Herman Wouk's *The Caine Mutiny* is a memorable example of this, maniacally clicking the steel balls in his hand as he defends his disciplinary code. Often we are not privy to the thoughts of a character at all, so that the conflicts must be expressed in a contradiction between the external methods of direct presentation, appearance, speech, and action. Character A may be speaking floods of friendly welcome, betraying his real feeling by backing steadily away. Character B, dressed in taffeta ruffles and ostrich plumes, may wail pityingly over the miseries of the poor. Notice that the notion of "betraying oneself" is important here: We're more likely to believe the evidence unintentionally given than deliberate expression.

A classic example of such self-betrayal is found in Leo Tolstoy's *The Death of Ivan Ilyich*, where the widow confronts her husband's colleague at the funeral.

. . . Noticing that the table was endangered by his cigarette ash, she immediately passed him an ashtray, saying as she did so: "I consider it an affectation to say that my grief prevents my attending to practical affairs. On the contrary, if anything can—I won't say console me, but—distract me, it is seeing to everything concerning him." She again took out her handkerchief as if preparing to cry, but suddenly, as if mastering her feeling, she shook herself and began to speak calmly. "But there is something I want to talk to you about."

It is no surprise either to the colleague or to us that Praskovya Federovna wants to talk about getting money.

Finally, character conflict can be expressed by creating a tension between the direct and the indirect methods of presentation, and this is a source of much irony. The author presents us with a judgment of the character and then lets him or her speak, appear, act, and/or think in contradiction of this judgment.

Sixty years had not dulled his responses; his physical reactions, like his moral ones, were guided by his will and strong character, and these could be seen plainly in his features. He had a long tube-like face with a long rounded open jaw and a long depressed nose.

FLANNERY O'CONNOR, *The Artificial Nigger*

Here what we see in the details of Mr. Head's features are not will and strong character but grimly unlikable qualities. "Tube-like" is an ugly image; an "open jaw" suggests stupidity; and "depressed" connotes more than shape, while the dogged repetition of "long" stretches the face grotesquely.

Jane Austen is a master of this ironic method, the authorial voice often having a naive goodwill toward the characters while the characters themselves prevent the reader from sharing it.

Mr. Woodhouse was fond of society in his own way. He liked very much to have his friends come and see him; and from various united causes, from his long residence at Hartfield, and his good nature, from his fortune, his house, and his daughter, he could command the visits of his own little circle in a great measure as he liked. He had not much intercourse with any families beyond that circle; his horror of late hours and large dinner parties made him unfit for any acquaintance but such as would visit him on his own terms. . . . Upon such occasions poor Mr. Woodhouse's feelings were in sad warfare. He loved to have the cloth laid, because it had been the fashion of his youth; but his conviction of suppers being very unwholesome made him rather sorry to see anything put on it; and while his hospitality would have welcomed his visitors to everything, his care for their health made him grieve that they would eat.

Emma

Here all the authorial generalizations about Mr. Woodhouse are generous and positive, whereas his actions and the "sad warfare" of his mind lead us to the conviction that we would just as soon not sup with this good-natured and generous man.

In addition to providing tension between methods of presentation, you can try a few other ways of making a character fresh and forceful in your mind before you start writing.

If the character is based on you or on someone you know, drastically alter the model in some external way: Change blond to dark or thin to thick; imagine the character as the opposite gender or radically alter the setting in which the character must act. Part of the trouble with writing directly from experience is that you know too much about it—what "they" did, how you felt. Under such circumstances it's hard to know whether everything in your mind is getting onto the page. An external alteration forces you to re-see, and so to see more clearly, and so to convey more clearly what you see.

On the other hand, if the character is created primarily out of your observation or invention and is unlike yourself, try to find an *internal* area that you have in common with the character. If you are a blond, slender young woman and the character is a fat, balding man, do you nevertheless have in common a love of French *haute cuisine*? Are you haunted by the same sort of dream? Do you share a fear of public performance or a susceptibility to fine weather?

I can illustrate these techniques only from my own writing, because I am the only author whose self I can identify with any certainty in fictional characters. In writing a recent novel, I wanted to open with a scene in which the heroine buries a dog in her backyard. I had recently buried a dog in my backyard. I wanted to capture the look and feel of red Georgia earth at sunrise, the tangle of roots, and the smell of decay. But I knew that I was likely to make the experience too much my own, too little my character's. I set about to make her not-me. I have long dark hair and an ordinary figure, and I tend to live in Levi's. I made Shaara Soole

> . . . big boned, lanky, melon-breasted, her best feature was a head of rusty barbed-wire hair that she tried to control with a wardrobe of scarves and headband things. Like most costume designers, she dressed with more originality than taste, usually on the Oriental or Polynesian side, sometimes with voluminous loops of thong and matte metal over an ordinary shirt. This was somewhat eccentric in Hubbard, Georgia, but Shaara may have been oblivious to her eccentricity, being so concerned to keep her essential foolishness in check.

Having thus separated Shaara from myself, I was able to bury the dog with her arms and through her eyes rather than my own. On the other hand, a few pages later I was faced with the problem of introducing her ex-husband, Boyd Soole. I had voluminous notes on this character, and I knew that he was almost totally unlike me. A man, to begin with, and a huge man, a theater director with a natural air of power and authority and very little interest in domestic affairs. I sat at my desk for several days, unable to make him move convincingly. My desk oppressed me, and I felt trapped and uncomfortable, my work thwarted, it seemed, by the very chair and typewriter. Then it occurred to me that Boyd was *also* sitting at a desk trying to work.

> The dresser at the Travelodge was some four inches too narrow and three inches too low. If he set his feet on the floor his knees would sit free of the drawer but would be awkwardly constricted left and right. If he crossed his legs, he could hook his right foot comfortably outside the left of the kneehole but would bruise his thigh at the drawer. If he shifted back he was placed at an awkward distance from his script. And in this position he could not work.

This passage did not instantly allow me to live inside Boyd Soole's skin, nor did it solve all my problems with his characterization. But it did let me get on with the story, and it gave me a flash of sympathy for him that later grew much more profound than I had foreseen.

Often, identifying what you have in common with the feelings of your character will also clarify what is important about him or her to the story—why, in fact, you chose to write about such a person at all. Even if the character is presented as a villain, you have something in common, and I don't mean something forgivable. If he or she is intolerably vain, watch your own private gestures in front of the mirror and borrow them. If he or she is cruel, remember how you enjoyed hooking the worm.

There is no absolute requirement that a writer need behave honestly in life; there is absolutely no such requirement. Great writers have been public hams, domestic dictators, emotional con artists, and Nazis. What is required for fine writing is honesty on the page—not how the character *should* react at the funeral, the surprise party, in bed, but how she or he *does*. In order to develop such honesty of observation on the page, you must begin with a willing honesty of observation (though mercifully not of behavior) in yourself.

Character: A Summary

It may be helpful to summarize such practical advice on character as this chapter and the previous chapter contain.

1. Keep a journal and use it to explore and build ideas for characters.
2. Know all the influences that go into the making of your character's type: age, gender, race, nationality, marital status, region, education, religion, profession.
3. Know the details of your character's life: what he or she does during every part of the day, thinks about, remembers, wants, likes and dislikes, eats, says, means.

4. Identify, heighten, and dramatize consistent inconsistencies. What does your character want that is at odds with whatever else the character wants? What patterns of thought and behavior work against the primary goal?

5. Focus sharply on how the character looks, on what she or he wears and owns, and on how she or he moves. Let us focus on it, too.

6. Examine the character's speech to make sure it does more than convey information. Does it characterize, accomplish exposition, and reveal emotion, intent, or change? Does it advance the conflict through no-dialogue? Speak it aloud: Does it "say"?

7. Build action by making your characters discover and decide. Make sure that what happens is action and not mere event or movement, that is, that it contains the possibility for human change.

8. Know what your character wants, both generally out of life, and specifically in the context of the story. Keeping that desire in mind, "think backward" with the character to decide what he or she would do in any situation presented.

9. Be aware of the five methods of presentation of character: authorial interpretation, appearance, speech, action, and thought; present the character differently in at least one of these ways than you do in the others.

10. If the character is based on a real model, including yourself, make a dramatic external alteration.

11. If the character is imaginary or alien to you, identify a mental or emotional point of contact.

~~~

My Man Bovanne

TONI CADE BAMBARA

Blind people got a hummin jones if you notice. Which is understandable completely once you been around one and notice what no eyes will force you into to see people, and you get past the first time, which seems to come out of nowhere, and it's like you in church again with fat-chest ladies and old gents gruntin a hum low in the throat to whatever the preacher be saying. Shakey Bee bottom lip all swole up with Sweet Peach and me explainin how come the sweet-potato bread was a dollar-quarter this time stead of dollar regular and he say uh hunh he understand, then he break into this *thizzin* kind of hum which is quiet, but fiercesome just the same, if you ain't ready for it. Which I wasn't. But I got used to it and the onliest time I had to say somethin bout it was when he was playin checkers on the stoop one time and he commenst to hummin quite churchy seem to me. So I says, "Look here Shakey Bee, I can't beat you and Jesus too." He stop.

So that's how come I asked My Man Bovanne to dance. He ain't my man mind you, just a nice ole gent from the block that we all know cause he fixes things and the kids like him. Or used to fore Black Power got hold their minds and mess em around till they can't be civil to ole folks. So we at this benefit for my niece's cousin who's runnin for somethin with this Black party somethin or other behind her. And I press up close to dance with Bovanne who blind and I'm hummin and he hummin, chest to chest like talkin. Not jammin my breasts into the man. Wasn't bout tits. Was about vibrations. And he dug it and asked me what color dress I had on and how my hair was fixed and how I was doin without a man, not nosy but nice-like, and who was at this affair and was the canapés dainty-stingy or healthy enough to get hold of proper. Comfy and cheery is what I'm tryin to get across. Touch talkin like the heel of the hand on the tambourine or on a drum.

But right away Joe Lee come up on us and frown for dancin so close to the man. My own son who knows what kind of warm I am about; and don't grown men all call me long distance and in the middle of the night for a little Mama comfort? But he frown. Which ain't right since Bovanne can't see and defend himself. Just a nice old man who fixes toasters and busted irons and bicycles and things and changes the lock on my door when my men friends get messy. Nice man. Which is not why they invited him. Grass roots you see. Me and Sister Taylor and the woman who does heads at Mamies and the man from the barber shop, we all there on account of we grass roots. And I ain't never been souther than Brooklyn Battery and no more country than the window box on my fire escape. And just yesterday my kids tellin me to take them countrified rags off my head and be cool. And now can't get Black enough to suit 'em. So everybody passin sayin My Man Bovanne. Big deal, keep steppin and don't even stop a minute to get the man a drink or one of them cute sandwiches or tell him what's goin on. And him standin there with a smile ready case someone do speak he want to be ready. So that's how come I pull him on the dance floor and we dance squeezin past the tables and chairs and all them coats and people standin round up in each other face talkin bout this and that but got no use for this blind man who mostly fixed skates and skooters for all these folks when they were just kids. So I'm pressed up close and we touch talkin with the hum. And here come my daughter cuttin her eye at me like she do when she tell me about my "apolitical" self like I got hoof and mouf disease and there ain't no hope at all. And I don't pay her no mind and just look up in Bovanne shadow face and tell him his stomach like a drum and he laugh. Laugh real loud. And here come my youngest, Task, with a tap on my elbow like he the third grade monitor and I'm cuttin up on the line to assembly.

"I was just talkin on the drums," I explained when they hauled me into the kitchen. I figured drums was my best defense. They can get ready for drums what with all this heritage business. And Bovanne stomach just like that drum Task give me when he come back from Africa. You just touch it and it hum thizzm, thizzm. So I stuck to the drum story. "Just drummin that's all."

"Mama, what are you talkin about?

"She had too much to drink," say Elo to Task cause she don't hardly say nuthin to me direct no more since that ugly argument about my wigs.

"Look here Mama," say Task, the gentle one. "We just trying to pull your coat. You were makin a spectacle of yourself out there dancing like that."

"Dancin like what?"

Task run a hand over his left ear like his father for the world and his father before that.

"Like a bitch in heat," say Elo.

"Well uhh, I was goin to say like one of them sex-starved ladies gettin on in years and not too discriminating. Know what I mean?"

I don't answer cause I'll cry. Terrible thing when your own children talk to you like that. Pullin me out the party and hustlin me into some stranger's kitchen in the back of a bar just like the damn police. And ain't like I'm old old. I can still wear me some sleeveless dresses without the meat hangin off my arm. And I keep up with some thangs through my kids. Who ain't kids no more. To hear them tell it. So I don't say nuthin.

"Dancin with that tom," say Elo to Joe Lee, who leanin on the folks' freezer. "His feet can smell a cracker a mile away and go into their shuffle number post haste. And them eyes. He could be a little considerate and put on some shades. Who wants to look into them blown-out fuses that—"

"Is this what they call the generation gap?" I say.

"Generation gap," spits Elo, like I suggested castor oil and fricassee possum in the milk-shakes or somethin. "That's a white concept for a white phenomenon. There's no generation gap among Black people. We are a col—"

"Yeh, well never mind," says Joe Lee. "The point is Mama . . . well, it's pride. You embarrass yourself and us too dancin like that."

"I wasn't shame." Then nobody say nuthin. Them standin there in they pretty clothes with drinks in they hands and gangin up on me, and me in the third-degree chair and nary a olive to my name. Felt just like the police got hold to me.

"First of all," Task say, holdin up his hand and tickin off the offenses, "the dress. Now that dress is too short, Mama, and too low-cut for a woman your age. And Tamu's going to make a speech tonight to kick off the campaign and will be introducin you and expecting you to organize the council of elders—"

"Me? Didn nobody ask me nuthin. You mean Nisi? She change her name?"

"Well, Norton was supposed to tell you about it. Nisi wants to introduce you and then encourage the older folks to form a Council of the Elders to act as an advisory—"

"And you going to be standing there with your boobs out and that wig on your head and that hem up to your ass. And people'll say, 'Ain't that the horny bitch that was grindin with the blind dude?'"

"Elo, be cool a minute," say Task, gettin to the next finger. "And then there's the drinkin. Mama, you know you can't drink cause next thing you know you be laughin loud and carryin on," and he grab another finger for the loudness. "And then there's the dancin. You been tattooed on the man for four records straight and slow draggin even on the fast numbers. How you think that look for a woman your age?"

"What's my age?"

"What?"

"I'm axin you all a simple question. You keep talkin bout what's proper for a woman my age. How old am I anyhow?" And Joe Lee slams his eyes shut and squinches up his face to figure. And Task run a hand over his ear and stare into his glass like the ice cubes goin calculate for him. And Elo just starin at the top of my head like she goin rip the wig off any minute now.

"Is your hair braided up under that thing? If so, why don't you take it off? You always did do a neat cornroll."

"Uh huh," cause I'm thinkin how she couldn't undo her hair fast enough talking bout cornroll so countrified. None of which was the subject. "How old, I say?"

"Sixtee-one or—"

"You a damn lie Joe Lee Peoples."

"And that's another thing," say Task on the fingers.

"You know what you all can kiss," I say, gettin up and brushin the wrinkles out my lap.

"Oh, Mama," Elo say, puttin a hand on my shoulder like she hasn't done since she left home and the hand landin light and not sure it supposed to be there. Which hurt me to my heart. Cause this was the child in our happiness fore Mr. Peoples die. And I carried that child strapped to my chest till she was nearly two. We was close is what I'm tryin to tell you. Cause it was more me in the child than the others. And even after Task it was the girlchild I covered in the night and wept over for no reason at all less it was she was a chub-chub like me and not very pretty, but a warm child. And how did things get to this, that she can't put a sure hand on me and say Mama we love you and care about you and you entitled to enjoy yourself cause you a good woman?

"And then there's Reverend Trent," say Task, glancin from left to right like they hatchin a plot and just now lettin me in on it. "You were suppose to be talking with him tonight, Mama, about giving us his basement for campaign headquarters and—"

"Didn nobody tell me nuthin. If grass roots mean you kept in the dark I can't use it. I really can't. And Reven Trent a fool anyway the way he tore into the widow man up there on Edgecomb cause he wouldn't take in three of them foster children and the woman not even comfy in the ground yet and the man's mind messed up and—"

"Look here," say Task. "What we need is a family conference so we can get all this stuff cleared up and laid out on the table. In the meantime I think we better get back into the other room and tend to business. And in the meantime, Mama, see if you can't get to Reverend Trent and—"

"You want me to belly rub with the Reven, that it?"

"Oh, damn," Elo say and go through the swingin door.

"We'll talk about all this at dinner. How's tomorrow night, Joe Lee?" While Joe Lee being self-important I'm wonderin who's doin the cookin and how come no body ax me if I'm free and do I get a corsage and things like that. Then Joe nod that it's O.K. and he go through the swingin door and just a little hubbub come through from the other room. Then Task smile his smile, lookin just like his daddy, and he leave. And it just me and this stranger's kitchen, which was a mess I wouldn't never let my kitchen look like. Poison you just to look at the pots. Then the door swing the other way and it's My Man Bovanne standin there sayin Miss Hazel but lookin at the deep fry and then at the steam table, and most surprised when I come up on him from the other direction and take him on out of there. Pass the folks pushin up towards the stage where Nisi and some other people settin and ready to talk, and folks gettin to the last of the sandwiches and the booze fore they settle down in one spot and listen serious. And I'm thinkin bout tellin Bovanne what a lovely long dress Nisi got on and the earrings and her hair piled up in a cone and the people bout to hear how we all gettin screwed and gotta form our own party and everybody there listenin and lookin. But instead I just haul the man on out of there, and Joe Lee and his wife look at me like I'm terrible, but they ain't said boo to the man yet. Cause he blind and old and don't nobody there need him since they grown up and don't need they skates fixed no more.

"Where we goin, Miss Hazel?" Him knowin all the time.

"First we gonna buy you some dark sunglasses. Then you comin with me to the supermarket so I can pick up tomorrow's dinner, which is goin to be a grand thing proper and you invited. Then we goin to my house."

"That be fine. I surely would like to rest my feet." Bein cute, but you got to let men play out they little show, blind or not. So he chat on bout how tired he is and how he appreciate me takin him in hand this way. And I'm thinkin I'll have him change the lock on my door first thing. Then I'll give the man a nice warm bath with jasmine leaves in the water and a little Epsom salt on the sponge to do his back. And then a good rubdown with rose water and olive oil. Then a cup of lemon tea with a taste in it. And a little talcum, some of that fancy stuff Nisi mother sent over last Christmas. And then a massage, a good face massage round the forehead which is the worryin part. Cause you gots to take care of the older folks. And let them know they still needed to run the mimeo machine and keep the spark plugs clean and fix the mailboxes for folks who might help us get the breakfast program goin, and the school for the little kids and the campaign and all. Cause old folks in the nation. That what Nisi was sayin and I mean to do my part.

"I imagine you are a very pretty woman, Miss Hazel."

"I surely am," I say just like the hussy my daughter always say I was.

Suggestions for Discussion

1. How is the narrator, Hazel, characterized by her syntax? Her imagery?

2. How does the dialogue of the children differentiate them from Hazel? From each other?

3. One of the difficulties of a story told in the first person is that the narrator can't describe herself from the outside. How does Hazel let us know what she looks like?

4. Take any passage of dialogue between mother and children and observe how consistently the characters are saying "no" to each other.

5. Identify moments of decision and discovery in the pattern of changes. How does Hazel change?

6. Where are Hazel's thoughts in contrast to her speech, action, and/or appearance?

Everything That Rises Must Converge

FLANNERY O'CONNOR

Her Doctor had told Julian's mother that she must lose twenty pounds on account of her blood pressure, so on Wednesday nights Julian had to take her downtown on the bus for a reducing class at the Y. The reducing class was designed for working girls over fifty, who weighed from 165 to 200 pounds. His mother was one of the slimmer ones, but she said ladies did not tell their age or weight. She would not ride the buses by herself at night since they had been integrated, and because the reducing class was one of her few pleasures, necessary for her health, and *free,* she said Julian could at least put himself out to take her, considering all she did for him. Julian did not like to consider all she did for him, but every Wednesday night he braced himself and took her.

She was almost ready to go, standing before the hall mirror, putting on her hat, while he, his hands behind him, appeared pinned to the door frame, waiting like Saint Sebastian for the arrows to begin piercing him. The hat was new and had cost her seven dollars and a half. She kept saying, "Maybe I shouldn't have paid that for it. No, I shouldn't have. I'll take it off and return it tomorrow. I shouldn't have bought it."

Julian raised his eyes to heaven. "Yes, you should have bought it," he said. "Put it on and let's go." It was a hideous hat. A purple velvet flap came down on one side of it and stood up on the other; the rest of it was green and looked like a cushion with the stuffing out. He decided it was less comical than jaunty and pathetic. Everything that gave her pleasure was small and depressed him.

She lifted the hat one more time and set it down slowly on top of her head. Two wings of gray hair protruded on their side of her florid face, but her eyes, sky-blue, were as innocent and untouched by experience as they must have been when she was ten. Were it not that she was a widow who had struggled fiercely to feed and clothe and put him through school and who was supporting him still, "until he got on his feet," she might have been a little girl that he had to take to town.

"It's all right, it's all right," he said. "Let's go." He opened the door himself and started down the walk to get her going. The sky was a dying violet and the houses stood out darkly against it, bulbous liver-colored monstrosities of a uniform ugliness though no two were alike. Since this had been a fashionable neighborhood forty years ago, his mother persisted in thinking they did well to have an apartment in it. Each house had a narrow collar of dirt around it in which sat, usually, a grubby child. Julian walked with his hands in his pockets, his head down and thrust forward and his eyes glazed with the determination to make himself completely numb during the time he would be sacrificed to her pleasure.

The door closed and he turned to find the dumpy figure, surmounted by the atrocious hat, coming toward him. "Well," she said, "you only live once and paying a little more for it, I at least won't meet myself coming and going."

"Some day I'll start making money," Julian said gloomily—he knew he never would—"and you can have one of those jokes whenever you take the fit." But first they would move. He visualized a place where the nearest neighbors would be three miles away on either side.

"I think you're doing fine," she said, drawing on her gloves. "You've only been out of school a year. Rome wasn't built in a day."

She was one of the few members of the Y reducing class who arrived in hat and gloves and who had a son who had been to college. "It takes time," she said, "and the world is in such a mess. This hat looked better on me than any of the others, though when she brought it out I said, 'Take that thing back. I wouldn't have it on my head,' and she said, 'Now wait till you see it on,' and when she put it on me I said, 'We-ull,' and she said, 'If you ask me, that hat does something for you and you do something for the hat, and besides,' she said, 'with that hat, you won't meet yourself coming and going.'"

Julian thought he could have stood his lot better if she had been selfish, if she had been an old hag who drank and screamed at him. He walked along, saturated in depression, as if in the midst of his martyrdom he had lost his faith. Catching sight of his long, hopeless, irritated face, she stopped suddenly with a grief-stricken look, and pulled back on his arm. "Wait on me," she said. "I'm going back to the house and take this thing off and tomorrow I'm going to return it. I was out of my head. I can pay the gas bill with that seven-fifty."

He caught her arm in a vicious grip. "You are not going to take it back," he said. "I like it."

"Well," she said, " I don't think I ought. . . ."

"Shut up and enjoy it," he muttered, more depressed than ever.

"With the world in the mess it's in," she said, "it's a wonder we can enjoy anything. I tell you, the bottom rail is on the top."

Julian sighed.

"Of course," she said, "if you know who you are, you can go anywhere." She said this every time he took her to the reducing class. "Most of them in it are not our kind of people," she said, "but I can be gracious to anybody. I know who I am."

"They don't give a damn for your graciousness," Julian said savagely. "Knowing who you are is good for one generation only. You haven't the foggiest idea where you stand now or who you are."

She stopped and allowed her eyes to flash at him. "I most certainly do know who I am," she said, "and if you don't know who you are, I'm ashamed of you."

"Oh hell," Julian said.

"Your great-grandfather was a former governor of this state," she said. "Your grandfather was a prosperous landowner. Your grandmother was a God-high."

"Will you look around you," he said tensely, "and see where you are now?" and he swept his arm jerkily out to indicate the neighborhood, which the growing darkness at least made less dingy.

"You remain what you are," she said. "Your great-grandfather had a plantation and two hundred slaves."

"There are no more slaves," he said irritably.

"They were better off when they were," she said. He groaned to see that she was off on that topic. She rolled onto it every few days like a train on an open track. He knew every stop, every junction, every swamp along the way, and knew the exact point at which her conclusion would roll majestically into the station: "It's ridiculous. It's simply not realistic. They should rise, yes, but on their own side of the fence."

"Let's skip it," Julian said.

"The ones I feel sorry for," she said, "are the ones that are half white. They're tragic."

"Will you skip it?"

"Suppose we were half white. We would certainly have mixed feelings."

"I have mixed feelings now," he groaned.

"Well let's talk about something pleasant," she said. "I remember going to Grandpa's when I was a little girl. Then the house had double stairways that went up to what was really the second floor—all the cooking was done on the first. I used to like to stay down in the kitchen on account of the way the walls smelled. I would sit with my nose pressed against the plaster and take deep breaths. Actually the place belonged to the Godhighs but your grandfather Chestny paid the mortgage and saved it for them. They were in reduced circumstances," she said, "but reduced or not, they never forgot who they were."

"Doubtless that decayed mansion reminded them," Julian muttered. He never spoke of it without contempt or thought of it without longing. He had seen it once when he was a child before it had been sold. The double stairways had rotted and been torn down. Negroes were living in it. But it remained in his mind as his mother had known it. It appeared in his dreams regularly. He would stand on the wide porch, listening to the rustle of oak leaves, then wander through the high-ceilinged hall into the parlor that opened onto it and gaze at the worn rugs and faded draperies. It occurred to him that it was he, not she, who could have appreciated it. He preferred its threadbare elegance to anything he could name and it was because of it that all the neighborhoods they had lived in had been a torment to him—whereas she had hardly known the difference. She called her insensitivity "being adjustable."

"And I remember the old darky who was my nurse, Caroline. There was no better person in the world. I've always had a great respect for my colored friends," she said. "I'd do anything in the world for them and they'd. . . ."

"Will you for God's sake get off that subject?" Julian said. When he got on a bus by himself, he made it a point to sit down beside a Negro, in reparation as it were for his mother's sins.

"You're mighty touchy tonight," she said. "Do you feel all right?"

"Yes, I feel all right," he said. "Now lay off."

She pursed her lips. "Well, you certainly are in a vile humor," she observed. "I just won't speak to you at all."

They had reached the bus stop. There was no bus in sight and Julian, his hands still jammed in his pockets and his head thrust forward, scowled down the empty street. The frustration of having to wait on the bus as well as ride on it began to creep up his neck like a hot hand. The presence of his mother was borne in upon him as she gave a pained sigh. He looked at her bleakly. She was holding herself very erect under the preposterous hat, wearing it like a banner of her imaginary dignity. There was in him an evil urge to break her spirit. He suddenly loosened his tie and pulled it off and put it in his pocket.

She stiffened. "Why must you look like *that* when you take me to town?" she said. "Why must you deliberately embarrass me?"

"If you'll never learn where you are," he said, "you can at least learn where I am."

"You look like a—thug," she said.

"Then I must be one," he murmured.

"I'll just go home," she said. "I will not bother you. If you can't do a little thing like that for me . . ."

Rolling his eyes upward, he put his tie back on. "Restored to my class," he muttered. He thrust his face toward her and hissed. "True culture is in the mind, the *mind*," he said, and tapped his head, "the mind."

"It's in the heart," she said, "and in how you do things and how you do things is because of who you *are*."

"Nobody in the damn bus cares who you are."

"I care who I am," she said icily.

The lighted bus appeared on top of the next hill and as it approached, they moved out into the street to meet it. He put his hand under her elbow and hoisted her up on the creaking step. She entered with a little smile, as if she were going into a drawing room where everyone had been waiting for her. While he put in the tokens, she sat down on one of the broad front seats for three which faced the aisle. A thin woman with protruding teeth and long yellow hair was sitting on the end of it. His mother moved up beside her and left room for Julian beside herself. He sat down and looked at the floor across the aisle where a pair of thin feet in red and white canvas sandals were planted.

His mother immediately began a general conversation meant to attract anyone who felt like talking. "Can it get any hotter?" she said and removed from her purse a folding fan, black with a Japanese scene on it, which she began to flutter before her.

"I reckon it might could," the woman with the protruding teeth said, "but I know for a fact my apartment couldn't get no hotter."

"It must get the afternoon sun," his mother said. She sat forward and looked up and down the bus. It was half filled. Everybody was white. "I see we have the bus to ourselves," she said. Julian cringed.

"For a change," said the woman across the aisle, the owner of the red and white canvas sandals. "I come on one the other day and they were thick as fleas—up front and all through."

"The world is in a mess everywhere," his mother said. "I don't know how we've let it get in this fix."

"What gets my goat is all those boys from good families stealing automobile tires," the woman with the protruding teeth said. "I told my boy, I said you may not be rich but you been raised right and if I ever catch you in any such mess, they can send you on to the reformatory. Be exactly where you belong."

"Training tells," his mother said. "Is your boy in high school?"

"Ninth grade," the woman said.

"My son just finished college last year. He wants to write but he's selling typewriters until he gets started," his mother said.

The woman leaned forward and peered at Julian. He threw her such a malevolent look that she subsided against the seat. On the floor across the aisle there was an abandoned newspaper. He got up and got it and opened it out in front of him. His mother discreetly continued the conversation in a lower tone but the woman across the aisle said in a loud voice, "Well that's nice. Selling typewriters is close to writing. He can go right from one to the other."

"I tell him," his mother said, "that Rome wasn't built in a day."

Behind the newspaper Julian was withdrawing into the inner compartment of his mind where he spent most of his time. This was a kind of mental bubble in which he established himself when he could not bear to be a part of what was going on around him. From it he could see out and judge but in it he was safe from any kind of penetration from without. It was the only place where he felt free of the general idiocy of his fellows. His mother had never entered it but from it he could see her with absolute clarity.

The old lady was clever enough and he thought that if she had started from any of the right premises, more might have been expected of her. She lived according to the laws of her own fantasy world, outside of which he had never seen her set foot. The law of it was to sacrifice herself for him after she had first created the necessity to do so by making a mess of things. If he had permitted her sacrifices, it was only because her lack of foresight had made them necessary. All of her life had been a struggle to act like a Chestny without the Chestny goods, and to give him everything she thought a Chestny ought to have; but since, said she, it was fun to struggle, why complain? And when you had won, as she had won, what fun to look back on the hard times! He could not forgive her that she had enjoyed the struggle and that she thought *she* had won.

What she meant when she said she had won was that she had brought him up successfully and had sent him to college and that he had turned out so well—good looking (her teeth had gone unfilled so that his could be straightened), intelligent (he realized he was too intelligent to be a success), and with a future ahead of him (there was of course no future ahead of him). She excused his gloominess on the grounds that he was still growing up and his radical ideas on his lack of practical experience. She said he didn't yet know a thing about "life," that he hadn't even entered the real world—when already he was as disenchanted with it as a man of fifty.

The further irony of all this was that in spite of her, he had turned out so well. In spite of going to only a third-rate college, he had, on his own initiative, come out with a first-rate education; in spite of growing up dominated by a small mind, he had ended up with a large one; in spite of all her foolish views, he was free of prejudice and unafraid to face facts. Most miraculous of all, instead of being blinded by love for her as she was for him, he had cut himself emotionally free of her and could see her with complete objectivity. He was not dominated by his mother.

The bus stopped with a sudden jerk and shook him from his meditation. A woman from the back lurched forward with little steps and barely escaped falling in his newspaper as she righted herself. She got off and a large Negro got on. Julian kept his paper lowered to watch. It gave him a certain satisfaction to see injustice in daily operation. It confirmed his view that with a few exceptions there was no one worth knowing within a radius of three hundred miles. The Negro was well dressed and carried a briefcase. He looked around and then sat down on the other end of the seat where the woman with the red and white canvas sandals was sitting. He immediately unfolded a newspaper and obscured himself behind it. Julian's mother's elbow at once prodded insistently into his ribs. "Now you see why I won't ride on these buses by myself," she whispered.

The woman with the red and white canvas sandals had risen at the same time the Negro sat down and had gone further back in the bus and taken the seat of the woman who had got off. His mother leaned forward and cast her an approving look.

Julian rose, crossed the aisle, and sat down in the place of the woman with the canvas sandals. From this position, he looked serenely across at his mother. Her face had turned an angry red. He stared at her, making his eyes the eyes of a stranger. He felt his tension suddenly lift as if he had openly declared war on her.

He would have liked to get in conversation with the Negro and to talk with him about art or politics or any subject that would be above the comprehension of those around him, but the man remained entrenched behind his paper. He was either ignoring the change of seating or had never noticed it. There was no way for Julian to convey his sympathy.

His mother kept her eyes fixed reproachfully on his face. The woman with the protruding teeth was looking at him avidly as if he were a type of monster new to her.

"Do you have a light?" he asked the Negro.

Without looking away from his paper, the man reached into his pocket and handed him a packet of matches.

"Thanks," Julian said. For a moment he held the matches foolishly. A NO SMOKING sign looked down upon him from over the door. This alone would not have deterred him; he had no cigarettes. He had quit smoking some months before because he could not afford it. "Sorry," he muttered and handed back the matches. The Negro lowered the paper and gave him an annoyed look. He took the matches and raised the paper again.

His mother continued to gaze at him but she did not take advantage of his momentary discomfort. Her eyes retained their battered look. Her face seemed to be unnaturally red, as if her blood pressure had risen. Julian allowed no glimmer of sympathy to show on his face. Having got the advantage, he wanted desperately to keep it and carry it through. He would have liked to teach her a lesson that would last her a while, but there seemed no way to continue the point. The Negro refused to come out from behind his paper.

Julian folded his arms and looked stolidly before him, facing her but as if he did not see her, as if he had ceased to recognize her existence. He visualized a scene in which, the bus having reached their stop, he would remain in his seat and when she said, "Aren't you going to get off?" he would look at her as at a stranger who had rashly addressed him. The corner they got off on was usually deserted, but it was well lighted and it would not hurt her to walk by herself the four blocks to the Y. He decided to wait until the time came and then decide whether or not he would let her get off by herself. He would have to be at the Y at ten to bring her back, but he could leave her wondering if he was going to show up. There was no reason for her to think she could always depend on him.

He retired again into the high-ceilinged room sparsely settled with large pieces of antique furniture. His soul expanded momentarily but then he became aware of his mother across from him and the vision shriveled. He studied her coldly. Her feet in little pumps dangled like a child's and did not quite reach the floor. She was training on him an exaggerated look of reproach. He felt completely detached from her. At that moment he could with pleasure have slapped her as he would have slapped a particularly obnoxious child in his charge.

He began to imagine various unlikely ways by which he could teach her a lesson. He might make friends with some distinguished Negro professor or lawyer and bring him home to spend the evening. He would be entirely justified but her blood pressure would rise to 300. He could not push her to the extent of making her have a stroke, and moreover, he had never been successful at making any Negro friends. He had tried to strike up an acquaintance on the bus with some of the better types, with ones that looked like professors or ministers or lawyers. One morning he had sat down next to a distinguished-looking dark brown man who had answered his questions with a sonorous solemnity but who had turned out to be an undertaker. Another day he had sat down beside a cigar-smoking Negro with a diamond ring on his finger, but after a few stilted pleasantries, the Negro had rung the buzzer and risen, slipping two lottery tickets into Julian's hand as he climbed over him to leave.

He imagined his mother lying desperately ill and his being able to secure only a Negro doctor for her. He toyed with that idea for a few minutes and then dropped it for a momentary vision of himself participating as a sympathizer in a sit-in demonstration. This was possible but he did not linger with it. Instead, he approached the ultimate horror. He brought home a beautiful suspiciously Negroid woman. Prepare yourself, he said. There is nothing you can do about it. This is the woman I've chosen. She's intelligent, dignified, even good, and she's suffered and she hasn't thought it *fun*. Now persecute us, go ahead and persecute us. Drive her out of here, but remember, you're driving me too. His eyes were narrowed and through the indignation he had generated, he saw his mother across the aisle, purple-faced, shrunken to the dwarf-like proportions of her moral nature, sitting like a mummy beneath the ridiculous banner of her hat.

He was tilted out of his fantasy again as the bus stopped. The door opened with a sucking hiss and out of the dark a large, gaily dressed, sullen-looking colored woman got on with a little boy. The child, who might have been four, had on a short plaid suit and a Tyrolean hat with a blue feather in it. Julian hoped that he would sit down beside him and that the woman would push in beside his mother. He could think of no better arrangement.

As she waited for her tokens, the woman was surveying the seating possibilities—he hoped with the idea of sitting where she was least wanted. There was something familiar-looking about her but Julian could not place what it was. She was a giant of a woman. Her face was set not only to meet opposition but to seek it out. The downward tilt of her large lower lip was like a warning sign: DON'T TAMPER WITH ME. Her bulging figure was encased in a green crepe dress and her feet overflowed in red shoes. She had on a hideous hat. A purple velvet flap came down on one side of it and stood up on the other; the rest of it was green and looked like a cushion with the stuffing out. She carried a mammoth red pocketbook that bulged throughout as if it were stuffed with rocks.

To Julian's disappointment, the little boy climbed up on the empty seat beside his mother. His mother lumped all children, black and white, into the common category, "cute," and she thought little Negros were on the whole cuter than little white children. She smiled at the little boy as he climbed on the seat.

Meanwhile the woman was bearing down upon the empty seat beside Julian. To his annoyance, she squeezed herself into it. He saw his mother's face change as the woman settled herself next to him and he realized with satisfaction that this was more objectionable to her than it was to him. Her face seemed almost gray and there was a look of dull recognition in her eyes, as if suddenly she had sickened at some awful confrontation. Julian saw that it was because she and the woman had, in a sense, swapped sons. Though his mother would not realize the symbolic significance of this, she would feel it. His amusement showed plainly on his face.

The woman next to him muttered something unintelligible to herself. He was conscious of a kind of bristling next to him, a muted growling like that of an angry cat. He could not see anything but the red pocketbook upright on the bulging green thighs. He visualized the woman as she had stood waiting for her tokens—the ponderous figure, rising from the red shoes upward over the solid hips, the mammoth bosom, the haughty face, to the green and purple hat.

His eyes widened.

The vision of the two hats, identical, broke upon him with the radiance of a brilliant sunrise. His face was suddenly lit with joy. He could not believe that Fate had thrust upon his mother such a lesson. He gave a loud chuckle so that she would look at him and see that he saw. She turned her eyes on him slowly. The blue in them seemed to have turned a bruised purple. For a moment he had an uncomfortable sense of her innocence, but it lasted only a second before principle rescued him. Justice entitled him to laugh. His grin hardened until it said to her as plainly as if he were saying aloud: Your punishment exactly fits your pettiness. This should teach you a permanent lesson.

Her eyes shifted to the woman. She seemed unable to bear looking at him and to find the woman preferable. He became conscious again of the bristling presence at his side. The woman was rumbling like a volcano about to become active. His mother's mouth began to twitch slightly at one corner. With a sinking heart, he saw incipient signs of recovery on her face and realized that this was going to strike her suddenly as funny and was going to be no lesson at all. She kept her eyes on the woman and an amused smile came over her face as if the woman were a monkey that had stolen her hat. The little Negro was looking up at her with large fascinated eyes. He had been trying to attract her attention for some time.

"Carver!" the woman said suddenly. "Come heah!"

When he saw that the spotlight was on him at last, Carver drew his feet up and turned himself toward Julian's mother and giggled.

"Carver!" the woman said. "You heah me? Come heah!"

Carver slid down from the seat but remained squatting with his back against the base of it, his head turned slyly around toward Julian's mother, who was smiling at him. The woman reached a hand across the aisle and snatched him to her. He righted himself and hung backwards on her knees, grinning at Julian's mother. "Isn't he cute?" Julian's mother said to the woman with the protruding teeth.

"I reckon he is," the woman said without conviction.

The Negress yanked him upright but he eased out of her grip and shot across the aisle and scrambled, giggling wildly, onto the seat beside his love.

"I think he likes me," Julian's mother said, and smiled at the woman. It was the smile she used when she was being particularly gracious to an inferior. Julian saw everything lost. The lesson had rolled off her like rain on a roof.

The woman stood up and yanked the little boy off the seat as if she were snatching him from contagion. Julian could feel the rage in her at having no weapon like his mother's smile. She gave the child a sharp slap across his leg. He howled once and then thrust his head into her stomach and kicked his feet against her shins. "Be-have," she said vehemently.

The bus stopped and the Negro who had been reading the newspaper got off. The woman moved over and set the little boy down with a thump between herself and Julian. She held him firmly by the knee. In a moment he put his hands in front of his face and peeped at Julian's mother through his fingers.

"I see yoooooooo!" she said and put her hand in front of her face and peeped at him.

The woman slapped his hand down. "Quit yo' foolishness," she said, "before I knock the living Jesus out of you!"

Julian was thankful that the next stop was theirs. He reached up and pulled the cord. The woman reached up and pulled it at the same time. Oh my God, he thought. He had the terrible intuition that when they got off the bus together, his mother would open her purse and give the little boy a nickel. The gesture would be as natural to her as breathing. The bus stopped and the woman got up and lunged to the front, dragging the child, who wished to stay on, after her. Julian and his mother got up and followed. As they neared the door, Julian tried to relieve her of her pocketbook.

"No," she murmured. "I want to give the little boy a nickel."

"No!" Julian hissed. "No!"

She smiled down at the child and opened her bag. The bus door opened and the woman picked him up by the arm and descended with him, hanging at her hip. Once in the street she set him down and shook him.

Julian's mother had to close her purse while she got down the bus step but as soon as her feet were on the ground, she opened it again and began to rummage inside. "I can't find but a penny," she whispered, "but it looks like a new one."

"Don't do it!" Julian said fiercely between his teeth. There was a streetlight on the corner and she hurried to get under it so she could better see into her pocketbook. The woman was heading off rapidly down the street with the child still hanging backward on her hand.

"Oh little boy!" Julian's mother called and took a few quick steps and caught up with them just beyond the lamp-post. "Here's a bright new penny for you," and she held out the coin, which shone bronze in the dim light.

The huge woman turned and for a moment stood, her shoulders lifted and her face frozen with frustrated rage, and stared at Julian's mother. Then all at once she seemed to explode like a piece of machinery that had been given one ounce of pressure too much. Julian saw the black fist swing out with the red pocketbook. He shut his eyes and cringed as he heard the woman shout, "He don't take nobody's pennies!" When he opened his eyes, the woman was disappearing down the street with the little boy staring wide-eyed over her shoulder. Julian's mother was sitting on the sidewalk.

"I told you not to do that," Julian said angrily. "I told you not to do that!"

He stood over her for a minute, gritting his teeth. Her legs were stretched out in front of her and her hat was on her lap. He squatted down and looked her in the face. It was totally expressionless. "You got exactly what you deserved," he said. "Now get up."

He picked up her pocketbook and put what had fallen out back in it. He picked the hat up off her lap. The penny caught his eye on the sidewalk and he picked that up and let it drop before her eyes into the purse. Then he stood up and leaned over and held his hands out to pull her up. She remained immobile. He sighed. Rising above them on either side were black apartment buildings, marked with irregular rectangles of light. At the end of the block a man came out of a door and walked off in the opposite direction. "All right," he said, "suppose somebody happens by and wants to know why you're sitting on the sidewalk?"

She took the hand and, breathing hard, pulled heavily up on it and then stood for a moment, swaying slightly as if the spots of light in the darkness were circling around her. Her eyes, shadowed and confused, finally settled on his face. He did not try to conceal his irritation. "I hope this teaches you a lesson," he said. She leaned forward and her eyes raked his face. She seemed trying to determine his identity. Then, as if she found nothing familiar about him, she started off with a headlong movement in the wrong direction.

"Aren't you going on to the Y?" he asked.

"Home," she muttered.

"Well, are we walking?"

For answer she kept going. Julian followed along, his hands behind him. He saw no reason to let the lesson she had had go without backing it up with an explanation of its meaning. She might as well be made to understand what had happened to her. "Don't think that was just an uppity Negro woman," he said. "That was the whole colored race which will no longer take your condescending pennies. That was your black double. She can wear the same hat as you, and to be sure," he added gratuitously (because he thought it was funny), "it looked better on her than it did on you. What all this means," he said, "is that the old world is gone. The old manners are obsolete and your graciousness is not worth a damn." He thought bitterly of the house that had been lost for him. "You aren't who you think you are," he said.

She continued to plow ahead, paying no attention to him. Her hair had come undone on one side. She dropped her pocketbook and took no notice. He stooped and picked it up and handed it to her but she did not take it.

"You needn't act as if the world had come to an end," he said, "because it hasn't. From now on you've got to live in a new world and face a few realities for a change. Buck up," he said, "it won't kill you."

She was breathing fast.

"Let's wait on the bus," he said.

"Home," she said thickly.

"I hate to see you behave like this," he said. "Just like a child. I should be able to expect more of you." He decided to stop where he was and make her stop and wait for a bus. "I'm not going any farther," he said, stopping. "We're going on the bus."

She continued to go on as if she had not heard him. He took a few steps and caught her arm and stopped her. He looked into her face and caught his breath. He was looking into a face he had never seen before. "Tell Grandpa to come get me," she said.

He stared, stricken.

"Tell Caroline to come get me," she said.

Stunned, he let her go and she lurched forward again, walking as if one leg were shorter than the other. A tide of darkness seemed to be sweeping her from him. "Mother!" he cried. "Darling, sweetheart, wait!" Crumpling, she fell to the pavement. He dashed forward and fell at her side, crying, "Mamma! Mamma!" He turned her over. Her face was fiercely distorted. One eye, large and staring, moved slightly to the left as if it had become unmoored. The other remained fixed on him, raked his face again, found nothing and closed.

"Wait here, wait here!" he cried and jumped up and began to run for help toward a cluster of lights he saw in the distance ahead of him. "Help, help!" he shouted, but his voice was thin, scarcely a thread of sound. The lights drifted farther away the faster he ran and his feet moved numbly as if they carried him nowhere. The tide of darkness seemed to sweep him back to her, postponing from moment to moment his entry into the world of guilt and sorrow.

Suggestions for Discussion

1. This story contains a conflict about "color," black and white. In what way does O'Connor use details of bright color—red, green, purple, yellow—to bring this conflict into focus? How do these colors further the plot?

2. Find four instances in which Julian's behavior contradicts his thoughts. Does his behavior nevertheless betray his thoughts?

3. How does the use of cliché help to characterize the mother through her speech? Examine the dialogue; how many things does it do besides convey information?

4. Plot the pattern of change through all of the discoveries and decisions. Note how deeds and actions result in and cause these dramatic changes in the characters.

5. The crisis action of the story is a discovery. What is it?

6. How, through his actions, do we understand the thoughts of the Negro man on the bus? How does O'Connor direct our sympathy toward him and away from Julian?

7. How does the green and purple hat help both to characterize Julian's mother and the Negro woman and to reveal the major conflict of the story?

RETROSPECT

1. Compare "My Man Bovanne," in which the younger generation berates the older, with "Girl," in which the older generation berates the younger. How are the generations contrasted?

2. How do the speech and actions of the doctor in "The Use of Force" contrast with his thoughts? What would be lost in this story if we did not know his thoughts?

3. Find the pattern of discovery and decision in "Mockingbird."

WRITING ASSIGNMENTS

1. Write a character sketch employing the four elements of direct presentation: appearance, action, speech, and thought. Use no authorial interpretation. Put one element in conflict with the other three.

2. Write a scene in which the central character does something palpably outrageous—violent, cruel, foolhardy, obscene. Let us, because we see into his or her mind, know that the character is behaving justly, kindly, or reasonably.

3. Write a character sketch describing the character both in generalizations (authorial interpretation) and in specific details. Let the details contradict the generalizations. ("Larry was the friendliest kid on the block. He had a collection of brass knucks he would let you see for fifty cents, and he would let you cock his BB gun for him as long as you were willing to hold the target.")

4. Write a scene in which a man (or boy) questions a woman (or girl) about her mother. Characterize all three.

5. Two friends are in love with the same person. One describes his or her feelings honestly and well; the other is unwilling or unable to do so, but betrays his or her feelings through appearance and action. Write the scene.

6. Write a scene in which the mood changes. When it's done take a look. Why did the mood change? Is there a discovery?

7. Nearly every writer under pressure of a deadline at some point succumbs to the temptation of writing a story about writing a story. These stories are rarely successful because they offer so few possibilities of external conflict and lively characterization. So write this story: You must write a short story, and you must therefore get your major character to do whatever he or she is to do in the story. But the character is too lazy, irritable, sick, suicidal, cruel, stupid, frivolous, or having too good a time. You must trick, cajole, or force the character into the story. Do you succeed?

6

CLIMATE CONTROL
Atmosphere

Narrative Place: Setting
Narrative Time

Your fiction must have an atmosphere because without it your characters will be unable to breathe.

Like many of the terms that relate to the elements of fiction, *atmosphere* has more than one meaning, sometimes referring to subject matter, sometimes to technique. Part of the atmosphere of a scene or story is its setting, which includes the locale, period, weather, and time of day. Part of the atmosphere is its *tone*, an attitude taken by the narrative voice that can be described not in terms of time and place, but as a quality—sinister, facetious, formal, solemn, wry, and so on. There is difficulty in discussing a term that has both a content meaning and a technical meaning: The two meanings need to be kept distinct for the sake of clarity; yet at the same time they are often inextricably mixed in the ultimate effect. A sinister atmosphere in a story might be partly achieved by syntax, rhythm, and word choice; partly by night, dampness, and a desolated landscape. We'll encounter the same difficulty discussing *point of view*, where complex literary techniques also include and make use of the mundane meaning of the phrase as "opinion." This chapter deals primarily with atmosphere as setting, the fictional boundaries in space and time, though it will not be possible to deal with those elements without reference to tone. Since tone, however, implies an attitude not only toward the setting, but also toward the characters and the reader, it will be more fully discussed in chapter 8 on point of view, under the heading "At What Distance?"

Narrative Place: Setting

HARMONY AND CONFLICT
BETWEEN CHARACTER AND BACKGROUND

If character is the foreground of fiction, setting is the background, and as in a painting's composition, the foreground may be in harmony or in conflict with the background. If we think of the Impressionist paintings of the late nineteenth century, we think of the harmony of, say, women with light-scattering parasols strolling against summer landscapes of light-scattering trees. By contrast, the Spanish painter José Cortijo has a portrait of a girl on her Communion day; she sits curled and ruffled, in a lace mantilla, on an ornately carved Mediterranean throne— against a backdrop of stark, harshly lit, poverty-stricken shacks. It will be clear from this illustration that where there is a conflict between background and foreground, between character and setting, there is already "narrative content," or the makings of a story.

But whether there is conflict between character and setting or the conflict takes place entirely in the foreground, within, between, or among the characters, the setting is important to our understanding of type and of what to expect, as well as to the emotional value that arises from the conflict. As we need to know a character's gender, race, and age, we need to know in what atmosphere she or he operates to understand the significance of the action.

The world and its creatures are essentially materialistic—composed of matter and in constant relation to matter. Our relation to place, time, and weather, like our relation to clothes and other objects, is charged with emotion more or less subtle, more or less profound. It is filled with judgment mellow or harsh. And it alters according to what happens to us. In some rooms you are always trapped; you enter them with grim purpose and escape them as soon as you can. Others invite you to settle in, to nestle or carouse. Some landscapes lift your spirits; others depress you. Cold weather gives you energy and bounce, or else it clogs your head and makes you huddle, struggling. You describe yourself as a "night person" or a "morning person." The house you loved as a child now makes you, precisely because you were once happy there, think of loss and death.

All such emotion can be used or heightened (or invented) to dramatic effect in fiction. Just as significant detail calls up a sense impression and also an abstraction, so the setting of a story imparts both information and emotion. Likewise, just as the rhythm of your prose may be more or less important but must work with and not against your intention, so the use of setting may be more or less vital, but it must work with and not against your ultimate meaning. In the Cortijo painting previously described, the communicant in the foreground is in disharmony with the houses in the background; but the contrast is part of the harmony of the composition as a whole: It is the point of the painting.

As I write, part of me is impatient with these speculations. Dully aware that every discussion of the elements of fiction includes of necessity the notions of atmosphere, setting, and tone, I have an impulse to deal with the matter summarily and get on to the next chapter: Events occur in time and through time; people move in space and through space. Therefore, let your story occur during some time and in some place, and take some attitude or other.

But part of me is aware of a dull March day outside my window, a stubbled field of muddy snow, the students' heels sucked by the thawing path, the rubble of winter without any sign that the contract for spring is in the mail. The river is frozen to the bridge and breaking up fitfully below; ice fidgets at the bank. This morning, stretching too far in a series of sit-ups, I pulled my back out of joint, and now my movements are confined; my spine reaches cautiously for the back of the chair, and my hand moves gingerly toward my tea. The dullness in myself looks for dullness in the day, finds it, and creates it there.

And so, observing this, part of me is impelled toward awe at the boundaries of time and space imposed on human beings and on their fictions, and yet always pulling them toward a wider context. Why must a story be set during some time and in some place, and why does the choice inevitably matter? Psychologists have determined that one of the earliest processes of a child's mental development is the differentiation between self and other. Until the infant discovers that its mother is not itself, it has no sense of self as we know it. Yet even before this discovery it has instinctive reactions to the elements, to warmth, cold, damp. As the mind develops it becomes aware of its environment, both social and physical, and hard on the heels of this awareness comes the attempt to control and manipulate: crying for mama, grasping the bars of the crib.

Biologists point out that the cells of our blood and bodies change according to the season, like the sap of trees, so that "spring fever" is a physical fact. The blood will thin and thicken in response to climate on the zones of the globe. The pupils of our eyes expand at night, contract by day. The new science of bioecology posits the theory that people adapt over generations to their habitat and that what we call nervous, mental, and emotional disorders may in fact be allergies of the blood and brain to food grown in alien soil.

Some linguists posit the theory that language itself originates in prepositions— that is, that spatial relationships are the primary function of the mind, and our perceptions of *above, below, toward, beyond,* and so on precede any other element in the structure of logical expression.

Whether or not these linguists are right, it is certainly so that since the rosy-fingered dawn came over the battlefield of Homer's *Iliad* (and no doubt well before that), poets and writers have used the context of history, night, storm, stars, sea, city, and plain to give their stories a sense of reaching out toward the universe. Sometimes the universe resonates with an answer. In his plays Shakespeare consistently drew parallels between the conflicts of the heavenly bodies and the conflicts of nations and characters. Whether or not an author deliberately uses this correspondence to suggest the influence of the macrocosm on the microcosm, a story's setting can give the significant sense of other without which, as in an infant's consciousness, there is no valid sense of self.

In "The Life You Save May Be Your Own," Flannery O'Connor uses the elements in a conscious Shakespearian way, letting the setting reflect and effect the theme.

> The old woman and her daughter were sitting on their own porch when Mr. Shiflet came up their road for the first time. The old woman slid to the edge of her chair and leaned forward, shading her eyes from the piercing sunset with her hand. The daughter could not see far in front of her and continued to play with her fingers. Although the old woman lived in this desolate spot with only her daughter, and she had never seen Mr. Shiflet before, she could tell, even from a distance, that he was a tramp and no one to be afraid of. His left coat sleeve was folded up to show there was only half an arm in it and his gaunt figure listed lightly to the side as if the breeze were pushing him. He had on a black town suit and a brown felt hat that was turned up in the front and down in the back and he carried a tin tool box by a handle. He came on at an amble, up her road, his face turned toward the sun which appeared to be balancing itself on the peak of a small mountain.

The focus in this opening paragraph of the story is on the characters and their actions, and the setting is economically, almost incidentally established: *porch, road, sunset, breeze, peak, small mountain.* What the passage gives us is a "type" of landscape, rural and harsh; the only adjectives in the description of the setting are "piercing," "desolate," and "small." But this general background works together with details of action, thought, and appearance to establish a great deal more that is both informational and emotional. The old woman's peering suggests that people on the road are not only unusual but suspicious. On the other hand, that she is reassured to see a tramp suggests both a period and a set of assumptions about country life. That Mr. Shiflet wears a "town suit" establishes him as a stranger to this set of assumptions. That the sun "appeared to be balancing itself" (we are not sure whether it is the old woman's observation or the author's) leaves us, at the end of the paragraph, with a sense of anticipation and tension.

Now, what happens in the story is this: Mr. Shiflet repairs the old woman's car and (in order to get the car) marries her retarded daughter. He abandons the daughter on their "honeymoon" and picks up a hitchhiker who insults both Mr. Shiflet and the memory of his mother. The hitchhiker jumps out. Mr. Shiflet curses and drives on.

Throughout the story, as in the first paragraph, the focus remains on the characters and their actions. Yet the landscape and the weather make their presence felt, subtly commenting on attitudes and actions. As Mr. Shiflet's fortunes wax promising and he expresses satisfaction with his own morality, "A fat yellow moon appeared in the branches of the fig tree as if it were going to roost there with the chickens." When, hatching his plot, he sits on the steps with the mother and daughter, "The old woman's three mountains were black against the sky." Once he has abandoned the girl, the weather grows "hot and sultry, and the country had flattened out. Deep in the sky a storm was preparing very slowly and without thunder." Once more there is a sunset, but this time the sun "was a reddening ball that through his windshield was slightly flat on the bottom and top," and this deflated sun reminds us of the "balanced" one about to be punctured by the peak in its inevitable decline. When the hitchhiker has left him, a cloud covers the sun, and Mr. Shiflet in his fury prays for the Lord to "break forth and wash the slime from this earth!" His prayer is apparently answered.

> After a few minutes there was a guffawing peal of thunder from behind and fantastic raindrops, like tin-can tops, crashed over the rear of Mr. Shiflet's car. Very quickly he stepped on the gas and with his stump sticking out the window he raced the galloping shower to Mobile.

The setting in this story, as this bald summary emphasizes, is deliberately used as a comment on the actions. The behavior of the elements, in ironic juxtaposition to the title, "The Life You Save May Be Your Own," makes clear that the "slime" Mr. Shiflet has damned may be himself. Yet the reader is never aware of this as a symbolic intrusion. The setting remains natural and realistically convincing, as incidental backdrop, until the heavens are ready to make their guffawing comment.

Robert Coover's settings rarely present a symbolic or sentient universe, but they produce in us an emotionally charged expectation of what is likely to happen here. The following passages are the opening paragraphs of three short stories from a single collection, *Pricksongs and Descants*. Notice how the three different settings are achieved not only by imagery and content, but also by the very different rhythms of the sentence structure.

> A pine forest in the midafternoon. Two children follow an old man, dropping breadcrumbs, singing nursery tunes. Dense earthy greens seep into the darkening distance, flecked and streaked with filtered sunlight. Spots of red, violet, pale blue, gold, burnt orange. The girl carries a basket for gathering flowers. The boy is occupied with the crumbs. Their song tells of God's care for little ones.
>
> "The Gingerbread House"

Situation: television panel game, live audience. Stage strobelit and cameras insecting about. Moderator, bag shape corseted and black suited behind desk/rostrum, blinking mockmodesty at lens and lamps, practised pucker on his soft mouth and brows arched in mild goodguy astonishment. Opposite him, the panel: Aged Clown, Lovely Lady and Mr. America, fat as the continent and bald as an eagle. There is an empty chair between Lady and Mr. A, which is now filled, to the delighted squeals of all, by a spectator dragged protesting from the Audience, nondescript introduced as Unwilling Participant, or more simply, Bad Sport. Audience: same as ever, docile, responsive, good-natured, terrifying. And the Bad Sport, you ask, who is he? fool! thou art!

"Panel Game"

She arrives at 7:40, ten minutes late, but the children, Jimmy and Bitsy, are still eating supper, and their parents are not ready to go yet. From the other rooms come the sounds of a baby screaming, water running, a television musical (no words: probably a dance number—patterns of gliding figures come to mind). Mrs. Tucker sweeps into the kitchen, fussing with her hair, and snatches a baby bottle full of milk out of a pan of warm water, rushes out again. "Harry!" she calls. "The babysitter's here already!"

"The Babysitter"

Here are three quite familiar places: a fairy-tale forest, a television studio, and a suburban house. In at least the first two selections, the locale is more consciously and insistently set than in the O'Connor opening, yet all three remain suggestive backdrops rather than active participants. Coover directs our attitude toward these places through imagery and tone. The forest is a neverland, and the time is "once upon a time," though there are grimmer than Grimm hints of violence about it. The television studio is a place of hysteria, chaos, and hypocrisy, whereas the American suburbia, where presumably such television shows are received, is boring rather than chaotic, not hysterical but merely hassled in a predictable sort of way.

In "The Gingerbread House," simple sentence structure helps establish the childlike quality appropriate to a fairy tale. But a more complex sentence intervenes, with surprising intensity of imagery: *dense, earthy, seep, darkening, flecked, streaked, filtered*. Because of this, the innocence of the tone is set askew, so that by the time we hear of "God's care for little ones," we fully and accurately expect a brutal disillusionment.

Note that although all fiction is bounded by place and time, the "place" and "time" may perfectly well be "no place" and "outside time." The failure to create an atmosphere, to bore or confuse us because we have no sense of where or when the story takes place, is always a fault. But an intensely created fantasy world makes new boundaries for the mind. *Once upon a time, long ago and far away, a dream, hell, heaven, time warp, black hole*, and the *subconscious* all have been the settings of excellent fiction. Outer space is an exciting setting precisely because its physical boundary is the outer edge of our familiar world. Obviously this does not absolve the writer from the necessity of giving outer space its own characteristics, atmosphere, and logic. If anything, these must be more intensely realized within the fiction, since we have less to borrow from in our own experience.

Setting can often, and in a variety of ways, arouse reader expectation and foreshadow events to come. In "The Gingerbread House," there is an implied conflict between character and setting, between the sentimentality of the children's flowers and nursery tunes and the threatening forest, so that we are immediately aware of the central conflict of the story: innocence versus violence.

But anticipation can also be aroused by an insistent single attitude toward setting, and in this case the reader, being a contrary sort of person, is likely to anticipate a change or paradox. The opening pages of E. M. Forster's A *Passage to India*, for instance, create an unrelenting portrait of the muddy dreariness of Chadrapore: *nothing extraordinary, rubbish, mean, ineffective, alleys, filth, made of mud, mud moving, abased, monotonous, rotting, swelling, shrinking, low but indestructible form of life.* The images are a little too one-sided, and as we might protest in life against a too fanatical condemnation of a place—isn't there anything good about it?—so we are led to expect (accurately again) that in the pages that follow, somehow beauty and mystery will break forth from the dross. Likewise—but in the opposite way—the opening pages of Woolf's Mrs. *Dalloway* burst with affirmation, the beauty of London and spring, love of life and love of life and love of life again! We suspect (accurately once more) that death and hatred lurk.

Where conflict between character and setting is immediately introduced, as it is in both "The Gingerbread House" and "Panel Game," it is usually because the character is unfamiliar with, or uncomfortable in, the setting. In "Panel Game" it's both. The television studio, which is in fact a familiar and unthreatening place to most of us, has been made mad. Partly, this is achieved by violating expected grammar. The sentences are not sentences. They are missing vital verbs and logical connectives, so that the images are squashed against each other. The prose is cluttered, effortful, negative; as a result, as reader you know the "delighted squeals of all" do not include your own, and you're ready to sympathize with the unwilling central character (you!).

ALIEN AND FAMILIAR SETTING

Many poets and novelists have observed that the function of literature is to make the ordinary fresh and strange. F. Scott Fitzgerald, on the other hand, advised a young writer that reporting extreme things as if they were ordinary was the starting point of fiction. Both of these views are true, and they are particularly true of setting. Whether a place is familiar or unfamiliar, comfortable or discomfiting in fiction has nothing to do with whether the reader actually knows the place and feels good there. It is an attitude taken, an assumption made. In his detective novels, Ross MacDonald assumes a familiarity toward California that is perfectly translatable into Japanese ("I turned left off the highway and down an old switch-back blacktop to a dead end"), whereas even the natives of North Hollywood must feel alien on Tom Wolfe's version of their streets.

> . . . endless scorched boulevards lined with one-story stores, shops, bowling alleys, skating rinks, taco drive-ins, all of them shaped not like rectangles but like trapezoids, from the way the roofs slant up from the back and the plate-glass fronts slant out as if they're going to pitch forward on the sidewalk and throw up.
>
> *The Kandy-Kolored Tangerine-Flake Streamline Baby*

The prose of Tom Wolfe, whether about rural North Carolina, Fifth Avenue, or Cape Kennedy, lives in a tone of constant astonishment. Ray Bradbury's outer space is pure down-home.

> It was quiet in the deep morning of Mars, as quiet as a cool black well, with stars shining in the canal waters, and, breathing in every room, the children curled with their spiders in closed hands.
>
> *Martian Chronicles*

The setting of the passage from Coover's "The Babysitter" is ordinary and is presented as ordinary. The sentences have standard and rather leisurely syntax; neither form nor image startles. In fact, there are few details of the sort that produce interesting individuality: The house is presented without a style; the children are named but not seen; Mrs. Tucker behaves in a way predictable and familiar to anyone in late-twentieth-century America. What Coover has in fact done is to present us with a setting so usual that (in the contrary way of readers) we begin to suspect that something unusual is afoot.

I have said of characterization that if the character is presented as typical, we would judge that character to be stupid or evil. The same is true of setting, but with results more varied and fruitful for an author's ultimate purpose. At the center of a fiction is a consciousness, one as individual and vital as the author can produce. If the setting remains dull and damnable, then there is conflict between character and setting, and this conflict can throw that individuality and vitality into relief. Many great stories and novels have relied on setting as a means of showing the intensity and variety of human consciousness by contrasting consciousness with a social or physical world that is rule-hampered, insincere, and routine. Gustave Flaubert's *Madame Bovary* comes instantly to mind: The fullness and exactitude of the portrait is partly achieved by the provinciality of the background. This provinciality, which is French and nineteenth century, remains typical to American readers of the 1990s, who are much more likely to have grown up in Coover's suburban house. It is Flaubert's tone that creates a sense of the familiar and the typical.

Much the same thing happens in "The Babysitter." The Tuckers, their house, their children, their car, their night out, and their babysitter remain unvaryingly typical through all the external actions in the course of the evening. Against this backdrop play the individual fantasies of the characters—brilliant, brutal, sexual, dangerous, and violent—which provides the conflict of the story.

One great advantage of being a writer is that you may create the world. Places and the elements have the significance and the emotional effect you give them in language. As a person you may be depressed by rain, but as an author you are free to make rain "mean" freshness, growth, bounty, and God. You may choose; the only thing you are not free to do is not to choose.

As with character, the first requisite of effective setting is to know it fully, to experience it mentally; the second is to create it through significant detail. What sort of place is this, and what are its peculiarities? What is the weather like, the light, the season, the time of day? What are the contours of the land and architecture? What are the social assumptions of the inhabitants, and how familiar and comfortable are the characters with this place and its life-style? These things are not less important in fiction than in life, but more, since their selection inevitably takes on significance.

AN EXERCISE IN SETTING

Here are a series of passages about war, set in various periods and places. The first is in Russia during the campaign of Napoleon, the second in Italy during World War I, the third on the island of Pianosa during World War II, the fourth during the Vietnam War, the fifth in a post-holocaust future.

Compare the settings. How do climate, period, imagery, and language contribute to each? To what degree is setting a sentient force? Is there conflict between character and setting? How does setting affect and/or reveal the attitude taken toward the war?

Several tens of thousands of the slain lay in diverse postures and various uniforms. . . . Over the whole field, previously so gaily beautiful with the glitter of bayonets and cloudlets of smoke in the morning sun, there now spread a mist of damp and smoke and a strange acid smell of saltpeter and blood. Clouds gathered and drops of rain began to fall on the dead and wounded, on the frightened, exhausted, and hesitating men, as if to say: "Enough, men! Enough! Cease . . . bethink yourselves! What are you doing?"

LEO TOLSTOY, *War and Peace*

In the late summer of that year we lived in a house in a village that looked across the river and plain to the mountains. In the bed of the river there were pebbles and boulders, dry and white in the sun, and the water was clear and swiftly moving and blue in the channels. Troops went by the house and down the road and the dust they raised powdered the leaves of the trees. The trunks of the trees too were dusty and the leaves fell early that year and we saw the troops marching along the road and the dust rising and leaves, stirred by the breeze, falling and the soldiers marching and afterward the road bare and white except for the leaves.

ERNEST HEMINGWAY, *A Farewell to Arms*

Their only hope was that it would never stop raining, and they had no hope because they all knew it would. When it did stop raining in Pianosa, it rained in Bologna. When it stopped raining in Bologna, it began again in Pianosa. If there was no rain at all, there were freakish, inexplicable phenomena like the epidemic of diarrhea or the bomb line that moved. Four times during the first six days they were assembled and briefed and then sent back. Once, they took off and were flying in formation when the control tower summoned them down. The more it rained, the worse they suffered. The worse they suffered, the more they prayed that it would continue raining.

JOSEPH HELLER, *Catch-22*

The rain fed fungus that grew in the men's boots and socks, and their socks rotted, and their feet turned white and soft so that the skin could be scraped off with a fingernail, and Stink Harris woke up screaming one night with a leech on his tongue. When it was not raining, a low mist moved across the paddies, blending the elements into a single gray element, and the war was cold and pasty and rotten. Lieutenant Corson, who came to replace Lieutenant Sidney Martin, contracted the dysentery. The trip-flares were useless. The ammunition corroded and the foxholes filled with mud and water during the nights, and in the mornings there was always the next village and the war was the same.

TIM O'BRIEN, *Going After Cacciato*

She liked the wild, quatrosyllabic lilt of the word, "Barbarian." Then, looking beyond the wooden fence, she saw a trace of movement in the fields beyond. It was not the wind among the young corn; or, if it was wind among the young corn, it carried her the whinny of a raucous horse. It was too early for poppies but she saw a flare of scarlet. She ceased to watch the Soldiers; instead she watched the movement flow to the fences and crash through them and across the tender wheat. Bursting from the undergrowth came horseman after horseman. . . . They flashed with curious curved plates of metal dredged up from the ruins. Their horses were bizarrely caparisoned with rags, small knives, bells and chains dangling from manes and tails, and man and horse together, unholy centaurs crudely daubed with paint, looked twice as large as life. They fired long guns. Confronted with the terrors of the night in the freshest hours of the morning, the gentle crowd scattered, wailing.

ANGELA CARTER, *Heroes and Villains*

Narrative Time

Literature is, by virtue of its nature and subject matter, tied to time in a way the other arts are not. A painting represents a frozen instant in time, and the "viewing time" is a matter of the viewer's choice; no external limits are imposed in order to say that you have seen the painting. Music takes a certain time to hear, and the timing of the various parts is of utmost importance, but the time scheme is self-enclosed and makes no reference to time in the world outside itself. A book takes time to read, but the reader chooses his or her rate and may put it down and take it up at will. Its vital relationship to time is content time, the period covered in the story. It is quite possible to write a story that takes about twenty minutes to read and covers about twenty minutes of action (Jean-Paul Sartre performed experiments in this "durational realism"), but no one has suggested it as a fictional requirement. Sometimes the period covered is telescoped, sometimes stretched. The history of the world up until now can be covered in a sentence; four seconds of crisis may take a chapter. It's even possible to do both at once: William Golding's entire novel *Pincher Martin* takes place between the time the drowning protagonist begins to take off his boots and the moment he dies with his boots still on. But when asked by a student, "How long does it *really* take?" Golding replied, "Eternity."

SUMMARY AND SCENE

Summary and *scene* are methods of treating time in fiction. A summary covers a relatively long period of time in relatively short compass; a scene deals with a relatively short period of time at length. Summary is a useful and often necessary device: to give information, fill in a character's background, let us understand a motive, alter pace, create a transition, leap moments or years. *Scene is always necessary to fiction.* A confrontation, a turning point, or a crisis occurs at given moments that take on significance *as moments* and cannot be summarized. The form of a story requires confrontation, turning points, and crises, and therefore requires scenes. It is quite possible to write a short story in a single scene, without any summary at all. It is not possible to write a successful story entirely in summary. One of the most common errors beginning fiction writers make is to summarize events rather than to realize them as moments.

In the following paragraph from Margaret Atwood's *Lady Oracle*, the narrator has been walking home from her Brownie troop with older girls who tease and terrify her with threats of a "bad man."

The snow finally changed to slush and then to water, which trickled down the hill of the bridge in two rivulets, one on either side of the path; the path itself turned to mud. The bridge was damp, it smelled rotten, the willow branches turned yellow, the skipping ropes came out. It was light again in the afternoons, and on one of them, when for a change Elizabeth hadn't run off but was merely discussing the possibilities with the others, a real man actually appeared.

He was standing at the far side of the bridge, a little off the path, holding a bunch of daffodils in front of him. He was a nice-looking man, neither old nor young, wearing a good tweed coat, not at all shabby or disreputable. He didn't have a hat on, his taffy-colored hair was receding and the sunlight gleamed on his high forehead.

The first paragraph of this quotation covers the way things were over a period of a few months and then makes a transition to one of the afternoons; the second paragraph specifies a particular moment. Notice that although summary sets us at a distance from the action, sense details remain necessary to its life: *snow, path, bridge, willow branches, skipping ropes.* These become more sharply focused as we concentrate on the particular moment. More important, the scene is introduced when an element of conflict and confrontation occurs. That the threatened "bad man" does appear and that he is surprisingly innocuous promises a turn of events and a change in the relationship among the girls. We need to see the moment when this change occurs.

Throughout *Lady Oracle,* which is by no means unusual in this respect, the pattern recurs: a summary leading up to, and followed by, a scene that represents a turning point.

> My own job was fairly simple. I stood at the back of the archery range, wearing a red leather change apron, and rented out the arrows. When the barrels of arrows were almost used up, I'd go down to the straw targets. . . . The difficulty was that we couldn't make sure all the arrows had actually been shot before we went down to clear the targets. Rob would shout, "Bows DOWN, please, arrows OFF the string," but occasionally someone would let an arrow go, on purpose or by accident. This was how I got shot. We'd pulled the arrows and the men were carrying the barrels back to the line; I was replacing a target face, and I'd just bent over.

The summaries in these two passages are of the two most common types, which I would call *sequential* and *circumstantial,* respectively. The summary in the first passage is sequential; it relates events in their sequence but compresses them: *snow finally changed to slush and then to water, willow branches turned yellow,* and then *skipping ropes came out;* the transition from winter to spring is made in a paragraph. The summary in the second excerpt is circumstantial because it describes the general circumstances during a period of time: This is how things were, this is what usually or frequently happened. The narrator in the second passage describes her job in such a way: *I stood at the back of the archery range. . . . I'd go down to the straw targets. . . . Rob would shout.* Again, when the narrator arrives at an event that changes her circumstance (*I got shot*), she focuses on a particular moment: *I was replacing a target face, and I'd just bent over.*

These two types of summary accurately represent two methods of the memory, which also drastically condenses. You might think of your past as a movement through time: *I was born in Arizona and lived there with my parents until I was eighteen; then I spent three years in New York before going on to England.* Or you might remember the way things were during a period of that time: *In New York we used to go* down Broadway for a midnight snack, and Judy would always dare us to some nonsense or other before we got back. But when you think of the events that significantly altered either the sequence or the circumstances of your life, your mind will present you with a scene: *Then one afternoon Professor Bovie stopped me in the hall after class and wagged his glasses at me. "Had you thought about studying in England?"*

Examining your own mind for these kinds of memory—sequential summary, circumstantial summary, and scene—will help make evident the necessity of scene in fiction. The moments that altered your life you remember at length and in detail; your memory tells you your story, and it is a great natural storyteller.

FLASHBACK

Flashback is one of the most magical of fiction's contrivances, easier and more effective in this medium than in any other, because the reader's mind is a swifter mechanism for getting into the past than anything that has been devised for stage or even film. All you must do is to give the reader smooth passage into the past, and the force of the story will be time-warped to whenever and wherever you want it.

Nevertheless, many beginning writers use unnecessary flashbacks. This happens because flashback can be a useful way to provide background to character or events, and is often seen as the easiest or only way. It isn't. Dialogue, narration, a reference or detail can often tell us all we need to know, and when that is the case, a flashback becomes cumbersome and overlong, taking us from the present where the story and our interest lie. Furthermore, these intrusive passages of childhood, motivation, and explanation tend to come early in the story, before we are caught up in the action. Then we wonder whether there is any story on its way.

If you are tempted to use flashback to fill in the whole past, try using your journal for exploring background. Write everything, fast. Then take a hard look at it to decide just how *little* of it you can use, how much of it the reader can infer, how you can sharpen an image to imply a scene or condense a grief into a line of dialogue. Trust the reader's experience of life to understand events from attitudes. And keep the present of the story moving.

Flashback is effectively used in fiction to *reveal* at the *right time*. It does not so much take us from, as contribute to, the central action of the story, so that as readers we suspend the forward motion of the narrative in our minds as our understanding of it deepens. David Madden, in *A Primer of the Novel for Readers and Writers*, says that "such time-shifts are most effective if the very fact of their occurrence contributes to the revelation of character and theme. . . ."

If you find that you need an excursion into the past to reveal, at some point, why the character reacts as she does, or how totally he is misunderstood by those around him, or some other point of emotional significance, then there are several ways to get the reader to cooperate.

Provide some sort of transition. A connection between what's happening in the present and what happened in the past will often best transport the reader, just as it does the character.

Avoid blatant transitions, such as "Henry thought back to the time . . ." and "I drifted back in memory. . . ." Assume the reader's intelligence and ability to follow a leap back.

> The kid in the Converse high-tops lifted off on the tips of his toes and slam-dunked it in.
>
> Joe'd done that once, in the lot off Seymour Street, when he was still four inches shorter than Ruppert and had already started getting zits. It was early fall, and. . . .

A graceful transition to the past allows you to summarize necessary background quickly, as in this example from James W. Hall's *Under Cover of Daylight.*

> Thorn watched as Sugarman made a quick inspection of the gallery. Thorn sat on the couch where he'd done his homework as a boy, the one that looked out across the seawall toward Carysfort light.
>
> That was how his nights had been once, read a little Thoreau, do some algebra, and look up, shifting his body so he could see through the louvers the fragile pulse of that marker light, and let his mind roam, first out the twelve miles to the reef and then pushing farther, out past the shipping lanes into a world he pictured as gaudy and loud, chaotic. Bright colors and horns honking, exotic vegetables and market stalls, and water, clear and deep and shadowy, an ocean of fish, larger and more powerful than those he had hauled to light. Beyond the reef.

If you are writing in the past tense, begin the flashback in the past perfect and use the construction "had (verb)" two or three times. Then switch to the simple past; the reader will be with you. If you are writing in the present tense, you may want to keep the whole flashback in the past.

Try to avoid a flashback within a flashback. If you find yourself tempted by this awkward shape, it probably means you're trying to let flashback carry too much of the story.

When the flashback ends, be very clear that you are catching up to the present again. Repeat an action or image that the reader will remember belongs to the basic time period of the story. Often simply beginning the paragraph with "Now . . ." will accomplish the reorientation.

"Flashback" is a term borrowed from film, and I want to borrow another—"slow motion"—to point out a correlation between narrative time and significant detail.

When people experience moments of great intensity, their senses become especially alert and they register, literally, more than usual. In extreme crisis people have the odd sensation that time is slowing down, and they see, hear, smell, remember ordinary sensations with extraordinary clarity. This psychological fact can work artistically in reverse: If you record detail with special focus and precision, it will create the effect of intensity. The phenomenon is so universal that it has become a film cliché to register a physical blow, gunshot, sexual passion, or extreme fear in slow motion. The old television show "Bionic Man" had as one of its conventions that when the bionic man ran at superhuman speeds, we saw him running in slow motion.

Ian McEwan, in *A Child in Time*, brilliantly demonstrates how the technique can work in fiction.

> The road was flanked by concrete irrigation ditches and made wide curves through miles of conifer plantation set well back beyond a wide swathe of tree stumps and dried out bracken. He had slept well the night before, he remembered later. He was relaxed but reasonably alert. His speed was somewhere between seventy and seventy-five, which dropped only a little as he came up behind a large pink lorry.
>
> In what followed, the rapidity of events was accommodated by the slowing of time. He was preparing to overtake when something happened—he did not quite see what—in the region of the lorry's wheels, a hiatus, a cloud of dust, and then something black and long snaked through a hundred feet towards him. It slapped the windscreen, clung there a moment and was whisked away before he had time to understand what it was. And then—or did this happen in the same moment?— the rear of the lorry made a complicated set of movements, a bouncing and swaying, and slewed in a wide spray of sparks, bright even in sunshine. Something curved and metallic flew off to one side. So far Stephen had had time to move his foot towards the brake, time to notice a padlock swinging on a loose flange, and 'Wash me please' scrawled in grime. There was a whinnying of scraped metal and new sparks, dense enough to form a white flame which seemed to propel the rear of the lorry into the air. He was applying first pressure to the brake as he saw the dusty, spinning wheels, the oily bulge of the differential, the camshaft, and now, at eye level, the base of the gear box. The upended lorry bounced on its nose once, perhaps twice, then lazily, tentatively, began to complete the somersault, bringing Stephen the inverted radiator grill, the downward flash of windscreen and a deep boom as the roof hit the road, rose again several feet, fell back, and surged along before him on a bed of flame. Then it swung its length round to block the road, fell on to its side and stopped abruptly as Stephen headed into it from a distance of less than a hundred feet and at a speed which he estimated, in a detached kind of way, to be forty-five miles an hour.

Now, in this slowing of time, there was a sense of a fresh beginning. He had entered a much later period in which all the terms and conditions had changed. So these were the new rules, and he experienced something like awe, as though he were walking alone into a great city on a newly discovered planet. There was space too for a little touch of regret, genuine nostalgia for the old days of spectacle, back then when a lorry used to caterpult so impressively before the impassive witness. Now was a more demanding time of effort and concentration. He was pointing the car towards a six-foot gap formed between a road sign and the front bumper of the motionless lorry. He had removed his foot from the brakes, reasoning—and it was as if he had just completed a monograph on the subject—that they were pulling the car to one side, interfering with his aim. Instead he was changing down through the gears and steering with both hands firmly, but not too tightly, on the wheel, ready to bring them up to cover his head if he missed. He beamed messages, or rather messages sprang from him, to Julie and Kate, nothing more distinct than pulses of alarm and love. There were others he should send to, he knew, but time was short, less than half a second, and fortunately they did not come to mind to confuse him. As he shifted to second and the small car gave out a protesting roar, it was clear that he must not think too hard, that he had to trust to a relaxed and dissociated thinking, that he must imagine himself into the gap. On the sound of this very word, which he must have spoken aloud, there was a brisk crunch of metal and glass and he was through and coming to a halt, with his door handle and wing mirror scattered across the road fifty feet behind.

Before the relief, before the shock, came an intense hope that the driver of the lorry had witnessed this feat of driving.

In this passage, McEwan consciously records the psychological phenomenon traced above, so that in effect he is writing metafiction, announcing his slow-motion device even as he describes the action. On the psychological level, anyone old enough to be reading the novel can almost inevitably identify with the experience of sensual slow-down. At the same time, part of our enjoyment is following the brilliance of the technique and knowing we're clever enough to get it.

It's also evident that the author is having a wonderful time. Beginning writers often rush through or skimp on the elements of setting and time, probably out of dreary memories of long descriptions they have read.

But when atmosphere is well created we do not experience it as description; we experience it. We yawn over passages in which authors have indulged themselves in plum-colored homilies on the beauties of nature or the wealth of decor. But just as dialogue that only offers information is too inert for the purposes of fiction, so too is description that only describes. The full realization of locale and period, the revelation of a character through architecture or of emotion through weather, the advancement of plot through changes in season and history, are among the pleasures of both writer and reader. Once you become adept at the skill of manipulating atmosphere, you will find that the necessity of setting your story some place and some time is a liberating opportunity.

How Far She Went

MARY HOOD

They had quarreled all morning, squalled all summer about the incidentals: how tight the girl's cut-off jeans were, the "Every Inch a Woman" T-shirt, her choice of music and how loud she played it, her practiced inattention, her sullen look. Her granny wrung out the last boiled dishcloth, pinched it to the line, giving the basin a sling and a slap, the water flying out in a scalding arc onto the Queen Anne's lace by the path, never mind if it bloomed, that didn't make it worth anything except to chiggers, but the girl would cut it by the everlasting armload and cherish it in the old churn, going to that much trouble for a week but not bending once—unbegged—to pick the nearest bean; she was sulking now. Bored. Displaced.

"And what do you think happens to a chigger if nobody ever walks by his weed?" her granny asked, heading for the house with that sidelong uneager unanswered glance, hoping for what? The surprise gift of a smile? Nothing. The woman shook her head and said it. "Nothing." The door slammed behind her. Let it.

"I hate it here!" the girl yelled then. She picked up a stick and broke it and threw the pieces—one from each hand—at the laundry drying in the noon. Missed. Missed.

Then she turned on her bare, haughty heel and set off high-shouldered into the heat, quick but not far, not far enough—no road was *that* long— only as far as she dared. At the gate, a rusty chain swinging between two lichened posts, she stopped, then backed up the raw drive to make a run at the barrier, lofting, clearing it clean, her long hair wild in the sun. Triumphant, she looked back at the house where she caught at the dark window her granny's face in its perpetual eclipse of disappointment, old at fifty. She stepped back, but the girl saw her.

"You don't know me!" the girl shouted, chin high, and ran till her ribs ached.

As she rested in the rattling shade of the willows, the little dog found her. He could be counted on. He barked all the way, and squealed when she pulled the burr from his ear. They started back to the house for lunch. By then the mailman had long come and gone in the old ruts, leaving the one letter folded now to fit the woman's apron pocket.

If bad news darkened her granny's face, the girl ignored it. Didn't talk at all, another of her distancings, her defiances. So it was as they ate that the woman summarized, "Your daddy wants you to cash in the plane ticket and buy you something. School clothes. For here."

Pale, the girl stared, defenseless only an instant before blurting out, "You're lying."

The woman had to stretch across the table to leave her handprint on that blank cheek. She said, not caring if it stung or not, "He's been planning it since he sent you here."

"I could turn this whole house over, dump it! Leave you slobbering over that stinking jealous dog in the dust!" The girl trembled with the vision, with the strength it gave her. It made her laugh. "Scatter the Holy Bible like confetti and ravel the crochet into miles of stupid string! I could! I will! I won't stay here!" But she didn't move, not until her tears rose to meet her color, and then to escape the shame of minding so much she fled. Just headed away, blind. It didn't matter, this time, how far she went.

The woman set her thoughts against fretting over their bickering, just went on unalarmed with chores, clearing off after the uneaten meal, bringing in the laundry, scattering corn for the chickens, ladling manure tea onto the porch flowers. She listened though. She always had been a listener. It gave her a cocked look. She forgot why she had gone into the girl's empty room, that ungirlish, tenuous lodging place with its bleak order, its ready suitcases never unpacked, the narrow bed, the contested radio on the windowsill. The woman drew the cracked shade down between the radio and the August sun. There wasn't anything else to do.

It was after six when she tied on her rough oxfords and walked down the drive and dropped the gate chain and headed back to the creosoted shed where she kept her tools. She took a hoe for snakes, a rake, shears to trim the grass where it grew, and seed in her pocket to scatter where it never had grown at all. She put the tools and her gloves and the bucket in the trunk of the old Chevy, its prime and rust like an Appaloosa's spots through the chalky white finish. She left the trunk open and the tool handles sticking out. She wasn't going far.

The heat of the day had broken, but the air was thick, sultry, weighted with honeysuckle in second bloom and the Nu-Grape scent of kudzu. The maple and poplar leaves turned over, quaking, silver. There wouldn't be any rain. She told the dog to stay, but he knew a trick. He stowed away when she turned her back, leaped right into the trunk with the tools, then gave himself away with exultant barks. Hearing him, her court jester, she stopped the car and welcomed him into the front seat beside her. Then they went on. Not a mile from her gate she turned onto the blue gravel of the cemetery lane, hauled the gearshift into reverse to whoa them, and got out to take the idle walk down to her buried hopes, bending all along to rout out a handful of weeds from between the markers of old acquaintance. She stood there and read, slow. The dog whined at her hem; she picked him up and rested her chin on his head, then he wriggled and whined to run free, contrary and restless as a child.

The crows called strong and bold MOM! MOM! A trick of the ear to hear it like that. She knew it was the crows, but still she looked around. No one called her that now. She was done with that. And what was it worth anyway? It all came to this: solitary weeding. The sinful fumble of flesh, the fear, the listening for a return that never came, the shamed waiting, the unanswered prayers, the perjury on the certificate—hadn't she lain there weary of the whole lie and it only beginning? and a voice telling her, "Here's your baby, here's your girl," and the swaddled package meaning no more to her than an extra anything, something store-bought, something she could take back for a refund.

"Tie her to the fence and give her a bale of hay," she had murmured, drugged, and they teased her, excused her for such a welcoming, blaming the anesthesia, but it went deeper than that; *she* knew, and the *baby* knew: there was no love in the begetting. That was the secret, unforgivable, that not another good thing could ever make up for, where all the bad had come from, like a visitation, a punishment. She knew that was why Sylvie had been wild, had gone to earth so early, and before dying had made this child in sudden wedlock, a child who would be just like her, would carry the hurting on into another generation. A matter of time. No use raising her hand. But she *had* raised her hand. Still wore on its palm the memory of the sting of the collision with the girl's cheek; had she broken her jaw? Her heart? Of course not. She said it aloud: "Takes more than that."

She went to work then, doing what she could with her old tools. She pecked the clay on Sylvie's grave, new-looking, unhealed after years. She tried again, scattering seeds from her pocket, every last possible one of them. Off in the west she could hear the pulpwood cutters sawing through another acre across the lake. Nearer, there was the racket of motorcycles laboring cross-country, insect-like, distracting.

She took her bucket to the well and hung it on the pump. She had half filled it when the bikers roared up, right down the blue gravel, straight at her. She let the bucket overflow, staring. On the back of one of the machines was the girl. Sylvie's girl! Her bare arms wrapped around the shirtless man riding between her thighs. They were first. The second biker rode alone. She studied their strangers' faces as they circled her. They were the enemy, all of them. Laughing. The girl was laughing too, laughing like her mama did. Out in the middle of nowhere the girl had found these two men, some moth-musk about her drawing them (too soon!) to what? She shouted it: "What in

God's—" They roared off without answering her, and the bucket of water tipped over, spilling its stain blood-dark on the red dust.

The dog went wild barking, leaping after them, snapping at the tires, and there was no calling him down. The bikers made a wide circuit of the churchyard, then roared straight across the graves, leaping the ditch and landing upright on the road again, heading off toward the reservoir.

Furious, she ran to her car, past the barking dog, this time leaving him behind, driving after them, horn blowing nonstop, to get back what was not theirs. She drove after them knowing what they did not know, that all the roads beyond that point dead-ended. She surprised them, swinging the Impala across their path, cutting them off; let them hit it! They stopped. She got out, breathing hard, and said, when she could, "She's underage." Just that. And put out her claiming hand with an authority that made the girl's arms drop from the man's insolent waist and her legs tremble.

"I was just riding," the girl said, not looking up.

Behind them the sun was heading on toward down. The long shadows of the pines drifted back and forth in the same breeze that puffed the distant sails on the lake. Dead limbs creaked and clashed overhead like the antlers of locked and furious beasts.

"Sheeeut," the lone rider said. "I told you." He braced with his muddy boot and leaned out from his machine to spit. The man the girl had been riding with had the invading sort of eyes the woman had spent her lifetime bolting doors against. She met him now, face to face.

"Right there, missy," her granny said, pointing behind her to the car.

The girl slid off the motorcycle and stood halfway between her choices. She started slightly at the poosh! as he popped another top and chugged the beer in one uptilting of his head. His eyes never left the woman's. When he was through, he tossed the can high, flipping it end over end. Before it hit the ground he had his pistol out and, firing once, winged it into the lake.

"Freaking lucky shot," the other one grudged.

"I don't need luck," he said. He sighted down the barrel of the gun at the woman's head. "POW!" he yelled, and when she recoiled, he laughed. He swung around to the girl; he kept aiming the gun, here, there, high, low, all around. "Y'all settle it," he said, with a shrug.

The girl had to understand him then, had to know him, had to know better. But still she hesitated. He kept looking at her, then away.

"She's fifteen," her granny said. "You can go to jail."

"You can go to hell," he said.

"Probably will," her granny told him. "I'll save you a seat by the fire." She took the girl by the arm and drew her to the car; she backed up, swung around, and headed out the road toward the churchyard for her tools and dog. The whole way the girl said nothing, just hunched against the far door, staring hard-eyed out at the pines going past.

The woman finished watering the seed in, and collected her tools. As she worked, she muttered, "It's your own kin buried here, you might have the decency to glance this way one time . . ." The girl was finger-tweezing her eyebrows in the side mirror. She didn't look around as the dog and the woman got in. Her granny shifted hard, sending the tools clattering in the trunk.

When they came to the main road, there were the men. Watching for them. Waiting for them. They kicked their machines into life and followed, close, bumping them, slapping the old fenders, yelling. The girl gave a wild glance around at the one by her door and said, "Gran'ma?" and as he drew his pistol, "Gran'ma!" just as the gun nosed into the open window. She frantically cranked the glass up between her and the weapon, and her granny, seeing, spat, "Fool!" She never had been one to pray for peace or rain. She stamped the accelerator right to the floor.

The motorcycles caught up. Now she braked, hard, and swerved off the road into an alley between the pines, not even wide enough for the school bus, just a fire scrape that came out a quarter mile from her own house, if she could get that far. She slewed on the pine straw, then righted, tearing along the dark tunnel through the woods. She had for the time being bested them; they were left behind. She was winning. Then she hit the wallow where the tadpoles were already five weeks old. The Chevy plowed in and stalled. When she got it cranked again, they were stuck. The tires spattered mud three feet up the near trunks as she tried to spin them out, to rock them out. Useless. "Get out and run!" she cried, but the trees were too close on the passenger side. The girl couldn't open her door. She wasted precious time having to crawl out under the steering wheel. The woman waited but the dog ran on.

They struggled through the dusky woods, their pace slowed by the thick straw and vines. Overhead, in the last light, the martins were reeling free and sure after their prey.

"Why? Why?" the girl gasped, as they lunged down the old deer trail. Behind them they could hear shots, and glass breaking as the men came to the bogged car. The woman kept on running, swatting their way clear through the shoulder-high weeds. They could see the Greer cottage, and made for it. But it was ivied-over, padlocked, the woodpile dry-rotting under its tarp, the electric meterbox empty on the pole. No help there.

The dog, excited, trotted on, yelping, his lips white-flecked. He scented the lake and headed that way, urging them on with thirsty yips. On the clay shore, treeless, deserted, at the utter limit of land, they stood defenseless, listening to the men coming on, between them and home. The woman pressed her hands to her mouth, stifling her cough. She was exhausted. She couldn't think.

"We can get under!" the girl cried suddenly, and pointed toward the Greers' dock, gap-planked, its walkway grounded on the mud. They splashed out to it, wading in, the woman grabbing up the telltale, tattletale dog in her arms. They waded out to the far end and ducked under. There was room between the foam floats for them to crouch neck-deep.

The dog wouldn't hush, even then; never had yet, and there wasn't time to teach him. When the woman realized that, she did what she had to do. She grabbed him, whimpering; held him; held him under till the struggle ceased and the bubbles rose silver from his fur. They crouched there then, the two of them, submerged to the shoulders, feet unsteady on the slimed lake bed. They listened. The sky went from rose to ocher to violet in the cracks over their heads. The motorcycles had stopped now. In the silence there was the glissando of locusts, the dry crunch of boots on the flinty beach, their low man-talk drifting as they prowled back and forth. One of them struck a match.

"—they in these woods we could burn 'em out."

The wind carried their voices away into the pines. Some few words eddied back.

"—lippy old smartass do a little work on her knees besides praying—"

Laughter. It echoed off the deserted house. They were getting closer.

One of them strode directly out to the dock, walked on the planks over their heads. They could look up and see his boot soles. He was the one with the gun. He slapped a mosquito on his bare back and cursed. The carp, roused by the troubling of the waters, came nosing around the dock, guzzling and snorting. The girl and her granny held still, so still. The man fired his pistol into the shadows, and a wounded fish thrashed, dying. The man knelt and reached for it, chuffing out his beery breath. He belched. He pawed the lake for the dead fish, cursing as it floated out of reach. He shot it again, firing at it till it sank and the gun was empty. Cursed that too. He stood then and unzipped and relieved himself of some of the beer. They had to listen to that. To know that about him. To endure that, unprotesting.

Back and forth on shore the other one ranged, restless. He lit another cigarette. He coughed. He called, "Hey! They got away, man, that's all. Don't get your shorts in a wad. Let's go."

"Yeah." He finished. He zipped. He stumped back across the planks and leaped to shore, leaving the dock tilting amid widening ripples. Underneath, they waited.

The bike cranked. The other ratcheted, ratcheted, then coughed, caught, roared. They circled, cut deep ruts, slung gravel, and went. Their roaring died away and away. Crickets resumed and a near frog bic-bic-bicked.

Under the dock, they waited a little longer to be sure. Then they ducked below the water, scraped out from under the pontoon, and came up into free air, slogging toward shore. It had seemed warm enough in the water. Now they shivered. It was almost night. One streak of light still stood reflected on the darkening lake, drew itself thinner, narrowing into a final cancellation of day. A plane winked its way west.

The girl was trembling. She ran her hands down her arms and legs, shedding water like a garment. She sighed, almost a sob. The woman held the dog in her arms; she dropped to her knees upon the random stones and murmured, private, haggard, "Oh, honey," three times, maybe all three times for the dog, maybe once for each of them. The girl waited, watching. Her granny rocked the dog like a baby, like a dead child, rocked slower and slower and was still.

"I'm sorry," the girl said then, avoiding the dog's inert, empty eye.

"It was him or you," her granny said, finally, looking up. Looking her over. "Did they mess with you? With your britches? Did they?"

"No!" Then, quieter, "No, ma'am."

When the woman tried to stand up she staggered, lightheaded, clumsy with the freight of the dog. "No, ma'am," she echoed, fending off the girl's "Let me." And she said again, "It was him or you. I know that. I'm not going to rub your face in it." They saw each other as well as they could in that failing light, in any light.

The woman started toward home, saying, "Around here, we bear our own burdens." She led the way along the weedy shortcuts. The twilight bleached the dead limbs of the pines to bone. Insects sang in the thickets, silencing at their oncoming.

"We'll see about the car in the morning," the woman said. She bore her armful toward her own moth-ridden dusk-to-dawn security light with that country grace she had always had when the earth was reliably progressing underfoot. The girl walked close behind her, exactly where *she* walked, matching her pace, matching her stride, close enough to put her hand forth (if the need arose) and touch her granny's back where the faded voile was clinging damp, the merest gauze between their wounds.

Suggestions for Discussion

1. Observe how scene and summary alternate in the first paragraph. What does each contribute?

2. What details help create in the reader a sense of familiarity with a setting that is in fact probably unfamiliar to most of us?

3. In what ways is each of the characters in harmony or conflict with the setting?

4. The girl tells us directly that she hates this place, but we are never directly given an image of the place she comes from. What do we know about it, and how?

5. In the two paragraphs on page 183 beginning, "The crows called strong . . . ," identify elements of scene, sequential summary, and circumstantial summary.

6. Apart from the bikers, what elements of the modern world seem to violate the setting?

7. Explain the irony of the refrains to do with leaving the place: "not far enough—no road was *that* long—only as far as she dared," "It didn't matter, this time, how far she went," "She wasn't going far," ". . . if she could get that far."

8. In the last three paragraphs of the story, how do elements of the setting symbolize reversal and resolution?

Waiting for Mr. Kim

CAROL ROH-SPAULDING

When Gracie Kang's elder twin sisters reached the age of eighteen, they went down to the Alameda County Shipyards and got jobs piecing battleships together for the U.S. Navy. This was the place to find a husband in 1945, if a girl was doing her own looking. They were Americans, after all, and they were of age. Her sisters caught the bus down to the waterfront every day and brought home their paychecks every two weeks. At night, they went out with their girlfriends, meeting boys at the cinema or the drugstore, as long as it was outside of Chinatown.

Gracie's parents would never have thought it was husbands they were after. Girls didn't choose what they were given. But the end of the war distracted everybody. While Mr. Kang tried to keep up with the papers and Mrs. Kang tried to keep up with the laundry, Sung-Sook slipped away one day with a black welder enrolled in the police academy and Sung-Ohk took off with a Chinatown nightclub singer from L.A. with a sister in the movies.

Escaped. Gracie had watched from the doorway that morning as Sung-Sook pulled on her good slip in front of the vanity, lifted her hair, breathed in long and slow. Her eyes came open, she saw Gracie's reflection. "Comeer," she said. "You never say goodbye." She kissed Gracie between the eyes. Gracie had only shrugged: "See you." Then Sung-Ohk from the bathroom: "This family runs a laundry, so where's all the goddamn towels?"

When the girls didn't come home, the lipstick and rouge wiped off their faces, to fold the four o'clock sheets, she understood what was what. On the vanity in the girls' room she found a white paper bell with sugar sprinkles. In silver letters, it read:

CALL TODAY!
MARRY TODAY!
YOUR WEDDING! YOUR WAY!
EIGHTEEN OR OVER?
WE WON'T SAY NAY!
(MAY BORROW VEIL AND BOUQUET)

As simple as having your hair done. Gracie sat at the vanity, thinking of the thousand spirits of the household her mother was always ticking off like a grocery list—spirit of the lamp, the clock, the ashtray. Spirit in the seat of your chair. Spirit of the stove, the closet, the broom, the shoes. Spirit of the breeze in the room, the Frigidaire. Gracie had always been willing to believe in them; she only needed something substantial to go on. Now, in her sisters' room, she felt that the spirits had been there, had moved on, to other inhabited rooms.

Those girls had escaped Thursday evenings with the old *chong-gaks*, who waited effortlessly for her father to give the girls away. No more sitting, knees together, in white blouses and circle skirts, with gritted smiles. Now Gracie would sit, the only girl, while her father made chitchat with Mr. Han and Mr. Kim. Number three daughter, much younger, the dutiful one, wouldn't run away. If her mother had had the say, the girls would have given their parents grandchildren by now. But she didn't have the say, and her father smiled his pleasant, slightly anxious smile at the *chong-gaks* and never ever brought up payment.

He was the one paying now. No one got dinner that night. Pots flew, plates rattled in the cabinets, the stove rumbled in the corner, pictures slid, clanked, tinkled. "Now we'll have a nigger for a grandson and a chink for a son-in-law, Mr. Kang!" her mother shouted. She cursed Korean, but had a gift for American slurs, translating the letter found taped to the laundry boiler into the horrors of marrying for love.

Gracie and Little Gene pressed themselves against the wall, squeezed around the Frigidaire, sidled to the staircase. They sat and backed up one step at a time, away from the stabs and swishes of the broom. "Or didn't you want Korean grandchildren, Mr. Kang? You're the one who let them fall into American love. Could I help it there aren't any good *chong-gaks* around? Thought we'd pack the girls off to Hawaii where the young ones are? Ha. I'd like to see the missionaries pay for that!"

Their father came into view below. Hurried, but with his usual dignity, he ducked and swerved as necessary. Silently, solemnly, he made for the closet, opened the door, and stepped in among the coats. The blows from first the bristled then the butted end of the broom came down upon the door.

Little Gene whispered, "I'm going outside."

"Fine," Gracie told him. "If you can make it to the door."

"Think I can't manage the window? I land in the trash bin, pretty soft!"

Gracie told him, "Bring me back a cigarette, then," and he left her there. A year younger than she and not very big for thirteen, he was still number one son. Gracie stuck her fingers in her mouth all the way to the knuckle, clamped down hard.

She chopped cabbage, scrubbed the bathhouses, washed and pressed and folded linen and laundry, dreaming up lives for her sisters. From their talk and their magazines, she knew how it should go. Sung-Sook stretched out by the pool in a leopard-print bathing suit with pointy bra cups and sipped colored drinks from thin glasses, leaving a pink surprise of lips at the rim. Somebody else served them, fetched them, cleaned them. Her husband shot cardboard men through the heart and came home to barbecue T-bones. Every night they held hands at the double feature. Sung-Ohk slipped into a tight Chinese-doll dress and jeweled cat-eyes, sang to smoky crowds of white people from out of town. Her lips grazed the mike as she whispered, "Thank you, kind people, thank you." In the second act, her husband, in a tux, dipped her, spun her, with slant-eyed-Gene-Kelly-opium flair. All the white people craned their necks and saw that Oriental women could have good legs.

They left Gracie and her mother with all the work. At first, her father tried to help out. He locked up the barbershop at lunch, crossed the street, passed through the kitchen, and stepped into Hell, as they called it. But her mother snapped down the pants press when she saw him and from a blur of steam shouted, "Fool for love! I'm warning you to get out of here, Mr. Kang!"

She bowed her head at the market now. She had stopped going to church. Lost face, it was called. And there was the worry of it. No one knew these men who took the girls away. Maybe one was an opium dealer and the other was a pimp. Maybe those girls were in for big disappointment, even danger. Her father twisted his hands, helpless and silent in the evenings. Her mother clanked the dishes into the sink, banged the washers shut, punched the buttons with her fists, helpless, too.

It was true he was a fool for love, as far as Gracie could tell. Her mother slapped at his hands when he came up behind her at the chopping board to kiss her hair—pretty brave, considering that knife. When her mother tried to walk behind him in the street, he stopped and tried to take her hand. Gracie and her mother were always nearly missing buses because she'd say, "Go on, Mr. Kang. We're coming," and they'd stay behind as she cleaned out her purse or took forever with her coat, just to have it the way she had learned it, her husband a few paces ahead, women behind. Maybe the girls would never have gotten away if he'd been firm about marriage, strict about love.

Where her parents were from, shamans could chase out the demon spirits from dogs, cows, rooms, people. Maybe her father had had the fool chased out of him, because when Thursday came around, he sat in the good chair with the Bible open on his knees, and Gracie sat beside him, waiting. Life was going to go on without her sisters. Her life. Gracie watched her father for lingering signs of foolishness. Above the donated piano, the cuckoo in the clock popped out seven times. As always, her father looked up with a satisfied air. He loved that bird. Her mother believed there was a spirit in the wooden box. The spirit was saying it was time.

Little Gene was free in the streets with that gang of Chinese boys. She waited for her cigarette and his stories—right now, he might be breaking into the high school, popping open the Coca-Cola machine, busting up some lockers. There weren't any Jap boys left to beat up on, and they stayed away from the mostly black neighborhoods or they'd get beat up themselves. Gracie sat with her hands clasped at her knees, worrying about him, admiring him a little.

First came the tap-tap of the missionary ladies from the United Methodist Church. Their hats looked like squat birds' nests through the crushed ice window. Every Thursday, they seemed to have taken such pains with their dresses and hats and shoes, Gracie couldn't think how they had lasted in the mountain villages of Pyongyang province. She had never been there herself, or been to mountains at all, but she knew there were tigers in Pyongyang.

Her father rose and assumed his visitors smile. "Everyone will be too polite to mention the girls, Gracie," he told her. That was the only thing at all he said about them to her.

The ladies stepped in, chins pecking. One bore a frosted cake, the other thrust forward a box of canned goods. American apologies. As though the girls had died, Gracie thought. Her father stiffened, but kept his smile.

"We think it's wonderful about the war," the cake lady began.

"Praise be to God that we've stopped the Japanese," the Spam lady went on. They looked at one another.

"The *Japanese* Japanese," said the second. She paused. "And we are so sorry about your country, Mr. Kang."

"But this is your country now," said the first.

Her father eased them onto more conversational subjects. They smiled, heads tilted, as Gracie pressed out "Greensleeves," "Colonial Days," "Jesus, We Greet Thee," on the piano. And at half past the hour, they were up and on their way out, accepting jars of *kimch'i* from her mother with wrinkle-nosed smiles.

The barbershop customers did not come by. Mr. Woo from the bakery and Mr. and Mrs. Lim from the Hunan restaurant stayed away. All the Chinese and Koreans knew about saving face. Except the *chong-gaks*, who knew better, surely, but arrived like clockwork anyway, a black blur and a white blur at the window. They always shuffled their feet elaborately on the doorstep before knocking, and her father used to say, "That's very Korean," to Sung-Sook and Sung-Ohk, who didn't bother to fluff their hair or straighten their blouses for the visitors. They used to moan, "Here come the old goats. Failure One and Failure Two." Her father only shushed them, saying, "Respect, daughters, respect." Gracie saw that he could have done better than that if he really expected the girls to marry these men, but after all, the girls were right. Probably her father could see that. They were failures. No families, even at their age. Little money, odd jobs, wasted lives. A week before, they had been only a couple of nuisances who brought her sticks of Beechnut gum and seemed never to fathom her sisters' hostility. They were that stupid, and now they were back. One Korean girl was as good as any other.

Gracie could actually tolerate Mr. Han. He had been clean and trim in his black suit, pressed shirt, and straight tie every Thursday evening since her sisters had turned sixteen. He was a tall, hesitant man with most of his hair, surprisingly good teeth, and little wire glasses so tight over his nose that the lenses steamed up when he was nervous. Everyone knew he had preferred Sung-Ohk, whose kindest remark to him ever was that he looked exactly like the Chinese servant in a Hollywood movie. He always perched on the piano bench as though he didn't mean to stay long, and he mopped his brow when Sung-Ohk glared at him. But he never pulled Gracie onto his lap to kiss her and pat her, and he never, as the girls called it, licked with his eyes.

He left that to Mr. Kim. Mr. Kim in the same white suit, white shirt, white tie, and white shoes which had never really been white, but always the color of pale urine. His teeth were brown from too much tea and sugar and opium. This wasn't her hateful imagination. She had washed his shirts ever since she'd started working. She knew the armpit stains that spread like an infection when she tried to soak them. The hairs and smudges of ash and something like pus in his sheets. She could smell his laundry even before she saw the ticket. His breath stank, too, like herring.

Mr. Kim found everything amusing. "It's been too warm, hasn't it, Mr. Kang?" he said by way of greeting. Then he chuckled, "I'm afraid our friend Mr. Han is almost done in by it."

"Yes, let me get you some iced tea," her father announced. "Mrs. Kang!"

Mr. Kim chuckled again at his companion. "Maybe his heart is suffering. Nearly sixty, you know. Poor soul. He's got a few years on me, anyway, haven't you, old man?"

Mr. Han lowered himself on the piano bench. "Yes, it's been too warm, too much for me."

His companion laughed like one above that kind of weakness. Then he said, "And how is Miss Kang? She's looking very well. She seems to be growing."

Gracie hunched her shoulders, looked anywhere but at him.

"Yes, she's growing," her father answered carefully. "She's still a child." The men smiled at each other with a lot of teeth showing, but their eyes were watchful. "Of course, she's a little lonesome nowadays," her father continued. Mr. Kim eyed him, then he seemed to catch on and slapped his knee—good joke. Mr. Han squinted in some sort of pain.

If Mr. Kim hadn't been in America even longer than her father had, with nothing to show for it but a rented room above the barbershop, then he might have been able to say, "What about this one, Mr. Kang? Are you planning to let her get away, too?" But if he'd had something to show for his twenty or so years in America, he wouldn't be sitting in her father's house and she wouldn't be waiting to be his bride.

Then from the piano bench: "Lonesome, Miss Kang?" Everybody looked. Mr. Han blinked, startled at the attention. He quietly repeated, "Have you, too, been lonesome?" Gracie looked down at her hands. Her father was supposed to answer, let him answer. At that moment, her mother entered, head bowed over the tea tray. Gracie could hear the spirit working in the cuckoo clock.

Her father had told her once that he'd picked cotton and grapes with the Mexicans in the Salinas Valley, and it got so hot you could fry meat on the railroad ties. But that was nothing compared to the sticky summers in Pyongyang, where the stench of human manure brought the bile to your throat. That was why he loved Oakland, he said, where the ocean breeze cleaned you out. It reminded him of his childhood visits to Pusan Harbor, when he'd traveled to visit his father who had been forced into the service of the Japanese. And it reminded him of the day he sailed back from America for his bride.

Bright days, fresh wind. Gracie imagined the women who had waited for the husbands who had never returned. Those women lived in fear, her mother had said. They were no good to marry if the men didn't come back, or if they did return but had no property, they had no legal status in America and no prospects in Korea. Plenty of the women did away with themselves, or their families sold them as concubines. "You think I'm lying?" she told Gracie. "I waited ten years for him. People didn't believe the letters he sent after a while. My family started talking about what to do with me, because I had other sisters waiting to marry, only I was the oldest and they had to get rid of me first!"

Gracie imagined those women, their hands tucked neatly in their bright sleeves, their smooth hair and ancient faces looking out over the water from high rooms. And she thought of Mr. Han gazing from his window out over the alley and between skyscrapers and telephone poles to his glimpse of the

San Francisco Bay. Where he was, the sky was black, starless in the city. Where she was, the sun rose, a brisk, hopeful morning.

On a morning like that, Gracie took the sheets and laundry across the street and up to the rented rooms. Usually the *chong-gaks* had coffee and a bun at the bakery and then strolled around the lake, but Gracie always knocked and set the boxes down.

Mr. Han's door inched open under her knuckles. The breeze in the bright room, the sterile light of morning in there, the cord rattling at the blinds. Something invisible crept out from the slit in the door and was with her in the hall.

"Mr. Han? Just your laundry, Mr. Han." Spirits of memory—she and Little Gene climbing onto his knees, reaching into his pockets for malted milk balls or sticks of gum. "Where are *your* children?" they'd asked. "Where is your stove? Where is your sink? Where is your mirror?" Mr. Han had always smiled, as though he were only hiding the things they named, could make them appear whenever he wanted.

She pushed the door open, and the spirits of memory mingled with the spirits of longing and desire. The bulb of the bare night light buzzed, like a recollection in a head full of ideas. Mr. Han lay half-on, half-off the bed. One shoe pressed firmly on the floor, as though half of him had had somewhere to go. The glasses dangled from the metal bed frame. That was where his head was, pressed against the bars. His eyes were rolled back, huge and amazed, toward the window. And at his throat, a stripe of beaded red, the thin lips of flesh puckering slightly, like the edges of a rose.

Spirits scuttered along the walls, swirled upwards, twisting in their airy, familiar paths. They pressed against the ceiling. They watched her in the corner. His spirit was near, she felt, in the white field of his pillow. Or in the curtains that puffed and lifted at the sill like a girl's skirt in the wind.

Gracie squatted and peered under the bed. The gleam there was a thing she had known all of her life, a razor from the barbershop. Clean, almost no blood, like his throat. She knew it was loss of air, not loss of blood, that did it. She knew because she'd heard about it before. Two or three of the neighborhood Japs had done the same, when they found that everything they thought they owned they no longer had a right to. They'd had three days to sell what they could and go. She didn't know where. She only knew that her father had been able to buy the barbershop and the bathhouse because of it.

Wind swelled in the hall, with the spirits of car horns, telephone wires, shop signs, traffic lights, and a siren, not for him. They were present at the new death—curious, laughing, implacable. They sucked the door shut. Gracie started. "Leaving now," she announced. "Mr. Han," she whispered to the *chong-gak*. Then she remembered he'd become part of something else, something weightless, invisible, near. She said it louder. "Mr. Han. I'm sorry for you, Mr. Han."

Mr. Kim ate with the Kangs that afternoon, after the ambulances had gone, and again in the evening. His fingers trembled. He lowered his head to the rice, unable to lift it to his mouth, scraping feebly with his chopsticks. Of the death he had one thing to say, which he couldn't stop saying: "I walked alone this morning. Why did I decide to walk alone, of all mornings?"

Mrs. Kang muttered guesses about what to do next, not about the body itself or the police inquiry or who was responsible for his room and his things, but about how best to give peace to the spirit of the *chong-gak*, who might otherwise torment the rest of their days. He didn't have a family of his own to torment. She'd prepared a plate of meat and rice and *kimch'i*, saying, "Where do I *put* this?"

Little Gene, jealous that Gracie had found the body and he hadn't, offered, "How 'bout on the sill? Then he can float by whenever. Or in his room? I'll stay in there all night and watch for him." Then he patted his stomach. "Or how 'bout right here?"

"Damn," her mother went on. "I wish now I'd paid more attention to the shamans. But we stayed away from those women unless we needed them. My family was afraid I'd get the call because I was sickly and talked in my sleep, and we have particularly restless ancestors. But I didn't have it in me. Was it food every day for a month or every month for a year? What a mystery. Now we'll have spirits till we all die."

"Girls shouldn't be shamans, anyway," Little Gene announced. "Imagine Gracie chasing spirits away."

Asshole, Gracie mouthed. Little Gene flipped her off. None of the adults understood the sign.

"You don't chase them, honey," Gracie's mother said to her. "You feed them and pay them and talk to them."

"Tell *him*," Gracie answered. "He's the one who brought it up."

"Feed everyone who's here first," Little Gene suggested. Gracie flipped him off in return.

"What's that you're doing with your fingers, Gracie?" he shot back. She put her finger to her lips and pointed at her father. His eyes were closed. He kept them that way, head bowed, lips moving.

"Fine," her mother announced. "Let's do Christian, Mr. Kang. It's simpler, as far as I'm concerned."

Mr. Kim lifted his head from his rice bowl, looking very old.

Her mother eyed him sternly. "Cheaper, too."

* * *

That night Gracie lay in her bed by the open window. Where was his spirit now? In heaven, at God's side? Or restlessly feeding on *bulgogi* and turnips in his room? Or somewhere else entirely, or nowhere at all? Please God or Thousand Spirits, she prayed. Let me marry for love. Please say I'm not waiting for Mr. Kim. It's fine with me if I'm a *chun-yo* forever.

They held a small service at the Korean United Methodist Church. Her father stood up and said a little about the hard life of a *chong-gak* in America, the loneliness of these men, the difficulties for Oriental immigrants. Gracie felt proud of him, though he was less convincing about heaven. No one even knew for certain if Mr. Han had converted.

Mr. Kim sat in white beside Gracie. "Thy kingdom come," he murmured, "thy will be done." And he reached out and took her hand, looking straight ahead to her father. His hand was moist. She could smell him.

"And forgive us our trespasses," she prayed.

"As we forgive those who trespass against us," he continued, and he squeezed her hand with the surety of possession, though her fingers slipped in his palm.

Gracie never got to the "amen." Instead, she leaned into his side, tilted her face to his cheek, and brought her lips to his ear. "You dirty old bastard," she whispered. Then she snatched her hand back and kept her head bowed, trembling. She wished she could pray that he would die, too, if it was the only way. From the corner of her eye, she could see Mr. Kim's offended hand held open on his knee. Sweat glistened in the creases of his palm. She would never be able to look into his eyes again. For a moment, pity and disgust swept through her. Then, as the congregation stood, she said her own prayer. It went, Please oh please oh please.

Little Gene stuck his head in the laundry room. "Hey, you! Mrs. Kim!"

Gracie flung a folded pillowcase at him.

"Whew. Step out of that hellhole for a minute. I've got something to show you."

He slid a cigarette from behind his ear and they went out the alley-side steps and shared it by the trash bin. "The day they give you away, I'll have this right under your window, see? I'll even stuff it with newspapers so you'll land easy."

"Nowhere to run," Gracie told him. It was the name of a movie they'd seen.

"Isn't Hollywood someplace? Isn't Mexico someplace?"

Gracie laughed out loud. "You coming?"

" 'Course I am. Mama's spirit crap is getting on my nerves."

Gracie shrugged. "You're too little to run away. Why should I need help from someone as little as you?"

Little Gene stood on tiptoe and sneered into her face. "Because I'm a boy."

Then he grinned and exhaled smoke through his nose and the sides of his mouth.

"Dragon-breath," she called him.

"Come on, Mrs. Kim. This way." They scrambled up the steps, took the staircase to the hall, then stepped through the door that led down again to the ground floor through an unlit passage to the old opium den. It was nothing but a storage room for old washers now, a hot box with a ceiling two stories above them. It baked, winter or summer, because it shared a wall with the boiler.

They'd hid there when they were little, playing hide-and-seek or creating stories about the opium dealers and the man who was supposed to have hung himself in there. They could never figure out where he might have hung himself from since the ceiling was so high and the walls so bare. They looked up in awe. Once, Little Gene thought he'd be clever, and he shut himself in the dryer. Gracie couldn't find him for the longest time, but when she came back for a second look, the round window was steamed up and he wasn't making any noise. She pulled him out. He was grinning, eyes vacant. "You stupid dumb stupid stupid kid."

Little Gene felt for the bulb on the wall, pulled the chain. Now the old dryer was somehow on its side. There were two busted washers and a cane chair. The air was secret, heavy with dust and heat. Gracie felt along the walls for loose bricks, pulled one out, felt around inside like they used to do, looking for stray nuggets or anything else that might have been hidden and forgotten by the Chinese who had lived there before.

Little Gene got on his hands and knees. "Lookit." He eased out a brick flush with the floor. "Lookit," he said again.

Gracie crouched. He crawled back to make way for her, then pushed her head down. "Down there, in the basement."

She saw dim, natural light, blackened redwood, steam-stained. The bathhouse. "So what? I clean 'em every day of my life."

"Just wait," he said.

Then the white blade of a man's back rose into view. Little Gene's hand was a spider up and down her side. "See him, Mrs. Kim? Bet you can't wait."

The back lowered, rose, lowered again, unevenly, painfully. She saw hair slicked back in seaweed streaks, tea-colored splotches on his back, the skin damp and speckled like the belly of a fish. Little Gene's hand was a spider again at her neck. Gracie slapped at him, crouched, looked again. "What the hell's he doing? Rocking himself?"

Little Gene only giggled nervously.

The eyes of Mr. Kim stared toward the thousand spirits, his mouth hung open. Then those eyes rolled back in his head, pupil-less, white, and still. "God, is he dying?" Gracie asked. If she moved a muscle, she would burst. "Is he dying?" she asked again. "Don't touch me," she told her brother, who was impatient with spidery hands.

Little Gene rolled his eyes. "That's all we need. He's not dying, stupid. Unless he dies every day." Life in a dim bathhouse, Gracie thought. Deaths in bright rooms.

A door slammed hard on the other side of the wall. Her mother cursed, called her name. Little Gene giggled and did the stroking motion at his crotch, then Gracie scrambled to her knees and pulled him up with her. He grabbed for the chain on the bulb. Dark. "Don't scream," he giggled.

"Gracie! Damn you!" her mother called.

Then his hands flew to her, one at her shoulder, the other, oily and sweet, cupping her open mouth.

A letter arrived the next Thursday. Sung-Sook had used her head and addressed it to the barbershop. Her father brought it up to her in the evening. Gracie was at her window, leaning out, watching the sky begin to gather color. "For 'Miss Gracie Kang,'" he read. "'Care of Mr. Park A. Kang.'" There was no return address. The paper smelled faintly like roses.

With his eyes, her father pleaded for news of them. He said, "You look like you're waiting for someone."

She shrugged. "It's Thursday." She wanted him to leave her alone until it was time to go downstairs and sit with Mr. Kim. Instead, he came to the window and looked out with her. "Where's your brother?"

"Wherever he feels like being."

He only smiled. Then he told her, "Mr. Kim has given me money. A lot of money."

She drew herself up. She couldn't look at him. "What money?"

"It's for a ticket, Gracie. He wants me to purchase him a ticket to Pusan and arrange some papers for him."

"Alone?" she asked.

"Alone."

She smiled out at the street, but asked again, "What money?"

Her father answered, "He will be happy to have a chance to tell you good-bye." And he left her at the window.

His money, she knew. Her father's. She kept still at the window. With her eyes closed, she saw farther than she had ever seen. "Did you hear that?" she said out loud, in case any spirits, celestial or domestic, were listening.

Then she carefully opened her letter. There was a piece of pale, gauzy paper, and a couple of photographs—a good thing, since the girls had stolen a bunch of family snapshots when they left.

> Dear Gracie,
>   I hope they let you see this. You're going to be an auntie now. Sung-Ohk's the lucky one, but me and El are really trying. For a baby, you know.

That's El in his rookie uniform and I'm in my wedding dress. We're at the Forbidden City, the club in San Francisco. Louie, that's Sung-Ohk's husband, got us in free on our wedding night. The other picture is of Louie and Sung-Ohk at Newport Beach. Isn't he handsome? Like El. We all live near the beach, ten minutes by freeway.

You'd love it here, but I guess you'd love it anywhere but Oakland. How are the old creeps, anyway? Maybe they'll die before Mom and Dad give you away, ha-ha.

Be good. Don't worry. We're going to figure something out. El says you can stay with us. Sung-Ohk sends her love. I do, too.

The letter fluttered in her hand in the window. She pulled open the drawer at her bedside table, folded the paper neatly back in its creases, and set it inside. Then she took out the only thing her sisters had left behind, the sugar-sprinkled, silver-lettered, instant-ceremony marriage advertisement. Gracie breathed in deeply, as her sister had done with the hope of her new life—as, perhaps, Mr. Han had done, with the hope of his release. Somewhere near, Little Gene laughed out loud in the street. Her mother banged dinner into the oven. Her father waited below, his Bible open on his knees, to greet the missionary ladies, to say goodbye to Mr. Kim. Below, a white, slow figure stepped from a door and headed across the street. Again, she breathed in. And what she took in was her own. Not everything had a name.

Suggestions for Discussion

1. By what details do you know the period, place, and background of the story? To what extent is Gracie in harmony with her background? To what extent is she in conflict?

2. The first half of the story is told largely in summary, the last half almost entirely in scenes. What function does this shape serve?

3. Many of the circumstantial summaries are nevertheless scenes, that is, they are examples of the sort of thing that went on. Identify a few such scenes.

4. On page 194 the scene beginning "she pushed open the door" is in slow motion. What is the effect of the extended detail?

5. There are no long flashbacks in this story, but there are economically presented elements of the past. Identify some of these.

6. In the dialogue at supper after Mr. Han's death, the characters are not being particularly honest or articulate about their feelings. How does the dialogue reveal what they feel?

RETROSPECT

1. Contrast the rural atmosphere of "Girl" and "How Far She Went." To what extent is setting an element of conflict in each story?

2. On page 76 of "The Things They Carried," there is a flashback to the time Jimmy Cross touched Martha's knee in a movie theater. How is the flashback introduced? Speculate on how much background is implied in this short passage and how much the author knew that he left out.

3. In "Mobili," how is the alien quality of the atmosphere conveyed?

4. Much of the story of "Orbiting" depends on a complicated past. Observe how Mukherjee alternates flashback with brief references.

WRITING ASSIGNMENTS

1. Write a scene, involving only one character, who is uncomfortable in his or her surroundings: socially inadequate, frightened, revolted, painfully nostalgic, or the like. Using active verbs in your description of the setting, build forceful conflict between the person and the place.

2. Write a scene with two characters in conflict over the setting: One wants to go, and one wants to stay. The more interesting the setting you choose, the more interesting the conflict will inevitably be.

3. Write a scene in a setting that is likely to be quite familiar to your readers (supermarket, dormitory, classroom, movie theater, suburban house, etc.) but that is unfamiliar, strange, outlandish, or outrageous to the central character. Let us feel the strangeness through the character's eyes.

4. Write a scene set in a strange, exotic place or a time far distant either in the past or the future, in which the setting is quite familiar to the central character. Convince us of the ordinariness of the place.

5. Write a scene in which the character's mood is at odds with the weather and make the weather nevertheless express her or his mood: The rain is joyful, the clear skies are threatening, the snow is comforting, the summer beach is chilling.

6. Write a scene containing a flashback in which the information about the past is crucial to an understanding of the present.

7. Write a scene that begins with a circumstantial summary and then moves to a scene in slow motion.

CALL ME ISHMAEL
Point of View, Part I

Who Speaks?
To Whom?
In What Form?

Point of view is the most complex element of fiction. Although it lends itself to analysis, definitions, and diagrams, it is finally a question of relationship among writer, characters, and reader—subject like any relationship to organic subtleties. We can discuss person, omniscience, narrative voice, tone, authorial distance, and reliability; but none of these things will ever pigeonhole a work in such a way that any other work may be placed in the exact same pigeonhole.

The first thing to do is to set aside the common use of the phrase "point of view" as being synonymous with "opinion," as in *It's my point of view that they all ought to be shot.* An author's view of the world as it is and as it ought to be will ultimately be revealed by his or her manipulation of the technique of point of view, but not vice versa—identifying the author's beliefs will not describe the point of view of the work. Rather than thinking of point of view as an opinion or belief, begin with the more literal synonym of "vantage point." Who is standing *where* to watch the scene?

Better, since we are dealing with a verbal medium, these questions might be translated: *Who speaks? To whom? In what form? At what distance from the action? With what limitations?* All these issues go into the determination of the point of view. Because *the author inevitably wants to convince us to share the same perspective,* the answers will also help reveal her or his final opinion, judgment, attitude, or message.

This chapter deals with the first three questions: *Who speaks? To whom? In what form?* Distance and limitations are considered in chapter 8.

Point of View

Who Speaks?

The Author	The Author	A Character
In: Third Person	In: Second Person	In: First Person
Editorial Omniscient	"You" as character	Central Narrator
Limited Omniscient	"You" as reader-turned-	Peripheral Narrator
Objective	character	

To Whom?

The Reader	Another Character or Characters	The Self
Characterized or Uncharacterized		

In What Form?

"Written Story," "Spoken Story," Reportage, Oratory, Monologue, Confessional, Journal, Diary, Interior Monologue, Stream of Consciousness, etc.

At What Distance?

Reader and Author ⟷ Narrator ⟷ Characters
Complete Identification ⟷ Complete Opposition
Temporal, Spatial, Moral, Intellectual, Aesthetic, Physical, Educational, Experiential

With What Limitations?

Reliable Narrator (or "Author") ⟷ Unreliable Narrator (or "Author")
on any of values listed above

Who Speaks?

The primary point-of-view decision that you as author must make before you can set down the first sentence of the story is *person.* This is the simplest and crudest subdivision that must be made in deciding who speaks. The story can be told in the third person. (*She walked out into the harsh sunlight*), the second person (*You walked out into the harsh sunlight*), or the first person (*I walked out into the harsh sunlight*). Third- and second-person stories are "told" by an author; first-person stories, by a character.

THIRD PERSON

Third person, in which the author is telling the story, can be subdivided again according to the degree of knowledge, or *omniscience*, the author assumes. Notice that since this is a matter of degree, the subdivisions are again only a crude indication of the variations possible. As an author you are free to decide how much you know. You may know every universal and eternal truth; you may know what is in the mind of one character but not what is in the mind of another; or you may know only what can be externally observed. You decide, and very early in the story you signal to the reader what degree of omniscience you have chosen. Once given, this signal constitutes a "contract" between author and reader, and it will be difficult to break the contract gracefully. if you have restricted yourself to the mind of James Lordly for five pages, as he observes the actions of Mrs. Grumms and her cats, you will violate the contract by suddenly dipping into Mrs. Grumms's mind to let us know what she thinks of James Lordly. We are likely to feel misused, and likely to cancel the contract altogether, if you suddenly give us the thoughts of the cats.

The *omniscient author*, sometimes referred to as the *editorial omniscient author* because she or he tells us directly what we are supposed to think, has total knowledge. As omniscient author you are God. You can:

1. Objectively report what is happening;
2. Go into the mind of any character;
3. Interpret for us that character's appearance, speech, actions, and thoughts, even if the character cannot do so;
4. Move freely in time or space to give us a panoramic, telescopic, microscopic, or historical view; tell us what has happened elsewhere or in the past or what will happen in the future;
5. Provide general reflections, judgments, and truths.

In all these aspects, we will accept what the omniscient author tells us. If you tell us that Ruth is a good woman, that Jeremy doesn't really understand his own motives, that the moon is going to explode in four hours and that everybody will be better off for it, we will believe you. Here is a paragraph that blatantly exhibits all five of these areas of knowledge.

(1) Joe glared at the screaming baby. (2) Frightened by his scowl, the baby gulped and screamed louder. I hate that thing, Joe thought. (3) But it was not really hatred that he felt. (4) Only two years ago he himself had screamed like that. (5) Children can't tell hatred from fear.

This illustration is awkwardly compressed, but an author well in control of his or her craft can move easily from one area of knowledge to another. In the first scene of *War and Peace*, Tolstoy describes Anna Scherer.

To be an enthusiast had become her social vocation, and sometimes even when she did not feel like it, she became enthusiastic in order not to disappoint the expectations of those who knew her. The subdued smile which, though it did not suit her faded features, always played around her lips, expressed as in a spoiled child, a continual consciousness of her charming defect, which she neither wished, nor could, nor considered it necessary to correct.

In two sentences Tolstoy tells us what is in Anna's mind, what the expectations of her acquaintances are, what she looks like, what suits her, what she can and cannot do; and he offers a general reflection on spoiled children.

The omniscient voice is the voice of the classical epic (*And Meleager, far-off, knew nothing of this, but felt his vitals burning with fever*), of the Bible (*So the Lord sent a pestilence upon Israel; and there fell seventy thousand men*), and of most nineteenth-century novels (*Tito put out his hand to help him, and so strangely quick are men's souls that in this moment, when he began to feel that his atonement was accepted, he had a darting thought of the irksome efforts it entailed*). But it is one of the manifestations of literature's movement downward in class from heroic to common characters, inward from action to the mind, that authors of the twentieth century have largely avoided the godlike stance of the omniscient author and have chosen to restrict themselves to fewer areas of knowledge.

The *limited omniscient viewpoint* is one in which the author may move with some, but not all, of the omniscient author's freedom. You may grant yourself the right, for example, to know what the characters in a scene are thinking but not to interpret their thoughts. You may interpret one character's thoughts and actions but see the others only externally. You may see with microscopic accuracy but not presume to reach any universal truths. The most commonly used form of the limited omniscient point of view is one in which the author can see events objectively and also grants himself or herself access to the mind of one character, but not to the minds of the others, nor to any explicit powers of judgment. This point of view is particularly useful for the short story because it very quickly establishes the point-of-view character or *means of perception*. The short story is so compressed a form that there is rarely time or space to develop more than one consciousness. Staying with external observation and one character's thoughts helps control the focus and avoid *awkward point-of-view shifts*.

But the form is also frequently used for the novel, as in Gail Godwin's *The Odd Woman*.

> It was ten o'clock on the evening of the same day, and the permanent residents of the household on the mountain were restored to routines and sobriety. Jane, on the other hand, sat by herself in the kitchen, a glass of Scotch before her on the cleanly wiped table, going deeper and deeper into a mood she could recognize only as unfamiliar. She could not describe it; it was both frightening and satisfying. It was like letting go and being taken somewhere. She tried to trace it back. When, exactly, had it started?

It is clear here that the author has limited her omniscience. She is not going to tell us the ultimate truth about Jane's soul, nor is she going to define for us the "unfamiliar" mood that the character herself cannot define. The author has the facts at her disposal, and she has Jane's thoughts, and that is all.

The advantage of the limited omniscient over the omniscient voice is immediacy. Here, because we are not allowed to know more than Jane does about her own thoughts and feelings, we grope *with* her toward understanding. In the process, a contract has been made between the author and the reader, and this contract must not now be broken. If at this point the author should step in and answer Jane's question, "When, exactly, had it started?" with, "Jane was never to remember this, but in fact it had started one afternoon when she was two years old," we would feel it as an abrupt and uncalled-for *authorial intrusion*.

Nevertheless, within the limits the author has set herself, there is fluidity and a range of possibilities. Notice that the passage begins with a panoramic observation (*ten o'clock, permanent residents, routines*) and moves to the tighter focus of a view, still external, of Jane (*sat by herself in the kitchen*), before moving into her mind. The sentence "She tried to trace it back" is a relatively factual account of her mental process, whereas in the next sentence, "When, exactly, had it started?" we are in Jane's mind, overhearing her question to herself.

Although this common form of the limited omniscient (objective reporting plus one mind) may seem very restricted, given all the possibilities of omniscience, it has a freedom that no human being has. In life you have full access to only one mind, your own; and you are also the one person you may not externally observe. As a fiction writer you can do what no human being can do, be simultaneously inside and outside a given character; it is this that E. M. Forster describes in *Aspects of the Novel* as "the fundamental difference between people in daily life and people in books."

> In daily life we never understand each other, neither complete clairvoyance nor complete confessional exists. We know each other approximately, by external signs, and these serve well enough as a basis for society and even for intimacy. But people in a novel can be understood completely by the reader, if the novelist wishes; their inner as well as their outer life can be exposed. And this is why they often seem more definite than characters in history, or even our own friends.

The *objective author* is not omniscient but impersonal. As an objective author, you restrict your knowledge to the external facts that might be observed by a human being; to the senses of sight, sound, smell, taste, and touch. In the story "Hills Like White Elephants," Ernest Hemingway reports what is said and done by a quarreling couple, both without any direct revelation of the characters' thoughts and without comment.

> The American and the girl with him sat at a table in the shade, outside the building. It was very hot and the express from Barcelona would come in forty minutes. It stopped at this junction for two minutes and went on to Madrid.
> "What should we drink?" the girl asked. She has taken off her hat and put it on the table.
> "It's pretty hot," the man said.
> "Let's drink beer."
> "Dos cervezas," the man said into the curtain.
> "Big ones?" a woman asked from the doorway.
> "Yes. Two big ones."
> The woman brought two glasses of beer and two felt pads. She put the felt pads and the beer glasses on the table and looked at the man and the girl. The girl was looking off at the line of hills. They were white in the sun and the country was brown and dry.

In the course of this story we learn, entirely by inference, that the girl is pregnant and that she feels herself coerced by the man into having an abortion. Neither pregnancy nor abortion is ever mentioned. The narrative remains clipped, austere, and external. What does Hemingway gain by this pretense of objective reporting? The reader is allowed to discover what is really happening. The characters avoid the subject, prevaricate, and pretend, but they betray their real meanings and feelings through gestures, repetitions, and slips of the tongue. The reader, focus directed by the author, learns by inference, as in life, so that we finally have the pleasure of knowing the characters better than they know themselves.

For the sake of clarity, the possibilities of third-person narration have been divided into the editorial omniscient, limited omniscient, and objective authors, but between the extreme stances of the editorial omniscient (total knowledge) and the objective author (external observation only), the powers of the limited omniscient are immensely variable. Because you are most likely to choose your authorial voice in this range, you need to be aware that you make your own rules and that, having made them, you must stick to them. Your position as a writer is analogous to that of a poet who may choose whether to write free verse or a ballad stanza. If the poet chooses the stanza, then he or she is obliged to rhyme. Beginning writers of prose fiction are often tempted to shift viewpoint when it is both unnecessary and disturbing.

> Leo's neck flushed against the prickly weave of his uniform collar. He concentrated on his buttons and tried not to look into the face of the bandmaster, who, however, was more amused than angry.

This is an awkward point-of-view shift because, having felt Leo's embarrassment with him, we are suddenly asked to leap into the bandmaster's feelings. The shift can be corrected by moving instead from Leo's mind to an observation that he might make.

> Leo's neck flushed against the prickly weave of his uniform collar. He concentrated on his buttons and tried not to look into the face of the bandmaster, who, however, was astonishingly smiling.

The rewrite is easier to follow because we remain with Leo's mind as he observes that the bandmaster is not angry. It further serves the purpose of implying that Leo fails to concentrate on his buttons, and so intensifies his confusion.

SECOND PERSON

First and third persons are most common in literature; the second person remains an idiosyncratic and experimental form, but it is worth mentioning because several twentieth-century authors have been attracted to its possibilities.

Person refers to the basic mode of a piece of fiction. In the third person, all the characters will be referred to as *he, she,* or *they.* In the first person, the character telling the story will refer to himself or herself as *I* and to other characters as *he, she,* or *they.* The second person is the basic mode of the story *only when a character* is referred to as *you.* When an omniscient author addresses the reader as *you* (*You will remember that John Doderring was left dangling on the cliff at Dover*), this does not alter the basic mode of the piece from third to second person. Only when "you" become an actor in the drama is the story or novel written in second person.

In *Even Cowgirls Get the Blues*, Tom Robbins exhibits both of these uses of the second person.

> If you could buckle your Bugs Bunny wristwatch to a ray of light, your watch would continue ticking but its hands wouldn't move.

The *you* involved here is a generalized reader, and the passage is written in the stance of an omniscient author delivering a general "truth."

But when the author turns to address his central character, Sissy Hankshaw, the basic mode of the narration becomes that of the second person.

> You hitchhike. Timidly at first, barely flashing your fist, leaning almost imperceptibly in the direction of your imaginary destination. A squirrel runs along a tree limb. You hitchhike the squirrel. A blue jay flies by. You flag it down.

The effect of this second-person narration is odd and original; the author observes Sissy Hankshaw, and yet his direct address implies an intimate and affectionate relationship that makes it easy to move further into her mind.

> Your thumbs separate you from other humans. You begin to sense a presence about your thumbs. You wonder if there is not magic there.

In this example it is a character clearly delineated and distinguished from the reader who is the *you* of the narrative. But the second person can also be used as a means of making the reader into a character, as in Robert Coover's story, "Panel Game," quoted in chapter 6.

> You squirm, viced by Lady (who excites you) and America (who does not, but bless him all the same), but your squirms are misread: Lovely Lady lifts lashes, crosses eyes, and draws breath excitedly. . . . Audience howls happily the while and who can blame them? You, Sport, resign yourself to pass the test in peace and salute them with a timid smile, squirm no more.

Here again the effect of the second person is unusual and complex. The author assigns you, the reader, specific characteristics and reactions, and thereby—assuming that you go along with his characterization of you—pulls you deeper and more intimately into the story.

It is unlikely that the second person will ever become a major mode of narration as the first and third are, but for precisely that reason you may find it an attractive experiment. It is startling and relatively unexplored.

A story is told in the first person when it is a character who speaks. The term "narrator" is sometimes loosely used to refer to any teller of a tale, but strictly speaking a story has a narrator only when it is told in the first person by one of the characters. This character may be the protagonist, the *I* telling *my* story, in which case that character is a *central narrator;* or the character may be telling a story about someone else, in which case he or she is a *peripheral narrator.*

In either case it's important to indicate early which kind of narrator we have so that we know who the story's protagonist is, as in the first paragraph of Alan Sillitoe's "The Loneliness of the Long-Distance Runner."

> As soon as I got to Borstal they made me a long-distance cross-country runner. I suppose they thought I was just the build for it because I was long and skinny for my age (and still am) and in any case I didn't mind it much, to tell you the truth, because running had always been made much of in our family, especially running away from the police.

The focus here is immediately thrown on the *I* of the story, and we expect that *I* to be the central character whose desires and decisions impel the action. But from the opening lines of R. Bruce Moody's *The Decline and Fall of Daphne Finn,* it is Daphne who is brought alive by attention and detail, while the narrator is established as an observer and recorder of his subject.

> "Is it really you?"
> Melodious and high, this voice descended to me from behind and above—as it seemed it was always to do—indistinct as bells in another country.
> Unable to answer in the negative, I turned from my desk, looked up, and smiled sourly.
> "Yes," I said, startling a face which had been peering over my shoulder, a face whose beauty it was apparent at the outset had made no concession to convention.
> It retreated as her feet staggered back.

The central narrator is always, as the term implies, at the center of the action; the peripheral narrator may be in virtually any position that is not the center. He or she may be the second most important character in the story, or may not be involved in the action at all but merely placed in a position to observe. The narrator may characterize himself or herself in detail or may remain detached and scarcely identifiable. It is even possible to make the first-person narrator plural, as William Faulkner does in "A Rose for Emily," where the story is told by a narrator identified only as one of "us," the people of the town in which the action has taken place.

That a narrator may be either central or peripheral, that a character may tell either his own story or someone else's, is both commonly assumed and obviously logical. But the author and editor Rust Hills, in his book *Writing in General and the Short Story in Particular,* takes interesting and persuasive exception to this idea. When point of view fails, Hills argues, it is always because the perception we are using for the course of the story is different from that of the character who is moved or changed by the action. Even when a narrator seems to be a peripheral observer and the story is "about" someone else, in fact it is the narrator who is changed, and must be, in order for us to be satisfied by our emotional identification with him or her.

> This, I believe, is what will always be the case in successful fiction: that either the character moved by the action will be the point-of-view character, or else the point-of-view character will *become* the character moved by the action. Call it Hills' Law.

Obviously, this view does not mean that we have to throw out the useful fictional device of the peripheral narrator. Hills uses the familiar examples of *The Great Gatsby* and *Heart of Darkness* to illustrate his meaning. In the former, Nick Carroway as a peripheral narrator observes and tells the story of Jay Gatsby, but by the end of the book it is Nick's life that has been changed by what he has observed. In the latter, Marlow purports to tell the tale of the ivory hunter Kurtz, even protesting that "I don't want to bother you much with what happened to me personally." By the end of the story, Kurtz (like Gatsby) is dead, but it is not the death that moves us so much as what, "personally," Marlow has learned *through* Kurtz and his death. The same can be said of *The Decline and Fall of Daphne Finn;* the focus of the action is on Daphne, but the pain, the passion, and the loss are those of her biographer. Even in "A Rose for Emily," where the narrator is a collective "we," it is the implied effect of Miss Emily on the town that moves us, the emotions of the townspeople that we share. Because we tend to identify with the means of perception in a story, we are moved with that perception; even when the overt action of the story is elsewhere, it is often the act of observation itself that provides the epiphany.

The thing to recognize about a first-person narrator is that because she or he is a character, she or he has all the limitations of a human being and cannot be omniscient. The narrator is confined to reporting what she or he could realistically know. More than that, although the narrator may certainly interpret actions, deliver dictums, and predict the future, these remain the fallible opinions of a human being; we are not bound to accept them as we are bound to accept the interpretations, truths, and predictions of the omniscient author. You may want us to accept the narrator's word, and then the most difficult part of your task, and the touchstone of your story's success, will be to convince us to trust and believe the narrator.

On the other hand, it may be an important part of your purpose that we should reject the narrator's opinions and form our own. In the latter case, the narrator is "unreliable," a phenomenon that will be taken up in chapter 8.

To Whom?

In choosing a point of view, the author implies an identity not only for the teller of the tale, but also for the audience.

THE READER

Most fiction is addressed to a literary convention, "the reader." When we open a book, we tacitly accept our role as a member of this unspecified audience. If the story begins, "I was born of a drunken father and an illiterate mother in the peat bogs of Galway during the Great Potato Famine," we are not, on the whole, alarmed. We do not face this clearly deceased Irishman who has crossed the Atlantic to take us into his confidence and demand, "Why are you telling me all this?"

Notice that the tradition of "the reader" assumes the universality of the audience. Most stories do not specifically address themselves to a segment or period of humanity, and they make no concessions to such difference as might exist between reader and author; they assume that anyone who reads the story can be brought around to the same understanding of it the author has. In practice most writers, though they do not acknowledge it in the text and may not admit it to themselves, are addressing someone *who can* be brought around to the same understanding as themselves. The author of a "Harlequin Romance" addresses the story to a generalized "reader" but knows that his or her likely audience is trained by repetition of the formula to expect certain Gothic features—rich lover, virtuous heroine, threatening house, colorful costume. Slightly less formulaic is the notion of "a *New Yorker* story," which is presumably what the author perceives that the editors perceive will be pleasing to the people who buy *The New Yorker*. Anyone who pens or types what he or she hopes is "literature" is assuming that his or her audience is literate, which leaves out better than half the world. My mother, distressed at the difficulty of my fictional style, used to urge me to write for "the masses," by which she meant subscribers to the *Reader's Digest*, whom she thought to be in need of cheering and escape. I considered this a very narrow goal until I realized that my own ambition to be "universal" was more exclusive still: I envisioned my audience as made up of people who would *not* subscribe to the *Reader's Digest*.

Nevertheless, the most common assumption of the tale-teller, whether omniscient author or narrating character, is that the reader is an amenable and persuasible Everyman, and that the telling needs no justification.

But there are various exceptions to this tendency which can be used to dramatic effect and which always involve a more definite characterizing of the receiver of the story. The author may address "the reader" but assign that reader specific traits that we, the actual readers, must then accept as our own if we are to accept the fiction. Nineteenth-century novelists had a tradition of addressing "You, gentle reader," "Dear reader," and the like, and this minimal characterization was a technique for implying mutual understanding. In "The Loneliness of the Long-Distance Runner," by Alan Sillitoe, on the other hand, the narrator divides the world into "us" and "you." We, the narrator and his kind, are the outlaws, all those who live by their illegal wits; you, the readers, are by contrast law-abiding, prosperous, educated, and rather dull. To quote again from "The Loneliness of the Long-Distance Runner":

> I suppose you'll laugh at this, me saying the governor's a stupid bastard when I know hardly how to write and he can read and write and add-up like a professor. But what I say is true right enough. He's stupid and I'm not, because I can see further into the likes of him than he can see into the likes of me.

The clear implication here is that the narrator can see further into the likes of us readers than we can see into the likes of him, and much of the effective irony of the story rests in the fact that the more we applaud and identify with the narrator, the more we must accept his condemning characterization of "us."

ANOTHER CHARACTER

More specifically still, the story may be told to *another character*, or *characters*, in which case we as readers "overhear" it; the teller of the tale does not acknowledge us even by implication. Just as the third-person author telling "her story" is theoretically more impersonal than the first-person character telling "my story," so "the reader" is theoretically a more impersonal receiver of the tale than another character. I insert the word "theoretically" because, with regard to point of view more than any other element of fiction, any rule laid down seems to be an invitation to rule breaking by some original and inventive author.

In the *epistolary* novel or story, the narrative consists entirely of letters written from one character to another, or between characters.

> I, Mukhail Ivanokov, stone mason in the village of Ilba in the Ukranian Soviet Socialist Republic, greet you and pity you, Charles Ashland, petroleum merchant in Titusville, Florida, in the United States of America. I grasp your hand.
>
> KURT VONNEGUT, "The Manned Missiles"

Or the convention of the story may be that of a monologue, spoken aloud by one character to another.

> May I, *monsieur,* offer my services without running the risk of intruding? I fear you may not be able to make yourself understood by the worthy ape who presides over the fate of this establishment. In fact, he speaks nothing but Dutch. Unless you authorize me to plead your case, he will not guess that you want gin.
>
> ALBERT CAMUS, *The Fall*

Again, the possible variations are infinite; the narrator may speak in intimate confessional to a friend or lover, or may present his case to a jury or a mob; she may be writing a highly technical report of the welfare situation, designed to hide her emotions; he may be pouring out his heart in a love letter he knows (and we know) he will never send.

In any of these cases, the convention employed is the opposite of that employed in a story told to "the reader." The listener as well as the teller is involved in the action; the assumption is not that we readers are there but that we are not. We are eavesdroppers, with all the ambiguous intimacy that position implies.

THE SELF

An even greater intimacy is implied if the character's story is as secret as a diary or as private as a mind, addressed to *the self* and not intended to be heard by anyone inside or outside the action.

In a *diary* or *journal,* the convention is that the thoughts are written, but not expected to be read by anyone except the writer.

> November 6
> Something has got into the Chief of my Division. When I arrived at the office he called me and began as follows: "Now then, tell me. What's the matter with you? . . . I know you're trailing after the Director's daughter. Just look at yourself—what are you? Just nothing. You haven't a penny to your name. Look in the mirror. How can you even think of such things?" The hell with him! Just because he's got a face like a druggist's bottle and that quiff of hair on his head all curled and pomaded.
>
> NIKOLAI GOGOL, *The Diary of a Madman*

The protagonist here is clearly using his diary to vent his feelings and does not intend it to be read by anyone else. Still, he has deliberately externalized his secret thoughts in a journal. Because the author has the power to enter a character's mind, the reader also has the power to eavesdrop on thoughts, read what is not written, hear what is not spoken, and share what cannot be shared.

Overheard thoughts are generally of two kinds, of which the most common is *interior monologue*, the convention being that we follow that character's thoughts in their sequence, though in fact the author, for our convenience, sets out those thoughts with a coherence and logic that no human mind ever possessed.

> I must organize myself. I must, as they say, pull myself together, dump this cat from my lap, stir—yes, resolve, move, do. But do what? My will is like the rosy dustlike light in this room: soft, diffuse, and gently comforting. It lets me do . . . anything . . . nothing. My ears hear what they happen to; I eat what's put before me; my eyes see what blunders into them; my thoughts are not thoughts, they are dreams. I'm empty or I'm full . . . depending; and I cannot choose. I sink my claws in Tick's fur and scratch the bones of his back until his rear rises amorously. Mr. Tick, I murmur, I must organize myself, I must pull myself together. And Mr. Tick rolls over on his belly, all ooze.
>
> WILLIAM H. GASS, "In the Heart of the Heart of the Country"

This interior monologue ranges, as human thoughts do, from sense impression to self-admonishment, from cat to light to eyes and ears, from specific to general and back again. But the logical connections between these things are all provided; the mind "thinks" logically and grammatically as if the character *were* trying to express himself.

Stream of consciousness acknowledges the fact that the human mind does not operate with the order and clarity of the monologue just quoted. Even what little we know of its operations makes clear that it skips, elides, makes and breaks images, leaps faster and further than any mere sentence can suggest. Any mind at any moment is simultaneously accomplishing dozens of tasks that cannot be conveyed simultaneously. As you read this sentence, part of your mind is following the sense of it; part of your mind is directing your hand to hold the book open; part of it is twisting your spine into a more comfortable position; part of it is still lingering on the last interesting image of this text, Mr. Tick rolling over on his belly, which reminds you of a cat you had once that was also *all ooze*, which reminds you that you're nearly out of milk and have to finish this chapter before the store closes . . . and so forth.

In *Ulysses*, James Joyce tried to catch the speed and multiplicity of the mind with the technique that has come to be known as stream of consciousness. The device is difficult and in many ways thankless: Since the speed of thought is so much faster than that of writing or speaking, and stream of consciousness tries to suggest the process as well as the content of the mind, it requires a more, not less, rigorous selection and arrangement than ordinary grammar requires. But Joyce and a very few other writers have handled stream of consciousness as an ebullient and exciting way of capturing the mind.

> Yes because he never did a thing like that before as ask to get his breakfast in bed with a couple of eggs since the *City Arms* hotel when he used to be pretending

to be laid up with a sick voice doing his highness to make himself interesting to that old faggot Mrs. Riordan that he thought he had a great leg of and she never left us a farthing for all masses for herself and her soul greatest miser ever was actually afraid to lay out 4d for her methylated spirit telling me all her ailments she had too much old chat in her about politics and earthquakes and the end of the world let us have a bit of fun first God help the world if all the women were her sort. . . .

JAMES JOYCE, Ulysses

The preceding two examples, of interior monologue and stream of consciousness, respectively, are written in the first person, so that we overhear the minds of narrator characters. Through the omniscient and limited omniscient authors we may also overhear the thoughts of the characters, and when this is the case there is a curious doubling or crossing of literary conventions. Say that the story is told by a limited omniscient author, who is therefore speaking to "the reader." But this author may also enter the mind of a character, who is speaking to himself or herself. The passage from *The Odd Woman* on page 206 is of this sort. Here is a still more striking example:

> Dusk was slowly deepening. Somewhere, he could not tell exactly where, a cricket took up a fitful song. The air was growing soft and heavy. He looked over the fields, longing for Bobo. . . .
> He shifted his body to ease the cold damp of the ground, and thought back over the day. Yeah, he'd been dam [sic] right about not wanting to go swimming. If he had followed his right mind he'd never have gotten into all this trouble.

RICHARD WRIGHT, "Big Boy Leaves Home"

Though this story, first published in 1938, makes use of an old style of dialect misspelling, Wright moves gracefully between the two voices. An authorial voice—educated, eloquent, and mature—tells us what is in Big Boy's mind: *he could not tell exactly where, longing for Bobo*; and a dialect voice lets us overhear Big Boy's thoughts, adolescent and uneducated: *Yeah, hed been dam right.* If either of these voices were absent, the passage would be impoverished; it needs the scope of the author and the immediacy of the character to achieve its effect.

In What Form?

The form of the story, like the teller and the listener, can be more or less specified as part of the total point of view. The form may announce itself without justification as a generalized *story*, either *written* or *spoken*; or it may suggest *report-*

age, *confessional, interior monologue,* or *stream of consciousness;* or it may be overtly identified as *monologue, oratory, journal,* or *diary.* The relationship between the teller of a tale and its receiver often automatically implies a form for the telling, so that most of the forms above have already been mentioned. The list is not exhaustive; you can tell your story in the form of a catalogue or a television commercial as long as you can devise a way to do so that also has the form of a story.

Form is important to point of view because the form in which a story is told indicates the degree of self-consciousness on the part of the teller; this will in turn affect the language chosen, the intimacy of the relationship, and the honesty of the telling. A written account will imply less spontaneity, on the whole, than one that appears to be spoken aloud, which suggests less spontaneity than thought. A narrator writing a letter to his grandmother may be less honest than he is when he tells the same facts aloud to his friend.

Certain relationships established by the narrative between teller and audience make certain forms more likely than others, but almost any combination of answers is possible to the questions, *Who speaks? To whom? In what form?* If you are speaking as an omniscient author to the literary convention of "the reader," we may assume that you are using the convention of "written story" as your form. But you might say:

> Wait, step over here a minute. What's this in the corner, stuffed down between the bedpost and the wall?

If you do this, you slip at least momentarily into the different convention of the spoken word—the effect is that we are drawn more immediately into the scene—and the point of view of the whole is slightly altered. A central narrator might be thinking, and therefore "talking to herself," while actually angrily addressing her thoughts to another character. Conversely, one character might be writing a letter to another but letting the conscious act of writing deteriorate into a betrayal of his own secret thoughts. Any complexities such as these will alter and inform the total point of view.

Here are the opening passages from a student short story in which the point of view is extremely complex. An adequate analysis of it will require, more than a definition or a diagram, a series of *yes but's* and *but also's.*

> Report: He is the light-bringer, the peerless one. She is the dark-water creature, the Queen of Fishes. I don't know why I say that except sometimes I get desperate for sheer sound. You would too if you went to St. Katherine's Day Academy where the D.H. Lawrence is in a locked cabinet in the library. I used to wonder why Tom sends me there except now I know it's his notion of a finishing school. "It's what your mother would have wanted," he says, tragic-eyed. But I know he's thinking about Vivian.
>
> I started my journal to show you what she's doing to him. He doesn't know. He

wouldn't. But I sit in on the seminar. I read the Eliot, the Rhys, the Muir, the MacDiarmid with them. They think I'm amusing, these long tall girls in *Rive Gauche* jeans and velour with Parker chrome mechanical pencils—engraved initials—and notebooks written all over: "Bring *The Green Helmet* to class Tues." and "talk to Dr. Johnson about Parents' Day Brunch" and phone numbers everywhere. I am a sort of mascot. They'd be surprised to know that I, their Tom's daughter, knows what they are at when they talk of regional sensibility in Muir and the mythic fallacy. Especially Vivian who comes to class early and stays late and comes for dinner and once "took Elaine shopping, isn't that nice?" God, I hated it. "Look, Elaine, that grey would just match your eyes. I'll bet Tom, I mean your father, would like that." I went home that day and cast a Mars number square against her for discord, discord, discord. But still she came back—back for Tom.

DIANE ROBERTS, "Lamia"

Who speaks? The passage is written in the first person—that much is easy. So it is a narrator who speaks, and this narrator tells us that she is peripheral: "I started my journal to show you what she's doing to him." But against this statement of the narrator's intention, we feel so much personal grief and bottled fury, and the focus of the narrative returns so insistently to what the *I* of the story is doing and feeling, that we are inclined to believe the real subject is not "what she's doing to him" but *what they're doing to me* and, therefore, to feel that we're dealing with a central narrator.

To whom? The narrator addresses a *you* who is clearly the convention of "the reader." Yet on several counts this notion doesn't bear pursuing. She is revealing bitter attitudes that couldn't be confessed to her father, so the *you* to whom she reveals them can scarcely include a reader sitting with printed pages. The reader who is the *you* of the narrative becomes so abstract that it might be the spirit of justice she addresses, or God. Yet the narrator makes little attempt to present a coherent account of background facts, which come out obliquely, subsidiary to the pent-up emotion—*I am a sort of mascot; They'd be surprised to know*—which suggests that she's really talking to herself.

In what form? She tells us twice: this is "a report" and "my journal." Neither is quite possible. The opening word "Report" is immediately contradicted by the dramatic imagery of "light-bringer" and "dark-water creature," so that we understand the word itself is an ironic attempt to claim logic and objectivity for an emotion that admits of neither. It's a journal, then, a diary of great intimacy. That's what it feels like; but how can a diary be addressed to a reader?

The amazing thing about all this is that we are not in the least confused! The paradoxes and contradictions of the narrative do not make us feel that the author is inept but, on the contrary, that she has captured with great precision the paradoxes and contradictions of the narrator's emotional state. We feel no awkward point-of-view shift because all the terms of the contract—those same paradoxes and contradictions—are laid out for us in the opening paragraph.

Clearly there is an author somewhere who is not the same person as this narrator, and who is directing us moment by moment to accept or reject, to believe or disbelieve, what the narrator tells us.

In order to deal with a viewpoint as complex as this, it will be necessary to deal not only with who speaks to whom in what form, but also with *distance* and *limitation*, subjects treated in chapter 8.

❦

The Masked Marvel's Last Toehold

RICHARD SELZER

Morning Rounds.

On the fifth floor of the hospital, in the west wing, I know that a man is sitting up in his bed, waiting for me. Elihu Koontz is seventy-five, and he is diabetic. It is two weeks since I amputated his left leg just below the knee. I walk down the corridor, but I do not go straight into his room. Instead, I pause in the doorway. He is not yet aware of my presence, but gazes down at the place in the bed where his leg used to be, and where now there is the collapsed leg of his pajamas. He is totally absorbed, like an athlete appraising the details of his body. What is he thinking, I wonder. Is he dreaming the outline of his toes? Does he see there his foot's incandescent ghost? Could he be angry? Feel that I have taken from him something for which he yearns now with all his heart? Has he forgotten so soon the pain? It was a pain so great as to set him apart from all other men, in a red-hot place where he had no kith or kin. What of those black gorilla toes and the soupy mess that was his heel? I watch him from the doorway. It is a kind of spying, I know.

Save for a white fringe open at the front, Elihu Koontz is bald. The hair has grown too long and is wilted. He wears it as one would wear a day-old laurel wreath. He is naked to the waist, so that I can see his breasts. They are the breasts of Buddha, inverted triangles from which the nipples swing, dark as garnets.

I have seen enough. I step into the room, and he sees that I am there.

"How did the night go, Elihu?"

He looks at me for a long moment. "Shut the door," he says.

I do, and move to the side of the bed. He takes my left hand in both of his, gazes at it, turns it over, then back, fondling, at last holding it up to his cheek. I do not withdraw from this loving. After a while he relinquishes my hand, and looks up at me.

"How is the pain?" I ask.

He does not answer, but continues to look at me in silence. I know at once that he has made a decision.

"Ever hear of The Masked Marvel?" He says this in a low voice, almost a whisper.

"What?"

"The Masked Marvel," he says. "You never heard of him?"

"No."

He clucks his tongue. He is exasperated.

All at once there is a recollection. It is dim, distant, but coming near.

"Do you mean the wrestler?"

Eagerly, he nods, and the breasts bob. How gnomish he looks, oval as the huge helpless egg of some outlandish lizard. He has very long arms, which, now and then, he unfurls to reach for things—a carafe of water, a get-well card. He gazes up at me, urging. He *wants* me to remember.

"Well . . . yes," I say. I am straining backward in time. "I saw him wrestle in Toronto long ago."

"Ha!" He smiles. "You saw *me*." And his index finger, held rigid and upright, bounces in the air.

The man has said something shocking, unacceptable. It must be challenged.

"You?" I am trying to smile.

Again that jab of the finger. "You saw *me*."

"No," I say. But even then, something about Elihu Koontz, those prolonged arms, the shape of his head, the sudden agility with which he leans from his bed to get a large brown envelope from his nightstand, something is forcing me toward a memory. He rummages through his papers, old newspaper clippings, photographs, and I remember . . .

It is almost forty years ago. I am ten years old. I have been sent to Toronto to spend the summer with relatives. Uncle Max has bought two tickets to the wrestling match. He is taking me that night.

"He isn't allowed," says Aunt Sarah to me. Uncle Max has angina.

"He gets too excited," she says.

"I wish you wouldn't go, Max," she says.

"You mind your own business," he says.

And we go. Out into the warm Canadian evening. I am not only abroad, I am abroad in the *evening!* I have never been taken out in the evening. I am terribly excited. The trolleys, the lights, the horns. It is a bazaar. At the Maple Leaf Gardens, we sit high and near the center. The vast arena is dark except for the brilliance of the ring at the bottom.

It begins.

The wrestlers circle. They grapple. They are all haunch and paunch. I am shocked by their ugliness, but I do not show it. Uncle Max is exhilarated. He leans forward, his eyes unblinking, on his face a look of enormous happiness. One after the other, a pair of wrestlers enter the ring. The two men join, twist, jerk, tug, bend, yank, and throw. Then they leave and are replaced by another pair. At last it is the main event. "The Angel vs. The Masked Marvel."

On the cover of the program notes, there is a picture of The Angel hanging from the limb of a tree, a noose of thick rope around his neck. The Angel hangs just so for an hour every day, it is explained, to strengthen his neck. The Masked Marvel's trademark is a black stocking cap with holes for the eyes and mouth. He is never seen without it, states the program. No one knows who The Masked Marvel really is!

"Good," says Uncle Max. "Now you'll see something." He is fidgeting, waiting for them to appear. They come down separate aisles, climb into the ring from opposite sides. I have never seen anything like them. It is The Angel's neck that first captures the eye. The shaved nape rises in twin columns to puff into the white hood of a sloped and bosselated skull that is too small. As though, strangled by the sinews of that neck, the skull had long since withered and shrunk. The thing about The Angel is the absence of any mystery in his body. It is simply *there*. A monosyllabic announcement. A grunt. One looks and knows everything at once, the fat thighs, the gigantic buttocks, the great spine from which hang knotted ropes and pale aprons of beef. And that prehistoric head. He is all of a single hideous piece, The Angel is. No detachables.

The Masked Marvel seems dwarfish. His fingers dangle kneeward. His short legs are slightly bowed as if under the weight of the cask they are forced to heft about. He has breasts that swing when he moves! I have never seen such breasts on a man before.

There is a sudden ungraceful movement, and they close upon one another. The Angel stoops and hugs The Marvel about the waist, locking his hands behind The Marvel's back. Now he straightens and lifts The Marvel as though he were uprooting a tree. Thus he holds him, then stoops again, thrusts one hand through The Marvel's crotch, and with the other grabs him by the neck. He rears and . . . The Marvel is aloft! For a long moment, The Angel stands as though deciding where to make the toss. Then throws. Was that board or bone that splintered there? Again and again, The Angel hurls himself upon the body of The Masked Marvel.

Now The Angel rises over the fallen Marvel, picks up one foot in both of his hands, and twists the toes downward. It is far beyond the tensile strength of mere ligament, mere cartilage. The Masked Marvel does not hide his agony, but pounds and slaps the floor with his hand, now and then reaching up toward The Angel in an attitude of supplication. I have never seen such suffering. And all the while his black mask rolls from side to side, the mouth pulled to a tight slit through which issues an endless hiss that I can hear from where I sit. All at once, I hear a shouting close by.

"Break it off! Tear off a leg and throw it up here!"

It is Uncle Max. Even in the darkness I can see that he is gray. A band of sweat stands upon his upper lip. He is on his feet now, panting, one fist pressed at his chest, the other raised warlike toward the ring. For the first time I begin to think that something terrible might happen here. Aunt Sarah was right.

"Sit down, Uncle Max," I say. "Take a pill, please."

He reaches for the pillbox, gropes, and swallows without taking his gaze from the wrestlers. I wait for him to sit down.

"That's not fair," I say, "twisting his toes like that."

"It's the toehold," he explains.

"But it's not *fair*," I say again. The whole of the evil is laid open for me to perceive. I am trembling.

And now The Angel does something unspeakable. Holding the foot of The Marvel at full twist with one hand, he bends and grasps the mask where it clings to the back of The Marvel's head. And he pulls. He is going to strip it off! Lay bare an ultimate carnal mystery! Suddenly it is beyond mere physical violence. Now I am on my feet, shouting into the Maple Leaf Gardens.

"Watch out," I scream. "Stop him. Please, somebody, stop him."

Next to me, Uncle Max is chuckling.

Yet The Masked Marvel hears me, I know it. And rallies from his bed of pain. Thrusting with his free heel, he strikes The Angel at the back of the knee. The Angel falls. The Masked Marvel is on top of him, pinning his shoulders to the mat. One! Two! Three! And it is over. Uncle Max is strangely still. I am gasping for breath. All this I remember as I stand at the bedside of Elihu Koontz.

Once again, I am in the operating room. It is two years since I amputated the left leg of Elihu Koontz. Now it is his right leg which is gangrenous. I have already scrubbed. I stand to one side wearing my gown and gloves. And . . . *I am masked.* Upon the table lies Elihu Koontz, pinned in a fierce white light. Spinal anesthesia has been administered. One of his arms is taped to a board placed at a right angle to his body. Into this arm, a needle has been placed. Fluid drips here from a bottle overhead. With his other hand, Elihu Koontz beats feebly at the side of the operating table. His head rolls from side to side. His mouth is pulled into weeping. It seems to me that I have never seen such misery.

An orderly stands at the foot of the table, holding Elihu Koontz's leg aloft by the toes so that the intern can scrub the limb with antiseptic solutions.

The intern paints the foot, ankle, leg, and thigh, both front and back, three times. From a corner of the room where I wait, I look down as from an amphitheater. Then I think of Uncle Max yelling, "Tear off a leg. Throw it up here." And I think that forty years later I am making the catch.

"It's not fair," I say aloud. But no one hears me. I step forward to break The Masked Marvel's last toehold.

Suggestions for Discussion

1. Who speaks in "The Masked Marvel's Last Toehold?" To whom? In what form?

2. Is the surgeon a peripheral or a central narrator? It is Elihu Koontz who loses his legs; how can the surgeon be said to be the one who is changed in the story?

3. How does the contrast between the surgeon's thoughts and his professional demeanor help characterize him?

4. The flashback beginning on page 220 moves back and forth between summary and scene. What is the function of each?

5. In the flashback the narrator re-creates his consciousness as a boy. How might the description differ if he were telling of the wrestling match from his adult perspective? What would be lost?

6. Suppose that the story were told from the point of view of The Masked Marvel. Could it be the same story?

⊷

The Wrysons

JOHN CHEEVER

The Wrysons wanted things in the suburb of Shady Hill to remain exactly as they were. Their dread of change—of irregularity of any sort—was acute, and when the Larkin estate was sold for an old people's rest home, the Wrysons went to the Village Council meeting and demanded to know what sort of old people these old people were going to be. The Wrysons' civic activities were confined to upzoning, but they were very active in this field, and if you were invited to their house for cocktails, the chances were that you would be asked to sign an upzoning petition before you got away. This was something more than a natural desire to preserve the character of the community. They seemed to sense that there was a stranger at the gates—unwashed, tirelessly scheming, foreign, the father of disorderly children who would ruin their rose garden and depreciate their real-estate investment, a man with a beard, a garlic breath, and a book. The Wrysons took no part in the intellectual life of the community. There was hardly a book in their house, and, in a place where even cooks were known to have Picasso reproductions hanging above their washstands, the Wrysons' taste in painting stopped at marine sunsets and bowls of flowers. Donald Wryson was a large man with thinning fair hair and the cheerful air of a bully, but he was a bully only in the defense of rectitude, class distinctions, and the orderly appearance of things. Irene Wryson was not a totally unattractive woman, but she was both shy and contentious—especially contentious on the subject of upzoning. They had one child, a little girl named Dolly, and they lived in a pleasant house on Alewives Lane, and they went in for gardening. This was another way of keeping up the appearance of things, and Donald Wryson was very critical of a neighbor who had ragged syringa bushes and a bare spot on her front lawn. They led a limited social life; they seemed to have no ambitions or needs in this direction, although at Christmas each year they sent out about six hundred cards. The preparation and addressing of these must have occupied their evenings for at least two weeks. Donald had a laugh like a jackass, and people who did not like him were careful not to sit in the same train coach with him. The Wrysons were stiff; they were inflexible. They seemed to experience not distaste but alarm when they found quack grass in their lawn or heard of a contemplated divorce among their neighbors. They were odd, of course. They were not as odd as poor, dizzy Flossie Dolmetch, who was caught forging drug prescriptions and was discovered to have been under the influence of morphine for three years. They were not as odd as Caruthers Mason, with his collection of two thousand lewd photographs, or as odd as Mrs. Temon, who, with those two lovely children in the next room— But why go on? They were odd.

Irene Wryson's oddness centered on a dream. She dreamed once or twice a month that someone—some enemy or hapless American pilot—had exploded a hydrogen bomb. In the light of day, her dream was inadmissible, for she could not relate it to her garden, her interest in upzoning, or her comfortable way of life. She could not bring herself to tell her husband at breakfast that she had dreamed about the hydrogen bomb. Faced with the pleasant table and its view of the garden—faced even with rain and snow—she could not find it in herself to explain what had troubled her sleep. The dream cost her much in energy and composure, and often left her deeply depressed. Its sequence of events varied, but it usually went like this.

The dream was set in Shady Hill—she dreamed that she woke in her own bed. Donald was always gone. She was at once aware of the fact that the bomb had exploded. Mattress stuffing and a trickle of brown water were coming through a big hole in the ceiling. The sky was gray—lightless—although there were in the west a few threads of red light, like those charming vapor trails we see in the air after the sun has set. She didn't know if these were vapor trails or some part of that force that would destroy the marrow in her bones. The gray air seemed final. The sky would never shine with light again. From her window she could see a river, and now, as she watched, boats began to come upstream. At first, there were only two or three. Then there were tens, and then there were hundreds. There were outboards, excursion boats, yachts, schooners with auxiliary motors; there were even rowboats. The number of boats grew until the water was covered with them, and the noise of motors rose to a loud din. The jockeying for position in this retreat up the river became aggressive and then savage. She saw men firing pistols at one another, and a rowboat, in which there was a family with little children, smashed and sunk by a cruiser. She cried, in her dream, to see this inhumanity as the world was ending. She cried, and she went on watching, as if some truth was being revealed to her—as if she had always known this to be the human condition, as if she had always known the world to be dangerous and the comforts of her life in Shady Hill to be the merest palliative.

Then in her dream she turned away from the window and went through the bathroom that connected their room and Dolly's. Her daughter was sleeping sweetly, and she woke her. At this point, her emotions were at their strongest. The force and purity of the love that she felt toward this fragrant child was an agony. She dressed the little girl and put a snowsuit on her and led her into the bathroom. She opened the medicine cabinet, the one place in the house that the Wrysons, in their passion for neatness, had not put in order. It was crowded with leftover medicines from Dolly's trifling illnesses—cough syrups, calamine lotion for poison ivy, aspirin, and physics. And the mild perfume of these remnants and the tenderness she had felt for her daughter when she was ill—as if the door of the medicine cabinet had been a window opening onto some dazzling summer of the emotions—made her cry again. Among the bottles was one that said "Poison," and she reached for this and unscrewed the top, and shook into her left hand a pill for herself and one for the girl. She told the trusting child some gentle lie, and was about to put the pill between her lips when the ceiling of the bathroom collapsed and they stood knee deep in plaster and dirty water. She groped around in the water for the poison, but it was lost, and the dream usually ended in this way. And how could she lean across the breakfast table and explain her pallor to her husky husband with this detailed vision of the end of the world? He would have laughed his jackass laugh.

Donald Wryson's oddness could be traced easily enough to his childhood. He had been raised in a small town in the Middle West that couldn't have had much to recommend it, and his father, an old-fashioned commercial traveler, with a hothouse rose in his buttonhole and buff-colored spats, had abandoned his wife and his son when the boy was young. Mrs. Wryson had few friends and no family. With her husband gone, she got a job as a clerk in an insurance office, and took up, with her son, a life of unmitigated melancholy and need. She never forgot the horror of her abandonment, and she leaned so heavily for support on her son that she seemed to threaten his animal spirits. Her life was a Calvary, as she often said, and the most she could do was to keep body and soul together.

She had been young and fair and happy once, and the only way she had of evoking these lost times was by giving her son baking lessons. When the nights were long and cold and the wind whistled around the four-family house where they lived, she would light a fire in the kitchen range and drop an apple peel onto the stove lid for the fragrance. Then Donald would put on an apron and scurry around, getting out the necessary bowls and pans, measuring out flour and sugar, separating eggs. He learned the contents of every cupboard. He knew where the spices and the sugar were kept, the nutmeats and the citron, and when the work was done, he enjoyed washing the bowls and pans and putting them back where they belonged. Donald loved these hours himself, mostly because they seemed to dispel the oppression that stood unlifted over those years of his mother's life—and was there any reason why a lonely boy should rebel against the feeling of security that he found in the kitchen on a stormy night? She taught him how to make cookies and muffins and banana bread and, finally, a Lady Baltimore cake. It was sometimes after eleven o'clock when their work was done. "We do have a good time together, don't we, son?" Mrs. Wryson would ask. "We have a lovely time together, don't we, you and me? Oh, hear that wind howling! Think of the poor sailors at sea." Then she would embrace him, she would run her fingers through his light hair, and sometimes, although he was much too big, she would draw him onto her lap.

All of that was long ago. Mrs. Wryson was dead, and when Donald stood at the edge of her grave he had not felt any very great grief. She had been reconciled to dying years before she did die, and her conversation had been full of gallant references to the grave. Years later, when Donald was living alone in New York, he had been overtaken suddenly, one spring evening, by a depression as keen as any in his adolescence. He did not drink, he did not enjoy books or movies or the theatre, and, like his mother, he had few friends. Searching desperately for some way to take himself out of his misery, he hit on the idea of baking a Lady Baltimore cake. He went out and bought the ingredients—deeply ashamed of himself—and sifted the flour and chopped the nuts and citron in the kitchen of the little walk-up apartment where he lived. As he stirred the cake batter, he felt his depression vanish. It was not until he had put the cake in the oven and sat down to wipe his hands on his apron that he realized how successful he had been in summoning the ghost of his mother and the sense of security he had experienced as a child in her kitchen on stormy nights. When the cake was done he iced it, ate a slice, and dumped the rest into the garbage.

The next time he felt troubled, he resisted the temptation to bake a cake, but he was not always able to do this, and during the eight or nine years he had been married to Irene he must have baked eight or nine cakes. He took extraordinary precautions, and she knew nothing of this. She believed him to be a complete stranger to the kitchen. And how could he at the breakfast table—all two hundred and sixteen pounds of him—explain that he looked sleepy because he had been up until three baking a Lady Baltimore cake, which he had hidden in the garage?

Given these unpleasant facts, then, about these not attractive people, we can dispatch them brightly enough, and who but Dolly would ever miss them? Donald Wryson, in his crusading zeal for upzoning, was out in all kinds of weather, and let's say that one night, when he was returning from a referendum in an ice storm, his car skidded down Hill Street, struck the big elm at the corner, and was demolished. Finis. His poor widow, either through love or dependence, was inconsolable. Getting out of bed one morning, a month or so after the loss of her husband, she got her feet caught in the dust ruffle and fell and broke her hip. Weakened by a long convalescence, she contracted pneumonia and departed this life. This leaves us with Dolly to account for, and what a sad tale we can write for this little girl. During the months in which her parents' will is in probate, she lives first on the charity and then on the forbearance of her neighbors. Finally, she is sent to live with her only relative, a cousin of her mother's, who is a schoolteacher in Los Angeles. How many hundreds of nights will she cry herself to sleep in bewilderment and loneliness. How strange and cold the world will seem. There is little to remind her of her parents except at Christmas, when, forwarded from Shady Hill, will come Greetings from Mrs. Sallust Trevor, who has been living in Paris and does not know about the accident; Salutations from the Parkers, who live in Mexico and never did get their lists straight; Season's Greetings from Meyers' Drugstore; Merry Christmas from the Perry Browns; Santissimas from the Oak Tree Italian Restaurant; A Joyeux Noël from Dodie Smith. Year after year, it will be this little girl's responsibility to throw into the wastebasket these cheerful holiday greetings that have followed her parents to and beyond the grave. . . . But this did not happen, and if it had, it would have thrown no light on what we know.

What happened was this: Irene Wryson had her dream one night. When she woke, she saw that her husband was not in bed. The air smelled sweet. Sweating suddenly, the beating of her heart strained with terror, she realized that the end had come. What could that sweetness in the air be but atomic ash? She ran to the window, but the river was empty. Half asleep and feeling cruelly lost as she was, she was kept from waking Dolly only by a healthy curiosity. There was smoke in the hallway, but it was not the smoke of any common fire. The sweetness made her feel sure that this was lethal ash. Led on by the smell, she went on down the stairs and through the dining room into the lighted kitchen. Donald was asleep with his head on the table and the room was full of smoke. "Oh, my darling," she cried, and woke him.

"I burned it," he said when he saw the smoke pouring from the oven. "I burned the damned thing."

"I thought it was the hydrogen bomb," she said.

"It's a cake," he said. "I burned it. What made you think it was the hydrogen bomb?

"If you wanted something to eat, you should have waked me," she said.

She turned off the oven, and opened the window to let out the smell of smoke and let in the smell of nicotiana and other night flowers. She may have hesitated for a moment, for what would the stranger at the gates—that intruder with his beard and his book—have made of this couple, in their nightclothes, in the smoke-filled kitchen at half past four in the morning? Some comprehension—perhaps momentary—of the complexity of life must have come to them, but it was only momentary. There were no further explanations. He threw the cake, which was burned to a cinder, into the garbage, and they turned out the lights and climbed the stairs, more mystified by life than ever, and more interested than ever in a good appearance.

Suggestions for Discussion

1. How, in the opening sentence, does the Wryson's desire that things "remain exactly as they were" prepare for the conflict?

2. Describe the point of view employed in the first long paragraph. Whose judgments can you identify? How? Where are the judgments supported by specific details and where are they undermined?

3. In the second paragraph we move into Irene Wryson's consciousness. How does this shift of viewpoint alter your sympathy?

4. Donald Wryson's section is presented mostly in flashback. How does that affect the point of view of the story?

5. Describe the consistent inconsistencies of the two characters.

6. "Given these unpleasant facts . . ." begins a fantasy of the Wrysons' demise. Whose fantasy?

7. At the end of the story the Wrysons are the same as they were at the beginning, only more so. How is the situation nevertheless the opposite of that at the beginning?

8. How would you describe the point of view of the story as a whole?

RETROSPECT

1. Who speaks in "Everything That Rises Must Converge"? To whom? In what form?

2. The first half of "The Mayor of the Sister City . . ." is told in what form? Describe how this affects the viewpoint of the story. Who is really telling it?

3. Who speaks in "Girl"? (Is this a trick question?) What would be lost if "Girl" were told in the omniscient?

WRITING ASSIGNMENTS

1. Write a short scene about the birth or death of anything. (You may interpret "anything" liberally—the birth or death of a person, plant, animal, machine, scheme, passion, etc.) Use all five areas of knowledge of the *editorial omniscient author*. Be sure to do the following: Give us the thoughts of more than one character, tell us something about at least one character that he or she doesn't know or realize, include some exposition from the past or the future, and provide at least one universal "truth."

2. Write a love scene, serious or comic, from the *limited omniscient* viewpoint, confining yourself to objective observation and the thoughts of one character. Make this character believe that the other loves her or him, while the external actions make clear to the reader that this is not so.

3. Write about your most interesting recent dream, using the viewpoint of the *objective author*. Without any comment or interpretation whatever, report the events (the more bizarre, the better) as they occur.

4. Write a scene from the point of view of a *peripheral narrator* who is not at all involved in the events he or she describes but who is placed in a position from which to observe them. Nevertheless, make the observing narrator the character who is moved by the action.

5. Write a letter from a *central narrator* to another character from whom the narrator wants a great deal of money. Convince us as readers that the money is deserved.

6. Place your character in an uncomfortable social situation and write a passage in which the character's thoughts are presented both in an *interior monologue* and aloud. Nothing else. Contrast the expressed with the unexpressed thoughts.

7. Write a scene in the *second person*, in which the reader is drawn into identifying with the protagonist.

8

ASSORTED LIARS
Point of View, Part II

At What Distance?
With What Limitations?

At What Distance?

As with the chemist at her microscope and the lookout in his tower, fictional point of view always involves the *distance*, close or far, of the perceiver from the thing perceived. Point of view in fiction, however, is immensely complicated by the fact that distance is not only, though it may be partly, spatial. It may also be temporal. Or the distance may be intangible and involve a judgment—moral, intellectual, and/or emotional. More complicated still, the narrator or characters or both may view the action from one distance, the author and reader from another.

> In any reading experience there is an implied dialogue among author, narrator, the other characters and the reader. Each of the four can range, in relation to each of the others, from identification to complete opposition, on any axis of value, moral, intellectual, aesthetic and even physical. . . . From the author's viewpoint, a successful reading of his book must eliminate all distance between [his] essential norms . . . and the norms of the postulated reader.
>
> WAYNE C. BOOTH, *The Rhetoric of Fiction*

Booth means that the author may ask us to identify completely with one character and totally condemn another. One character may judge another harshly while the author suggests that we should qualify that judgment. Author, characters, and reader are always in the dialogue, but if there is also a narrator, that narrator may think himself morally superior while the author behind his back makes sure that we will think him morally deficient. Further, the four members of the dialogue may operate differently in various areas of value: The character calls the narrator stupid and ugly; the narrator thinks herself ugly but clever; the author and the reader know that she is both intelligent and beautiful. The result is an *authorial distance*, or what John Gardner termed *psychic distance*—the distance the reader perceives between himself or herself and the fiction.

Any complexity or convolution of judgments among author, narrator, and characters can make successful fiction. The one relationship in the dialogue in which there must not be any opposition is between author and reader. We may find the characters and/or the narrator bad, stupid, and tasteless and still applaud the book as just, brilliant, and beautiful. But if the hero's agony strikes us as ridiculous, if the comedy leaves us cold—if we say that the *book* is bad, stupid, or tasteless—then we are in opposition to the author on some axis of value and reject his or her "point of view" in the sense of "opinion." Ultimately, the reader must accept the "essential norms"—the attitudes and judgments—of the author, even if only provisionally, whether these are the norms of the characters or not, if the fiction is going to work.

I can think of no exception to this rule, and it is not altered by experimental plays and stories in which the writer's purpose is to embarrass, anger, or disgust us. Our acceptance of such experiments rests on our understanding that the writer did want to embarrass, anger, or disgust us, just as we accept being frightened by a horror story because we know that the writer set out to frighten us. If we think the writer is disgusting by accident, ineptitude, or moral depravity, then we are "really" disgusted and the fiction does not work.

It is a frustrating experience for many beginning (and established) authors to find that, whereas they meant the protagonist to appear sensitive, their readers find him self-pitying; whereas he meant her to be witty, the readers find her vulgar. When this happens there is a failure of authorial, or psychic, distance: The author did not have sufficient perspective on the character to convince us to share his or her judgment. I recall one class in which a student author had written, with excellent use of image and scene, the story of a young man who fell in love with an exceptionally beautiful young woman, and whose feelings turned to revulsion when he found out she had had a mastectomy. The most vocal feminist in the class loved this story, which she described as "the exposé of a skuzzwort." This was not, from the author's point of view, a successful reading of his story.

The notion of authorial distance may be clarified by drawing a parallel with acting. Assume that you go on successive nights to see Tom Cruise in *Risky Business* and *Born on the Fourth of July*. In both, you're aware of Cruise-the-actor—his face, his voice, the way he moves, the characteristic expressions that he brings to both roles. At the same time you're willing to accept his identity now as a gangly, greedy teenager, now as a grunt on a mission to Vietnam. While Joel Goodson stumbles and dances his way toward entrepreneurial success, you identify with his comically shallow goals and hope he will succeed, and you understand that Cruise-the-actor wishes you so to identify. While Ron Kovic suffers the loss of his limbs and grows toward political awareness, you identify with his critical attitude and his commitment, and you understand that Cruise-the-actor wishes you so to identify. In one of them, you judge with the actor that money is a fine thing; in the other, you choose with the actor an honorable poverty. Neither judgment attaches to Cruise-the-actor.

The same phenomenon occurs between writer and reader of fiction. We may judge Moll Flanders to be materialistic; the Godfather, brutal; and Popeye, psychotic. But we understand that the author has directed us toward these judgments and do not think Defoe materialistic, Puzo brutal, or Faulkner psychotic. A significant difference is that the actor has various physical and vocal means to direct our judgment; the writer's resources are the selection and arrangement of words alone. Only as an omniscient author may you "tell" us what your attitude is—and even then you may opt not to. If you purport to be objective, or if you are speaking through the mouth or mind of a character or narrator, then you must show us by implication, through your *tone*.

The word "tone," applied to fiction, is a metaphor derived from music and also commonly—and metaphorically—used to describe color and speech. When we speak of a "tone of voice" we mean, as in fiction, that an attitude is conveyed, and this attitude is determined by the situation and by the relation of the persons involved in the situation. Tone can match, emphasize, alter, or contradict the meaning of the words.

The situation is that Louise stumbles into her friend Judy's apartment, panting, hair disheveled, coat torn, and face blanched. Judy rushes to support her. "You look awful! What happened?" Here the tone conveys alarm, openness, and a readiness to sympathize.

Judy's son wheels in grinning, swinging a baseball bat, shirt torn, mud splattered, and missing a shoe. "You look awful! What happened?" Judy's tone is angry, exasperated.

Louise's ex-boyfriend drops by that night decked out in a plaid polyester sports coat and an electric blue tie. "You look awful! What happened?" Louise says, her tone light, but cutting, so that he knows she means it.

Judy's husband comes back from a week in Miami and takes off his shirt to model his tan. "You look awful! What happened?" she teases, playful and flirting, so that he knows she means he looks terrific.

In each of these situations the attitude is determined by the situation and the emotional relationships of the persons involved, and in life as in acting the various tones would be conveyed by vocal means—pitch, tempo, plosion, nasality—reinforced by posture, gesture, and facial expression. When we apply the word "tone" to fiction, we tacitly acknowledge that we must do without these helpful signs. The author, of course, may describe pitch, posture, and the like, or may identify a tone as "cutting" or "playful," but these verbal and adverbial aids describe only the tone used among characters, whereas the fictional relationship importantly includes an author who must also convey identification or distance, sympathy or judgment, and who must choose and arrange words so that they match, emphasize, alter, or contradict their inherent meaning.

SPATIAL AND TEMPORAL DISTANCE

The author's or narrator's attitude may involve distance in time or space or both. When a story begins, "Long ago and far away," we are instantly transported by a tone we recognize as belonging to fairy tale, fantasy, and neverland. The year 1890 may be long ago and the Siberian salt mines far away, but if the author is going to expose prison conditions in czarist Russia, he had better take another tone.

Anytime you (or your narrator) begin by telling us that the events you are relating took place in the far past, you distance us, making a submerged promise that the events will come to an end, since they "already have." This, of course, may be a device to lure us into the story, and you may—almost certainly do—want to draw us into closer and deeper involvements as the story progresses.

> That spring, when I had a great deal of potential and no money at all, I took a job as a janitor. That was when I was still very young and spent money very freely, and when, almost every night, I drifted off to sleep lulled by sweet anticipation of that time when my potential would suddenly be realized and there would be capsule biographies of my life on the dust jackets of many books.
>
> JAMES ALAN McPHERSON, "Gold Coast"

Here a distance in time indicates the attitude of the narrator toward his younger self, and his indulgent, self-mocking tone (*lulled by sweet anticipation of that time when my potential would suddenly be realized*) invites us as readers to identify with the older, narrating self. We know that he is no longer lulled by such fantasies, and, at least for the duration of the story, neither are we. That is, we are close to the narrator, distanced from him as a young man, so that the distance in time also involves distance in attitude. The story "Gold Coast" continues to reinforce this distance, the temporal involving us in the emotional.

> I then became very rich, with my own apartment, a sensitive girl, a stereo, two speakers, one tattered chair, one fork, a job, and the urge to acquire. . . .

Now, all of us either know, or are, people who would consider a job, an apartment, and a sensitive girl very real prosperity. But the author forces us to take a longer perspective than we might in life by including the contrast between "very rich" and "one fork" and "the urge to acquire." Only toward the end of the story, when the narrator himself is moved by his memory, does he let us share the emotion of the younger self.

In the next passage, the author makes use of space to establish an impersonal and authoritative tone.

> An unassuming young man was traveling, in midsummer, from his native city of Hamburg, to Davos-Platz in the Canton of Grisons, on a three weeks' visit.
>
> From Hamburg to Davos is a long journey—too long, indeed, for so brief a stay. It crosses all sorts of country; goes up hill and down dale, descends from the plateau of Southern Germany to the shore of Lake Constance, over its bounding waves and on across marshes once thought to be bottomless.
>
> THOMAS MANN, *The Magic Mountain*

Here Mann distances us from the young man by characterizing him perfunctorily, not even naming him, and describes the place travelogue style, inviting us to take a panoramic view. This choice of tone establishes a remoteness that is emotional as well as geographical, and would do so even if the reader happened to be a native of Grisons. Again, we will eventually become intimately involved with Davos and the unassuming young man, who is in for a longer stay than he expects.

By closing the literal distance between the reader and the subject, the intangible distance can be closed as well.

> Her face was half an inch from my face. The curtain flapped at the open window and her pupils pulsed with the coming and going of the light. I know Jill's eyes; I've painted them. They're violent and taciturn, a ring of gas-blue points like cold explosion to the outside boundary of iris, the whole held back with its brilliant lens. A detonation under glass.
>
> JANET BURROWAY, *Raw Silk*

In the extreme closeness of this focus, we are brought emotionally close, invited to share the narrator's perspective of Jill's explosive eyes.

It will be obvious that using time and space as a means of controlling the reader's emotional closeness or distance involves all the elements of atmosphere discussed in chapter 6. This is true of familiarity, which invites identification with a place, and of strangeness, which alienates. And it is true of summary, which distances, and of scene, which draws us close. If you say, "There were twelve diphtheria outbreaks in Coeville over the next thirty years," you invite us to take a detached historical attitude. But if you say, "He forced his finger into her throat and tilted her toward the light to see, as he'd expected, the grayish membrane reaching toward the roof of her mouth and into her nose," the doctor may remain detached, but we as readers cannot.

There is a grammatical technique very often misused involving distance and the use of time as *tense*. Most fiction in English is written in the *past tense* (*She put her foot on the shovel and leaned all her weight against it*). The author's constant effort is to give this past the immediacy of the present. A story may be written in the *present tense* (*She puts her foot on the shovel and leans all her weight against it*). The effect of the present tense, somewhat self-consciously, is to reduce distance and increase immediacy: we are there. Generally speaking, the tense once established *should not be changed*.

> Danforth got home about five o'clock in the morning and fixed himself a peanut butter sandwich. He eats it over the sink, washing it down with half a carton of chocolate milk. He left the carton on the sink and stumbled up to bed.

The change of tense in the second sentence is pointless; it violates the reader's sense of time to have the action skip from past to present and back again and produces no compensating effect.

There are times, however, when a change of tense can be functional and effective. In the story "Gold Coast," we are dealing with two time frames, one having to do with the narrator's earlier experiences as a janitor, and one in which he acknowledges the telling.

> I left the rug on the floor because it was dirty and too large for my new apartment. I also left the two plates given me by James Sullivan, for no reason at all. Sometimes I want to go back to get them, but I do not know how to ask for them or explain why I left them in the first place.

The tense change here is logical and functional: It acknowledges the past of the "story" and the present of the "telling"; it also incidentally reinforces our emotional identification with the older, narrating self.

Sometimes, however, a shift into the present tense without a strictly logical justification can achieve the effect of intensity and immediacy, so that the emotional distance between reader and character is diminished.

> When alone he had a dreadful and distressing desire to call someone, but he knew beforehand that with others present it would be still worse. "Another dose of morphine—to lose consciousness. I will tell him, the doctor, that he must think of something else. It's impossible, impossible, to go on like this."
>
> An hour and another pass like that. But now there's a ring at the doorbell. Perhaps it's the doctor? It is. He comes in fresh, hearty, plump and cheerful.
>
> LEO TOLSTOY, *The Death of Ivan Ilyich*

This switch from the past to the present draws us into the character's anguish and makes the doctor's arrival more intensely felt. Notice that Ivan Ilyich's thoughts—

"Another dose of morphine"—which occur naturally in the present tense, serve as a transition from past to present so that we are not jolted by the change. In *The Death of Ivan Ilyich*, Tolstoy keeps the whole scene of the doctor's visit in the present tense, while Ivan Ilyich's consciousness is at a pitch of pain, contempt for the doctor, and hatred for his wife; then, as the focus moves to the wife, the tense slips back into the past.

> The thrill of hatred he feels for her makes him suffer from her touch.
> Her attitude towards him and his disease is still the same. Just as the doctor had adopted a certain relation to his patient which he could not abandon, so had she formed one toward him . . . and she could not now change that attitude.

The present tense can be effectively employed to depict moments of special intensity, but it needs both to be saved for those crucial moments and to be controlled so carefully in the transition that the reader is primarily aware of the intensity, rather than the tense.

INTANGIBLE DISTANCE

Spatial and temporal distance, then, can imply distance in the attitude of the teller toward his or her material. But authorial distance may also be implied through tone without any tangible counterpart.

Tone itself is an intangible, and there are probably as many possible tones as there are possible situations, relationships, and sentences. But in a very general way, we will trust, in literature as in life, a choice of words that seems appropriate in intensity or value to the meaning conveyed. If the intensity or value seems inappropriate, we will start to read between the lines. If a woman putting iodine on a cut says "Ouch," we don't have to search for her meaning. But if the cut is being stitched up without anesthetic, then "Ouch" may convey courage, resignation, and trust. If she says "Ouch" when her lover strokes her cheek, then we read anger and recoil into the word.

In the same way, you as author manipulate intensity and value in your choice of language, sometimes matching meaning, sometimes contradicting, sometimes overstating, sometimes understating, to indicate your attitude to the reader.

> She was a tall woman of imperious mien, handsome, with definite black eyebrows. Her smooth black hair was parted exactly. For a few moments she stood steadily watching the miners as they passed along the railway; then she turned toward the brook course. Her face was calm and set, her mouth was closed with disillusionment.
>
> D. H. LAWRENCE, "Odor of Chrysanthemums"

There is in this passage no discrepancy between the thing conveyed and the intensity with which it is conveyed, and we take the words at face value, accepting that the woman is as the author says she is. The phrase "imperious mien" has itself an imperious tone about it (I doubt one would speak of a *real cool mien*). The syntax is as straightforward as the woman herself. (Notice how the rhythm alters with "For a few moments," so that the longest and most flowing clause follows the passing miners.) You might describe the tone of the passage as a whole as "calm and set."

The next example is quite different.

> Mrs. Herriton did not believe in romance, nor in transfiguration, nor in parallels from history, nor in anything that may disturb domestic life. She adroitly changed the subject before Philip got excited.
>
> E. M. FORSTER, *Where Angels Fear to Tread*

This is clearly also a woman of "imperious mien," and the author purports, like the first, to be informing us of her actions and attitudes. But unlike the first example, the distance here between the woman's attitude and the author's is apparent. It is possible to "believe in" both romance and transfiguration, which are concepts. If Lawrence should say of the woman in "Odor of Chrysanthemums" that "she did not believe in romance, nor in transfiguration," we would accept it as a straightforward part of her characterization. But how can one believe in parallels? *Belief* is too strong a word for *parallels*, and the discrepancy makes us suspicious. Not to "believe" in "anything that may disturb domestic life" is a discrepancy of a severer order, unrealistic and absurd. The word "adroitly" presents a value judgment, one of praise. But placed as it is between "anything that may disturb domestic life" and "before Philip got excited," it shows us that Mrs. Herriton is manipulating the excitement out of domestic life.

Irony. Discrepancies of intensity and value are *ironic.* Any time there is a discrepancy between what is said and what we are to accept as the truth, we are in the presence of an irony. There are three basic types of irony.

Verbal irony is a rhetorical device in which the author (or character) says one thing and means another. Mrs. Herriton "adroitly changed the subject" is a form of verbal irony. When the author goes on to say, "Lilia tried to assert herself, and said that she should go to take care of [her mother]. It required all Mrs. Herriton's kindness to prevent her," there is further verbal irony in the combination of "required" and "kindness."

Dramatic irony is a device of plot in which the reader or audience knows more than the character does. The classical example of dramatic irony is *Oedipus Rex*, where the audience knows that Oedipus himself is the murderer he seeks. There is a dramatic irony in *The Death of Ivan Ilyich,* as Ilyich persists in ignoring the pain from his fall, protesting to himself that it's nothing, while the reader knows that it will lead to his death.

Cosmic irony is an all-encompassing attitude toward life, which takes into account the contradictions inherent in the human condition. The story "Everything That Rises Must Converge," in which Julian's contemptuous desire to get away from his mother is fulfilled, and he is devastated by it, demonstrates cosmic irony.

Any of these types of irony will inform the author's attitude toward the material and will be reflected in his or her tone. Any of them will involve authorial distance, since the author means, knows, or wishes to take into account—and also intends the reader to understand—something not wholly conveyed by the literal meaning of the words.

In the two passages quoted above, we may say that the first, from Lawrence, is without irony; the second, from Forster, contains an irony presented by the author, understood by the reader, and directed against the character described.

The following passage, again about a woman of imperious mien, is more complex because it introduces the fourth possible member of the narrative dialogue, the narrator; and it also contains temporal distance.

> She was a tall woman with high cheekbones, now more emphasized than ever by the loss of her molar teeth. Her lips were finer than most of her tribe's and wore a shut, rather sour expression. Her eyes seemed to be always fixed on the distance, as though she didn't "see" or mind the immediate, but dwelt in the eternal. She was not like other children's grandmothers we knew, who would spoil her grandchildren and had huts "just outside the hedge" of their sons' homesteads. Grandmother lived three hills away, which was inexplicable.
>
> JONATHAN KARIARA, "Her Warrior"

This paragraph begins, like Lawrence's, without irony, as a strong portrait of a strong woman. Because we trust the consistent tone of the first two sentences, we also accept the teller's smile "as though she didn't 'see' or mind the immediate," which emphasizes without contradicting. Up to this point the voice seems to have the authority of an omniscient author, but in the fourth sentence the identity of the narrator is introduced—one of the woman's grandchildren. Because the past tense is used, and even more, because the language is measured and educated, we instantly understand that the narrator is telling of his childhood perceptions from an adult, temporally distanced perspective. Curiously, the final word of the final sentence presents us with a contradiction of everything we have just found convincing. It cannot be "inexplicable" that this woman lived three hills away, because it has already been explained to us that she lived in deep and essential remoteness.

This irony is not directed primarily against the character of the grandmother but by the narrator against himself as a child. Author, narrator, and reader all concur in an intellectual distance from the child's mind and its faulty perceptions. At the same time, there is perhaps a sympathetic identification with the child's hurt, and therefore there results a residual judgment of the grandmother.

With What Limitations?

In each of the passages excerpted in the section "Intangible Distance" we trust the teller of the tale. We may find ourselves in opposition to characters perceived or perceiving, but we identify with the attitudes, straightforward or ironic, of the authors and narrators who present us these characters. We share, at least for the duration of the narrative, their norms.

THE UNRELIABLE NARRATOR

It is also possible to mistrust the teller. Authorial distance may involve not a deliberate attitude taken by the speaker, but distance on the part of the author from the narrator. The answer to the question, *Who speaks?* may itself necessitate a judgment, and again this judgment may imply opposition of the author (and reader) on any scale of value—moral, intellectual, aesthetic, or physical—and to these I would add educational and experiential (probably the list can be expanded further).

If the answer to *Who speaks?* is *a child, a bigot, a jealous lover, an animal, a schizophrenic, a murderer, a liar,* any of these may imply that the narrator speaks with *limitations* we do not necessarily share. To the extent that the narrator displays and betrays such limitations, she or he is an *unreliable narrator;* and the author, without a word to call his own, must let the reader know that the story is not to be trusted.

Here is a fourth woman, imperious and sour, who tells her own story.

> But that's why I have an understanding of the girl Ginny downstairs and her kids. They're runty, underdeveloped. No sun, no beef. Noodles, beans, cabbage. Well, my mother off the boat knew better than that. . . .
>
> Five ladies on the block, old friends, nosy, me not included, got up a meeting and wrote a petition to Child Welfare. I already knew it was useless, as the requirement is more than dirt, drunkenness, and a little once-in-a-way whoring. That is probably something why the children in our city are in such a state. I've noticed it for years, though it's not my business. Mothers and fathers get up when they wish, half being snuggled in relief, go to bed in the afternoon with their rumpy bumpy sweethearts pumping away before 3 p.m. (So help me.) Child Welfare does not show its concern. No matter who writes them. People of influence, known in the district, even the district leader, my cousin Leonie . . .
>
> GRACE PALEY, "Distance"

We mistrust every judgment this woman makes, but we are also aware of an author we do trust, manipulating the narrator's tone to expose her. The outburst is fraught with ironies (including perhaps the title, "Distance"), but because the narrator is unaware of them, they are directed against herself. She claims "understanding" and "concern" for what she exhibits as invective. She claims respectability, which she lamely bolsters by name-dropping her mother and her cousin, while her own language is "rumpy bumpy" lascivious. Her syntax betrays ignorance and her bristling intensity is spent on the wrong values, and "that is probably something why" author and reader side with Ginny and her kids in direct opposition to the narrator.

In this case the narrator is wholly unreliable, and we're unlikely to accept any judgment she could make. But it is also possible for a narrator to be reliable in some areas of value and unreliable in others. Mark Twain's Huckleberry Finn is a famous case in point. Here Huck has decided to free his friend Jim, and he is astonished that Tom Sawyer is going along with the plan.

> Well, one thing was dead sure; and that was, that Tom Sawyer was in earnest and was actuly going to help steal that nigger out of slavery. That was the thing that was too many for me. Here was a boy that was respectable, and well brung up; and had a character to lose; and folks at home that had characters; and he was bright and not leather-headed; and knowing and not ignorant; and not mean, but kind; and yet here he was, without any more pride, or rightness, or feeling, than to stoop to this business, and make himself a shame, and his family a shame, before everybody. I *couldn't* understand it, no way at all.

The extended irony in this excerpt is that slavery should be defended by the respectable, the bright, the knowing, the kind, and those of character. We reject Huck's assessment of Tom as well as the implied assessment of himself as worth so little that he has nothing to lose by freeing a slave. Huck's moral instincts are better than he himself can understand. (Notice, incidentally, how Huck's lack of education is communicated by word choice and syntax and how sparse the misspellings are.) So author and reader are in intellectual opposition to Huck the narrator, but morally identify with him.

The unreliable narrator—who has become one of the most popular characters in modern fiction—is far from a newcomer to literature and in fact predates fiction. Every drama contains characters who speak for themselves and present their own cases, and from whom we are partly or wholly distanced in one area of value or another. So we identify with Othello's morality but mistrust his logic, trust Faust's intellect but not his ethics, admire Barney Fife's heart of gold but not his courage. As these examples suggest, the unreliable narrator always presents us with dramatic irony, because we always "know" more than he or she does about the characters, the events, and the significance of both.

The following five passages—one a lyric and four prose fiction—represent narrations by five relatively mad madmen. How mad is each? To whom does each speak? In what form? Which of their statements are reliable? Which are unreliable? Which of them admit to madness? Is the admission reliable? What ironies can you identify, and against whom is each directed? What is the attitude of the author behind the narrator? By what choice and arrangement of words do you know this?

I met my old lover
   On the street last night
   She seemed so glad to see me
   I just smiled
   And we talked about some old times
   And we drank ourselves some beers
   Still crazy after all these years . . .

I'm not the kind of man
   Who tends to socialize
   I seem to lean on
   Old familiar ways
   And I ain't no fool for love songs
   That whisper in my ears
   Still crazy after all these years . . .

Now I sit by the window
   And I watch the stars
   I fear I'll do some damage
   One fine day
   But I would not be convicted
   By a jury of my peers . . .
   Still crazy after all these years.

PAUL SIMON, "Still Crazy After All These Years"

The doctor advised me not to insist too much on looking so far back. Recent events, he says, are equally valuable for him, and above all my fancies and dreams of the night before. But I like to do things in their order, so directly I left the doctor (who was going to be away from Trieste for some time). I bought and read a book on psychoanalysis, so that I might begin from the very beginning, and make the doctor's task easier. It is not difficult to understand, but very boring. I have stretched myself out after lunch in an easy chair, pencil and paper in hand. All the lines have disappeared from my forehead as I sit here with mind completely relaxed. I seem to be able to see my thoughts as something quite apart from myself. I can watch them rising, falling, their only form of activity. I seize my pencil in order to remind them that it is the duty of thought to manifest itself. At once the wrinkles collect on my brow as I think of the letters that make up every word.

ITALO SVEVO, *Confessions of Zeno*

Madrid, Februarius the thirtieth

So I'm in Spain. It all happened so quickly that I hardly had time to realize it. This morning the Spanish delegation finally arrived for me and we all got into the carriage. I was somewhat bewildered by the extraordinary speed at which we traveled. We went so fast that in half an hour we reached the Spanish border. But then, nowadays there are railroads all over Europe and the ships go so fast too. Spain is a strange country. When we entered the first room, I saw a multitude of people with shaven heads. I soon realized, though, that these must be Dominican or Capuchin monks because they always shave their heads. I also thought that the manners of the King's Chancellor, who was leading me by the hand, were rather strange. He pushed me into a small room and said: "You sit quiet and don't you call yourself King Ferdinand again or I'll beat the nonsense out of your head." But I knew that I was just being tested and refused to submit.

NIKOLAI GOGOL, *The Diary of a Madman*

Pushed back into sleep as I fight to emerge, pushed back as they drown a kitten, or a child fighting to wake up, pushed back by voices and lullabies and bribes and bullies, punished by tones of voices and by silences, gripped into sleep by medicines and syrups and dummies and dope.

Nevertheless I fight, desperate, like a kitten trying to climb out of the slippy-sided zinc pail it has been flung in, an unwanted, unneeded cat to drown, better dead than alive, better asleep than awake, but I fight, up and up into the light, greeting dark now as a different land, a different texture, a different state of the Light.

DORIS LESSING, *Briefing for a Descent into Hell*

Come into my cell. Make yourself at home. Take the chair; I'll sit on the cot. No? You prefer to stand by the window? I understand. You like my little view. Have you noticed that the narrower the view the more you can see? For the first time I understand how old ladies can sit on their porches for years.

Don't I know you? You look very familiar. I've been feeling rather depressed and I don't remember things very well. I think I am here because of that or because I committed a crime. Perhaps it's both. Is this a prison or a hospital or a prison hospital? A Center for Aberrant Behavior? So that's it. I have behaved aberrantly. In short, I'm in the nuthouse.

WALKER PERCY, *Lancelot*

UNRELIABILITY IN OTHER VIEWPOINTS

I have said that a narrator cannot be omniscient, although he or she may be reliable. It may seem equally plausible that the phenomenon of unreliability can apply only to a narrator, who is by definition a fallible human being. But the subtleties of authorial distance are such that it is possible to indicate unreliability through virtually any point of view. If, for example, you have chosen a limited omniscient viewpoint including only external observation and the thoughts of one character, then it may be that the character's thoughts are unreliable and that he or she misrepresents external facts. Then you must make us aware through tone that you know more than you have chosen to present. William Golding, in *The Inheritors*, tells his story in the third person, but through the eyes and thoughts of a Neanderthal who has not yet developed the power of deductive reasoning.

> The man turned sideways in the bushes and looked at Lok along his shoulder. A stick rose upright and there was a lump of bone in the middle. . . . Suddenly Lok understood that the man was holding the stick out to him but neither he nor Lok could reach across the river. He would have laughed if it were not for the echo of screaming in his head. The stick began to grow shorter at both ends. Then it shot out to full length again.
>
> The dead tree by Lok's ear acquired a voice.
>
> "Clop!"
>
> His ears twitched and he turned to the tree. By his face there had grown a twig: a twig that smelt of other, and of goose, and of the bitter berries that Lok's stomach told him he must not eat.

The imaginative problem here, imaginatively embraced, is that we must supply the deductive reasoning of which our point-of-view character is incapable. Lok has no experience of bows or poison arrows, nor of "men" attacking each other, so his conclusions are unreliable. "Suddenly Lok understood" is an irony setting us in opposition to the character's intellect; at the same time, his innocence makes him morally sympathetic. Since the author does not intervene to interpret for us, the effect is very near that of an unreliable narrator.

Other experiments abound. Isaac Loeb Peretz tells the story of "Bontsha the Silent" from the point of view of the editorial omniscient, privy to the deliberations of the angels, but with Yiddish syntax and "universal truths" so questionable that the omniscient voice itself is unreliable. Conversely, Faulkner's *The Sound and the Fury* is told through several unreliable narrators, each with an idiosyncratic and partial perception of the story, so that the cumulative effect is of an omniscient author able not only to penetrate many minds but also to perceive the larger significance.

I'm conscious that this discussion of point of view contains more analysis than advice, and this is because very little can be said to be right or wrong about point of view as long as the reader ultimately identifies with the author; as long, that is, as you make it work. In *Aspects of the Novel* E. M. Forster speaks vaguely, but with undeniable accuracy, of "the power of the writer to bounce the reader into accepting what he says." He then goes on to prove categorically that Dickens's *Bleak House* is a disaster, "Logically . . . all to pieces, but Dickens bounces us, so that we do not mind the shiftings of the view-point."

The one imperative is that the reader must bounce with, not against, the author.

Virtually any story can be told from virtually any point of view and convey the same attitude of the author.

Suppose, for example, that you are going to write this story: Two American soldiers, one a seasoned corporal and the other a newly arrived private, are sent on a mission in a Far Eastern "police action" to kill a sniper. They track, find, and capture the Oriental, who turns out to be a fifteen-year-old boy. The corporal offers to let the private pull the trigger, but he cannot. The corporal kills the sniper and triumphantly cuts off his ear for a trophy. The young soldier vomits; ashamed of himself, he pulls himself together and vows to do better next time.

Your attitude as author of this story is that war is inhumane and dehumanizing.

You may write the story from the point of view of the editorial omniscient, following the actions of the hunters and the hunted, going into the minds of corporal, private, and sniper, ranging the backgrounds of each and knowing the ultimate pointlessness of the death, telling us, in effect, that war is inhumane and dehumanizing.

Or you may write it from the point of view of the corporal as an unreliable narrator, proud of his toughness and his expertise, condescending to the private, certain the Orientals are animals, glorying in his trophy, betraying his inhumanity.

Between these two extremes of total omniscience and total unreliability, you may take any position of the middle ground. The story might be written in the limited omniscient, presenting the thoughts only of the anxious private and the external actions of the others. It might be written objectively, with a cold and detached accuracy of military detail. It might be written by a peripheral narrator, a war correspondent, from interviews and documents; as a letter home from the private to his girl; as a field report from the corporal; as an interior monologue of the young sniper during the seconds before his death.

Any of these modes could contain your meaning, any of them fulfill your purpose. Your central problem as a writer might prove to be the choosing. But whatever your final choice of point of view in the technical sense, your point of view in the sense of *opinion*—that war is inhumane and dehumanizing—could be suggested.

The Era of Great Numbers

LEE K. ABBOTT

Head coach Woody Knapp stood in the center of his office, a manorial layout that put him in mantic frame of mind. He had parquet floors, coromandel screens, a cream brocade sectional sofa, a mile of Marie Antoinette moldings. Through a window which opened onto the players' locker room, he saw backfield coach Nate Creer methodically beating a sophomore second-string scatback named Krebs. Coach Knapp had one thought, possibly warm-hearted, about the relationship of discipline to pedagogy; and another, this about what it meant to play football in the twenty-first century.

Near his desk his publicist, Lefty Mantillo, was on the phone, answering questions from a reporter for a special issue of *Jane's Fighting Ships*.

"They wonder if you'll use the Umayyad," Lefty said, "and how gravitons might complement the game plan."

Coach Knapp watched Nate Creer pummeling the benchwarmer. Groans were heard, as were thumps and bone-noise. He was reminded of the Turner painting of Piazza San Marco, *Juliet and Her Nurse*.

"Tell them I agree with Einstein," Coach Knapp said. "Football, like nature, is simple and beautiful."

Lefty had come to the team from the night world of rock 'n' roll. He had made famous The Unfinished Business of Childhood, a band that took turmoil as a theme to speak for the beleaguered.

"They're interested in the pregame meal," Lefty said.

Coach adjusted his tie. It was silk, crafted by the adjunct faculty in the Division of Careless Movements.

"Mango sorbet," Coach began. "A milk concoction."

"They like that," Lefty told him.

Coach read the rest: West Beach Café taquito, beignets, grillades, Mardi Gras King cake, hearts-of-palm salad, Cat Château Petrus, lobster medallions and rosettes of chestnut puree.

"One more question," Lefty said.

Lefty had the bald, thickly veined egghead of a B-movie Martian. He was said to have had in the old days an affiliation with the Montonero guerrillas of Argentina, a single-minded group with an explicit interest in hemispheric chaos.

"They want to know the pregame talk," Lefty was saying. "Chapter and verse, your perspective."

The pregame talk, Coach announced, would be the usual—about grief, how it is total and deep. "As I see it," he concluded, "we have three choices: move, ascend or vanish."

Nate Creer was finished with his player. Coach Knapp saw a puddle on the floor—necessary private fluids, perhaps—and he heard the sound of something pulpy, but in cleats, scraping toward the showers.

"Remember," Coach said, "truth is indifferent and men with guns are everywhere."

When Creer entered the room, Lefty exited in a flourish. Creer had been with Coach Knapp from the beginning, the intramural squads in the Louisiana playing fields of the Organization of American States. His virtues were a scientist's attention to detail, plus the wry imagination of a sneak-thief. He was thought to have a wife somewhere—in the First Republic of Albuquerque?—whose face had the texture of igneous rock.

"What was that beating all about?" Coach asked.

"Sloth," Creer said. "I spoke about digging deep within the self. I used the words 'ontology' and 'entelechy.' I appealed to the old conventions of manhood, of self-worth. I respected our differences within the mutuality of shared purpose. I aimed to address the issues of sacrifice, which leads to the loftimost, and puerilism, which does not. Then I pounded the stuffings out of him."

Coach Knapp picked up his briefcase, his silver whistle. "You mentioned Aquinas, I trust. And Vasco da Gama."

Nate Creer nodded. "Lordy," he said, "I love it when they smartmouth."

Woody Knapp walked through the locker room slowly. The air was stale, yellow, heavy. Several odors reached him: unguents, ointments, salves. His people, his players, were monodonists, ligubriates, inspired by Saracens. They spoke Igorot, Kimbundu, fluent New Orleans. Missing eyes, ears, toes, one or two limbs, they believed in firmaments, unified fields, what infants yearn for. In one locker, he noticed a two-page discussion of spasm-dose ratios, nuclear throw-weights; in another, a beaded reticule. He could see skull caps, djellabas, a garter belt, a life-size china snow leopard. They wore shawls, prophylacteries, vinyl jumpsuits. Coach Knapp heard a tape player somewhere, a tune called "More Facts About Life." It mentioned the pineal gland, what to do with the floccose. Like snowfall in July, its effect was eerie. One wall—this of Pentelic marble—was covered with graffiti unique to the intimate acts of man: birth, death, sport. The gods here were Cytrons and Maronites, metal constructions from the firms of Mattel and Fisher-Price in the old ages; and the atmosphere seemed basinesque, Caribbean, having to do with body-whomping and sly ways of using sweat. It brought to mind flickering torches, low but constant fevers, what can be accomplished by heedlessness.

At the entrance to the tunnel that led under the stands to the stadium, Coach Knapp met Eppley Franks, the editor of the alumni quarterly, *The Vulgate*. He was the ghostwriter for Coach's autobiography, *The Era of Great Numbers*.

"I got the galleys back yesterday," Franks was saying. His eyes were full of flecks and various luminous colors. In addition to talk linking him to specific jungle-spawned narcotics, he was said to like all things thalloid and most spore-bearing creatures.

"They want to delete the chain mail," he was saying. "They're in conference now about the anga coats and Mrs. K's silk turban. Textiles upset them."

"What do they want to substitute?"

Eppley Franks pawed through a folder of documents at his feet. His was the handwriting of an Ostrogoth, but he had the virtue of a prose style direct enough to cause excruciating pain.

"There's talk of Huns, Hittites. I heard the name Ramses Two once. There's concern with subtext. 'Despotic' is a word that gets mentioned a lot."

"Where do we stand on this?" Coach wondered.

Eppley Franks glanced at his notes. At one time he'd apparently written on ox hide.

"Statute supports us on this one. We have Bishop De Quadra, Lord Robert. Prothalamion's our big gun. They, of course, control the paper and ink."

Coach Knapp was watching the cheerleaders practicing in the near end-zone. They seemed to have come from the only cities in the world: Islamabad and Trenton, New Jersey. Lithe and sufficiently buxom, they had a cheer artful and acrobatic enough to serve increase and weal.

"Touch my hand," Coach said. "What do you hear?"

"I hear compromise," Franks said. "Expediency."

Coach was watching the smokes in the southern distances—pink and yellow and green. Fires were said to be still smoldering in El Paso. There were rumors of fierce, eccentric hot winds and the habits of displaced housewives. One heard stories—set in other regions of the baked, white deserts—of hungry dogs and the howling food fleeing them.

"One more thing, Coach."

The cheerleaders were chanting about gore.

"Speak to me, Eppley. I'm in a hurry."

"No more philosophizing, okay? I'm getting grief from just about everybody. Stick to the basics, they say. Carnage, things you've won, why everybody loves you."

In his observation tower near the fifty-yard line, Coach Knapp was approached by his defensive line coordinator, Teak Warden. His was the face of a monast—bony, hollow-eyed, mean. At his belt flopped a walkie-talkie.

"I am lonely," Teak said. In his manner was the suggestion of loud voices, hanging meat. "I like to toy with my food. I'm starting to hear songs. I'm beginning to assign gender to inanimate objects, concepts. A phrase keeps popping up: 'the curves of time.' I can't sleep, I fear my bedclothes."

On a scrimmage field beyond the open end of the stadium stood the marching band, practicing a brassy, optimistic composition, basic oom-pah-pah with a fair amount of human shrieking in it. They had instruments of hair, vinework, dried fibers—flutes, bouzoukis, shells, bells. They liked to prance on the field at halftime, all five hundred of them, to form words or symbols. At the TCU game in Fort Worth, they'd spelled out a single declarative sentence: *Being is not different from nothingness.* They had names for man's slangy parts and knew where angst came from.

"I'm working on a purer vision," Teak was saying. "I keep seeing a place like this—vast, silent, full of rubble."

The walkie-talkie came to life: "Victor-Zulu-King, this is Almighty, do you copy?"

In the distance, the clouds were beasts, serpents, civil ruin.

"I had a dream the other night," Teak said.

"Why are you telling me this?"

"It was profound. Religious. There was horror involved."

Down below, Coach's players were yammering in Pali, Tamil, Oriya. Moving in slow motion, the linebackers raised their fists, grunting. In helmets and pads, they brought to mind vaulted cisterns, limestone caves, the lamps the holy worship by.

"We're a serious people," Coach Knapp said.

Teak Warden nodded. "Ain't that the truth?"

"It's a lyric mode we seek, something to satisfy the animal in us. Wistfulness extends, diminishes our purpose. There is danger of ambiguity, of winding down."

The walkie-talkie crackled again: "Almighty, Almighty, this is Victor-Zulu-King, we have contact. Repeat: we have contact, do you copy?"

"These are sad times, Teak Warden," Coach said.

"The saddest."

A hot wind had come up, like jet exhaust.

"We're in a strange business."

"Affirmative," Teak Warden said.

"There is the laying on of hands," Coach said, "and the hurling of bodies. Information is exchanged. We objectify, polarize. Screams are heard. There is hooting and other meaningful tumult."

"There are chains of being," Teak Warden said. "We are pre-science. I'm thinking matrix. I'm thinking the moral life, a negotiation of same."

Coach was watching the grandstands opposite him, tier upon tier of seats and gleaming metal benches. Plastered to the upper walls were banners from the pep club: "Refute Belief," "Visual Messages Are Not Discursive," "Self-Expression Requires No Artistic Form." There were impressive drawings from *Tractatus Logico-Philosophicus* and *The Ape and the Child*. Conference flags were whipping back and forth: Griffons, Knave-life, The Hidden Iman.

"Teak," Coach said, "who is that?"

He indicated a figure squatting beside a meager fire high up in the stands. It was a man, certainly, who seemed wrapped in a half-century of north-country outerwear.

The walkie-talkie hissed to life again. Someone was calling for help. "Accept no higher being," a voice said. "Let's go out there and thwart somebody."

"Don't know," Teak Warden said. "Student, possibly."

"Whose?"

Teak Warden waved, and yonder, out of the clothes, shot an arm. It snapped up and down several times, then disappeared. Something about it suggested delirium.

"Ours," Teak said, "definitely ours."

On the field, defensive line coach Archie Weeks, carrying a brushed-aluminum briefcase, had assembled his players in a semicircle. A dozen pens stuck out of his breast pocket. His view of sport was admirably cerebral. He was now referring to a chalkboard dense with numbers and letters, arrows and stars. He was very nimble for someone who sweated and twitched.

"I want penetration," he was saying. "Give me an emotion, lower organs. I want a rising up and a putting asunder."

His players—Cud, Onan, Redman, Univac, the Prince of Darkness—were serious, attentive. They had majors from every page in the catalogue: disquiet, vigor, happenstance. They were beef with heads that swiveled a little.

"I take failure personally," Archie Weeks was saying. "I want luridness out there tomorrow. Verve approaching madness."

Coach Knapp remained to one side. There would be several more lectures by his assistants, then he would have to say something. He was watching the mountains in the east. They were called the Organs and seemed associated with conditions best explained in poetry: rue, torment, befuddlement. Between them and him—indeed, all around, from horizon to horizon—lay the desert full of stunted trees, scrub, spines, thorns, savage hooks. People were believed to be out there—tribes of very unpleasant, dark-minded citizens. They had sores and mangy pelts, and every now and then they roared out of the spectacular wastes to watch football.

"I'm talking about conspiracies," Archie Weeks was saying. "Insinuations, betrayals. I'm talking about piling on, about getting one's licks in."

Next was Gene Jenks, offensive line coach. He looked like circus property. He had the need to lean into people's faces and yowl.

Gene Jenks spoke of the ideal sportsman. A half-winged creature, it could be any of the human colors, but it knew everything: how wish works, what to say when the glands call. It was a machine. Something with many fine parts. A quiet, high-speed operation with uncommonly expressive shoulder-work. It had a chemical description and delightful physical properties. It had girth and heft, and slammed about in the current hubbub being heroic.

"Things could be worse," Gene Jenks said. "Things could be much worse."

Vigorous applause greeted Coach Knapp when he stepped to the center of his players. He had visited each of their homes—their tents, cabins, lean-tos, caves. He had seen what they'd eaten, how they'd prepared themselves, and they had confessed to him their joys, their nightmares. Mesomorphs, hairy, porcine, thick as tree stumps—they were all the ilks folks come in. They read Erasmus, Cato, referred to themselves as loin or chop. Many of them slept upright and appeared better for it. They had thick parts and amusing ways of getting from hither to yon. They did not mumble. Nor did they lose direction, wander off. One would address them and, at the signal, they would go. Footwear was vital to them, as were rigor and single-mindedness. What did one say to such beings? He had met their parents, their distant relations. He'd met their mates—names came to him: Lulu, Jo Ann, Dottie. These women were life principles and part of winning itself. Coach's players believed in ritual and magic. They carried lucky thread, well-thumbed coins, medals that promised protection against smite itself. They had special words: *miasma, columbine, Umgang.* They were held together—apart from the claim of the larger world—by tape and plastic, by miracle fabrics and bolts. One did not speak to them directly. One used an elaborate rhetoric of colors and numbers, a code of doing and being done to. "Blue, forty-six, slant left," one would say, and an instant later there would be a pile of very satisfied sportsmen. All over the fallen world such exchanges were being made: language became action and the human measure of it. Unusually large men were speaking to almost round things and beating each other for the sake of them. This was not war. It was earth and wind, fire and water. It was biology and the shedding of unnecessary parts. One said, "Red, dish-right, on eight," and immediately there was a collision and the crawling away from it.

"Sleep, eat, wash," Coach Knapp said, at last. "This is what we do. When we work, life is easy. We get to go places and hear ourselves talked about. This is what I like. Don't disappoint me."

In the locker room Coach Knapp came upon one of his people reading a book. The player was a free safety—a former woodchopper named Herkie Walls, Coach believed—and he wore a T-shirt with a picture of the new universe. There were curlicues, as well as runes, objects made important by desire. The kind of collapsed, special ruin hope had once lived in.

"I have questions," the kid said. "I have doubts, grow depressed. My vocabulary's shrinking."

A wind had risen, steady and full of faraway dirts.

Coach Knapp gestured to the book: "What're you reading?"

Herkie Walls held the thing aloft, his playbook. It was open to the pages relevant to humbug and derring-do.

"I could have been a thousand things," the kid said. His eyes suggested fear. "For one birthday I received a field jacket. It was khaki, its hem bordered with formal Kufic lettering. I preferred to wear it with polychrome sateen. I had the need to stand out and be incorrigible."

Tension was involved here, a wariness. Worry was one parameter of

Coach's profession; faith, the other. Eleven, sometimes twelve times a year he ushered his people onto one turf or another. He gave instructions, rules, rubrics. He urged them toward the manifest in themselves, put before them images of fleece and flax. He reminded his people what their opponents were: creatures without spawn, vermiculate matter that ambled on two legs. Coach Knapp created stories, narratives featuring a random collection of humans who find themselves in a remote, austere venue. In every version, the endings were identical: this collection—this cadre of gristle and girth—discovers unfamiliar and surprising things and returns to the world changed in some way.

"Where are you from, free safety?"

Almost black with blood, a hand appeared, pointed. "The Province of Florida, I think. You recruited me."

A light went on in Coach Knapp's memory. He saw—anew and in a way quite compelling—a thatched hut, a puny fire, a mewling thing. The common elements.

"I said you were a state of mind, I believe. I said if you ran very swiftly and were acceptably violent, you would be admired."

A smile came to the free safety, Herkie Walls. He had been bamboozled, the floor of his self given way, and now he was not.

"Thinking is a performing art, Coach. That's what you said."

Like father and son, they consulted the playbook. Its pages, light and precious as human skin, were garish with hexagons, exotic birds, palmette stars. Its language ran from border to border and defined the seat the self sits in. The product of a dozen minds, it avoided terms like "capitulation" and "surrender." Unlike the playbooks of the olden, icier ages—the times of Sooners and Razorbacks and Nittany Lions—this volume trafficked in parables, allegories, fables. It was to be read in a wild, silent place; it made the muscles tight and strong, set the organs tingling. Among other things, it spoke of love, which was the things that happened and what we said about them. Though it mentioned sulphur and brimstone, what speeds the stupid travel at, its effect was hortatory; its purpose, to heal and to promote fellowship.

"So what do we know now?" Coach asked.

In the kid's open locker was fabric that recalled mirth and what swine are for.

"We know one meaning of life," the kid said. "We've learned to discriminate, not to be deflected or deferred."

"We have learned not to read between the lines," Coach said. "To speak clearly and to hoist heavy things."

"Fucking A," the kid said.

Coach Knapp made his way across campus in his customary manner, in a straight line, his step springy as modernity itself. The sky had turned greenish-yellow, what blasphemy was said to look like once upon a time. Everywhere was evidence of scholarship: scrolls, cudgels, sacks to tote. In front of the music building, a dozen students dressed in shimmer stood in a precise file. They had fierce, determined faces, what kamikazes were thought to look like, and muttered into their fists. Admissions reported that there were thousands of students now—the craven and the mighty, fans of one science or another. They resembled hounds or crawling quadripeds. Some had affiliated themselves with social clubs, drawn near one another by a shared interest in bombast or rowdiness. They were cowboys, memphitites, janissaries. To class, they brought jackstays, epodes, sporules. They dedicated themselves to epigraphy, to sponsion, to what inflammation means. In keeping with tradition, Coach Knapp had attended their parties. They celebrated complexity, nuance. They were the gummata, the kinematic. At the School of Applied Practice, they traveled in groups. One heard them in the early morning, theirs a singsong that had to do with kindredness. In other hours, one heard screech and riot given syntax. They painted their residences to resemble objects of desire and people they'd once loved.

"What is it we subscribe to?" one group was saying now. Their leader was a senior named Don, and around him in a ragged circle sat the females he hunkered with. They believed in tigers burning bright and gnarled trees of mystery.

"Where are we going?" Don hollered.

"Up," was the answer.

Don had a worried-man's face, a creased thing suffused with darkness. Soon he would graduate and toil in the outlands.

"When are we going?"

"Now," they said.

On the steps nearby, uncommonly rigid and sharp-eyed, had gathered the matriculants of the Department of Poesy. Each affected the face of his favorite versifier: Rah, the Sylphides, Lex Luthor. These were to be the next generation of literateurs, Coach knew. They would produce books, tracts, documents that refuted the accepted wisdom. In the end, another generation would come along. Tricks would be played, points of view offered, positions debated. Scholars would hear of afflatus, disquisitions, stuff in dreadful tongues.

In its way, writing was like football itself: there was contact and joy at the end of it.

Outside the President's door sat a secretary using the phone. Several things about her—her whichaway hair, her upcast eyeballs, one hand sawing in the air—said motherhood, a concern for others.

"Are you listening?" she was saying as Coach Knapp stepped by her. "First, it appears with green eyes, copper skin, a mouth tender as a child's. It has horns, fangs, forked appendages. It sprouts, blossoms, shrivels, has tendrils, converts easily to liquid. It serenades, wheedles, cajoles, barks. Its body is indescribable—features of goat, canine, scale of fish. It's made of dross, it's made of sputum. It causes a bloody flux."

The President was waiting. He was part Arab, part something else. Oklahoman maybe. Nobody knew. One of seven cousins who owned the college, he had discovered something in the Wadi, in the Heights, in the Gulf. It was a process, a refinement, a radical personal philosophy. Soon there was capital, assets, plunder, booty. Things were organized and produced. Titles were conferred. The cousins owned goods, services, personalities. Their logo—and the team's own name—was an arrangement of tiny but essential bones that had to do with longevity.

"I've been thinking about reality," the President said. "Particularly its specifications, the hardware vital to it. It's a big subject."

The President had a seal's slick hair, as well as the hands and precious feet of a jazz dancer. He liked to host parties that involved glee and out-of-body travel.

"Let us stand by the window," the man said. "We can watch."

Coach Knapp could still hear the secretary in the other room. "It's under the Ns," she was saying. "'Nosology,' 'nostic,' 'nostril'—in there somewhere. It ravishes, torments, has gall. What a marvel it is."

In the distance, half in the shadows of the stadium itself, Coach Knapp saw his players moving like an army. They carried torches, penlights, smoky kerosene lamps, and they were headed for their dormitory, an exclusive facility that towered over its neighbors. Once inside, they'd prepare themselves. They would review, recapitulate, speculate. Out would go furniture, accoutrements, luxuries; in would come victuals and liquids, what the creature in them cried for. They were men who yearned for that agreement which could be found only in another man's bulky arms.

"I adore these moments," the President remarked.

"As do I," Coach Knapp said.

"Pads, headgear, scurrying in one direction—I am enamoured of the whole thing."

"It is a spirit," Coach said. "Relationships, various coordinations. I'm humbled by the purity of it."

The men stood shoulder to shoulder. Below, on a stubbled, litter-strewn acre known as The Square of Past Mistakes, a pep rally was beginning.

"Still," the President said, "there are issues to guard against."

"One hopes to have a positive effect," Coach Knapp said. "Yet it is seldom the kids say anything to you. There's a barrier, I create it. My people don't call me Woody. My father's people used to call him Moe, and often I think it would be nice to be called Woody, to be friends. But that's not my job. My job is to treat them brutally; theirs, to love it."

From the other room came that voice again, the secretary. "'Geniculation,'" she was saying, "the state of being geniculate."

Down below, the coach for the other team was being burned in effigy. His people were the Dukes, their mascot the dainty porringer of Count Ugo Malatesta. They were big, it was rumored. Like storybook farm life. And strong. They had one play, Wild Pinch Ollie, which did not involve the ball but which called upon an underclassman named Ham to lift his arms and pray in an annoying voice.

"I have the need to reveal myself to you," the President said. "I can trust you, I feel. I have confessions. At times, I am quite bad. I am headstrong, for example. I don't know any Greek. I give money away. Other times, I am surprised by my own goodness. I am generous to my wives. I like to breed. Ideas come to me, I scribble them down, attempt to bring them to fruition. I can make a scarf joint."

"You would have been an excellent weakside linebacker."

"Yes," the President said, "when one dashes off the field, there shouldn't be anything left."

"It's unfortunate you're not a coach," Woody Knapp said. "We could study film together, confide in each other. At halftime, you could stand up and make one hundred youngsters feel very inadequate."

"I could have been responsible for recruiting, say. Or the defensive backfield."

"You could show them what the world looks like and why there is so much screaming."

The fire below was beautiful. In the past, fans had charred the likenesses of Gator and Bruin. This season they would incinerate the Schismata, the Tartars. This year the Gentoo, the hymenopterous insects, the Galbanum— all the disagreeable, seductive notions they stood for—would go up in flames. The same songs would be heard, "Tell Me What You Know" and "All Hail the Power." Insights would be advanced, meanings detailed. Months from now one would have numbers to measure achievement.

"One more thing, Coach."

"Yes."

"Explain, please, the Strong G Wham."

Woody Knapp's hands fluttered like birds. He described movements, a frame of reference, what work the heart did. He discussed action in terms of phylum, genre, a specific ligament. He offered metaphor. Deep structure. Deconstruction. Tool and man.

"Check Magoo," he said. "Stem to cover Three. Willie Sam Flop One. The Cat's gotta get into the middle. Up blasts the Monster. Think turnover.

Rover has deep responsibility, Red Ryder the underbody. We defoliate and make a Sweep. Then there's the Nether Parts."

"And Little Piggy?"

"Little Piggy stays home."

Outside, in the twilight, Coach Knapp moved quickly but deliberately. It was one of his precepts. "Pick a place and go to it," he would say. "Conceive and act." All around him, by contrast, wandered the distracted and the aimless. Sport—especially sport that required pain and constant doctoring—would have made everyone more saintly. There were things that could be understood only at the bottom of a mound of flesh. Coming toward him, accelerating like a steam train, charged Lefty Mantillo, the publicist. He was wearing a new outfit now, one of bangles and chrome hasps, his evening dress.

"I'm glad I found you," he said. "I got an inspiration."

Coach Knapp could see a line of lights on the mesa above the valley. Fans, he thought. Like players, they moved in bunches now. They wore red, or black, and had the look of humans who scrambled dawn to dusk. They could not gambol. Neither could they cavort.

"We do a movie," Lefty was saying, "a feature. Super eight, three-quarter tape, noise reduction—the works. We charge your mother's name. Serena, Philomel—something with lilt. We allude to catamites. You moralize, hector. I have ideas for vistas, soft focus, stop-action, you in the misty twilight, leaves on the ground, billowy cloudwork. A narrator. Flow and irony. We loop in the bullshit in post-production."

Coach Knapp was saddened by the image of himself. There was so much to learn nowadays—where beautiful women came from, what to make of metaphysics, the subtleties of the shuddery arts.

"The first reel's all special effects," Lefty continued. "Birth, youth, rites of passage. The second, I don't know yet. Hoopla, maybe. Hurly-burly. Bad things happen. You emerge. Football enters the current times."

"I like it," Coach said.

"I hums, sahib. It says tie-in, promotion, scratch 'n' sniff. It's killer material, that's what it is. Contemplative but with the rough stuff left in."

"I have to go, Lefty."

Mantillo's eyes went out of focus, came back. He hugged himself as if something—a crucial tissue, a fluid—were about to spill out.

"Ten-four, Coach. I gotta get back to work. I'm excited, I tell you. It's like getting aroused. I love this art business."

Coach Knapp ducked around one corner. And another. Direction signs stood up all over, from the folks in Orientation: ESCHEW GLUTTONY; THE TIMES ARE NEVER SO BAD; GO BACK, THIS IS NOT FOR YOU. A few people in that department were former players who held convocations to propose answers to impossible questions. They quoted Karl Barth, the Wallendas, seers from the dark atomic years. "Suck it in," they ordered. "Stand up tall. Don't be a drag-ass."

Now Coach Knapp was aware of someone following him. There was shambling, a trepidation. Nerve was being summoned. Soon there would be a clearing of the throat. Then speech.

"Who are you?" Coach asked.

Out of the gloom shuffled a figure, something wrought. It was the person in the stands earlier in the afternoon, the one who'd waved.

"I know you," Coach said. "Your name is Griggs. Emile, possibly. You were called the Snake, I believe. This was ages ago. The Lizard. A member of the reptile family."

The man came closer, smiling.

"Height, six-two. Weight, one ninety-six. I never forget these statistics. Your favorite dinner, what you dreamed. You attended school in Cupertino, I remember. Had trouble with world geography."

"Culver," the man said. "It's not there anymore."

Griggs looked like the poorly fitted parts of many other men. His posture said "Assemble with care." It said "Close cover before striking."

"What do you want, Mr. Griggs?"

"Football," he answered. "I want to wear what everyone else does. I want to take directions from somebody named Lance or Butch. I want knowledge alien to the outside world."

A fiber had let go in Coach Knapp, a link to memory. Here was ash, here was dust.

"Are you still fast?"

Griggs raced away, darted back. "I'm fast."

"Are you strong, mean?"

"I could apply myself," Griggs said. "Things could be applied to me."

"What about age?" Coach said. "You must be middle, late thirties."

"I have wisdom," Griggs insisted. "I know things. The fornix, for example. How to foregather, where to look for ground water. I have enthusiasm."

"I could've used you ten years ago."

Griggs edged forward, his posture an underling's.

"You could use me now," he said. "I could be a conduit, a transitor, your voice in the muddle. I could be a moral value. Truth, say. Something vaunted, an idealization. I'd be a whirlwind."

A noise composed of yowling and shouting had risen in the west. Coach Knapp believed it the cries those in history were famous for. Ideas, in the form of people, were colliding. Bad, or weak, ideas would be seen in the morning like trash on a beach.

"You are staying nearby?" Coach asked.

Griggs nodded. He had a residence. Four stakes in the dirt, a rag to crawl under in the dark.

"Go there," Coach said.

"You'll call for me?"

Coach thought he might.

"I could offer myself elsewhere," Griggs said. "I have a list—opponents, those without scruple. I can't take much more wandering. I thirst, I hunger."

Griggs was moving off, bent and sly, the animal half of him alert and watchful. In the distance, the shrieking had become speech, then prattle again. A concord was being reached, disunion overlooked.

"Griggs?" Coach called. "What's your greatest thrill?"

The man had a smile like daylight.

"To break the plane of the goal line," he yelled back. "I want to vault forward and dance by myself in front of eighty thousand people."

Outside his office, Coach Knapp found Nate Creer interrogating a player. The kid was strapped to a chair, a gooseneck lamp over his head, its light a noontime glare. Around them, on the floor, were scattered groundnuts, alkaloids, an overnight bag. "We've been here a while," Creer explained. The kid was in shock, eyes bulging, sweating.

Nate was name-calling. "Hydroid dipstick, muck-faced fart-breath," he was screaming. "Colewort motherhumper. Salmon slime!"

"What's the problem here?" Coach asked.

"He says he's hurt."

The kid's face went three or four directions.

"I'm hurt," the kid said. "I'm hurt."

"He denies he's a dickweed."

"I deny," the kid blubbered. "I deny."

"He swears on his mother, his father."

The kid's jaw dropped. He swore, he swore.

"What's his story?"

"The usual," Nate began. "Parturition, a time of running about unsupervised, body hair. Hormones, friendship—the years all run together. A succession of pets, an allowance. A world view develops, life becomes complicated. An attitude is adopted. Vocabulary expands, paperwork accumulates. Courtship, a tearful reunion, admissions of guilt. There is commingling, disappointment."

"Then what?"

Nate Creer pounded his fist in exasperation.

"Then this squirrel-faced, rat-eyed squamoid yellow-belly fractures his wrist."

Up went the kid's arm. Knobby and blue, it looked like a peculiarly cunning but soft club.

"I figure an hour more, then I let him go," Nate Creer said. "I got things to say here, a position to defend."

"This is a bad sign, Nate."

The man shrugged. "Bad signs are everywhere, Coach. I tend to ignore them."

In his office, Coach Woody Knapp kept the lights off. The dark had its comforts. It encouraged reflection, maximum self-awareness. It allowed for a summing up, a casting forward. He would be home in an hour. There would be food, badinage. Mrs. Knapp, Helen, would tend to him. All had been done that could be. There would be sleep, morning. Time would shrink, disappear. Then he would be back here again, his people ready, his advice delivered. There would be football then.

And nothing else.

Suggestions for Discussion

1. "The Era of Great Numbers" is told in the limited omniscient point of view, an objective author plus Woody Knapp's consciousness. How objective is the objective author?

2. How would you describe the distance between author, reader, Knapp, and the other characters?

3. Find four or five examples of irony—you won't have to look far. How is the discrepancy between tone and substance presented?

4. Analyze the paragraph on page 250 beginning "Vigorous applause greeted Coach Knapp. . . ." As in "The Things They Carried," specifics and abstractions are alternated in a long list, but here the effect is comic rather than moving. Why?

5. How would you describe the temporal and spatial distance of this story? To what extent is the setting familiar, to what extent alien?

6. How does the passive voice achieve a comic effect (for example, "Groans were heard, as were thumps and bone-noise")?

7. Identify several passages of dialogue that do more than one thing at a time. How do the characters' syntax and word choice reveal them? Where do their actions contradict their words?

I and I

JOHN HOLMAN

You would like to go home. These drug runs are getting tiring. Besides, Mississippi makes you nervous. You look past your sun-darkened elbow out the window of the van at the house Rusty has sent you to. It is low, thick-looking, and made of red brick. Looks like a kiln. Stiff yuccas sprout from the bristling yard, and a dead palm tree bends against the right corner of the house. Timmy leans his sweaty face from the back, over your shoulder. "Rusty sure know how to pick 'em, don't he?" he says, breathing hotly on your ear.

Joyless puts the van in reverse and backs into the driveway, hiding the out-of-state license plates. His dreads hang heavy on his shoulders, and flop rigidly when he moves his head. You don't envy his heat. His hair is seasoned copper-colored, today like a network of heated wires. He brushes back the locks and steps from the van. For a moment, you look out across the highway at the red neon beer sign in the window of the convenience store. Timmy nudges you and says, "Let's go."

Joyless has the key and opens the door. The house is unfurnished, with many rooms. The front room is lavender with a wide brick fireplace, and the air is stuffy and dim. While Timmy finds the thermostat and turns on the air conditioning, you walk through the house as if inspecting a hotel. You can't imagine anyone living here. Every room is a different color—carpets purple, pink, blue, green. Matching drapes shaped like suffocation hang in the windows. They have funeral parlor folds, garish colors of Dracula lips.

"I'll take the green room," Joyless says.

"The blue one for me," Timmy says.

You have your pick of the reds. You choose the front room because it is near a door and has lavender blinds instead of drapes.

When everyone awakens you are joined in the front room, listening to your cassette player, your quart of beer half empty. Your friends are barefoot and naked to the waist. Their long toes sink deep into the carpet, leaving dark, clawlike scars.

"I'm hungry," you say. "We passed a Morrison's on the way."

"That should do," Joyless says, sitting down cross-legged opposite you, his silver scimitar swinging from the thin chain around his neck.

"I'm hungry to leave this place," Timmy says. "In my sleep I heard screaming. How many brothers been offed in this state?"

"Those were bats you heard," you say. "In the chimney, there."

The screeches sound from the chimney, and Timmy covers his ears. "No sleep for me tonight," he says. You look at Joyless and smile.

Joyless wears his name in Arabic on a Timmy-made silver bracelet. He reaches under his hair and pulls out a joint. He smokes hard until his head is lost in a cloud, a ragged orb of smoke. He passes the joint to Timmy. "I caught some lizards," he says. "Built a cage for them. There's all kinds of junk out back."

He gets up and returns with a makeshift wire mesh cage housing two small lizards and dried grass and sticks. He sets it down and the lizards turn bright green. "For the children," he says. "When we get home."

"They won't survive that long," Timmy says, twisting a short strand of his own early dreads. "Not through Florida and then all the way back."

"We'll feed them," Joyless says.

You wonder if Timmy's four-year-old would be afraid of them. You envision her stomping the cage determinedly the way she stomps on ants.

In Morrison's, Joyless has his hair under a brown knit hat so that his head looks like a beehive. He chooses french fries and vegetables, and nods at a couple pointing at him. He is used to it, and takes off the hat. Timmy chooses fish, and you take the chicken with a dish of cherry Jell-O filled with cottage cheese. You get two glasses of water and notice the check-out girl staring.

"Your hair," she says to Joyless. "What do you do with it?" She is a pretty girl with yellowish skin and water-bright eyes.

Joyless gives her a steely look. "What do you think?" he says. "They are antennae tuned to black hole mystery. They drip honey. Lie down, I'll show you what I do with them."

"Very interesting. I guess you have to get used to it, huh?"

"It grows on you," Joyless says.

The girl gives him his price total, and Joyless finds a table by a wall. He is thin, and seems to spring when he walks, his long feet slewed in blue canvas shoes.

You give the girl your address and invite her over tonight. Timmy talks to her awhile about friends of hers.

At the table you wonder why no one else is staring. The room is nearly full. Old women with ice blue or blond hair, and men in farmer caps, hunch over their plates. Parents coax their children to eat. And teenagers wearing university T-shirts gesture brusquely with their forks. If you were them, you think, you would stare. You and your friend are not a complementary sight.

"Could be these folks are culturally deprived," Timmy says.

Joyless spreads his arms to take in the whole room. "I and I," he says.

"I think that girl might show tonight," you say.

You drink a full glass of water, take a breath, and start on the other one. Your tongue is cold. You lick your lips and catch the eye of the check-out girl.

"Much love and fear in her," Joyless says. "She won't come without a crowd."

"Let's hope not," Timmy says. "I need a party to help keep me awake."

"We have drugs for that," Joyless says. "And you have to drive tomorrow. Sleep."

"Not with bats in the tomb."

You finish eating and leave the cafeteria. Outside is golden and ninety-three degrees. A time and temperature sign gives you the numbers in computer digitals. You complain about the heat, the lack of wind. You feel as if a rubber glove were fitted to your face.

"It's not hot, really," Timmy says. He has rolled up the sleeves of his T-shirt, and his face and shoulders shine. Joyless's knit hat hangs out the back pocket of his army camouflage pants. He lifts his face, his eyes closed, to the setting sun, and walks basking that way until you reach the van. Because of the heat, you dread getting into the van. It is a dark green Dodge with black carpet on the floor and interior walls. You offer to drive to avoid having to ride in the back, and Timmy grabs the passenger seat and turns on the radio, searching for "the black spot," he says. Joyless sprawls on the floor in the back between the two benchlike couches and lights up a joint. Before you leave the parking lot, he passes it to you. You would like to see a movie, to watch TV. "I wonder who won the Braves game," Timmy says.

When you get to the house, you walk across the highway to the convenience store to buy more beer. You think you should feel free, but you are vaguely frightened. Maybe you are developing agoraphobia. Heat waves rise from the pavement. A few cars whiz under the traffic light. Tall dry grass grows in the median. Small shirtless children play in the dirt yards of the project housing next to the store. You're glad you will never have to get used to this place.

The store is a Jr. Food Mart, with Jr. himself painted as a big, dark-haired Howdy Doody look-alike on the sign above the entrance. Inside, two musky little girls stand on bare tiptoes at the counter to buy lime-flavored Push-Ups and an assortment of grape and lemon candy. There is a different man at the cash register from when you were here before.

You get the beer from the glass-encased cooler. Just as you pull out a six-pack, another takes its place. Startled, you stand there until someone's hands appear behind the cans placing beer in the cooler from the back. "You scared me," you say, but the person doesn't answer. You take out another six-pack and go to the front.

At the counter, the little girls have left, and the attendant you thought was a man turns out to be a coal black young woman with a fresh, short haircut, and wearing a man's white tank-top undershirt. As she bags the beer you gaze at the dark nipples under the tight-fitting shirt.

"You're not from around here, are you?" she asks.

You try, but you can't think of anything. "I give up."

"Fifty-dollar bills are rare in this store. You here to stay or just passing through?"

"Spending the night."

"You're lucky." Two of her top front teeth are edged with gold. Her skin looks smooth and very soft.

"My friends and I are staying across the street. You should come over when you get finished here."

"Yeah? I was thinking about it. I saw you pull up over there. We like to welcome new folks to the area, you know?"

You smile, take your change, and walk with the beer to the house. Joyless and Timmy are preparing the package of cocaine to be delivered. You tell them about the girl at the store, and Timmy is pleased, but Joyless looks annoyed.

You look at the Kleenex box he is wrapping with a sheet of newspaper.

"Timmy and I will make the delivery. You ought to hang around. Too many people know we're here already."

Joyless and Timmy are gone a long time. You look out back for crickets, and manage to catch another lizard, too. You put them all in the cage, and drink while listening to the tape player. It is a muffled tape recorded from the radio on a cheap cassette. When darkness falls, you look for lamps, but nothing is in the closets except empty coat hangers. You find a light bulb in the ceiling fixture of the green room, and you have to jump several times before unscrewing it. You use the same technique to install it in the front room ceiling. The bats start screeching, and you turn up the volume of the tape player.

Joyless and Timmy have been gone at least three hours. You wonder what you will do if it turns out they're busted. You try the radio to hear the time. You can't call the police. You will wait awhile longer and then call Rusty.

Car lights glance off the blinds, and you turn down the music to listen for the sound of the engine. It is not the van. A car door closes, and footsteps crunch on the gravel driveway. You go to the window and peep through a slit in the blinds. The car is a new Chevrolet, but you cannot see who is at the door. There is a knock and you leave the window. You wait for another knock but it doesn't come. Instead, there are footsteps again, and the close of the car door. You are afraid to go back to the window, not wanting to be seen. For a while the car sits in the driveway, the motor running. Then it leaves. The bats are screaming in the chimney.

You go through the house making sure all the doors and windows are locked, and you hide all the coke in your suitcase in a back closet. Then you turn off the light and peep out the window again, noticing that the convenience store is still open. Maybe the Chevy belonged to the girl at Morrison's. In the darkness, something tickles your foot, and you think maybe the lizards are loose. Hopping up, you turn on the light and see two roaches run to the corner of the room. You throw your shoe at them. The light stays on.

Your respect for Rusty is waning. You used to marvel at his resourcefulness, the way he always found you places to stay in any city you needed to visit. A Realtor friend who owed him a favor offered him this house with air conditioning or one with furniture. Right now you would like a rocking chair, and some pictures on the walls.

You lie with your ear to the tape player, eventually losing yourself in the reggae. You must have dozed, because someone is at the door again. This time the van is out there. Timmy is calling your name.

You let them in. They stand on the threshold carrying brown sacks of cooking equipment and a two-pound bag of shrimp. Behind them the light of the convenience store is out. A car, the Chevy, pulls into the driveway behind the van. You all look, and the girl from Morrison's gets out. She is alone, and no longer in her green and white uniform; instead she is wearing blue shorts and a white jersey with the word *Bruisers* printed on the front.

"I'm a star," she says, shaking her fists above her head. "A grand slam in the bottom of the twelfth. How do you like me, guys?"

"I love a winner," Timmy says.

Joyless laughs and shakes her hand.

"Where've you guys been?" she asks. You ask if she likes shrimp.

Inside you boil the shrimp while the girl explains the tricks of playing third base for the B&G Grill Bruisers. *B&G* is printed in blue script on the back of the jersey above the number 12. Making sure she doesn't hear, you tell Joyless where the coke is, and he squats in the living room laying out lines on a mirror between his feet.

Soon, you and the girl serve up the shrimp, passing out paper plates and paper towels. Joyless sets aside the mirror of coke, and Timmy gets up to wash his hands. When he returns, the convenience store girl arrives, wearing a fresh tank top and loose white pants with orange birds printed on them. Timmy is delighted. He says he won't have to sleep with bats.

"Do you expect to sleep with me instead?" says the convenience store girl.

"Forgive me, no," Timmy says. "I won't have to sleep at all."

Soon there is a pile of shrimp skins on all the plates. Joyless talks about sleeping with the moon. "At night on the mountain you scoot over to make room for it, it rises so close. Then when morning, you look down through mist at lush green pasteled by a rainbow in the valley."

The softball girl wants to know what mountain.

"My mountain," Joyless says. "In Columbia."

"Joyless is from Boston," you say. "He has multiple biographies."

"I'm a talented surgeon," he says.

"We are house painters on vacation," Timmy says. "On our way to Florida. You ladies care to come along?"

They both say they can't.

You go over and thump the lizard cage. They are either dead or asleep, turned dark gray. You remember the bright green of their day. You thump some more. The convenience store girl moves over and kneels beside you. Suddenly one of the lizards brightens, and its throat swells flashing red. "It has a song inside," she says. You look at her as if she is crazy.

You stay up late doing the coke. The girls talk about their town. They had never met before, having gone to different high schools, but they have seen each other at parties. They say how much they want to travel, and you and Timmy make them like you with tales of big cities. Joyless is a mystic and a poet, you say. And a terrible painter. When he paints walls he paints the windowpanes, too, and you have to clean it off. They laugh and like Joyless, too. Timmy gets out his kit and shines his silver jewelry. He gives each girl a ring he has made.

They leave before sunup, and you search for another cassette to play, something you haven't heard. Joyless puffs on a large joint, the smoke curling in his hair like a ghost wig. Everything is always strange, you think. The bats, for now, are quiet.

Timmy bends to the mirror on the carpet and pulls up his eyelid. He turns his head from side to side and then lifts the other lid. "Home they hiring at Lockheed," he says.

Joyless takes another big puff. You stare at Timmy, wondering if he would really go to work. Joyless passes you the joint. He smiles at you and looks at the cage. "Let's paint it," he says.

Suggestions for Discussion

1. Why did Holman choose the second person for this story? Why did he title it "I and I"? Recast a couple of paragraphs in the third person and observe the change in effect.

2. On what scale of values is this narrator reliable, and on what scale unreliable?

3. The story recounts an evening in which a group of friends run drugs, risk danger, make money, meet girls, throw a party. How does Holman achieve the atmosphere of dreariness and strain?

4. Explain the irony of "You stare at Timmy, wondering if he would really go to work."

5. How do time, place, and tone inform the authorial distance of "I and I"?

6. How many discoveries and decisions make up the pattern of change that is the action? What is changed?

RETROSPECT

1. How many time periods are involved in "The Masked Marvel's Last Toehold"? To what extent does the narrator retain an adult perspective on the child's experience? To what extent does he enter that experience and see it from the child's viewpoint?

2. Is the protagonist of "Rape Fantasies" an unreliable narrator? How and to what extent?

3. Show how the narrator of "My Man Bovanne" is more reliable than her more educated children.

WRITING ASSIGNMENTS

1. Choose a crucial incident from a child's life (your own or invented) and write about it from the temporally distanced perspective of an adult narrator.

2. Rewrite the same incident in the child's language from the point of view of the child as narrator.

3. Write a passage from the point of view of a central narrator who is spatially distanced from the events he or she describes. Make the contrast significant—write of a sea voyage from prison, of home from an alien country, of a closet from a mountaintop, or the like.

4. Write a short scene from the point of view of anything nonhuman (a plant, object, animal, Martian, angel). We may sympathize or not with the perceptions of the narrator, but try to imagine or invent the terms, logic, and frame of reference this character would use.

5. Write from the point of view of a narrator who passes scathing judgments on another character, but let us know that the narrator really loves or envies the other.

6. Let your narrator begin with a totally unacceptable premise—illogical, ignorant, bigoted, insane. In the passage, let us gradually come to sympathize with his or her view.

7. Take any assignment you have previously done and recast it from another point of view. This may (but will not simply) involve changing the person in which it is written. Alter the means of perception or point-of-view character so that we have an entirely different perspective on the events. But let your attitude as author remain the same.

9

IS AND IS NOT
Comparison

Types of Metaphor and Simile
Metaphoric Faults to Avoid
Allegory
Symbol
The Objective Correlative

As the concept of distance implies, every reader reading is a self-deceiver. We simultaneously "believe" a story and know that it is a faction, a fabrication. Our belief in the reality of the story may be so strong that it produces physical reactions—tears, trembling, sighs, gasps, a headache. At the same time, as long as the fiction is working for us, we know that our submission is voluntary; that we have, as Samuel Taylor Coleridge pointed out, suspended disbelief. "It's just a *movie*," says the exasperated father as he takes his shrieking six-year-old out to the lobby. For the father the fiction is working; for the child it is not.

The necessity of disbelief was demonstrated for me some years ago with the performance of a play that ended with too "good" a hanging. The harness was too well hidden, the actor too adept at purpling and bloating his face when the trap fell. Consternation rippled through the audience: My God, they've hanged the *actor*. Because the illusion was too like reality, the illusion was destroyed and the audience was jolted from its belief in the story back into the real world of the performance.

Simultaneous belief and awareness of illusion are present in both the content and the craft of literature, and what is properly called artistic pleasure derives from the tension of this *is and is not*.

The content of a plot tells us that something happens that does not happen, that people who do not exist behave in such a way, and that the events of life—which we know to be random, unrelated, and unfinished—are necessary, patterned, and come to closure. When someone declares interest or pleasure in a story "because it really happened," he or she is expressing an unartistic and antiartistic preference, subscribing to the lie that events can be accurately translated into the medium of words. Pleasure in artistry comes precisely when the illusion rings true without, however, destroying the knowledge that it is an illusion.

In the same way, the techniques of every art offer us the tension of things that are and are not *alike*. This is true of poetry, in which rhyme is interesting because *tend* sounds like *mend* but not exactly like; it is true of music, whose interest lies in variations on a theme; of composition, where shapes and colors are balanced in asymmetry. And it is the fundamental nature of metaphor, from which literature derives.

Just as the content of a work must not be too like life to destroy the knowledge that it is an illusion, so the likenesses in the formal elements of art must not be too much alike. Rich rhyme, in which *tend* rhymes with *contend* and *pretend*, is boring and restrictive, and virtually no poet chooses to write a whole poem in it. Repetitive tunes jingle; symmetrical compositions tend toward decor.

Metaphor is the literary device by which we are told that something is, or is like, something that it clearly is not, or is not exactly like. What a good metaphor does is surprise us with the unlikeness of the two things compared while at the same time convincing us of the aptness or truth of the likeness. A bad metaphor fails to surprise or to convince or both.

Types of Metaphor and Simile

The simplest distinction between types of comparison, and usually the first one grasped by beginning students of literature, is between *metaphor* and *simile*. A simile makes a comparison with the use of *like* or *as*, a metaphor without. Though this distinction is technical, it is not entirely trivial, for a metaphor demands a more literal acceptance. If you say, "a woman is a rose," you ask for an extreme suspension of disbelief, whereas "a woman is like a rose" is more sophisticated form, acknowledging the artifice in the statement.

Historically, metaphor preceded simile, originating in a purely sensuous comparison. When we speak of "the eyes of a potato," or "the eye of the needle," we mean simply that the leafbud and the thread hole *look like* eyes. We don't mean to suggest that the potato or the needle can *see*. The comparisons do not suggest any essential or abstract quality to do with sight.

Both metaphor and simile have developed, however, so that the resonance of comparison is precisely in the essential or abstract quality that the two objects share. When a writer speaks of "the eyes of the houses" or "the windows of the soul," the comparison of eyes to windows does contain the idea of transmitting vision between the inner and the outer. When we speak of "the king of beasts," we don't mean that a lion wears a crown or sits on a throne (though it is relevant that in children's stories the lion often does precisely that, in order to suggest a primitive physical likeness); we mean that king and lion share abstract qualities of power, position, pride, and bearing.

In both metaphor and simile a physical similarity can yield up a characterizing abstraction. So "a woman" may be either "a rose" or "like a rose." The significance of either lies not in the physical similarity but in the essential qualities that such similarity implies: slenderness, suppleness, fragrance, beauty, color—and perhaps the hidden threat of thorns.

Every metaphor and simile I have used so far is either a cliché or a dead metaphor (both of which will be discussed later): Each of them may at one time have surprised by their aptness, but by now each has been used so often that the surprise is gone. I wished to use familiar examples in order to clarify that *resonance of comparison depends on the abstractions conveyed in the likeness of the things compared.* A good metaphor reverberates with the essential; this is the writer's principle of choice.

So Flannery O'Connor, in "A Good Man Is Hard to Find," describes the mother as having "a face as round and innocent as a cabbage." A soccer ball is also round and innocent; so is a schoolroom globe; so is a street lamp. But if the mother's face had been as round and innocent as any of these things, she would be a different woman altogether. A cabbage is also rural, heavy, dense, and cheap, and so it conveys a whole complex of abstractions about the woman's class and mentality. There is, on the other hand, no innocence in the face of Shrike, in Nathanael West's *Miss Lonelyhearts,* who "buried his triangular face like a hatchet in her neck."

Sometimes the aptness of comparison is achieved by taking it from an area of reference relevant to the thing compared. In *Dombey and Son,* Charles Dickens describes the ships' instrument maker, Solomon Gills, as having "eyes as red as if they had been small suns looking at you through a fog." The simile suggests a seascape, whereas in *One Flew Over the Cuckoo's Nest,* Ken Kesey's Ruckly, rendered inert by shock therapy, has eyes "all smoked up and gray and deserted inside like blown fuses." But the metaphor may range further from its original, in which case the abstraction conveyed must strike us as strongly and essentially appropriate. William Faulkner's Emily Grierson in "A Rose for Emily" has "haughty black eyes in a face the flesh of which was strained across the temple and about the eyesockets as you imagine a lighthouse-keeper's face ought to look." Miss Emily has no connection with the sea, but the metaphor reminds us not only of her sternness and self-sufficiency, but also that she has isolated herself in a locked house. The same character as an old woman has eyes that "looked like two pieces of coal pressed into a lump of dough," and the image domesticates her, robs her of her light.

Both metaphors and similes can be *extended*, meaning that the writer continues to present aspects of likeness in the things compared.

> There was a white fog . . . standing all around you like something solid. At eight or nine, perhaps, it lifted as a shutter lifts. We had a glimpse of the towering multitude of trees, of the immense matted jungle, with the blazing little ball of sun hanging over it—all perfectly still—and then the shutter came down again, smoothly, as if sliding in greased grooves.
>
> JOSEPH CONRAD, *Heart of Darkness*

Notice that Conrad moves from a generalized image of "something solid" to the specific simile "as a shutter lifts"; reasserts the simile as a metaphor, "then the shutter came down again"; and becomes still more specific in the extension "as if sliding in greased grooves." Also note that Conrad emphasizes the dumb solidity of the fog by comparing the larger natural image with the smaller domestic one. Metaphor may equally work when the smaller or more ordinary image is compared with one larger or more intense, as in this example from Katherine Anne Porter's "Flowering Judas."

> Sometimes she wishes to run away, but she stays. Now she longs to fly out of this room, down the narrow stairs, and into the street where the houses lean together like conspirators under a single mottled lamp.

A *conceit*, which can be either metaphor or simile, is a comparison of two things radically and startlingly unlike—in Samuel Johnson's words, "yoked by violence together." A conceit is as far removed as possible from the purely sensuous comparison of "the eyes of the potato." It compares two things that have very little or no immediately apprehensible similarity; and so it is the nature of the conceit to be long. The author must explain to us, sometimes at great length, why these things can be said to be alike. When John Donne compares a flea to the Holy Trinity, the two images have no areas of reference in common, and we don't understand. He must explain to us that the flea, having bitten both the poet and his lover, now has the blood of three souls in its body.

The conceit is more common to poetry than to prose because of the density of its imagery, but it can be used to good effect in fiction. In *The Day of Locust*, Natanael West uses a conceit in an insistent devaluation of love. The screenwriter Claude Estee says:

> Love is like a vending machine, eh? Not bad. You insert a coin and press home the lever. There's some mechanical activity inside the bowels of the device. You receive a small sweet, frown at yourself in the dirty mirror, adjust your hat, take a firm grip on your umbrella and walk away, trying to look as though nothing had happened.

"Love is like a vending machine" is a conceit; if the writer didn't explain to us in what way love is like a vending machine, we'd founder trying to figure it out. So he goes on to develop the vending machine in images that suggest not "love" but seamy sex. The last image—"trying to look as though nothing had happened"—has nothing to do with the vending machine; we accept it because by this time we've fused the two ideas in our minds.

Tom Robbins employs conceit in *Even Cowgirls Get the Blues*, in a playfully self-conscious, mock-scientific comparison of Sissy Hankshaw's thumbs to a pearl.

> As for the oyster, its rectal temperature has never been estimated, although we must suspect that the tissue heat of the sedentary bivalve is as far below good old 98.6 as that of the busy bee is above. Nonetheless, the oyster, could it fancy, should fancy its excremental equipment a hot item, for what other among Creation's crapping creatures can convert its bodily wastes to treasure?
>
> There is a metaphor here, however strained. The author is attempting to draw a shaky parallel between the manner in which the oyster, when beset by impurities or disease, coats the offending matter with its secretions—and the manner in which Sissy Hankshaw, adorned with thumbs that many might consider morbid, coated the offending digits with glory.

The vignette of the oyster is a frivolous digression, relevant only in the making of the pearl. The comparison of pearl and thumbs is a conceit because sensuous similarity is not the point: Sissy's thumbs are not necessarily pale or shiny. The similarity is in the abstract idea of converting "impurities" to "glory."

A *dead metaphor* is one so familiar that it has in effect ceased to be a metaphor; it has lost the force of the original comparison and acquired a new definition. Fowler's *Modern English Usage* uses the word "sift" to demonstrate the dead metaphor, one that has "been used so often that speaker and hearer have ceased to be aware the the words used are not literal."

> Thus, in *The men were sifting the meal* we have a literal use of *sift;* in *Satan hath desired to have you, that he may sift you as wheat, sift* is a live metaphor; in *the sifting of evidence,* the metaphor is so familiar that it is about equal chances whether *sifting* or *examination* will be used, and that a sieve is not present to the thought.

English abounds in dead metaphors. *Abounds* is one, where the overflowing of liquid is not present to the thought. When a man *runs* for office, his legs are not present to the thought, nor is an arrow when we speak of his *aim*, hot stones when we go through an *ordeal*, headgear when someone *caps* a joke. Unlike clichés, dead metaphors enrich the language. There is a residual resonance from the original metaphor but no pointless effort on the part of the mind to resolve the tension of like and unlike. English is fertile with metaphors (including those eyes of the potato and the needle) that have died and been resurrected as *idiom*, a "manner of speaking."

Metaphoric Faults to Avoid

Comparison is not a frivolity. It is, on the contrary, the primary business of the brain. Some eighteenth-century philosophers spoke of the human mind as a *tabula rasa*, a blank sheet on which sense impressions were recorded, compared, and grouped. Now we're more likely to speak of the mind as a "computer" (notice that both images are metaphors), "storing" and "sorting" "data." What both acknowledge is that comparison is the basis of all learning and all reasoning. When a child burns his hand on the stove and his mother says, "It's hot," and then goes toward the radiator and the mother says, "It's hot," the child learns not to burn his fingers. But the goal of reasoning is fact, toward a mode of behavior. When we speak of "the flames of torment," our impulse is comprehension and compassion. The goal of literary comparison is not fact but perception, toward scope of understanding.

Nevertheless, metaphor is a dirty word in some critical circles, because of the strain of the pursuit. Clichés, mixed metaphors, similes that are inept, unapt, obscure, or done to death mar good prose and tax the patience of the most willing reader. After eyes have been red suns, burnt-out fuses, lighthouse keepers, and lumps of coal, what else can they be?

The answer is, always something. But because by definition metaphor introduces an alien image into the flow of the story, metaphor is to some degree always self-conscious. Badly handled, it calls attention to the writer rather than the meaning and produces a sort of hiccup in the reader's involvement. A good metaphor fits so neatly that it fuses to and illuminates the meaning; or, like the Robbins passage quoted above, it acknowledges its self-consciousness so as to take the reader into the game. Generally speaking, where metaphors are concerned, less is more and, if in doubt, don't.

(Now I want to analyze the preceding paragraph. It contains at least seven dead metaphors: *alien*, *flow*, *handled*, *calls*, *fits*, *fuses*, and *illuminates*. A metaphor is not a foreigner; a story is not water; we do not take comparisons in our fingers; they have no vocal cords; they are not puzzle pieces; they do not congeal; and they give off no light rays. But each of these words has acquired a new definition and so settles into its context without strain. At the same time, the metaphoric echoes of these words make them more interesting than their abstract synonyms: *introduces an image from a different context into the meaning of the story . . . badly written, it makes us aware of the writer . . . a good metaphor is so directly relevant that it makes the meaning more understandable*—these abstract synonyms contain no imagery, and so they make for flatter writing. I have probably used what Fowler speaks of as a "moribund or dormant, but not stone-dead" metaphor when I speak of Robbins "taking the reader into the game." If I were Robbins, I'd probably have said. "inviting the reader to sit down at the literary pinochle table," which is a way of acknowledging that "taking the reader into the game" is a familiar metaphor; that is, it's a way of taking us into the game. I have used one live metaphor—"produces a sort of hiccup in the reader's involvement"—and I think I will leave it there to defend itself.)

There are more *don't*'s than *do*'s to record for the writing of metaphor and simile, because every good comparison is its own justification by virtue of being apt and original.

To study good metaphor, read. In the meantime, avoid the following:

Cliché metaphors are metaphors on their way to being dead. They are inevitably apt comparisons; if they were not, they wouldn't have been repeated often enough to become clichés. But they have not acquired new definitions, and so the reader's mind must make the imaginative leap to an image. The image fails to surprise, and we blame the writer for this expenditure of energy without a payoff. The metaphor is not original. Or, to put it a worse way:

> Clichés are *the last word* in bad writing, and it's *a crying shame* to see all you *bright young things* spoiling your *deathless prose* with phrases *as old as the hills*. You must *keep your nose to the grindstone*, because *the sweet smell of success* only comes to those who *march to the tune of a different drummer*.

It's a sad fact that because you have been born into the twentieth century, you may not say that eyes are like pools or stars, and you should be very wary of saying that they flood with tears. These have been so often repeated that they've become shorthand for emotions (attractions in the first and second instances, grief in the third) without the felt force of those emotions. Anytime you as writer record an emotion without convincing us to feel that emotion, you introduce a fatal distance between author and reader. Therefore, neither may your characters be hawk-eyed nor eagle-eyed; nor may they have ruby lips or pearly teeth or peaches-and-cream complexions or necks like swans or thighs like hams. I once gave a character spatulate fingers—and have been worrying about it ever since. If you sense—and you may—that the moment calls for the special intensity of metaphor, you may have to sift through a whole stock of clichés that come readily to mind before you find the fresh comparison that is both apt and startling.

Nevertheless, *pools* and *stars* have become clichés for *eyes* because they capture and manifest something essential about the nature of eyes. As long as eyes continue to contain liquid and light, there will be a new way of saying so. And a metaphor freshly pursued can even take advantage of the shared writer-reader consciousness of familiar images. Here William Golding, in *The Inheritors*, describes his Neanderthal protagonist's first tears, which mark his evolution into a human being.

> There was a light now in each cavern, lights faint as the starlight reflected in the crystals of a granite cliff. The lights increased, acquired definition, brightened, lay each sparkling at the lower edge of a cavern. Suddenly, noiselessly, the lights became thin crescents, went out, and streaks glistened on each cheek. The lights appeared again, caught among the silvered curls of the beard. They hung, elon-

gated, dropped from curl to curl and gathered at the lowest tip. The streaks on the cheeks pulsed as the drops swam down them, a great drop swelled at the end of a hair of the beard, shivering and bright. It detached itself and fell in a silver flash.

In this sharply focused and fully extended metaphor of eyes as caverns, Golding asks us to draw on a range of familiar light imagery: starlight, crystal, and crescent moon, silver. The light imagery usually associated with eyes attaches to the water imagery of tears, though neither eyes nor tears are named. There is a submerged acknowledgment of cliché, but there is no cliché; Golding has reinvested the familiar images with their comparative and emotional force.

In both serious and comic writing, the consciousness of the familiar can be a peripheral advantage if you find a new way of exploiting it. It is a cliché to say, "You'll break my heart," but when Linda Ronstadt sings, "Break my mind, break my mind . . . ," the heart is still there, and the old image takes on new force. Although you may not say *her eyes are like pools,* you may probably say *her eyes are like the scummy duck pond out back,* and we'll find it comic partly because we know the cliché is lurking under the scum.

Cliché can also be useful as a device for establishing authorial distance toward a character or narrator. If the author tells us that Rome wasn't built in a day, we're likely to think the author has little to contribute to human insight; but if a character says so, in speech or thought, the judgment attaches to the character rather than to the author.

> The door closed and he turned to find the dumpy figure, surmounted by the atrocious hat, coming toward him. "Well," she said, *"you only live once* and paying a little more for it, I at least won't *meet myself coming and going."*
> "Some day I'll start making money . . ."
> "I think you're doing fine," she said, drawing on her gloves. "You've only been out of school a year. *Rome wasn't built in a day."*
>
> (*italics mine*)
> FLANNERY O'CONNOR, "Everything That Rises Must Converge"

Though you can exploit the familiar by acknowledging it in a new way, it is never sufficient to put a cliché in quotation marks: *They hadn't seen each other for "eons."* Writers are sometimes tempted to do this in order to indicate that they know a cliché when they see one. Unfortunately, quotation marks have no power to renew emotion. All they say is, "I'm being lazy and I know it."

Farfetched metaphors are the opposite of clichés; they surprise but are not apt. As the dead metaphor *farfetched* suggests, the mind must travel too far to carry back the likeness, and too much is lost on the way. When such a comparison does work, we speak laudatorily of a "leap of the imagination." But when it does not, what we face is in effect a failed conceit: The explanation of what is alike about these two things does not convince. Very good writers in the search for originality sometimes fetch too far. Ernest Hemingway's talent was not for metaphor, and on the rare occasions that he used a metaphor, he was likely to strain. In this passage from *A Farewell to Arms*, the protagonist has escaped a firing squad and is fleeing the war.

> You had lost your cars and your men as a floorwalker loses the stock of his department in a fire. There was, however, no insurance. You were out of it now. You had no more obligation. If they shot floorwalkers after a fire in the department store because they spoke with an accent they had always had, then certainly the floorwalkers would not be expected to return when the store opened again for business. They might seek other employment; if there was any other employment and the police did not get them.

Well, this doesn't work. We may be willing to see the likeness between stock lost in a department store fire and men and cars lost in a military skirmish; but "they" *don't* shoot floorwalkers as they shoot prisoners of war; and although a foreign accent might be a disadvantage behind enemy lines, it is hard to see how floorwalkers could be killed because of one, although it might make it hard for them to get hired in the first place, if. . . . The mind twists trying to find any illuminating or essential logic in the comparison of a soldier to a floorwalker, and fails, so that the protagonist's situation is trivialized in the attempt.

Mixed metaphors are so called because they ask us to compare the original image with things from two or more different areas of reference: *As you walk the path of life, don't founder on the reefs of ignorance.* Life can be a path or a sea, but it cannot be both at the same time. The point of metaphor is to fuse two images in a single tension. The mind is adamantly unwilling to fuse three.

Separate metaphors or similes too close together, especially if they come from areas of reference very different in value or tone, disturb in the same way the mixed metaphor does. The mind doesn't leap; it staggers. The cliché paragraph on page 274 gives an example of metaphors packed too closely. Here is another example, less cliché.

> They fought like rats in a Brooklyn sewer. Nevertheless her presence was the axiom of his heart's geometry, and when she was away you would see him walking up and down the street dragging his cane along the picket fence like an idle boy's stick.

Any of these metaphors or similes might be acceptable by itself, but rats, axioms, and boys' sticks connote three different areas and tones, and two sentences cannot contain them all.

Mixed metaphors and metaphors too close together may be used for comic or characterizing effect. *The New Yorker* has been amusing its readers for decades with a filler item called "Block That Metaphor." But the laugh is always on the writer/speaker, and put-down humor, like a bad pun, is more likely to produce a snicker than an insight. Just as writers are sometimes tempted to put a cliché in quotation marks, they are sometimes tempted to mix metaphors and then apologize for it, in some such phrase as "to mix the metaphor," or, "if I may be permitted a mixed metaphor." It doesn't work. Don't apologize and don't mix.

Obscure and *overdone metaphors* falter because the author has misjudged the difficulty of the comparison. The result is either confusion or an insult to the reader's intelligence. In the case of obscurity, a similarity in the author's mind isn't getting onto the page. One student described the spines on a prickly pear cactus as being "slender as a fat man's fingers." I was completely confused by this. Was it ironic, that the spines weren't slender at all? Ah no, he said, hadn't I noticed how startling it was when someone with a fleshy body had bony fingers and toes? The trouble here was that the author knew what he meant but had left out the essential abstraction in the comparison, the startling quality of the contrast: "the spines of the fleshy prickly pear, like slender fingers on a fat man."

In this case, the simile was underexplained. It's probably a more common impulse—we're so anxious to make sure the reader gets it—to explain the obvious. In the novel *Raw Silk*, I had the narrator describe quarrels with her husband, "which I used to face with my dukes up in high confidence that we'd soon clear the air. The air can't be cleared now. We live in marital Los Angeles. This is the air—polluted, poisoned." A critic friend pointed out to me that anybody who didn't know about L. A. smog wouldn't get it anyway, and that all the last two words did was ram the comparison down the reader's throat. He was right. "The air can't be cleared now. We live in marital Los Angeles. This is the air." The rewrite is much stronger because it neither explains nor exaggerates; and the reader enjoys supplying the metaphoric link.

Metaphors using *topical references,* including celebrity names, can work as long as a sense of the connection is given; don't rely for effect on knowledge that the reader may not have. To write, "He looked just like Michael Jackson," is to make Jackson do your job; and if the reader happens to be a Beethoven buff, or Hungarian, or reading your story in the twenty-first century, there may be no was of knowing what the reference refers to. "He had the liquid, androgynous movements of Michael Jackson" will convey the sense even for someone who doesn't own a television. Likewise, "She was as beautiful as Theda Bara" may not mean much to you, whereas if I say, "She had the saucer eyes and satin hair of Theda Bara," you'll get it, close enough.

Allegory

Allegory is a narrative form in which comparison is structural rather than stylistic. An allegory is a continuous fictional comparison of events, in which the action of the story represents a different action or a philosophical idea. The simplest illustration of an allegory is a fable, in which, for example, the race between the tortoise and the hare is used to illustrate the philosophical notion that "the race is not always to the swift." Such a story can be seen as an extended simile, with the original figure of the comparison suppressed: The tortoise and the hare represent types of human beings, but people are never mentioned and the comparison takes place in the reader's mind. George Orwell's *Animal Farm* is a less naive animal allegory, exploring ideas about corruption in a democratic society. Muriel Spark's *The Abbey* is a historical allegory, representing, without any direct reference to Richard Nixon, the events of Nixon's presidential term through allegorical machinations in a nunnery. The plots of such stories are self-contained, but their significance lies in the reference to outside events or ideas.

Allegory is a tricky form. In the hands of Dante, John Bunyan, Edmund Spenser, John Keats, Franz Kafka, Henrik Ibsen, and Samuel Beckett, it has yielded works of the highest philosophical insight. But most allegories seem to smirk. A naive philosophical fable leads to a simpleminded idea that can be stated in a single phrase; a historical allegory relies on our familiarity with, for example, the Watergate scandal or the tribulations of the local football team, and so appeals to a limited and insular readership.

Symbol

A *symbol* differs from metaphor and simile in that it need not contain a comparison. A symbol is an object or event that, by virtue of association, represents something more or something other than itself. Sometimes an object is invested arbitrarily with such meaning, as a flag represents a nation and patriotism. Sometimes a single event stands for a whole complex of events, as the crucifixion of Christ stands as well for resurrection and redemption. Sometimes an object is invested with a complex of qualities through its association with the event, like the cross itself. These symbols are not metaphors; the cross represents redemption but is not similar to redemption, which cannot be said to be wooden or T-shaped. The mother's hat in "Everything That Rises Must Converge" is such a symbol; it cannot be said to "resemble" desegregation, but in the course of the story it comes to represent the tenacious nostalgia of gentility and the aspirations of the new black middle class, and therefore the unacknowledged "converging" of equality.

Nevertheless, most literary symbols, including this one, do in the course of the action derive their extra meaning from some sort of likeness on the level of emotional or ideological abstraction. The hat is not "like" desegregation, but the action of the story reveals that both women are able to buy such a hat and choose it; this is a concrete example of equality, and so represents the larger concept of equality.

Margaret Drabble's novel *The Garrick Year* recounts the disillusionment of a young wife and mother who finds no escape from her situation. The book ends with a family picnic in an English meadow and the return home.

> On the way back to the car, Flora dashed at a sheep that was lying in the path, but unlike all the others it did not get up and move: it stared at us instead with a sick and stricken indignation. Flora passed quickly on, pretending for pride's sake that she had not noticed its recalcitrance; but as I passed, walking slowly, supported by David, I looked more closely and I saw curled up and clutching at the sheep's belly a real snake. I did not say anything to David: I did not want to admit that I had seen it, but I did see it, I can see it still. It is the only wild snake that I have ever seen. In my book on Herefordshire it says that that part of the country is notorious for its snakes. But "Oh, well, so what," is all that one can say, the Garden of Eden was crawling with them too, and David and I managed to lie amongst them for one whole pleasant afternoon. One just has to keep on and to pretend, for the sake of the children, not to notice. Otherwise one might just as well stay at home.

The sheep is a symbol of the young woman's emotional situation. It does resemble her, but only on the level of the abstractions: sickness, indignation, and yet resignation at the fatal dangers of the human condition. There is here a metaphor that could be expressed as such (*she was sick and resigned as the sheep*), but the strength of the symbol is that such literal expression does not take place: We let the sheep stand in the place of the young woman while it reaches out to the larger significance.

A symbol may also begin as and grow from a metaphor, so that it finally contains more qualities than the original comparison. In John Irving's novel *The World According to Garp*, the young Garp mishears the word "undertow" as "under toad" and compares the danger of the sea to the lurking fantasies of his childish imagination. Throughout the novel the "under toad" persists, and it comes symbolically to represent all the submerged dangers of ordinary life, ready to drag Garp under just when he thinks he is swimming under his own power. Likewise, the African continent in *Heart of Darkness* is dark like the barbaric reaches of the soul; but in the course of the novella we come to understand that darkness is shot with light and light with darkness, that barbarity and civilization are inextricably intermixed, and that the heart of darkness is the darkness of the heart.

One important distinction in the use of literary symbols is between those symbols of which the character is aware, and therefore "belong" to him or her, and those symbols of which only writer and reader are aware, and therefore belong to the work. This distinction is often important to characterization, theme, and distance. In the passage quoted from *The Garrick Year*, the narrator is clearly aware of the import of the sheep, and her awareness suggests her intelligence and the final acceptance of her situation, so that we identify with her in recognizing the symbol. The mother in "Everything That Rises Must Converge," on the other hand, does not recognize the hat as a symbol, and this distances us from her perception. She is merely disconcerted and angered that a black woman can dress in the same style she does, whereas for author and reader the coincidence symbolizes a larger convergence.

Sometimes the interplay between these types of symbol—those recognized by the characters and those seen only by writer and reader—can enrich the story in scope or irony. In *The Inheritors*, from which I've quoted several times, the Neanderthal tribe has its own religious symbols—a root, a grave, shapes in the ice cap—that represent its life-cycle worship. But in the course of the action, flood, fire, and a waterfall recall biblical symbols that allow the reader to supply an additional religious interpretation, which the characters would be incapable of doing. Again, in "Everything That Rises Must Converge," the mother sees her hat as representing, first, her taste and pride, and later the outrageousness of black presumption. For the reader it has the opposite and ironic significance, as a symbol of equality.

Symbols are subject to all the same faults as metaphor: cliché, strain, obscurity, obviousness, and overwriting. For these reasons, and because the word "Symbolism" also describes a particular late-nineteenth-century movement in French poetry, with connotations of obscurity, dream, and magical incantation, *symbolism* as a method has sometimes been treated with scorn in the hard-nosed twentieth century.

Yet is seems to me incontrovertible that the writing process is inherently and by definition symbolic. In the structuring of events, the creation of character and atmosphere, the choice of object, detail, and language, you are selecting and arranging toward the goal that these elements should signify more than their mute material existence. If this were not so, then you would have no principle of choice and might just as well write about any other sets of events, characters, and objects. If you so much as say, "as innocent as a cabbage," the image is minutely symbolic, not a statement of fact but selected to mean something more and something other than itself.

There is another and more mundane reason that symbol cannot be avoided in literature, and should not, which is that people also, constantly, function symbolically. We must do so because we rarely know exactly what we mean, and if we do we are not willing to express it, and if we are willing we are not able, and if we are able we are not heard, and if we are heard we are not understood. Words are unwieldy and unyielding, and we leap past them with intuition, body language, tone, and symbol. "Is the oven supposed to be on?" he asks. He is only peripherally curious about whether the oven is supposed to be on. He is really complaining: *You're scatterbrained and extravagant with the money I go out and earn.* "If I don't preheat it, the muffins won't crest," she says, meaning: *You didn't catch me this time! You're always complaining about the food, and God knows I wear myself out trying to please you.* "We used to have *salade niçoise* in the summertime," he recalls, meaning: *Don't be so damn triumphant. You're still extravagant, and you haven't got the class you* used to have when we were young. "We used to keep a garden," she says, meaning: *You're always away on weekends and never have time to do anything with me because you don't love me anymore; I think you have a mistress.* "What do you expect of me!" he explodes, and neither of them is surprised that ovens, muffins, salads, and gardens have erupted. When people say "we quarreled over nothing," this is what they mean. They quarreled over symbols.

The Objective Correlative

But the conflict in a fiction cannot be "over nothing," and as a writer you must search for the concrete external manifestations that are adequate to the inexpressible feeling. T. S. Eliot used the term "objective correlative" to describe this process and this necessity.

> The only way of expressing emotion in the form of art is by finding an "objective correlative"; in other words, a set of objects, a situation, a chain of events which shall be the formula of that particular emotion; such that when the external facts, which must terminate in sensory experience, are given, the emotion is immediately invoked.
>
> *The Sacred Wood*

Some critics have argued that Eliot's *objective correlative* is really no more than a synonym for *symbol*, but the term and its definition make several important distinctions:

1. An "objective correlative" contains and evokes an *emotion*. Unlike many other sorts of symbols—scientific formulae, notes of music, the letters of the alphabet—the purpose of artistic symbol is to invoke emotion.

2. Some kinds of symbol—religious or political, for example—also arouse emotion, but they do so by virtue of one's acceptance of a general community of belief not specific to the context in which that symbol is used. The wine that represents the blood of Christ will evoke the same general emotion in Venice, Buenos Aires, and New York. But an artistic symbol arouses an emotion specific to the work and does not rely on sympathy or belief outside that work. Mentioning the wine of the Communion ceremony in a story cannot be relied on to produce religious emotion in the reader; indeed, the author may choose to make it arouse some other emotion entirely.

3. The elements of a story are interrelated in such a way that the specific objects, situation, and events produce a *specific* emotion. The "romance" and "pity" invoked by *Romeo and Juliet* are not the same romance and pity invoked by *Anna*

Karenina or *Gone With the Wind*, because the external manifestations in each work (which, being external "terminate in sensory experience") define the nature of the emotion.

4. The objects, situation, and events of a particular work contain its particular effect; conversely, if they do not contain the desired emotional effect, that effect cannot be produced in that work, either by its statement in abstractions or by appeal to outside symbols. The "objective" sensory experience (objects, situation, events) must be "co-relative" to the emotion, each corresponding to the other, for that is *the only way* of expressing emotion in the form of art.

When literary symbols fail, it is most often in this difficult and essential mutuality. In a typical example, we begin the story in a room of a dying woman alone with her collection of perfume bottles. The story ranges back over her rich and sensuous life, and at the end we focus on an empty perfume bottle. It is meant to move us at her death, but it does not. Yet the fault is not in the perfume bottle. Presumably a perfume bottle may express mortality as well as a hat may express racial equality. The fault is in the use of the symbol, which has not been integrated into the texture of the story. We would need to be convinced, perhaps, of the importance this woman placed on perfume as essence, need to know how the collection has played a part in the conflicts of her life, perhaps to see her fumbling now toward her favorite, so that we could emotionally equate the spilling or evaporation of the scent with her own spirit.

Writers of the first rank have had this difficulty dealing with the two holocausts of World War II, the extermination camps and the bombing of Hiroshima and Nagasaki, not because fact is stranger than fiction, but because the two horrors are of such magnitude that it is almost impossible to find a particular series of objects, situations, and events adequate to invoke the emotion of the historical facts. Arthur Miller's play *Incident at Vichy*, Lina Wertmuller's film *Seven Beauties*, and William Styron's novel *Sophie's Choice*—all these seem to some extent to borrow from the emotion invoked by the extermination camps rather than to co-relate the facts and the emotions.

A symbolic object, situation, or event may err because it is insufficiently integrated into the story, and so seems to exist for its own sake rather than to emanate naturally from the characters' lives. It may err because the objective correlative is inadequate to the emotion it is supposed to evoke. Or it may err because it is too heavy or heavy-handed; that is, the author keeps pushing the symbol at us, nudging us in the ribs to say: Get it? In any of these cases we will say that the symbol is *artificial*—a curious word in the critical vocabulary, analogous to the charge of a *formula* plot, since *art*, like *form*, is a word of praise. All writing is "artificial," and when we charge it with being so, we mean that it isn't artificial enough, that the artifice has not concealed itself so as to give the illusion of the natural, and that the artificer must go back to work.

Signs and Symbols

VLADIMIR NABOKOV

I

For the fourth time in as many years they were confronted with the problem of what birthday present to bring a young man who was incurably deranged in his mind. He had no desires. Man-made objects were to him either hives of evil, vibrant with a malignant activity that he alone could perceive, or gross comforts for which no use could be found in his abstract world. After eliminating a number of articles that might offend him or frighten him (anything in the gadget line for instance was taboo), his parents chose a dainty and innocent trifle: a basket with ten different fruit jellies in ten little jars.

At the time of his birth they had been married already for a long time; a score of years had elapsed, and now they were quite old. Her drab gray hair was done anyhow. She wore cheap black dresses. Unlike other women of her age (such as Mrs. Sol, their next-door neighbor, whose face was all pink and mauve with paint and whose hat was a cluster of brookside flowers), she presented a naked white countenance to the fault-finding light of spring days. Her husband, who in the old country had been a fairly successful businessman, was now wholly dependent on his brother Isaac, a real American of almost forty years' standing. They seldom saw him and had nicknamed him "the Prince."

That Friday everything went wrong. The underground train lost its life current between two stations, and for a quarter of an hour one could hear nothing but the dutiful beating of one's heart and the rustling of newspapers. The bus they had to take next kept them waiting for ages; and when it did come, it was crammed with garrulous high-school children. It was raining hard as they walked up the brown path leading to the sanitarium. There they waited again; and instead of their boy shuffling into the room as he usually did (his poor face blotched with acne, ill-shaven, sullen, and confused), a nurse they knew, and did not care for, appeared at last and brightly explained that he had again attempted to take his life. He was all right, she said, but a visit might disturb him. The place was so miserably understaffed, and things got mislaid or mixed up so easily, that they decided not to leave their present in the office but to bring it to him next time they came.

She waited for her husband to open his umbrella and then took his arm. He kept clearing his throat in a special resonant way he had when he was upset. They reached the bus-stop shelter on the other side of the street and he closed his umbrella. A few feet away, under a swaying and dripping tree, a tiny half-dead unfledged bird was helplessly twitching in a puddle.

During the long ride to the subway station, she and her husband did not exchange a word; and every time she glanced at his old hands (swollen veins, brown-spotted skin), clasped and twitching upon the handle of his umbrella, she felt the mounting pressure of tears. As she looked around trying to hook her mind onto something, it gave her a kind of soft shock, a mixture of compassion and wonder, to notice that one of the passengers, a girl with dark hair and grubby red toenails, was weeping on the shoulder of an older woman. Whom did that woman resemble? She resembled Rebecca Borisovna, whose daughter had married one of the Soloveichiks—in Minsk, years ago.

The last time he had tried to do it, his method had been, in the doctor's words, a masterpiece of inventiveness; he would have succeeded, had not an envious fellow patient thought he was learning to fly—and stopped him. What he really wanted to do was to tear a hole in his world and escape.

The system of his delusions had been the subject of an elaborate paper in a scientific monthly, but long before that she and her husband had puzzled it out for themselves. "Referential mania," Herman Brink had called it. In these very rare cases the patient imagines that everything happening around him is a veiled reference to his personality and existence. He excludes real people from the conspiracy—because he considers himself to be so much more intelligent than other men. Phenomenal nature shadows him wherever he goes. Clouds in the staring sky transmit to one another, by means of slow signs, incredibly detailed information regarding him. His inmost thoughts are discussed at nightfall, in manual alphabet, by darkly gesticulating trees. Pebbles or stains or sun flecks form patterns representing in some awful way messages which he must intercept. Everything is a cipher and of everything he is the theme. Some of the spies are detached observers, such are glass surfaces and still pools; others, such as coats in store windows, are prejudiced witnesses, lynchers at heart; others again (running water, storms) are hysterical to the point of insanity, have a distorted opinion of him and grotesquely misinterpret his actions. He must be always on his guard and devote every minute and module of life to the decoding of the undulation of things. The very air he exhales is indexed and filed away. If only the interest he provokes were limited to his immediate surroundings—but alas it is not! With distance the torrents of wild scandal increase in volume and volubility. The silhouettes of his blood corpuscles, magnified a million times, flit over vast plains; and still farther, great mountains of unbearable solidity and height sum up in terms of granite and groaning firs the ultimate truth of his being.

II

When they emerged from the thunder and foul air of the subway, the last dregs of the day were mixed with the street lights. She wanted to buy some fish for supper, so she handed him the basket of jelly jars, telling him to go home. He walked up to the third landing and then remembered he had given her his keys earlier in the day.

In silence he sat down on the steps and in silence rose when some ten minutes later she came, heavily trudging upstairs, wanly smiling, shaking her head in deprecation of her silliness. They entered their two-room flat and he at once went to the mirror. Straining the corners of his mouth apart by means of his thumbs, with a horrible masklike grimace he removed his new hopelessly uncomfortable dental plate and severed the long tusks of saliva connecting him to it. He read his Russian-language newspaper while she laid the table. Still reading, he ate the pale victuals that needed no teeth. She knew his moods and was also silent.

When he had gone to bed, she remained in the living room with her pack of soiled cards and her old albums. Across the narrow yard where the rain tinkled in the dark against some battered ash cans, windows were blandly alight and in one of them a black-trousered man with his bare elbows raised could be seen lying supine on an untidy bed. She pulled the blind down and examined the photographs. As a baby he looked more surprised than most babies. From a fold in the album, a German maid they had had in Leipzig and her fat-faced fiancé fell out. Minsk, the Revolution, Leipzig, Berlin, Leipzig, a slanting house front badly out of focus. Four years old, in a park: moodily, shyly, with puckered forehead, looking away from an eager squirrel as he would from any other stranger. Aunt Rosa, a fussy, angular, wild-eyed old lady, who had lived in a tremulous world of bad news, bankruptcies, train accidents, cancerous growths—until the Germans put her to death, together with all the people she had worried about. Age six—that was when he drew wonderful birds with human hands and feet, and suffered from insomnia like a grown-up man. His cousin, now a famous chess player. He again, aged about eight, already difficult to understand, afraid of the wallpaper in the passage, afraid of a certain picture in a book which merely showed an idyllic landscape with rocks on a hillside and an old cart wheel hanging from the branch of a leafless tree. Aged ten: the year they left Europe. The shame, the pity, the humiliating difficulties, the ugly, vicious, backward children he was with in that special school. And then came a time in his life, coinciding with a long convalescence after pneumonia, when those little phobias of his which his parents had stubbornly regarded as the eccentricities of a prodigiously gifted child hardened as it were into a dense tangle of logically interacting illusions, making him totally inaccessible to normal minds.

This, and much more, she accepted—for after all living did mean accepting the loss of one joy after another, not even joys in her case—mere possibilities of improvement. She thought of the endless waves of pain that for some reason or other she and her husband had to endure; of the invisible giants hurting her boy in some unimaginable fashion; of the incalculable amount of tenderness contained in the world; of the fate of this tenderness, which is either crushed, or wasted, or transformed into madness; of neglected children humming to themselves in unswept corners; of beautiful weeds that cannot hide from the farmer and helplessly have to watch the shadow of his simian stoop leave mangled flowers in its wake, as the monstrous darkness approaches.

III

It was past midnight when from the living room she heard her husband moan; and presently he staggered in, wearing over his nightgown the old overcoat with astrakhan collar which he much preferred to the nice blue bathrobe he had.

"I can't sleep," he cried.

"Why," she asked, "why can't you sleep? You were so tired."

"I can't sleep because I am dying," he said and lay down on the couch.

"Is it your stomach? Do you want me to call Dr. Solov?"

"No doctors, no doctors," he moaned. "To the devil with doctors! We must get him out of there quick. Otherwise we'll be responsible. Responsible!" he repeated and hurled himself into a sitting position, both feet on the floor, thumping his forehead with his clenched fist.

"All right," she said quietly, "we shall bring him home tomorrow morning."

"I would like some tea," said her husband and retired to the bathroom.

Bending with difficulty, she retrieved some playing cards and a photograph or two that had slipped from the couch to the floor: knave of hearts, nine of spades, ace of spades, Elsa and her bestial beau.

He returned in high spirits, saying in a loud voice:

"I have it all figured out. We will give him the bedroom. Each of us will spend part of the night near him and the other part on this couch. By turns. We will have the doctor see him at least twice a week. It does not matter what the Prince says. He won't have to say much anyway because it will come out cheaper."

The telephone rang. It was an unusual hour for their telephone to ring. His left slipper had come off and he groped for it with his heel and toe as he stood in the middle of the room, and childishly, toothlessly, gaped at his wife. Having more English than he did, it was she who attended the calls.

"Can I speak to Charlie," said a girl's dull little voice.

"What number you want? No. That is not the right number."

The receiver was gently cradled. Her hand went to her old tired heart.

"It frightened me," she said.

He smiled a quick smile and immediately resumed his excited monologue.

They would fetch him as soon as it was day. Knives would have to be kept in a locked drawer. Even at his worst he presented no danger to other people.

The telephone rang a second time. The same toneless anxious young voice asked for Charlie.

"You have the incorrect number. I will tell you what you are doing: you are turning the letter O instead of the zero."

They sat down to their unexpected festive midnight tea. The birthday present stood on the table. He sipped noisily; his face was flushed; every now and then he imparted a circular motion to his raised glass so as to make the sugar dissolve more thoroughly. The vein on the side of his bald head where there was a large birthmark stood out conspicuously and although he had shaved that morning, a silvery bristle showed on his chin. While she poured him another glass of tea, he put on his spectacles and re-examined with pleasure the luminous yellow, green, red little jars. His clumsy moist lips spelled out their eloquent labels: apricot, grape, peach, plum, quince. He had got to crab apple, when the telephone rang again.

Suggestions for Discussion

1. In the third paragraph of the story we read, "The underground train lost its life current between two stations . . ."; and at the beginning of section II, "they emerged from the thunder and foul air of the subway." How do these metaphors relate to the situation of the story and to its symbolic pattern?

2. Is the "tiny half-dead unfledged bird . . . helplessly twitching in a puddle" at the end of the fourth paragraph of the first section a symbol? Of what?

3. The "referential mania" described on page 284 is the symbolic system of a madman, in which every natural phenomenon means something other and something more than itself. What distance do we take on this system when we first encounter it? How has that distance altered by the end of the story?

4. What place do the following have in the symbolic meaning of the story: The description of Aunt Rosa on page 285? The shadow of the farmer's "simian stoop" at the end of section II on page 286? The old woman's explanation, "you are turning the letter O instead of the zero," on this page?

5. This is a "Lady or the Tiger" tale, ending with an unanswered and unanswerable question. Why has Nabokov chosen this form for this particular story? Who do you think is on the other end of the telephone at the third call? What significance does it have for the symbolic meaning of the story if it should be the wrong-number caller again? The hospital?

The Ones Who Walk Away from Omelas

URSULA K. LE GUIN

With a clamor of bells that set the swallows soaring, the Festival of Summer came to the city. Omelas, bright-towered by the sea. The rigging of the boats in harbor sparkled with flags. In the streets between houses with red roofs and painted walls, between old moss-grown gardens and under avenues of trees, past great parks and public buildings, processions moved. Some were decorous: old people in long stiff robes of mauve and grey, grave master workmen, quiet, merry women carrying their babies and chatting as they walked. In other streets the music beat faster, a shimmering of gong and tambourine, and the people went dancing, the procession was a dance. Children dodged in and out, their high calls rising like the swallows' crossing flights over the music and singing. All the processions wound towards the north side of the city, where on the great water-meadow called the Green Fields boys and girls, naked in the bright air, with mud-stained feet and ankles and long, lithe arms, exercised their restive horses before the race. The horses wore no gear at all but a halter without bit. Their manes were braided with streamers of silver, gold, and green. They flared their nostrils and pranced and boasted to one another; they were vastly excited, the horse being the only animal who has adopted our ceremonies as his own. Far off to the north and west the mountains stood up half encircling Omelas on her bay. The air of morning was so clear that the snow still crowning the Eighteen Peaks burned with white-gold fire across the miles of sunlit air, under the dark blue of the sky. There was just enough wind to make the banners that marked the racecourse snap and flutter now and then. In the silence of the broad green meadows one could hear the music winding through the city streets, farther and nearer and ever approaching, a cheerful faint sweetness of the air that from time to time trembled and gathered together and broke out into the great joyous clanging of the bells.

Joyous! How is one to tell about joy? How describe the citizens of Omelas?

They were not simple folk, you see, though they were happy. But we do not say the words of cheer much any more. All smiles have become archaic. Given a description such as this one tends to make certain assumptions. Given a description such as this one tends to look next for the King, mounted on a splendid stallion and surrounded by his noble knights, or perhaps in a golden litter borne by great-muscled slaves. But there was no king. They did not use swords, or keep slaves. They were not barbarians. I do not know the rules and laws of their society, but I suspect that they were singularly few. As they did without monarchy and slavery, so they also got on without the stock exchange, the advertisement, the secret police, and the bomb. Yet I repeat that these were not simple folk, not dulcet shepherds, noble savages, bland utopians. They were not less complex than us. The trouble is that we have a bad habit, encouraged by pedants and sophisticates, of considering happiness as something rather stupid. Only pain is intellectual, only evil interesting. This is the treason of the artist: a refusal to admit the banality of evil and the terrible boredom of pain. If you can't lick 'em, join 'em. If it hurts, repeat it. But to praise despair is to condemn delight, to embrace violence is to lose hold of everything else. We have almost lost hold; we can no longer describe a happy man, nor make any celebration of joy. How can I tell you about the people of Omelas? They were not naïve and happy children— though their children were, in fact, happy. They were mature, intelligent, passionate adults whose lives were not wretched. O miracle! but I wish I could describe it better. I wish I could convince you. Omelas sounds in my words like a city in a fairy tale, long ago and far away, once upon a time. Perhaps it would be best if you imagined it as your own fancy bids, assuming it will rise to the occasion, for certainly I cannot suit you all. For instance, how about technology? I think that there would be no cars or helicopters in and above the streets; this follows from the fact that the people of Omelas are happy people. Happiness is based on a just discrimination of what is necessary, what is neither necessary nor destructive, and what is destructive. In the middle category, however—that of the unnecessary but undestructive, that of comfort, luxury, exuberance, etc.—they could perfectly well have central heating, subway trains, washing machines, and all kinds of marvelous devices not yet invented here, floating light-sources, fuelless power, a cure for the common cold. Or they could have none of that: it doesn't matter. As you like it. I incline to think that people from towns up and down the coast have been coming in to Omelas during the last days before the Festival on very fast little trains and double-decked trams and that the train station of Omelas is actually the handsomest building in town, though plainer than the magnificent Farmers' Market. But even granted trains, I fear that Omelas so far strikes some of you as goody-goody. Smiles, bells, parades, horses, bleh. If so, please add an orgy. If an orgy would help, don't hesitate. Let us not, however, have temples from which issue beautiful nude priests and priestesses already half in ecstasy and ready to copulate with any man or woman, lover or stranger, who desires union with the deep godhead of the blood, although that was my first idea. But really it would be better not to have any temples in Omelas—at least, not manned temples. Religion yes, clergy no. Surely the beautiful nudes can just wander about, offering themselves like divine soufflés to the hunger of the needy and the rapture of the flesh. Let them join the processions. Let tambourines be struck above the copulations, and the glory of desire be proclaimed upon the gongs, and (a not unimportant point) let the offspring of these delightful rituals be beloved and looked after by all. One thing I know there is none of in Omelas is guilt. But what else should there be? I thought at first there were no drugs, but that is puritanical. For those who like it, the faint insistent sweetness of *drooz* may perfume the ways of the city, *drooz* which first brings a great lightness and brilliance to the mind and limbs, and then after some hours a dreamy languor, and wonderful visions at last of the very arcana and inmost secrets of the Universe, as well as exciting the pleasure of sex beyond all belief; and it is not habit-forming. For more modest tastes I think there ought to be beer. What else, what else belongs in the joyous city? The sense of victory, surely, the celebration of courage. But as we did without clergy, let us do without soldiers. The joy built upon successful slaughter is not the right kind of joy; it will not do; it is fearful and it is trivial. A boundless and generous contentment, a magnanimous triumph felt not against some outer enemy but in communion with the finest and fairest in the souls of all men everywhere and the splendor of the world's summer: this is what swells the hearts of the people of Omelas, and the victory they celebrate is that of life. I really don't think many of them need to take *drooz*.

Most of the processions have reached the Green Fields by now. A marvelous smell of cooking goes forth from the red and blue tents of the provisioners. The faces of small children are amiably sticky; in the benign grey beard of a man a couple of crumbs of rich pastry are entangled. The youths and girls have mounted their horses and are beginning to group around the starting line of the course. An old woman, small, fat, and laughing, is passing out flowers from a basket, and tall young men wear her flowers in their shining hair. A child of nine or ten sits at the edge of the crowd, alone, playing on a wooden flute. People pause to listen, and they smile, but they do not speak to him, for he never ceases playing and never sees them, his dark eyes wholly rapt in the sweet, thin magic of the tune.

He finishes, and slowly lowers his hands holding the wooden flute.

As if that little private silence were the signal, all at once a trumpet sounds from the pavillion near the starting line: imperious, melancholy, piercing. The horses rear on their slender legs, and some of them neigh in answer. Sober-faced, the young riders stroke the horses' necks and soothe them, whispering, "Quiet, quiet, there my beauty, my hope. . . ." They begin to form in rank along the starting line. The crowds along the racecourse are like a field of grass and flowers in the wind. The Festival of Summer has begun.

Do you believe? Do you accept the festival, the city, the joy? No? Then let me describe one more thing.

In the basement under one of the beautiful public buildings of Omelas, or perhaps in the cellar of one of its spacious private homes, there is a room. It has one locked door, and no window. A little light seeps in dustily between cracks in the boards, secondhand from a cobwebbed window somewhere across the cellar. In one corner of the little room a couple of mops, with stiff, clotted, foul-smelling heads, stand near a rusty bucket. The floor is dirt, a little damp to the touch, as cellar dirt usually is. The room is about three paces long and two wide: a mere broom closet or disused tool room. In the room a child is sitting. It could be a boy or a girl. It looks about six, but actually is nearly ten. It is feeble-minded. Perhaps it was born defective, or perhaps it has become imbecile through fear, malnutrition, and neglect. It picks its nose and occasionally fumbles vaguely with its toes or genitals, as it sits hunched in the corner farthest from the bucket and two mops. It is afraid of the mops. It finds them horrible. It shuts its eyes, but it knows the mops are still standing there; and the door is locked; and nobody will come. The door is always locked; and nobody ever comes, except that sometimes—the child has no understanding of time or interval—sometimes the door rattles terribly and opens, and a person, or several people, are there. One of them may come in and kick the child to make it stand up. The others never come close, but peer in at it with frightened, disgusted eyes. The food bowl and the water jug are hastily filled, the door is locked, the eyes disappear. The people at the door never say anything, but the child, who has not always lived in the tool room, and can remember sunlight and its mother's voice, sometimes speaks. "I will be good," it says. "Please let me out. I will be good!" They never answer. The child used to scream for help at night, and cry a good deal, but not it only makes a kind of whining, "eh-haa, eh-haa," and it speaks less and less often. It is so thin there are no calves to its legs; its belly protrudes; it lives on a half-bowl of corn meal and grease a day. It is naked. Its buttocks and thighs are a mass of festered sores, as it sits in its own excrement continually.

They all know it is there, all the people of Omelas. Some of them have come to see it, others are content merely to know it is there. They all know that it has to be there. Some of them understand why, and some do not, but they all understand that their happiness, the beauty of their city, the tenderness of their friendships, the health of their children, the wisdom of their scholars, the skill of their makers, even the abundance of their harvest and the kindly weathers of their skies, depend wholly on this child's abominable misery.

This is usually explained to children when they are between eight and twelve, whenever they seem capable of understanding; and most of those who come to see the child are young people, though often enough an adult comes, or comes back, to see the child. No matter how well the matter has been explained to them, these young spectators are always shocked and sickened at the sight. They feel disgust, which they had thought themselves superior to. They feel anger, outrage, impotence, despite all the explanations. They would like to do something for the child. But there is nothing they can do. If the child were brought up into the sunlight out of that vile place, if it were cleaned and fed and comforted, that would be a good thing, indeed; but if it were done, in that day and hour all the prosperity and beauty and delight of Omelas would wither and be destroyed. Those are the terms. To exchange all the goodness and grace of every life in Omelas for that single, small improvement: to throw away the happiness of thousands for the chance of the happiness of one: that would be to let guilt within the walls indeed.

The terms are strict and absolute; there may not even be a kind word spoken to the child.

Often young people go home in tears, or in a tearless rage, when they have seen the child and faced this terrible paradox. They may brood over it for weeks or years. But as time goes on they begin to realize that even if the child could be released, it would not get much good of its freedom: a little vague pleasure of warmth and food, no doubt, but little more. It is too degraded and imbecile to know any real joy. It has been afraid too long ever to be free of fear. Its habits are too uncouth for it to respond to humane treatment. Indeed, after so long it would probably be wretched without walls about it to protect it, and darkness for its eyes, and its own excrement to sit in. Their tears at the bitter injustice dry when they begin to perceive the terrible justice of reality and to accept it. Yet it is their tears and anger, the trying of their generosity and the acceptance of their helplessness, which are perhaps the true source of the splendor of their lives. Theirs is no vapid, irresponsible happiness. They know that they, like the child, are not free. They know compassion. It is the existence of the child, and their knowledge of its existence, that makes possible the nobility of their architecture, the poignancy of their music, the profundity of their science. It is because of the child that they are so gentle with children. They know that if the wretched one were not snivelling in the dark, the other one, the flute-player, could make no joyful music as the young riders line up in their beauty for the race in the sunlight of the first morning of summer.

Now do you believe in them? Are they more credible? But there is one more thing to tell, and this is quite incredible.

At times one of the adolescent girls or boys who go to see the child does not go home to weep or rage, does not, in fact, go home at all. Sometimes also a man or woman much older falls silent for a day or two, and then leaves home. These people go out into the street, and walk down the street alone. They keep walking, and walk straight out of the city of Omelas, through the beautiful gates. They keep walking across the farmlands of Omelas. Each one goes alone, youth or girl, man or woman. Night falls; the traveler must pass down the village streets, between the houses with yellow-lit windows, and on out into the darkness of the fields. Each alone, they go west or north, towards the mountains. They go on. They leave Omelas, they walk ahead into the darkness, and they do not come back. The place they go towards is a place even less imaginable to most of us than the city of happiness. I cannot describe it at all. It is possible that it does not exist. But they seem to know where they are going, the ones who walk away from Omelas.

Suggestions for Discussion

1. Is "The Ones Who Walk Away from Omelas" an allegory? What situation might it stand for without mentioning?

2. Is the story metafiction? Look over the section on metafiction on page 51 and consider "storytelling" as the subject or theme.

3. Is the story based on the birth model? Consider whether conflict is central to its structure. (See pages 42–43.)

4. Is it a story at all? Who are its characters?

5. How does the child operate as a symbol? Of what?

6. Who speaks? Who is the "I" in this story? How would you describe the point of view?

7. Describe the indescribable place toward which those who walk away from Omelas go. What does it symbolize?

RETROSPECT

Explain how each of the following metaphors or symbols operates in its context:

1. The excerpt from *The Writing Life:* digging instruments (page 27).

2. "Everything That Rises Must Converge": "while he, his hands behind him, appeared pinned to the door frame, waiting like Saint Sebastian for the arrows to begin piercing him" (page 151).

3. "Orbiting": scars (page 123); the dagger and the carving knife (page 124).

4. "Waiting for Mr Kim": "white paper bell with sugar sprinkles" (pages 188–189).

5. "The Wrysons": Irene Wryson's dream (pages 224–225; Donald Wryson's baking (page 226–227).

WRITING ASSIGNMENTS

1. Write a passage using at least three cliché metaphors, finding a way to make each fresh and original.

2. Take any dead metaphor and write a comic or serious scene that reinvests the metaphor with its original comparative force. Here are a few sample suggestions (your own will be better).

Sifting the evidence. (The lawyer uses a colander, a tea strainer, two coffee filters, and a garlic press to decide the case.)

Speakeasy. (Chicago, 1916. A young libertine tricks a beautiful but repressed young woman into an illegal basement bar. He thinks drink will loosen her up. What it loosens is not her sensuality but her tongue, and what she says he doesn't want to hear.)

Peck on the cheek.

(Alfred Hitchcock has done this one already, perhaps?)

Bus terminal.	*Don't spoil your lunch.*
Advertising jingle.	*Broken home.*
Soft shoulders.	*Good-bye.*

3. Write two one-page scenes, each containing an extended metaphor or simile. In one, compare an ordinary object to something of great size or significance. In the other, compare a major thing or phenomenon to something smaller and more mundane or less intense.

4. Write a short scene involving a conflict between two people over an object. Let the object take on symbolic significance. It may have the same significance to the two people, of a different significance to each.

5. Let an object smaller than a breadbox symbolize hope, redemption, or love to the central character. Let it symbolize something else entirely to the reader.

6. List all the clichés you can think of to describe a pair of blue eyes. Then write a paragraph in which you find a fresh, new metaphor for blue eyes.

10

I GOTTA USE WORDS
WHEN I TALK TO YOU
Theme

Idea and Morality in Theme
How Fictional Elements Contribute to Theme
Developing Theme as You Write

How does a fiction mean?

Most literature textbooks begin a discussion of theme by warning that theme is not the *message*, not the *moral*, and that the *meaning* of a piece cannot be paraphrased. Theme contains an idea but cannot be stated as an idea. It suggests a morality but offers no moral. Then what is theme, and how as a writer can you pursue that rich resonance?

First of all, theme is what a story is about. But that is not enough, because a story may be "about" a dying Samurai or a quarreling couple or two kids on a trampoline, and those are not the themes of those stories. A story is also "about" an abstraction, and if the story is significant, that abstraction may be very large; yet thousands of stories are about love, other thousands about death, several thousands about both love and death, and to say this is to say little about the theme of any of them.

I think it might be useful to borrow an idea from Existentialist philosophy, which asks the question: *What is what is?* That is, what is the nature of that which exists? We might start to understand theme if we ask the question: *What about what it's about?* What does the story have to say about the idea of abstraction that seems to be contained in it? What attitudes or judgments does it imply? Above all, how do the techniques particular to fiction contribute to our experience of those ideas and attitudes in the story?

Idea and Morality in Theme

Literature is stuck with ideas in a way other arts are not. Music, paradoxically the most abstract of the arts, creates a logical structure that need make no reference to the world outside itself. It may express a mood, but it need draw no conclusions. Shapes in painting and sculpture may suggest forms in the physical world, but they need not represent the world, and they need contain no message. But words mean. The grammatical structure of the simplest sentence contains a concept, whatever else it may contain, so that an author who wishes to treat words solely as sound or shape may be said to make strange music or pictures but not literature.

Yet those who choose to deal in the medium of literature consistently denigrate concepts and insist on the value of the particular instance. Here is Vladimir Nabokov's advice to a reader.

> . . . fondle details. There is nothing wrong about the moonshine of generalization *after* the sunny trifles of the book have been lovingly collected. If one begins with a ready-made generalization, one begins at the wrong end and travels away from the book before one has started to understand it.

Joan Didion parallels the idea from the other side of the typewriter in an essay on "Why I Write."

> I am not a scholar. I am not in the least an intellectual, which is not to say that when I hear the word "intellectual" I reach for my gun, but only to say that I do not think in abstracts. During the years when I was an undergraduate at Berkeley I tried, with a kind of hopeless late-adolescent energy, to buy some temporary visa into the world of ideas, to forge for myself a mind that could deal with the abstract.
>
> In short I tried to think. I failed. My attention veered inexorably back to the specific, to the tangible, to what was generally considered, by everyone I knew then and for that matter have known since, the peripheral. I would try to contemplate the Hegelian dialectic and would find myself concentrating instead on the flowering pear tree outside my window and the particular way the petals fell on the floor.

Didion takes a Socratic stance here, ironically pretending to naïveté and modesty as she equates "thinking" with "thinking in the abstract." Certainly her self-deprecation is ironic in light of the fact that she is not only a novelist but also one of the finest intellects among our contemporary essayists. But she acknowledges an assumption that's both very general and very seriously taken, that *thought* means *dealing with the abstract,* and that abstract thought is more real, central, and valid than specific concrete thought.

What both these passages suggest is that a writer of fiction approaches concepts, abstractions, generalizations, and truths through their particular embodiments—showing, not telling. "Literature," says John Ciardi, "is never only about ideas, but about the experience of ideas." T. S. Eliot points out that the creation of this experience is of itself an intellectual feat.

> We talk as if thought was precise and emotion was vague. In reality there is precise emotion and there is vague emotion. To express precise emotion requires as great intellectual power as to express precise thought.

The value of the literary experience is that it allows us to judge an idea at two levels of consciousness, the rational and the emotional (or the neocortical and the limbic), simultaneously. The kind of "truth" that can be told through thematic resonance is many-faceted and can acknowledge the competing of many truths, exploring paradox and contradiction.

There is a curious prejudice built into our language that makes us speak of telling *the* truth but telling *a* lie. No one supposes that all conceivable falsehood can be wrapped up in a single statement called "the lie"; lies are manifold, varied, and specific. But truth is supposed to be absolute: the truth, the whole truth, and nothing but the truth. This is, of course, impossible nonsense, and *telling a lie* is a truer phrase than *telling the truth.* Fiction does not have to tell *the* truth, but *a* truth.

Anton Chekov wrote that "the writer of fiction should not try to solve such questions as those of God, pessimism and so forth." What is "obligatory for the artist," he said, is not "solving a problem," but "stating a problem correctly." John Keats went even further in pursuing a definition of "the impersonality of genius." "The only means of strengthening one's intellect is to make up one's mind about nothing—to let the mind be a thoroughfare for all thoughts." And he defined genius itself as *negative capability,* "that is when a man is capable of being in uncertainties, mysteries and doubts, without any irritable reaching after fact and reason."

A story, then, speculates on a possible truth. It is not an answer or a law but a supposition, an exploration. Every story reaches in its climax and resolution an interim solution to a specifically realized dilemma. But it offers neither a final solution nor the Final Solution.

The contrast with the law here is relevant. Abstract reasoning works toward generalization and results in definitions, laws, and absolute judgments. Imaginative reasoning and concrete thought work toward instances and result in emotional experience, revelation, and the ability to contain life's paradoxes in tension—which may explain the notorious opposition of writers to the laws and institutions of their time. Lawmakers struggle to define a moral position in abstract terms such that it will justly account for every instance to which it is applied. (This is why the language of law is so tedious and convoluted.) Poets and novelists continually goad them by producing instances for which the law does not account and referring by implication to the principle behind and beyond the law. (This is why the language of literature is so dense and compact.)

The idea that is proposed, supposed, or speculated on in a fiction may be simple and idealistic, like the notion in "Cinderella" that the good and beautiful will triumph. Or it may be profound and unprovable, like the theme in *Oedipus Rex* that man cannot escape his destiny but may be ennobled in the attempt. Or it may be deliberately paradoxical and offer no guidelines that can be used in life, as in Jane Austen's *Persuasion,* where the heroine, in order to adhere to her principles, must follow advice given on principles less sound than her own.

In any case, while exploring an idea the writer inevitably conveys an attitude toward that idea. Rust Hills puts it this way.

> . . . coherence in the world [an author] creates is constituted of two concepts he holds, which may be in conflict: one is his world view, his sense of the way the world is; and the other is his sense of morality, the way the world ought to be.

Literature is a persuasive art, and we respond to it with the tautology of literary judgment, that a fiction is "good" if it's "good." No writer who fails to convince us of the validity of his or her vision of the world can convince us of his or her greatness. The Victorians used literature to teach piety, and the Aesthetes asserted that Victorian piety was a deadening lie. Albert Camus believed that no serious writer in the twentieth century could avoid political commitment, whereas for Joyce the true artist could be a God but *must not* be a preacher. Each of these stances is a moral one. Those who defend escape literature do so on the grounds that people *need* to escape. Those who defend hardcore pornography argue that we can't prove an uncensored press makes for moral degeneracy, whereas it can be historically demonstrated that a censored press makes for political oppression. Anarchistic, nihilistic, and antisocial literature is always touted as offering a neglected truth. I have yet to hear anyone assert that literature leads to laziness, madness, and brutality and then say that it doesn't matter.

The writer, of course, may be powerfully impelled to impose a limited vision of the world as it ought to be, and even to tie that vision to a social institution, wishing not only to persuade and convince but also to propagandize. But because the emotional force of literary persuasion is in the realization of the particular, the writer is doomed to fail. The greater the work, the more it refers us to some permanent human impulse rather than a given institutional embodiment of that impulse. Fine writing expands our scope by continually presenting a new way of seeing, a further possibility of emotional identification; it flatly refuses to become a law. I am not a Roman Catholic like Gerard Manley Hopkins and cannot be persuaded by his poetry to become one; but in a moment near despair I can drive along an Illinois street in a Chevrolet station wagon and take strength from the lines of a Jesuit in the Welsh wasteland. I am not a communist as Bertolt Brecht was and cannot be convinced by his plays to become one; but I can see the hauteur of wealth displayed on the Gulf of Mexico and recognize, from a parable of the German Marxist, the difference between a possession and a belonging.

In the human experience, emotion, judgment, and logic are inextricably mixed, and we make continual cross-reference between and among them. *You've just got the sulks today.* (I pass judgment on your emotion.) *What do you think of this idea?* (How do you judge this logic?) *Why do I feel this way?* (What is the logic of this emotion?) *It makes no sense to be angry about it.* (I pass judgment on the logic of your emotion.) Literature attempts to fuse three areas of experience organically, denying the force of none of them, positing that no one is more real than the others. This is why I have insisted throughout this book on detail and scene (immediate felt experience), the essential abstractions conveyed therein (ideas), and the attitude implied thereby (judgment).

Not all experience reveals, but all revelation comes through experience. Books aspire to become a part of that revelatory experience, and the books that are made in the form of fiction attempt to do so by re-creating the experience of revelation.

How Fictional Elements Contribute to Theme

Whatever the idea and attitudes that underlie the theme of a story, that story will bring them into the realm of experience through its particular and unique pattern. Theme involves emotion, logic, and judgment, all three—but the pattern that forms the particular experience of that theme is made up of every element of fiction this book has discussed: the arrangement, shape, and flow of the action, as performed by the characters, realized in their details, seen in their atmosphere, from a unique point of view, through the imagery and the rhythm of the language.

This book, for example, contains six stories that may be said to have "the generation gap" as a major theme: "Girl," "How Far She Went," "Orbiting," "My Man Bovanne," "Waiting for Mr. Kim," and "Ralph the Duck." Some of these are written from the point of view of a member of the older generation, some from the point of view of the younger. In some conflict is resolved by bridging the gap; in others it is not. The characters are variously poor, middle class, rural, urban, male, female, adolescent, middle-aged, old, black, white, Oriental. The imagery variously evokes food, sex, speed, torture, blindness, death, and writing. It is in the different uses of the elements of fiction that each story makes unique what it has to say about, and what attitude it takes toward, the idea of "the generation gap."

What follows is as short a story as you are likely to encounter in print. It is spare in the extreme—almost, as its title suggests, an outline. Yet the author has contrived in this miniscule compass to direct every fictional element we have discussed toward the exploration of several large themes.

〰️

A Man Told Me the Story of His Life

GRACE PALEY

Vicente said: I wanted to be a doctor. I wanted to be a doctor with my whole heart.

I learned every bone, every organ in the body. What is it for? Why does it work?

The school said to me: Vicente, be an engineer. That would be good. You understand mathematics.

I said to the school: I want to be a doctor. I already know how the organs connect. When something goes wrong, I'll understand how to make repairs.

The school said: Vicente, you will really be an excellent engineer. You show on all the tests what a good engineer you will be. It doesn't show whether you'll be a good doctor.

I said: Oh, I long to be a doctor. I nearly cried. I was seventeen. I said: But perhaps you're right. You're the teacher. You're the principal. I know I'm young.

The school said: And besides, you're going into the army.

And then I was made a cook. I prepared food for two thousand men.

Now you see me. I have a good job. I have three children. This is my wife, Consuela. Did you know I saved her life?

Look, she suffered pain. The doctor said: What is this? Are you tired? Have you had too much company? How many children? Rest overnight, then tomorrow we'll make tests.

The next morning I called the doctor. I said: She must be operated immediately. I have looked in the book. I see where her pain is. I understand what the pressure is, where it comes from. I see clearly the organ that is making trouble.

The doctor made a test. He said: She must be operated at once. He said to me: Vicente, how did you know?

I think it would be fair to say that this story is about the waste of Vicente's talent through the bad guidance of authority. I'll start by saying, then, that *waste* and *power* are its central themes. How are the elements of fiction arranged in the story to present them?

The *conflict* is between Vicente and the figures of authority he encounters: teacher, principal, army, doctor. His desire at the beginning of the story is to become a doctor (in itself a figure of authority), and this desire is thwarted by persons of increasing power. In the *crisis action* what is at stake is his wife's life. In this "last battle" he succeeds as a doctor, so that the *resolution* reveals the *irony* of his having been denied in the first place.

The story is told from the *point of view* of a *first-person central narrator*, but with an important qualification. The title, "A Man Told Me the Story of His Life," and the first two words, "Vicente said," posit a *peripheral narrator* reporting what Vicente said. If the story were titled "My Life" and began, "I wanted to be a doctor," Vicente might be making a public appeal, a boast of how wronged he has been. As it is, he told his story privately to the barely sketched author who now wants it known, and this leaves Vicente's modesty intact.

The modesty is underscored by the simplicity of his *speech*, a *rhythm* and word choice that suggest educational *limitations* (perhaps that English is a second language). At the same time, that simplicity helps us *identify* with Vicente morally. Clearly, if he has educational limitations, it is not for want of trying to get an education! His credibility is augmented by *understatement*, both as a youth—"Perhaps you're right. You're the teacher."—and as a man—"I have a good job. I have three children." This apparent acceptance makes us trust him at the same time as it makes us angry on his behalf.

It's consistent with the spareness of the language that we do not have an accumulation of minute or vivid details, but the degree of *specificity* is nevertheless a clue to where to direct our sympathy. In the title Vicente is just "A Man." As soon as he speaks he becomes an individual with a name. "The School," collective and impersonal, speaks to him, but when he speaks it is to "the teacher, the principal," and when he speaks of his wife she is "Consuela."

Moreover, the *sense details* are so arranged that they relate to each other in ways that give them *metaphoric* and *symbolic significance*. Notice, for example, how Vicente's desire to become a doctor "with my whole heart" is immediately followed by, "I learned every bone, every organ. . . ." Here the factual anatomical study refers us back to the heart that is one of those organs, suggesting by implication that Vicente is somebody who knows what a heart is. He knows how things "connect."

An engineer, of course, has to know how things connect and how to make repairs. But so does a doctor, and the authority figures of the school haven't the imagination to see the connection. The army, by putting him to work in a way that involves both connections and anatomical parts, takes advantage of his by-now clear ability to order and organize things—he feeds two thousand men—but it is too late to repair the misdirection of such talents. We don't know what his job is now; it doesn't matter, it's the wrong one.

As a young man Vicente asked, "What is it for? Why does it work?", revealing a natural fascination with the sort of question that would, of course, be asked on an anatomy test. But no such test is given, and the tests that are given are irrelevant. His wife's doctor will "make tests," but like the school authorities he knows less than Vicente does, and so impersonally asks insultingly personal questions. In fact you could say that all the authorities of the story fail the test.

This analysis, which is about two and a half times as long as the story, doesn't begin to exhaust the possibilities for interpretation, and you may disagree with any of my suggestions. But it does indicate how the techniques of characterization, plot, detail, point of view, image, and metaphor all reinforce the themes of waste and power. The story is so densely conceived and developed that it might fairly be titled "Connections," "Tests," "Repairs," "What Is It For?", or "How Did You Know?"—any one could lead us toward the themes of waste and the misguidance of authority.

Not every story is or needs to be as intensely interwoven in its elements as "A Man Told Me the Story of His Life," but the development of theme always involves such interweaving to a degree. It is a standard to work toward.

Developing Theme as You Write

In an essay, your goal is to say as clearly and directly as possible what you mean. In fiction, your goal is to make people and make them do things, and, ideally, never to "say what you mean" at all. Theoretically, an outline can never harm an essay: this is what I have to say, and I'll say it through points A, B, and C. But if a writer sets out to write a story to illustrate an idea, the fiction will almost inevitably be thin. Even if you begin with an outline, as many writers do, it will be an outline of the action and not of your "points." You may not know the meaning of the story until the characters begin to tell you what it is. You'll begin with an image of a person or a situation that seems vaguely to embody something important, and you'll learn as you go what that something is. Likewise, what you mean will emerge in the reading experience and take place in the reader's mind, "not," as the narrator says of Marlowe's tales in Heart of Darkness, "inside like a kernel but outside, enveloping the tale which brought it out."

But at some point in the writing process, you may find yourself impelled by, under pressure of, or interested primarily in your theme more than your plot. It will seem that you must set yourself this lonely, austere, and tortuous task because you do have something to say. At this point you will, and you should, begin to let that sorting-comparing-cataloging neocortical portion of your triune human brain go to work on the stuff of your story. John Gardner describes the process in The Art of Fiction.

Theme, it should be noticed, is not imposed on the story but evoked from within it—initially an intuitive but finally an intellectual act on the part of the writer. The writer muses on the story idea to determine what it is in it that has attracted him, why it seems to him worth telling. Having determined . . . what interests him—and what chiefly concerns the major character . . . he toys with various ways of telling his story, thinks about what has been said before about (his theme), broods on every image that occurs to him, turning it over and over, puzzling it, hunting for connections, trying to figure out—before he writes, while he writes, and in the process of repeated revisions—what it is he really thinks. . . . Only when he thinks out a story in this way does he achieve not just an alternative reality or, loosely, an imitation of nature, but true, firm art—fiction as serious thought.

This process—worrying a fiction until its theme reveals itself, connections occur, images recur, a pattern emerges—is more conscious than readers know, beginning writers want to accept, or established writers are willing to admit. It has become a popular—a cliché—stance for modern writers to claim that they haven't the faintest idea what they meant in their writing. *Don't ask me; read the book. If I knew what it meant, I wouldn't have written it. It means what it says.* When an author makes such a response, it is well to remember that an author is a professional liar. What he or she means is not that there are no themes, ideas, or meanings in the work but that these are not separable from the pattern of fictional experience in which they are embodied. It also means that, having done the difficult writerly job, the writer is now unwilling also to do the critic's work. But beginning critics also resist. Students irritated by the analysis of literature often ask, "How do you know she did that on purpose? How do you know it didn't just happen to come out that way?" The answer is: You don't. But what is on the page is on the page. An author no less than a reader or critic can see an emerging pattern, and the author has both the possibility and the obligation of manipulating it. When you have put something on the page, you have two possibilities, and only two: You may cut it or you are committed to it. Gail Godwin asks:

But what about the other truths you lost by telling it that way? . . .
Ah, my friend, that is my question too. The choice is always a killing one. One option must die so that another may live. I do little murders in my workroom every day.

Often the choice to commit yourself to a phrase, an image, a line of dialogue will reveal, in a minor convulsion of understanding, what you mean. I have written no story or novel in which this did not occur in trivial or dramatic ways. I once sat bolt upright at 4:00 A.M. in a strange town with the realization that my sixty-year-old narrator, in a novel full of images of hands and manipulation, had been lying to me for two hundred pages. Sometimes the realistic objects or actions of a work will begin to take on metaphoric or symbolic associations with your theme, producing a crossing of references, or what Richmond Lattimore calls a "symbol complex." In a novel about a woman who traveled around the world, I dealt with images of dangerous water and the danger of losing her balance, both physically and mentally. At some point I came up with—or, as it felt, was given—the image of a canal, the lock in which water finds its balance. This unforeseen connection gave me the purest moment of pleasure I had in writing that book. Yet I dare say no reader could identify it as a moment of particular intensity; nor, I hope, would any reader be consciously aware that the themes of danger and balance joined there.

Although I can address myself to what Grace Paley ultimately chose to publish as "A Man Told Me the Story of His Life," I cannot recount the theme-worrying *process* of any writer except myself, so I would like to try briefly to outline one such experience.

I quoted earlier from a novel that begins with the burial of a dog. When I began writing I did not know why I wanted this scene in the book, let alone at the powerful position of its opening. I complained in my journal of the time, "It has nothing to do with the plot."

The book is about a theater director, his first wife, who is a costume designer, and his second wife, who does not particularly know herself. The director is directing a play called *The Nuns*, in which three men dressed as nuns murder a young Spanish heiress, bury her, and later dig her up. The director is having trouble communicating with his son. He is also frightened of becoming like his father, who killed himself, while his current wife is frightened of becoming like her mother, who is a prim and colorless bore. The two wives are nervous about meeting each other. The first wife has not quite put the marriage behind her, and is afraid of falling in love with the theater carpenter.

Now, the structure of this book follows the seven-week rehearsal period of the play, and I knew it was to be called *Opening Night*—or, as it turned out, *Opening Nights*. As I wrote I began to discover that all the characters were having trouble "opening up" to each other. I began to notice that there were a lot of windows, doors, keys, and locks in their houses, apartments, motels, offices, and cars. Flowers tended to open here and there. Reading the newspaper one morning before I sat down to the desk I learned that it had been a bad year for earthquakes (a lot of earthquakes went into the book). I thought about how, in an earthquake, the earth can open up and close again—or else not. This was true also of my characters' hearts. Some sexual parallels presented themselves. As the plot developed I realized that a major reason my characters were having trouble opening up was that each had failed to deal with a significant person in the past, either a parent or a spouse. In order to get on with their lives, each had to dig up the past and get it properly buried again. *And of course I had to dig up that dog.*

I have had a good time writing this flippant outline, but it represents a tiny fraction of a process that took seven years, during which I twice decided to give up the novel and once decided to give up writing altogether. And even now, if someone asks me what the book is "about," I answer: *It's about a costume designer in a crummy little town in southern Georgia, whose ex-husband comes to work in the same town.* In other words, I answer with character and plot, which is what my interlocutor wants to know about. But in doing so I feel dishonest and detached. I could answer more truthfully and with more enthusiasm: *It's about digging up graves* (but that would give the false impression that it's a horror novel); or: *It's about dreams coming true* (which would give the equally false impression that it's a romance); or: *It's about professionalism, trash and treasure, getting rid of the past, opening and openings, permission, the occult as a metaphor for the horrors of ordinary life* (none of which, I think, would give much impression at all). Jane Austen once wrote her sister that the theme of her novel *Mansfield Park* was "ordination." In the two hundred years since that letter, critics have written many times the number of words in the novel trying to explain what she meant. And yet the novel is well understood, forcefully experienced, and intelligently appreciated. The difficulty is not in understanding the book but in applying the "kernel" definition to its multiplicity of ideas and richness of theme.

The fusion of elements into a unified pattern is the nature of creativity, a word devalued in latter years to the extent that is has come to mean a random gush of self-expression. God, perhaps, created out of the void; but in the world as we know it, all creativity, from the sprouting of an onion to the painting of *Guernica*, is a matter of selection and arrangement. A child learns to draw one circle on top of another, to add two triangles at the top and a line at the bottom, and in this particular pattern of circles, triangles, and lines has made a creature of an altogether different nature: a cat! The child draws one square on top of another and connects the corners and has made three dimensions where there are only two. And although these are tricks that can be taught and learned, they partake of the essential nature of creativity, in which several elements are joined to produce not merely a whole that is greater than the sum of its parts, but a whole that is something altogether other. At the conception of a fetus or a short story, there occurs a conjunction of two unlike things, whether cells or ideas, that have never been joined before. Around this conjunction other cells, other ideas accumulate in a deliberate pattern. That pattern is the unique personality of the creature, and if the pattern does not cohere, it miscarries or is stillborn.

The organic unity of a work of literature cannot be taught—or, if it can, I have not discovered a way to teach it. I can suggest from time to time that concrete image is not separate from character, which is revealed in dialogue and point of view, which may be illuminated by simile, which may reveal theme, which is contained in plot as water is contained in an apple. But I cannot tell you how to achieve this; nor, if you achieve it, will you be able to explain very clearly how you have done so. Analysis separates in order to focus; it assumes that an understanding of the parts contributes to an understanding of the whole, but it does not produce the whole. Scientists can determine with minute accuracy the elements, in their proportions, contained in a piece of human skin. They can gather these elements, stir and warm them, but they will not be skin. A good critic can show you where a metaphor does or does not illuminate character, where the character does or does not ring true in an action. But the critic cannot tell you how to make a character breathe; the breath is talent and can be neither explained nor produced.

No one can tell you what to mean, and no one can tell you how. I am conscious of having avoided the phrase *creative writing* in these pages, largely because all of us who teach creative writing find the words sticking in our throats. I myself would like to see courses taught in creative algebra, creative business administration, creative nursing, and creative history. I also fully and seriously intend one day to teach an advanced seminar in destructive writing (polemic, invective, libel, actionable obscenity, and character defamation). The mystique and the false glamour of the writing profession grow partly out of a mistaken belief that people who can express profound ideas and emotions have ideas and emotions more profound than the rest of us. It isn't so. The ability to express is a special gift with a special craft to support it and is spread fairly equally among the profound, the shallow, and the mediocre.

All the same, I am abashedly conscious that the creative exists—in algebra and nursing as in words—and that it mysteriously surfaces in the trivia of human existence: numbers, bandages, words. In the unified pattern of a fiction there is even something to which the name of magic may be given, where one empty word is placed upon another and tapped with a third, and a flaming scarf or a long-eared hope is pulled out of the tall black heart. The most magical thing about this magic is that once the trick is explained, it is not explained, and the better you understand how it works, the better it will work again.

Birth, death, work, and love continue to occur. Their meanings change from time to time and place to place, and new meanings engender new forms, which capture and create new meanings until they tire, while birth, death, work, and love continue to recur. Something to which we give the name of "honor" seems to persist, though in one place and time it is embodied in choosing to die for your country, in another, choosing not to. A notion of "progress" survives, though it is expressed now in technology, now in ecology, now in the survival of the fittest, now in the protection of the weak. There seems to be something corresponding to the human invention of "love," though it takes its form now in tenacious loyalty, now in letting go.

Ideas are not new, but the form in which they are expressed is constantly renewed, and new forms give life to what used to be called (in the old form) the eternal verities. An innovative writer tries to forge, and those who follow try to perfect, forms that so fuse with meaning that form itself expresses.

Cathedral

RAYMOND CARVER

This blind man, an old friend of my wife's, he was on his way to spend the night. His wife had died. So he was visiting the dead wife's relatives in Connecticut. He called my wife from his in-laws'. Arrangements were made. He would come by train, a five-hour trip, and my wife would meet him at the station. She hadn't seen him since she worked for him one summer in Seattle ten years ago. But she and the blind man had kept in touch. They made tapes and mailed them back and forth. I wasn't enthusiastic about his visit. He was no one I knew. And his being blind bothered me. My idea of blindness came from the movies. In the movies, the blind moved slowly and never laughed. Sometimes they were led by seeing-eye dogs. A blind man in my house was not something I looked forward to.

That summer in Seattle she had needed a job. She didn't have any money. The man she was going to marry at the end of the summer was in officers' training school. He didn't have any money, either. But she was in love with the guy, and he was in love with her, etc. She'd seen something in the paper: HELP WANTED—*Reading to Blind Man*, and a telephone number. She phoned and went over, was hired on the spot. She'd worked with this blind man all summer. She read stuff to him, case studies, reports, that sort of thing. She helped him organize his little office in the county social-service department. They'd become good friends, my wife and the blind man. How do I know these things? She told me. And she told me something else. On her last day in the office, the blind man asked if he could touch her face. She agreed to this. She told me he touched his fingers to every part of her face, her nose— even her neck! She never forgot it. She even tried to write a poem about it. She was always trying to write a poem. She wrote a poem or two every year, usually after something really important had happened to her.

When we first started going out together, she showed me the poem. In the poem she recalled his fingers and the way they had moved around over her face. In the poem, she talked about what she had felt at the time, about what went through her mind when the blind man touched her nose and lips. I can remember I didn't think much of the poem. Of course, I didn't tell her that. Maybe I just don't understand poetry. I admit it's not the first thing I reach for when I pick up something to read.

Anyway, this man who'd first enjoyed her favors, the officer-to-be, he'd been her childhood sweetheart. So okay. I'm saying that at the end of the summer she let the blind man run his hands over her face, said goodbye to him, married her childhood etc., who was now a commissioned officer, and she moved away from Seattle. But they'd kept in touch, she and the blind man. She made the first contact after a year or so. She called him up one night from an Air Force base in Alabama. She wanted to talk. They talked. He asked her to send him a tape and tell him about her life. She did this. She sent the tape. On the tape, she told the blind man about her husband and about their life together in the military. She told the blind man she loved her husband but she didn't like it where they lived and she didn't like it that he was a part of the military-industrial thing. She told the blind man she'd written a poem and he was in it. She told him that she was writing a poem about what it was like to be an Air Force officer's wife. The poem wasn't finished yet. She was still writing it. The blind man made a tape. He sent her the tape. She made a tape. This went on for years. My wife's officer was posted to one base and then another. She sent tapes from Moody AFB, McGuire, McConnell, and finally Travis, near Sacramento, where one night she got to feeling lonely and cut off from people she kept losing in that moving-around life. She got to feeling she couldn't go it another step. She went in and swallowed all the pills and capsules in the medicine chest and washed them down with a bottle of gin. Then she got into a hot bath and passed out.

But instead of dying, she got sick. She threw up. Her officer—why should he have a name? he was the childhood sweetheart, and what more does he want?—came home from somewhere, found her, and called the ambulance. In time, she put it all on a tape and sent the tape to the blind man. Over the years, she put all kinds of stuff on tapes and sent the tapes off lickety-split. Next to writing a poem every year, I think it was her chief means of recreation. On one tape, she told the blind man she'd decided to live away from her officer for a time. On another tape, she told him about her divorce. She and I began going out, and of course she told her blind man about it. She told him everything, or so it seemed to me. Once she asked me if I'd like to hear the latest tape from the blind man. This was a year ago. I was on the tape, she said. So I said okay, I'd listen to it. I got us drinks and we settled down in the living room. We made ready to listen. First she inserted the tape into the player and adjusted a couple of dials. Then she pushed a lever. The tape squeaked and someone began to talk in this loud voice. She lowered the volume. After a few minutes of harmless chitchat, I heard my own name in the mouth of this stranger, this blind man I didn't even know! And then this: "From all you've said about him, I can only conclude—" But we were interrupted, a knock at the door, something, and we didn't ever get back to the tape. Maybe it was just as well. I'd heard all I wanted to.

Now this same blind man was coming to sleep in my house.

"Maybe I could take him bowling," I said to my wife. She was at the draining board doing scalloped potatoes. She put down the knife she was using and turned around.

"If you love me," she said, "you can do this for me. If you don't love me, okay. But if you had a friend, any friend, and the friend came to visit, I'd make him feel comfortable." She wiped her hands with the dish towel.

"I don't have any blind friends," I said.

"You don't have *any* friends," she said. "Period. Besides," she said, "goddamn it, his wife's just died! Don't you understand that? The man's lost his wife!"

I didn't answer. She'd told me a little about the blind man's wife. Her name was Beulah. Beulah! That's a name for a colored woman.

"Was his wife a Negro?" I asked.

"Are you crazy?" my wife said. "Have you just flipped or something?" She picked up a potato. I saw it hit the floor, then roll under the stove. "What's wrong with you?" she said "Are you drunk?"

"I'm just asking," I said.

Right then my wife filled me in with more detail than I cared to know. I made a drink and sat at the kitchen table to listen. Pieces of the story began to fall into place.

Beulah had gone to work for the blind man the summer after my wife had stopped working for him. Pretty soon Beulah and the blind man had themselves a church wedding. It was a little wedding—who'd want to go to such a wedding in the first place?—just the two of them, plus the minister and the minister's wife. But it was a church wedding just the same. It was what Beulah had wanted, he'd said. But even then Beulah must have been carrying the cancer in her glands. After they had been inseparable for eight years—my wife's word, *inseparable*—Beulah's health went into a rapid decline. She died in a Seattle hospital room, the blind man sitting beside the bed and holding on to her hand. They'd married, lived and worked together, slept together—had sex, sure—and then the blind man had to bury her. All this without his having ever seen what the goddamned woman looked like. It was beyond my understanding. Hearing this, I felt sorry for the blind man for a little bit. And then I found myself thinking what a pitiful life this woman must have led. Imagine a woman who could never see herself as she was seen in the eyes of her loved one. A woman who could go on day after day and never receive the smallest compliment from her beloved. A woman whose husband could never read the expression on her face, be it misery or something better. Someone who could wear makeup or not—what difference to him? She could, if she wanted, wear green eye-shadow around one eye, a straight pin in her nostril, yellow slacks and purple shoes, no matter. And then to slip off into death, the blind man's hand on her hand, his blind eyes streaming tears—I'm imagining now—her last thought maybe this: that he never even knew what she looked like, and she on an express to the grave.

Robert was left with a small insurance policy and half of a twenty-peso Mexican coin. The other half of the coin went into the box with her. Pathetic.

So when the time rolled around, my wife went to the depot to pick him up. With nothing to do but wait—sure, I blamed him for that—I was having a drink and watching the TV when I heard the car pull into the drive. I got up from the sofa with my drink and went to the window to have a look.

I saw my wife laughing as she parked the car. I saw her get out of the car and shut the door. She was still wearing a smile. Just amazing. She went around to the other side of the car to where the blind man was already starting to get out. This blind man, feature this, he was wearing a full beard! A beard on a blind man! Too much, I say. The blind man reached into the back seat and dragged out a suitcase. My wife took his arm, shut the car door, and, talking all the way, moved him down the drive and then up the steps to the front porch. I turned off the TV. I finished my drink, rinsed the glass, dried my hands. Then I went to the door.

My wife said, "I want you to meet Robert. Robert, this is my husband. I've told you all about him." She was beaming. She had this blind man by his coat sleeve.

The blind man let go of his suitcase and up came his hand.

I took it. He squeezed hard, held my hand, and then he let it go.

"I feel like we've already met," he boomed.

"Likewise," I said. I didn't know what else to say. Then I said, "Welcome. I've heard a lot about you." We began to move then, a little group, from the porch into the living room, my wife guiding him by the arm. The blind man was carrying his suitcase in his other hand. My wife said things like "To your left here, Robert. That's right. Now watch it, there's a chair. That's it. Sit down right here. This is the sofa. We just bought this sofa two weeks ago."

I started to say something about the old sofa. I'd liked that old sofa. But I didn't say anything. Then I wanted to say something else, small-talk, about the scenic ride along the Hudson. How going *to* New York, you should sit on the right-hand side of the train, and coming *from* New York, the left-hand side.

"Did you have a good train ride?" I said. "Which side of the train did you sit on, by the way?"

"What a question, which side!" my wife said. "What's it matter which side?" she said.

"I just asked," I said.

"Right side," the blind man said. "I hadn't been on a train in nearly forty years. Not since I was a kid. With my folks. That's been a long time. I'd nearly forgotten the sensation. I have winter in my beard now," he said. "So I've been told, anyway. Do I look distinguished, my dear?" the blind man said to my wife.

"You look distinguished, Robert," she said. "Robert," she said. "Robert, it's just so good to see you."

My wife finally took her eyes off the blind man and looked at me. I had the feeling she didn't like what she saw. I shrugged.

I've never met, or personally known, anyone who was blind. This blind man was late forties, a heavy-set, balding man with stooped shoulders, as if he carried a great weight there. He wore brown slacks, brown shoes, a light-brown shirt, a tie, a sports coat. Spiffy. He also had this full beard. But he didn't use a cane and he didn't wear dark glasses. I'd always thought dark glasses were a must for the blind. Fact was, I wished he had a pair. At first glance, his eyes looked like anyone else's eyes. But if you looked close, there was something different about them. Too much white in the iris, for one thing, and the pupils seemed to move around in the sockets without his knowing it or being able to stop it. Creepy. As I stared at his face, I saw the left pupil turn in toward his nose while the other made an effort to keep in one place. But it was only an effort, for that eye was on the roam without his knowing it or wanting it to be.

I said, "Let me get you a drink. What's your pleasure? We have a little of everything. It's one of our pastimes."

"Bub, I'm a Scotch man myself," he said fast enough in this big voice.

"Right," I said. Bub! "Sure you are. I knew it."

He let his fingers touch his suitcase, which was sitting alongside the sofa. He was taking his bearing. I didn't blame him for that.

"I'll move that up to your room," my wife said.

"No, that's fine," the blind man said loudly. "It can go up when I go up."

"A little water with the Scotch?" I said.

"Very little," he said.

"I knew it," I said.

He said, "Just a tad. The Irish actor, Barry Fitzgerald? I'm like that fellow. When I drink water, Fitzgerald said, I drink water. When I drink whiskey, I drink whiskey." My wife laughed. The blind man brought his hand up under his beard. He lifted his beard slowly and let it drop.

I did the drinks, three big glasses of Scotch with a splash of water in each. Then we made ourselves comfortable and talked about Robert's travels. First the long flight from the West Coast to Connecticut, we covered that. Then from Connecticut up here by train. We had another drink concerning that leg of the trip.

I remembered having read somewhere that the blind didn't smoke because, as speculation had it, they couldn't see the smoke they exhaled. I thought I knew that much and that much only about blind people. But this blind man smoked his cigarette down to the nubbin and then lit another one. This blind man filled his ashtray and my wife emptied it.

When we sat down at the table for dinner, we had another drink. My wife heaped Robert's plate with the cube steak, scalloped potatoes, green beans. I buttered him up two slices of bread. I said, "Here's bread and butter for you." I swallowed some of my drink. "Now let us pray," I said, and the blind man lowered his head. My wife looked at me, her mouth agape. "Pray the phone won't ring and the food doesn't get cold," I said.

We dug in. We ate everything there was to eat on the table. We ate like there was no tomorrow. We didn't talk. We ate. We scarfed. We grazed that table. We were into serious eating. The blind man had right away located his foods, he knew just where everything was on his plate. I watched with admiration as he used his knife and fork on the meat. He'd cut two pieces of meat, fork the meat into his mouth, and then go all out for the scalloped potatoes, the beans next, and then he'd tear off a hunk of buttered bread and eat that. He'd follow this up with a big drink of milk. It didn't seem to bother him to use his fingers once in a while, either.

We finished everything, including half a strawberry pie. For a few moments, we sat as if stunned. Sweat beaded on our faces. Finally, we got up from the table and left the dirty plates. We didn't look back. We took ourselves into the living room and sank into our places again. Robert and my wife sat on the sofa. I took the big chair. We had us two or three more drinks while they talked about the major things that had come to pass for them in the past ten years. For the most part, I just listened. Now and then I joined in. I didn't want him to think I'd left the room, and I didn't want her to think I was feeling left out. They talked of things that had happened to them—to them!—these past ten years. I waited in vain to hear my name on my wife's sweet lips: "And then my dear husband came into my life"—something like that. But I heard nothing of the sort. More talk of Robert. Robert had done a little of everything, it seemed, a regular blind jack-of-all-trades. But most recently he and his wife had had an Amway distributorship, from which, I gathered, they'd earned their living, such as it was. The blind man was also a ham radio operator. He talked in his loud voice about conversations he'd had with fellow operators in Guam, in the Philippines, in Alaska, and even in Tahiti. He said he'd have a lot of friends there if he ever wanted to go visit those places. From time to time, he'd turn his blind face toward me, put his hand under his beard, ask me something. How long had I been in my present position? (Three years.) Did I like my work? (I didn't.) Was I going to stay with it? (What were the options?) Finally, when I thought he was beginning to run down, I got up and turned on the TV.

My wife looked at me with irritation. She was heading toward a boil. Then she looked at the blind man and said "Robert, do you have a TV?"

The blind man said, "My dear, I have two TVs. I have a color set and a black-and-white thing, an old relic. It's funny, but if I turn the TV on, and I'm always turning it on, I turn on the color set. It's funny, don't you think?"

I didn't know what to say to that. I had absolutely nothing to say to that. No opinion. So I watched the news program and tried to listen to what the announcer was saying.

"This is a color TV," the blind man said. "Don't ask me how, but I can tell."

"We traded up a while ago," I said.

The blind man had another taste of his drink. He lifted his beard, sniffed it, and let it fall. He leaned forward on the sofa. He positioned his ashtray on the coffee table, then put the lighter to his cigarette. He leaned back on the sofa and crossed his legs at the ankles.

My wife covered her mouth, and then she yawned. She stretched. She said, "I think I'll go upstairs and put on my robe. I think I'll change into something else. Robert, you make yourself comfortable," she said.

"I'm comfortable," the blind man said.

"I want you to feel comfortable in this house," she said.

"I am comfortable," the blind man said.

After she'd left the room, he and I listened to the weather report and then to the sports roundup. By that time, she'd been gone so long I didn't know if she was going to come back. I thought she might have gone to bed. I wished she'd come back downstairs. I didn't want to be left alone with a blind man. I asked him if he wanted another drink, and he said sure. Then I asked if he wanted to smoke some dope with me. I said I'd just rolled a number. I hadn't, but I planned to do so in about two shakes.

"I'll try some with you," he said.

"Damn right," I said. "That's the stuff."

I got our drinks and sat down on the sofa with him. Then I rolled us two fat numbers. I lit one and passed it. I brought it to his fingers. He took it and inhaled.

"Hold it as long as you can," I said. I could tell he didn't know the first thing.

My wife came back downstairs wearing her pink robe and her pink slippers.

"What do I smell?" she said.

"We thought we'd have us some cannabis," I said.

My wife gave me a savage look. Then she looked at the blind man and said, "Robert, I didn't know you smoked."

He said, "I do now, my dear. There's a first time for everything. But I don't feel anything yet."

"This stuff is pretty mellow," I said. "This stuff is mild. It's dope you can reason with," I said. "It doesn't mess you up."

"Not much it doesn't, bub," he said, and laughed.

My wife sat on the sofa between the blind man and me. I passed her the number. She took it and toked and then passed it back to me. "Which way is this going?" she said. Then she said, "I shouldn't be smoking this. I can hardly keep my eyes open as it is. That dinner did me in. I shouldn't have eaten so much."

"It was the strawberry pie," the blind man said. "That's what did it," he said, and he laughed his big laugh. Then he shook his head.

"There's more strawberry pie," I said.

"Do you want some more, Robert?" my wife said.

"Maybe in a little while," he said.

We gave our attention to the TV. My wife yawned again. She said, "Your bed is made up when you feel like going to bed, Robert. I know you must have had a long day. When you're ready to go to bed, say so." She pulled his arm. "Robert?"

He came to and said, "I've had a real nice time. This beats tapes, doesn't it?"

I said, "Coming at you," and I put the number between his fingers. He inhaled, held the smoke, and then let it go. It was like he'd been doing it since he was nine years old.

"Thanks, bub," he said. "But I think this is all for me. I think I'm beginning to feel it," he said. He held the burning roach out for my wife.

"Same here," she said. "Ditto. Me, too." She took the roach and passed it to me. "I may just sit here for a while between you two guys with my eyes closed. But don't let me bother you, okay? Either one of you. If it bothers you, say so. Otherwise, I may just sit here with my eyes closed until you're ready to go to bed," she said. "Your bed's made up, Robert, when you're ready. It's right next to our room at the top of the stairs. We'll show you up when you're ready. You wake me up now, you guys, if I fall asleep." She said that and then she closed her eyes and went to sleep.

The news program ended. I got up and changed the channel. I sat back down on the sofa. I wished my wife hadn't pooped out. Her head lay across the back of the sofa, her mouth open. She'd turned so that her robe had slipped away from her legs, exposing a juicy thigh. I reached to draw her robe back over her, and it was then that I glanced at the blind man. What the hell! I flipped the robe open again.

"You say when you want some strawberry pie," I said.

"I will," he said.

I said, "Are you tired? Do you want me to take you up to your bed? Are you ready to hit the hay?"

"Not yet," he said. "No, I'll stay up with you, bub. If that's all right. I'll stay up until you're ready to turn in. We haven't had a chance to talk. Know what I mean? I feel like me and her monopolized the evening." He lifted his beard and he let it fall. He picked up his cigarettes and his lighter.

"That's all right," I said. Then I said, "I'm glad for the company."

And I guess I was. Every night I smoked dope and stayed up as long as I could before I fell asleep. My wife and I hardly ever went to bed at the same time. When I did go to sleep, I had these dreams. Sometimes I'd wake up from one of them, my heart going crazy.

Something about the church and the Middle Ages was on the TV. Not your run-of-the-mill TV fare. I wanted to watch something else. I turned to other channels. But there was nothing on them, either. So I turned back to the first channel and apologized.

"Bub, it's all right," the blind man said. "It's fine with me. Whatever you want to watch is okay. I'm always learning something. Learning never ends. It won't hurt me to learn something tonight. I got ears," he said.

We didn't say anything for a time. He was leaning forward with his head turned at me, his right ear aimed in the direction of the set. Very disconcerting. Now and then his eyelids drooped and then they snapped open again. Now and then he put his fingers into his beard and tugged, like he was thinking about something he was hearing on the television.

On the screen, a group of men wearing cowls was being set upon and tormented by men dressed in skeleton costumes and men dressed as devils. The men dressed as devils wore devil masks, horns, and long tails. This pageant was part of a procession. The Englishman who was narrating the thing said it took place in Spain once a year. I tried to explain to the blind man what was happening.

"Skeletons," he said. "I know about skeletons," he said, and he nodded.

The TV showed this one cathedral. Then there was a long, slow look at another one. Finally, the picture switched to the famous one in Paris, with its flying buttresses and its spires reaching up to the clouds. The camera pulled away to show the whole of the cathedral rising above the skyline.

There were times when the Englishman who was telling the thing would shut up, would simply let the camera move around over the cathedrals. Or else the camera would tour the countryside, men in fields walking behind oxen. I waited as long as I could. The I felt I had to say something. I said, "They're showing the outside of this cathedral now. Gargoyles. Little statues carved to look like monsters. Now I guess they're in Italy. Yeah, they're in Italy. There's paintings on the walls of this one church."

"Are those fresco paintings, bub?" he asked, and he sipped from his drink.

I reached for my glass. But it was empty. I tried to remember what I could remember. "You're asking me are those frescoes?" I said. "That's a good question. I don't know."

The camera moved to a cathedral outside Lisbon. The differences in the Portuguese cathedral compared with the French and Italian were not that great. But they were there. Mostly the interior stuff. Then something occurred to me, and I said, "Something has occurred to me. Do you have any idea what a cathedral is? What they look like, that is? Do you follow me? If somebody says cathedral to you, do you have any notion what they're talking about? Do you know the difference between that and a Baptist church, say?"

He let the smoke dribble from his mouth. "I know they took hundreds of workers fifty or a hundred years to build," he said. "I just heard the man say that, of course. I know generations of the same families worked on a cathedral. I heard him say that, too. The men who began their life's work on them, they never lived to see the completion of their work. In that wise, bub, they're no different from the rest of us, right?" He laughed. Then his eyelids drooped again. His head nodded. He seemed to be snoozing. Maybe he was imagining himself in Portugal. The TV was showing another cathedral now. This one was in Germany. The Englishman's voice droned on. "Cathedrals," the blind man said. He sat up and rolled his head back and forth. "If you want the truth, bub, that's about all I know. What I just said. What I heard him say. But maybe you could describe one to me? I wish you'd do it. I'd like that. If you want to know, I really don't have a good idea."

I stared hard at the shot of the cathedral on the TV. How could I even begin to describe it? But say my life depended on it. Say my life was being threatened by an insane guy who said I had to do it or else.

I stared some more at the cathedral before the picture flipped off into the countryside. There was no use. I turned to the blind man and said, "To begin with, they're very tall." I was looking around the room for clues. "They reach way up. Up and up. Toward the sky. They're so big, some of them have to have these supports. To help hold them up, so to speak. These supports are called buttresses. They remind me of viaducts, for some reason. But maybe you don't know viaducts, either? Sometimes the cathedrals have devils and such carved into the front. Sometimes lords and ladies. Don't ask me why this is," I said.

He was nodding. The whole upper part of his body seemed to be moving back and forth.

"I'm not doing so good, am I?" I said.

He stopped nodding and leaned forward on the edge of the sofa. As he listened to me, he was running his fingers through his beard. I wasn't getting through to him, I could see that. But he waited for me to go on just the same. He nodded, like he was trying to encourage me. I tried to think what else to say. "They're really big," I said. "They're massive. They're built of stone. Marble, too, sometimes. In those olden days, when they built cathedrals, men wanted to be close to God. In those olden days, God was an important part of everyone's life. You could tell this from their cathedral-building. I'm sorry," I said, "but it looks like that's the best I can do for you. I'm just no good at it."

"That's all right, bub," the blind man said. "Hey, listen. I hope you don't mind my asking you. Can I ask you something? Let me ask you a simple question, yes or no. I'm just curious and there's no offense. You're my host. But let me ask if you are in any way religious? You don't mind my asking?"

I shook my head. He couldn't see that, though. A wink is the same as a nod to a blind man. "I guess I don't believe in it. In anything. Sometimes it's hard. You know what I'm saying?"

"Sure, I do," he said.

"Right," I said.

The Englishman was still holding forth. My wife sighed in her sleep. She drew a long breath and went on with her sleeping.

"You'll have to forgive me," I said. "But I can't tell you what a cathedral looks like. It just isn't in me to do it. I can't do any more than I've done."

The blind man sat very still, his head down, as he listened to me.

I said, "The truth is, cathedrals don't mean anything special to me. Nothing. Cathedrals. They're something to look at on late-night TV. That's all they are."

It was then that the blind man cleared his throat. He brought something up. He took a handkerchief from his back pocket. Then he said, "I get it, bub. It's okay. It happens. Don't worry about it," he said. "Hey, listen to me. Will you do me a favor? I got an idea. Why don't you find us some heavy paper? And a pen. We'll do something. We'll draw one together. Get us a pen and some heavy paper. Go on, bub, get the stuff," he said.

So I went upstairs. My legs felt like they didn't have any strength in them. They felt like they did after I'd done some running. In my wife's room, I looked around. I found some ballpoints in a little basket on her table. And then I tried to think where to look for the kind of paper he was talking about.

Downstairs, in the kitchen, I found a shopping bag with onion skins in the bottom of the bag. I emptied the bag and shook it. I brought it into the living room and sat down with it near his legs. I moved some things, smoothed the wrinkles from the bag, spread it out on the coffee table.

The blind man got down from the sofa and sat next to me on the carpet.

He ran his fingers over the paper. He went up and down the sides of the paper. The edges, even the edges. He fingered the corners.

"All right," he said. "All right, let's do her."

He found my hand, the hand with the pen. He closed his hand over my hand. "Go ahead, bub, draw," he said. "Draw. You'll see. I'll follow along with you. It'll be okay. Just begin now like I'm telling you. You'll see. Draw," the blind man said.

So I began. First I drew a box that looked like a house. It could have been the house I lived in. Then I put a roof on it. At either end of the roof, I drew spires. Crazy.

"Swell," he said. "Terrific. You're doing fine," he said. "Never thought anything like this could happen in your lifetime, did you, bub? Well, it's a strange life, we all know that. Go on now. Keep it up."

I put in windows with arches. I drew flying buttresses. I hung great doors. I couldn't stop. The TV station went off the air. I put down the pen and closed and opened my fingers. The blind man felt around over the paper. He moved the tips of his fingers over the paper, all over what I had drawn, and he nodded.

"Doing fine," the blind man said.

I took up the pen again, and he found my hand. I kept at it. I'm no artist. But I kept drawing just the same.

My wife opened up her eyes and gazed at us. She sat up on the sofa, her robe hanging open. She said, "What are you doing? Tell me, I want to know."

I didn't answer her.

The blind man said, "We're drawing a cathedral. Me and him are working on it. Press hard," he said to me. "That's right. That's good," he said. "Sure. You got it, bub. I can tell. You didn't think you could. But you can, can't you? You're cooking with gas now. You know what I'm saying? We're going to really have us something here in a minute. How's the old arm?" he said. "Put some people in there now. What's a cathedral without people?"

My wife said, "What's going on? Robert, what are you doing? What's going on?"

"It's all right," he said to her. "Close your eyes now," the blind man said to me.

I did it. I closed them just like he said.

"Are they closed?" he said. "Don't fudge."

"They're closed," I said.

"Keep them that way," he said. He said, "Don't stop now. Draw."

So we kept on with it. His fingers rode my fingers as my hand went over the paper. It was like nothing else in my life up to now.

Then he said, "I think that's it. I think you got it," he said. "Take a look. What do you think?"

But I had my eyes closed. I thought I'd keep them that way for a little longer. I thought it was something I ought to do.

"Well?" he said. "Are you looking?"

My eyes were still closed. I was in my house. I knew that. But I didn't feel like I was inside anything.

"It's really something," I said.

Suggestions for Discussion

1. How do the structure and tone of the narrator's sentences help to characterize him?

2. The narrator uses sloppy generalizations (*she read stuff, that sort of thing*, etc., *more detail than I cared to know*) and clichés (*enjoyed her favors, jack-of-all-trades, pooped out, hit the hay*). How do these tricks of speech contribute to the theme?

3. By contrast, on page 309 the narrator imagines the blind man's wife in grotesque details. Immediately thereafter he refers to the blind man for the first time by his name, Robert. Why?

4. The story is called "Cathedral." It is about a blind man's visit. How do the ideas of *cathedral* and *blindness* relate to each other as themes?

5. Do you consider "jealousy" a theme of the story? Why or why not?

6. The story contains realistic details having to do with the inability to hear, to remember, to describe, to understand, and also with the drugging effects of food, nicotine, alcohol, and cannabis. How do these contribute to the idea that the blind man can see more vividly or exactly than the narrator?

7. On page 315 Robert makes a little speech about learning. How does it relate to the narrator's experience in the story?

8. What discoveries does the narrator make in the course of the evening that prepare us for the discovery he makes at the end?

Ralph the Duck

FREDERICK BUSCH

I woke up at 5:25 because the dog was vomiting. I carried seventy-five pounds of heaving golden retriever to the door and poured him onto the silver, moonlit snow. "Good boy," I said because he'd done his only trick. Outside he retched, and I went back up, passing the sofa on which Fanny lay. I tiptoed with enough weight on my toes to let her know how considerate I was while she was deserting me. She blinked her eyes. I swear I heard her blink her eyes. Whenever I tell her that I hear her blink her eyes, she tells me I'm lying; but I can hear the damp slap of lash after I have made her weep.

In bed and warm again, noting the red digital numbers (5:29) and certain that I wouldn't sleep, I didn't. I read a book about men who kill each other for pay or for their honor. I forget which, and so did they. It was 5:45, the alarm would buzz at 6:00, and I would make a pot of coffee and start the wood stove; I would call Fanny and pour her coffee into her mug; I would apologize because I always did, and then she would forgive me if I hadn't been too awful—I didn't think I'd been that bad—and we would stagger through the day, exhausted but pretty sure we were all right, and we'd sleep that night, probably after sex, and then we'd waken in the same bed to the alarm at 6:00, or the dog, if he'd returned to the frozen deer carcass he'd been eating in the forest on our land. He loved what made him sick. The alarm went off, I got into jeans and woolen socks and a sweatshirt, and I went downstairs to let the dog in. He'd be hungry, of course.

I was the oldest college student in America, I thought. But of course I wasn't. There were always ancient women with their parchment for skin who graduated at seventy-nine from places like Barnard and the University of Georgia. I was only forty-two, and I hardly qualified as a student. I patrolled the college at night in a Bronco with a leaky exhaust system, and I went from room to room in the classroom buildings, kicking out students who were studying or humping in chairs—they'd do it *anywhere*—and answering emergency calls with my little blue light winking on top of the truck. I didn't carry a gun or a billy, but I had a flashlight that took six batteries and I'd used it twice on some of my overprivileged northeastern-playboy part-time classmates. On Tuesdays and Thursdays I would awaken at 6:00 with my wife, and I'd do my homework, and work around the house, and go to school at 11:30 to sit there for an hour and a half while thirty-five stomachs growled with hunger and boredom, and this guy gave instruction about books. Because I was on the staff, the college let me take a course for nothing every term. I was getting educated, in a kind of slow-motion way—it would have taken me something like fifteen or sixteen years to graduate, and I would no doubt get an F in gym and have to repeat—and there were times when I respected myself for it. Fanny often did, and that was fair incentive.

I am not unintelligent. *You are not an unintelligent writer,* my professor wrote on my paper about Nathaniel Hawthorne. We had to read short stories, I and the other students, and then we had to write little essays about them. I told how I saw Kafka and Hawthorne in similar light, and I was not unintelligent, he said. He ran into me at dusk one time, when I answered a call about a dead battery and found out it was him. I jumped his Buick from the Bronco's battery, and he was looking me over, I could tell, while I clamped onto the terminals and cranked it up. He was a tall, handsome guy who never wore a suit. He wore khakis and sweaters, loafers or sneaks, and he was always talking to the female students with the brightest hair and best builds. But he couldn't get a Buick going on a ice-cold night, and he didn't know enough to look for cells going bad. I told him he was going to need a new battery and he looked me over the way men sometimes do with other men who fix their cars for them.

"Vietnam?"

I said, "Too old."

"Not at the beginning. Not if you were an adviser. So-called. Or one of the Phoenix Project fellas?"

I was wearing a watch cap made of navy wool and an old Marine fatigue jacket. Slick characters like my professor like it if you're a killer or at least a onetime middleweight fighter. I smiled like I knew something. "Take it easy," I said, and I went back to the truck to swing around the cemetery at the top of the campus. They'd been known to screw in down-filled sleeping bags on horizontal stones up there, and the dean of students didn't want anybody dying of frostbite while joined at the hip to a matriculating fellow resident of our northeastern camp for the overindulged.

He blinked his high beams at me as I went. "You are not an unintelligent driver," I said.

Fanny had left me a bowl of something made with sausages and sauerkraut and potatoes, and the dog hadn't eaten too much more than his fair share. He watched me eat his leftovers and then make myself a king-sized drink composed of sourmash whiskey and ice. In our back room, which is on the northern end of the house, and cold for sitting in that close to dawn, I sat and watched the texture of the sky change. It was going to snow, and I wanted to see the storm come up the valley. I woke up that way, sitting in the rocker with its loose right arm, holding a watery drink, and thinking right away of the girl I'd convinced to go back inside. She'd been standing outside her dormitory, looking up at a window that was dark in the midst of all those lighted panes—they never turned a light off, and often left the faucets run half the night—crying onto her bathrobe. She was barefoot in shoe-pacs, the brown ones so many of them wore unlaced, and for all I know she was naked under the robe. She was beautiful, I thought, and she was somebody's red-headed daughter, standing in a quadrangle how many miles from home weeping.

"He doesn't love anyone," the kid told me. "He doesn't love his wife—I mean his ex-wife. And he doesn't love the ex-wife before that, or the one before that. And you know what? He doesn't love me. I don't know anyone who *does!*"

"It isn't your fault if he isn't smart enough to love you," I said, steering her toward the truck.

She stopped. She turned. "You know him?"

I couldn't help it. I hugged her hard, and she let me, and then she stepped back, and of course I let her go. "Don't you *touch* me! Is this sexual harassment? Do you know the rules? Isn't this sexual harassment?"

"I'm sorry," I said at the door to the truck. "But I think I have to be able to give you a grade before it counts as harassment."

She got in. I told her we were driving to the dean of students' house. She smelled like marijuana and something very sweet, maybe one of those coffee-with-cream liqueurs you don't buy unless you hate to drink.

As the heat of the truck struck her, she started going kind of clay-gray-green, and I reached across her to open the window.

"You touched my breast!" she said.

"It's the smallest one I've touched all night, I'm afraid."

She leaned out the window and gave her rendition of my dog.

But in my rocker, waking up, at whatever time in the morning in my silent house, I thought of her as someone's child. Which made me think of ours, of course. I went for more ice, and I started on a wet breakfast. At the door of the dean of students' house, she'd turned her chalky face to me and asked, "What grade would you give me, then?"

It was a week composed of two teachers locked out of their offices late at night, a Toyota with a flat and no spare, an attempted rape on a senior girl walking home from the library, a major fight outside a fraternity house (broken wrist and significant concussion), and variations on breaking-and-entering. I was scolded by the director of nonacademic services for embracing a student who was drunk; I told him to keep his job, but he called me back because I was right to hug her, he said, and also wrong, but what the hell, and would I please stay. I thought of the fringe benefits—graduation in only sixteen years—so I went back to work.

My professor assigned a story called "A Rose for Emily," and I wrote him a paper about the mechanics of corpse fucking, and how, since she clearly couldn't screw her dead boyfriend, she was keeping his rotten body in bed because she truly loved him. I called the paper "True Love." He gave me a B and wrote *See me, pls.* In his office after class, his feet up on his desk, he trimmed a cigar with a giant folding knife he kept in his drawer.

"You got to clean the hole out," he said, "or they don't draw."

"I don't smoke," I said.

"Bad habit. Real *habit*, though. I started in smoking 'em in Georgia, in the service. My C.O. smoked 'em. We collaborated on a brothel inspection one time, and we ended up smoking these with a couple of women—" He waggled his eyebrows at me, now that his malehood was established.

"Were the women smoking them too?"

He snorted laughter through his nose while the greasy smoke came curling off his thin, dry lips. "They were pretty smoky, I'll tell ya!" Then he propped his feet—he was wearing cowboy boots that day—and he sat forward. "It's a little hard to explain. But—hell. You just don't say *fuck* when you write an essay for a college prof. Okay?" Like a scoutmaster with a kid he'd caught in the outhouse jerking off: "All right? You don't wanna do that."

"Did it shock you?"

"Fuck, no, it didn't shock me. I just told you. It violates certain proprieties."

"But if I'm writing it to you, like a letter—"

"You're writing it for posterity. For some mythical reader someplace, not just me. You're making a *statement.*"

"Right. My statement said how hard it must be for a woman to fuck with a corpse."

"And a point worth making. I said so. Here."

"But you said I shouldn't say it."

"No. Listen. Just because you're talking about fucking, you don't have to say *fuck.* Does that make it any clearer?"

"No."

"I wish you'd lied to me just now," he said.

I nodded. I did too.

"Where'd you do your service?" he asked.

"Baltimore. Baltimore, Maryland."

"What's in Baltimore?"

"Railroads. I liaised on freight runs of army matériel. I killed a couple of bums on the rod with my bare hands, though."

He snorted again, but I could see how disappointed he was. He'd been banking on my having been a murderer. Interesting guy in one of my classes, he must have told some terrific woman at an overpriced meal: I just *know* the guy was a rubout specialist in the Nam, he had to have said. I figured I should come to work wearing my fatigue jacket and a red bandanna tied around my head. Say "Man" to him a couple of times, hang a fist in the air for grief and solidarity, and look terribly worn, exhausted by experiences he was fairly certain that he envied me. His dungarees were ironed, I noticed.

On Saturday we went back to the campus because Fanny wanted to see a movie called *The Seven Samurai.* I fell asleep, and I'm afraid I snored. She let me sleep until the auditorium was almost empty. Then she kissed me awake. "Who was screaming in my dream?" I asked her.

"Kurosawa," she said.

"Who?"

"Ask your professor friend."

I looked around, but he wasn't there. "Not an un-weird man," I said.

We went home and cleaned up after the dog and put him out. We drank a little Spanish brandy and went upstairs and made love. I was fairly premature, you might say, but one way and another by the time we fell asleep we were glad to be there with each other, and glad that it was Sunday coming up the valley toward us, and nobody with it. The dog was howling at another dog someplace, or at the moon, or maybe just his moon-thrown shadow on the snow. I did not strangle him when I opened the back door and he limped happily past me and stumbled up the stairs. I followed him into our bedroom and groaned for just being satisfied as I got into bed. You'll notice I didn't say fuck.

He stopped me in the hall after class on a Thursday, and asked me How's it goin, just one of the kickers drinking sour beer and eating pickled eggs and watching the tube in a country bar. How's it goin. I nodded. I wanted a grade from the man, and I did want to learn about expressing myself. I nodded and made what I thought was a smile. He'd let his mustache grow out and his hair grow longer. He was starting to wear dark shirts with lighter ties. I thought he looked like someone in *The Godfather*. He still wore those light little loafers or his high-heeled cowboy boots. His corduroy pants looked baggy. I guess he wanted them to look that way. He motioned me to the wall of the hallway, and he looked and said, "How about the Baltimore stuff?"

I said "Yeah?"

"Was that really true?" He was almost blinking, he wanted so much for me to be a damaged Vietnam vet just looking for a bell tower to climb into and start firing from. The college didn't have a bell tower you could get up into, though I'd once spent an ugly hour chasing a drunken ATO down from the roof of the observatory. "You were just clocking through boxcars in Baltimore?"

I said, "Nah."

"I thought so!" He gave a kind of sigh.

"I killed people," I said.

"You know, I could have sworn you did," he said.

I nodded, and he nodded back. I'd made him so happy.

The assignment was to write something to influence somebody. He called it Rhetoric and Persuasion. We read an essay by George Orwell and "A Modest Proposal" by Jonathan Swift. I liked the Orwell better, but I wasn't comfortable with it. He talked about "niggers," and I felt him saying it two ways.

I wrote "Ralph the Duck."

Once upon a time, there was a duck named Ralph who didn't have any feathers on either wing. So when the cold wind blew, Ralph said, Brr, and shivered and shook.

What's the matter? Ralph's mommy asked.

I'm *cold*, Ralph said.

Oh, the mommy said. Here. I'll keep you warm.

So she spread her big, feathery wings, and hugged Ralph tight, and when the cold wind blew, Ralph was warm and snuggly, and fell fast asleep.

•   •   •

The next Thursday, he was wearing canvas pants and hiking boots. He mentioned kind of casually to some of the girls in the class how whenever there was a storm he wore his Lake District walking outfit. He had a big, hairy sweater on. I kept waiting for him to make a noise like a mountain goat. But the girls seemed to like it. His boots made a creaky squeak on the linoleum of the hall when he caught up with me after class.

"As I told you," he said, "it isn't unappealing. It's just—not a college theme."

"Right," I said. "Okay. You want me to do it over?"

"No," he said. "Not at all. The D will remain your grade. But I'll read something else if you want to write it."

"This'll be fine," I said.

"Did you understand the assignment?"

"Write something to influence someone—Rhetoric and Persuasion."

We were at his office door and the redheaded kid who had gotten sick in my truck was waiting for him. She looked at me like one of us was in the wrong place, which struck me as accurate enough. He was interested in getting into his office with the redhead, but he remembered to turn around and flash me a grin he seemed to think he was known for.

Instead of going on shift a few hours after class, the way I'm supposed to, I told my supervisor I was sick, and I went home. Fanny was frightened when I came in, because I don't get sick and I don't miss work. She looked at my face and she grew sad. I kissed her hello and went upstairs to change. I always used to change my clothes when I was a kid, as soon as I came home from school. I put on jeans and a flannel shirt and thick wool socks, and I made myself a dark drink of sourmash. Fanny poured herself some wine and came into the cold northern room a few minutes later. I was sitting in the rocker, looking over the valley. The wind was lining up a lot of rows of cloud so that the sky looked like a baked trout when you lift the skin off. "It'll snow," I said to her.

She sat on the old sofa and waited. After a while, she said, "I wonder why they always call it a mackerel sky?"

"Good eating, mackerel," I said.

Fanny said, "Shit! You're never that laconic unless you feel crazy. What's wrong? Who'd you punch out at the playground?"

"We had to write a composition," I said.

"Did he like it?"

"He gave me a D."

"Well, you're familiar enough with D's. I never saw you get this low over a grade."

"I wrote about Ralph the Duck."

She said, "You did?" She said, "Honey." She came over and stood beside the rocker and leaned into me and hugged my head and neck. "Honey," she said. "Honey."

It was the worst of the winter's storms, and one of the worst in years. That afternoon they closed the college, which they almost never do. But the roads were jammed with snow over ice, and now it was freezing rain on top of that, and the only people working at the school that night were the operator who took emergency calls and me. Everyone else had gone home except the students, and most of them were inside. The ones who weren't were drunk, and I kept on sending them in and telling them to act like grown-ups. A number of them said they were, and I really couldn't argue. I had the bright beams on, the defroster set high, the little blue light winking, and a thermos of sourmash and hot coffee that I sipped from every time I had to get out of the truck or every time I realized how cold all that wetness was out there.

About eight o'clock, as the rain was turning back to snow and the cold was worse, the roads impossible, just as I was done helping a county sander on the edge of the campus pull a panel truck out of a snowbank, I got the emergency call from the college operator. We had a student missing. The roommates thought the kid was headed for the quarry. This meant I had to get the Bronco up on a narrow road above the campus, above the old cemetery, into all kinds of woods and rough track that I figured would be chocked with ice and snow. Any kid up there would really have to want to be there, and I couldn't go in on foot, because you'd only want to be there on account of drugs, booze, or craziness, and either way I'd be needing blankets and heat, and then a fast ride down to the hospital in town. So I dropped into four-wheel drive to get me up the hill above the campus, bucking snow and sliding on ice, putting all the heater's warmth up onto the windshield because I couldn't see much more than swarming snow. My feet were still cold from the tow job, and it didn't seem to matter that I had on heavy socks and insulated boots I'd coated with waterproofing. I shivered, and I thought of Ralph the Duck.

I had to grind the rest of the way, from the cemetery, in four-wheel low, and in spite of the cold I was smoking my gearbox by the time I was close enough to the quarry—they really did take a lot of rocks for the campus buildings from there—to see I'd have to make my way on foot to where she was. It was a kind of scooped-out shape, maybe four or five stories high, where she stood—well, wobbled is more like it. She was as chalky as she'd been the last time, and her red hair didn't catch the light anymore. It just lay on her like something that had died on top of her head. She was in a white nightgown that was plastered to her body. She had her arms crossed as if she wanted to be warm. She swayed, kind of, in front of the big, dark, scooped-out rock face, where the trees and brush had been cleared for trucks and earthmovers. She looked tiny against all the darkness. From where I stood, I could see the snow driving down in front of the lights I'd left on, but I couldn't see it near her. All it looked like around her was dark. She was shaking with the cold, and she was crying.

I had a blanket with me, and I shoved it down the front of my coat to keep it dry for her, and because I was so cold. I waved. I stood in the lights and I waved. I don't know what she saw—a big shadow, maybe. I surely didn't reassure her, because when she saw me she backed up, until she was near the face of the quarry. She couldn't go any farther.

I called, "Hello! I brought a blanket. Are you cold? I thought you might want a blanket."

Her roommates had told the operator about pills, so I didn't bring her the coffee laced with mash. I figured I didn't have all that much time, anyway, to get her down and pumped out. The booze with whatever pills she'd taken would make her die that much faster.

I hated that word. Die. It made me furious with her. I heard myself seething when I breathed. I pulled my scarf and collar up above my mouth. I didn't want her to see how close I might come to wanting to kill her because she wanted to die.

I called, "Remember me?"

I was closer now. I could see the purple mottling of her skin. I didn't know if it was cold or dying. It probably didn't matter much to distinguish between them right now, I thought. That made me smile. I felt the smile, and I pulled the scarf down so she could look at it. She didn't seem awfully reassured.

"You're the sexual harassment guy," she said. She said it very slowly. Her lips were clumsy. It was like looking at a ventriloquist's dummy.

"I gave you an A," I said.

"When?"

"It's a joke," I said. "You don't want me making jokes. You want me to give you a nice warm blanket, though. And then you want me to take you home."

She leaned against the rock face when I approached. I pulled the blanket out, then zipped my jacket back up. The snow had stopped, I realized, and that wasn't really a very good sign. It felt like an arctic cold descending in its place. I held the blanket out to her, but she only looked at it.

"You'll just have to turn me in," I said. "I'm gonna hug you again."

She screamed, "No more! I don't want any more hugs!"

But she kept her arms on her chest, and I wrapped the blanket around her and stuffed a piece into each of her tight, small fists. I didn't know what to do for her feet. Finally, I got down on my haunches in front of her. She crouched down too, protecting herself.

"No," I said. "No. You're fine."

I took off the woolen mittens I'd been wearing. Mittens keep you warmer than gloves because they trap your hand's heat around the fingers and palms at once. Fanny had knitted them for me. I put a mitten as far onto each of her feet as I could. She let me. She was going to collapse, I thought.

"Now, let's go home," I said. "Let's get you better."

With her funny, stiff lips, she said, "I've been very self-indulgent and weird and I'm sorry. But I'd really like to die." She sounded so reasonable that I found myself nodding in agreement as she spoke.

"You can't just die," I said.

"Aren't I dying already? I took all of them, and then"—she giggled like a child, which of course is what she was—"I borrowed different ones from other people's rooms. See, this isn't some teenage cry for like *help*. Understand? I'm seriously interested in death and I have to like stay out here a little longer and fall asleep. All right?"

"You can't do that," I said. "You ever hear of Vietnam?"

"I saw that movie," she said. "With the opera in it? *Apocalypse?* Whatever."

"I was there!" I said. "I killed people! I helped to kill them! And when they die, you see their bones later on. You dream about their bones and blood on the ends of the splintered ones, and this kind of mucous stuff coming out of their eyes. You probably heard of guys having dreams like that, didn't you? Whacked-out Vietnam vets? That's me, see? So I'm telling you, I know about dead people and their eyeballs and everything falling out. And people keep dreaming about the dead people they knew, see? You can't make people dream about you like that! It isn't fair!"

"You dream about me?" She was ready to go. She was ready to fall down, and I was going to lift her up and get her to the truck.

"I will," I said. "If you die."

"I want you to," she said. Her lips were hardly moving now. Her eyes were closed. "I want you all to."

I dropped my shoulder and put it into her waist and picked her up and carried her down to the Bronco. She was talking, but not a lot, and her voice leaked down my back. I jammed her into the truck and wrapped the blanket around her better and then put another one down around her feet. I strapped her in with the seat belt. She was shaking, and her eyes were closed and her mouth open. She was breathing. I checked that twice, once when I strapped her in, and then again when I strapped myself in and backed up hard into a sapling and took it down. I got us into first gear, held the clutch in, leaned over to listen for breathing, heard it—shallow panting, like a kid asleep on your lap for a nap—and then I put the gear in and howled down the hillside on what I thought might be the road.

We passed the cemetery. I told her that was a good sign. She didn't respond. I found myself panting too, as if we were breathing for each other. It made me dizzy, but I couldn't stop. We passed the highest dorm, and I dropped the truck into four-wheel high. The cab smelled like burnt oil and hot metal. We were past the chapel now, and the observatory, the president's house, then the bookstore. I had the blue light winking and the V-6 roaring, and I drove on the edge of out-of-control, sensing the skids just before I slid into them, and getting back out of them as I needed to. I took a little fender off once, and a bit of the corner of a classroom building, but I worked us back on course, and all I needed to do now was negotiate the sharp left turn around the Administration Building past the library, then floor it for the straight run to the town's main street and then the hospital.

I was panting into the mike, and the operator kept saying, "Say again?"

I made myself slow down some, and I said we'd need stomach pumping, and to get the names of the pills from her friends in the dorm, and I'd be there in less than five or we were crumpled up someplace and dead.

"Roger," the radio said. "Roger all that." My throat tightened and tears came into my eyes. They were helping us, they'd told me: Roger.

I said to the girl, whose head was slumped and whose face looked too blue all through its whiteness, "You know, I had a girl once. My wife, Fanny. She and I had a small girl one time."

I reached over and touched her cheek. It was cold. The truck swerved, and I got my hands on the wheel. I'd made the turn past the Ad Building using just my left. "I can do it in the dark," I sang to no tune I'd ever learned. "I can do it with one hand." I said to her, "We had a girl child, very small. Now, I do *not* want you dying."

I came to the campus gates doing fifty on the ice and snow, smoking the engine, grinding the clutch, and I bounced off a wrought iron fence to give me the curve going left that I needed. On a pool table, it would have been a bank shot worth applause. The town cop picked me up and got out ahead of me and let the street have all the lights and noise it could want. We banged up to the emergency room entrance and I was out and at the other door before the cop on duty, Elmo St. John, could loosen his seat belt. I loosened hers, and I carried her into the lobby of the ER. They had a gurney, and doctors, and they took her away from me. I tried to talk to them, but they made me sit down and do my shaking on a dirty sofa decorated with drawings of little spinning wheels. Somebody brought me hot coffee, I think it was Elmo, but I couldn't hold it.

"They won't," he kept saying to me. "They won't."

"What?"

"You just been sitting there for a minute and a half like St. Vitus dancing, telling me, 'Don't let her die. Don't let her die.'"

"Oh."

"You all *right?*"

"How about the kid?"

"They'll tell us soon."

"She better be all right."

"That's right."

"She—somebody's gonna have to tell me plenty if she isn't."

"That's right."

"She better not die this time," I guess I said.

Fanny came downstairs to look for me. I was at the northern windows, looking through the mullions down the valley to the faint red line along the mounds and little peaks of the ridge beyond the valley. The sun was going to come up, and I was looking for it.

Fanny stood behind me. I could hear her. I could smell her hair and the sleep on her. The crimson line widened, and I squinted at it. I heard the dog limp in behind her, catching up. He panted and I knew why his panting sounded familiar. She put her hands on my shoulders and arms. I made muscles to impress her with, and then I let them go, and let my head drop down until my chin was on my chest.

I didn't think you'd be able to sleep after that," Fanny said.

"I brought enough adrenaline home to run a football team."

"But you hate being a hero, huh? You're hiding in here because somebody's going to call, or come over, and want to talk to you—her parents for shooting sure, sooner or later. Or is that supposed to be part of the service up at the playground? Saving their suicidal daughters. Almost dying to find them in the woods and driving too fast for *any* weather, much less what we had last night. Getting their babies home. The bastards." She was crying. I knew she would be, sooner or later. I could hear the soft sound of her lashes. She sniffed and I could feel her arm move as she felt for the tissues on the coffee table.

"I have them over here," I said. "On the windowsill."

"Yes." She blew her nose, and the dog thumped his tail. He seemed to think it one of Fanny's finer tricks, and he had wagged for her for thirteen years whenever she'd done it. "Well, you're going to have to talk to them."

"I will," I said. "I will." The sun was in our sky now, climbing. We had built the room so we could watch it climb. "I think that jackass with the smile, my prof? She showed up a lot at his office, the last few weeks. He called her 'my advisee,' you know? The way those guys sound about what they're achieving by getting up and shaving and going to work and saying the same thing every day? Every year? Well, she was his advisee, I bet. He was shoving home the old advice."

"She'll be okay," Fanny said. "Her parents will take her home and love her up and get her some help." She began to cry again, then she stopped. She blew her nose, and the dog's tail thumped. She kept a hand between my shoulder and my neck. "So tell me what you'll tell a waiting world. How'd you talk her out?"

"Well, I didn't, really. I got up close and picked her up and carried her is all."

"You didn't say *anything*?"

"Sure I did. Kid's standing in the snow outside of a lot of pills, you're gonna say something."

"So what'd you *say*?"

"I told her stories," I said. "I did Rhetoric and Persuasion."

Fanny said, "Then you go in early on Thursday, you go in half an hour early, and you get that guy to jack up your grade."

Suggestions for Discussion

1. What is "Ralph the Duck" about? What does it say about what it's about?

2. Consider the following in their relation to the theme of "Ralph the Duck":
   "He loved what made him sick." (See page 320.)
   ". . . not unintelligent . . ."
   grades
   ". . . and I did want to learn about expressing myself." (See page 324.)
   sexual harassment
   Rhetoric and Persuasion

3. What does Ralph the Duck symbolize to the narrator and his wife? Does it operate differently as a symbol in the story?

4. Describe the plot of "Ralph the Duck." What is the relation of the theme to the plot?

5. Take any passage of dialogue from the story and show how it does more than one thing at a time.

RETROSPECT

1. What is "The Ones Who Walk Away from Omelas" about, and what does it say about what it's about?

2. Consider the themes of insanity, secret communication, helplessness, and chance in "Signs and Symbols."

3. Which of the stories in this volume offer an inversion of a "truth" that you ordinarily accept about, for instance, the nature of reality, sanity, time, goodness? How successfully does each offer its alternative truth?

4. In which of the stories in this volume can a central character be said to "find" himself or herself in the crisis and resolution? How do emotion, judgment, and logic fuse in these epiphanies to suggest theme?

WRITING ASSIGNMENTS

These five exercises are arranged in order of ascending difficulty. The first is the easiest, and it is likely to produce a bad story. If it produces a bad story, it will be invaluably instructive to you, and you will be relieved of the onus of ever doing it again. If it produces a good story, then you have done something else, something more, and something more original than the assignment asks for. If you prefer to do exercise 4 or 5, then you may already have doomed yourself to the writing craft and should prepare to be very poor for a few years while you discover what place writing will have in your life.

1. Take a simple but specific political, religious, scientific, or moral idea. It may be one already available to us in a formula of words, or it may be one of your own, but it should be possible to state it in less than ten words. Write a short story that illustrates the idea. Do not state the idea at all. Your goals are two: that the idea should be perfectly clear to us so that it could be extracted as a moral or message, and that we should feel we have experienced it.

2. Take as your title a common proverb or maxim, such as *power corrupts, honesty is the best policy, walk softly and carry a big stick, haste makes waste.* Let the story make the title ironic, that is, explore a situation in which the advice or statement does not apply.

3. Taking as a starting point some incident or situation from your own life, write a story with one of the following themes: nakedness, blindness, thirst, noise, borders, chains, clean wounds, washing, the color green, dawn. The events themselves may be minor (a story about a slipping bicycle chain may ultimately be more effective than one about a chain gang). Once you have decided on the structure of the story, explore everything you think, know, or believe about your chosen theme and try to incorporate that theme in imagery, dialogue, event, character, and so forth.

4. Identify the belief you hold most passionately and profoundly. Write a short story that explores an instance in which this belief is untrue.

5. Write a short story that you have wanted to write all term and have not written because you knew it was too big for you and you would fail. You may fail. Write it anyway.

11

PLAY IT AGAIN, SAM
Revision

Worry It and Walk Away
Criticism
Revision Questions
An Example of the Revision Process

The creative process is not all inventive; it is partly corrective, critical, nutritive, and fostering—a matter of getting this creature to be the best that it can be. William C. Knott, in *The Craft of Fiction,* cogently observes that "anyone can write—and almost everyone you meet these days is writing. However, only the writers know how to rewrite. It is this ability alone that turns the amateur into a pro."

Revising is a process more dreaded than dreadful. The resistance to rewriting is, if anything, greater than the resistance to beginning in the first place. Yet the chances are that once you have committed yourself to a first draft, you'll be unable to leave it in an unfinished and unsatisfying state. You'll be *unhappy* until it's right. Making it right will involve a second commitment, to seeing the story fresh and creating it again with the advantage of this re-vision.

You may have to "see-again" more than once. The process of revision involves external and internal insight; you'll need your conscious critic, your unconscious, and readers you trust. You may need each of them several times, not necessarily in that order.

Worry It and Walk Away

To write your first draft, you banished the internal critic. Now make him or her welcome. Revision is work, but the strange thing is that you may find you can concentrate on the work for much longer than you could play at freedrafting. It has occurred to me that writing a first draft is very like tennis or softball—I have to be psyched for it, energy level up, alert, on my toes. A few hours is all I can manage, and at the end of it I'm wiped out. Revision is like careful carpentry, and if I'm under a deadline or just determined to get this thing crafted and polished, I can be good for twelve hours of it.

The first round of rewrites is probably a matter of letting your misgivings surface. Focus for a while on what seems awkward, overlong, undeveloped, flat, or flowery. Tinker. Tighten. Sharpen. More important at this stage than finishing any given page or phrase is that you're getting to know your story in order to open it to new possibilities. You will also get tired of it; you may feel stuck.

Then put it away. *Put it away.* Don't look at it for a matter of days or weeks—until you feel fresh on the project. In addition to getting some distance on your story, you're mailing it to your unconscious. Carolyn Bly says, "Here is the crux of it: between the conscious and unconscious mind we are more complex and given to concept than we are in the conscious mind."

"Complex" means that you can begin to see your story organically; "concept" means that you may discover what it is really about.

Rollo May, in *The Courage to Create,* makes a similar point.

> Everyone uses from time to time such expressions as, "a thought pops up," an idea comes "from the blue" or "dawns" or "comes as though out of a dream," or "it suddenly hit me." These are various ways of describing a common experience: the breakthrough of ideas from some depth below the level of awareness.

May describes getting stuck doing research on a psychological study; the evidence contradicted his theory that children rejected by their mothers would universally display symptoms of anxiety. He sat for long hours moiling and baffled, "caught by an insoluble problem."

> Late one day, putting aside my books and papers in the little office I used in that shelter house, I walked down the street toward the subway. I was tired. I tried to put the whole troublesome business out of my mind. About fifty feet away from the entrance to the Eighth Street station, it suddenly struck me "out of the blue," as the not-unfitting expression goes, that those young women who didn't fit my hypothesis *were all from the proletarian class.* . . . I saw at that instant that it is not

rejection by the mother that is the original trauma which is the source of anxiety; it is rather *rejection that is lied about.*

Here, May solves a logical problem not by consciously working it out, but by letting it go. In the process he sees a new connection and realizes what his project is about—not rejection after all, but dishonesty.

It is my experience that such connections and such realizations occur over and over again in the course of writing a short story or novel. Often I will believe that because I know who my characters are and what happens to them, I know what my story is about—and often I find I'm wrong, or that my understanding is shallow or incomplete.

In the first draft of my most recent novel, for instance, I opened with the sentence, "It took a hundred and twelve bottles of champagne to see the young Poindexters off to Arizona." A page later one character whispered to another that the young Mr. Poindexter in question had "consumption." I worked on this book for a year (taking my characters off to Arizona where they dealt with the desert heat, lack of water, alcoholism, loss of religion, and the development of mining interests and the building trade) before I saw the connection between "consumption" and "champagne." When I understood that simple link, I understood the overarching theme—surely latent in the idea from the moment it had taken hold of me—between tuberculosis, spiritual thirst, consumerism, and addiction, all issues of "consumption."

It might seem dismaying that you should see what your story is about only after you have written it. Try it; you'll like it. Nothing is more exhilarating than the discovery that a complex pattern has lain in your mind ready to unfold.

Note that in the early stages of revision, both the worrying and the walking away are necessary. Perhaps it is bafflement itself that plunges us to the unconscious space where the answer lies.

Criticism

Once you have thought your story through, drafted it, and worked on it to the best of your ability, someone else's eyes can help to refresh the vision of your own. Wise professionals rely on the help of an agent or editor at this juncture (although even the wisest still smart at censure); anyone can rely on the help of friends, family, or classmates. The trick to making good use of criticism is to be utterly selfish about it. Be greedy for it. Take it all in. Ultimately you are the laborer, the arbiter, *and* the boss in any dispute about your story, so you can afford to consider any problem and any solution. Most of us feel not only committed to what we have put on the page, but also defensive on its behalf—wanting, really, only to be told that it is a work of genius or, failing that, to find out that we have gotten away with it. Therefore, the first exigency of revision is that you learn to hear, absorb, and accept criticism.

It used to be popular to speak of "constructive criticism" and "destructive criticism," but these are misleading terms, suggesting that positive suggestions are useful and negative criticism useless. In practice the opposite is usually the case. You're likely to find that the most constructive thing a reader can do is say *I don't believe this, I don't like this, I don't understand this,* pointing to precisely the passages that made you uneasy. This kind of laying-the-finger-on-the-trouble-spot produces an inward groan, but it's also satisfying; you know just where to go to work. Often the most destructive thing a reader can do is offer you a positive suggestion—*Why don't you have him crash the car?*—that is irrelevant to your vision of the story. Be suspicious of praise that is too extravagant, of blame that is too general. If your impulse is to defend the story or yourself, still the impulse. Behave as if bad advice were good advice, and give it serious consideration. You can reject it after you have explored it for anything of use it may offer.

Once again, walk away—Kenneth Atchity, in *A Writer's Time,* advises compulsory "vacations" at crucial points in the revising process—and let the criticism cook until you feel ready, impatient, to get back to writing.

When you feel that you have acquired enough distance from the story to see it anew, go back to work. Make notes of your plans, large and small. Talk to yourself in your journal about what you want to accomplish and where you think you have failed. Let your imagination play with new images or passages of dialogue. Keep a copy of the story as it is so that you can always go back to the original, and then be ruthless with another copy. Eudora Welty advises cutting sections apart and then pinning them back together so that they can be easily re- and re-arranged.

Revision Questions

As you plan the revision and as you rewrite, you will know (and your critics will tell you) what problems are unique to your story. There are also general, almost universal, pitfalls that you can avoid if you ask yourself the following questions:

What is my story about? Another way of saying this is: *What is the pattern of change?* Once this pattern is clear, you can check your draft to make sure you've included all the crucial moments of discovery and decision. Is there a crisis action?

Are there irrelevant scenes? Remember that it is a common impulse to try to cover too much ground. Tell your story in the fewest possible scenes; cut down on summary and unnecessary flashback. These dissipate energy and lead you to tell rather than show.

*　　　*　　　*

Why should the reader turn from the first page to the second? Is the language fresh? Are the characters alive? Does the first sentence, paragraph, page introduce real tension? If it doesn't, you have probably begun at the wrong place. If you are *unable* to find a way to introduce tension on the first page, you may have to doubt whether you have a story after all.

Is it original? Almost every writer thinks first, in some way or other, of the familiar, the usual, the given. This character is a stereotype, that emotion is too easy, that phrase is a cliché. First-draft laziness is inevitable, but it is also a way of being dishonest. A good writer will comb the work for clichés and labor to find the exact, the honest, and the fresh.

Is it clear? Although ambiguity and mystery provide some of our most profound pleasures in literature, beginning writers are often unable to distinguish between mystery and muddle, ambiguity and sloppiness. You may want your character to be rich with contradiction, but we still want to know whether that character is male or female, black or white, old or young. We need to be oriented on the simplest level of reality before we can share your imaginative world. Where are we? When are we? Who are they? How do things look? What time of day or night is it? What's the weather? What's happening?

Is it self-conscious? Probably the most famous piece of advice to the rewriter is William Faulkner's "kill all your darlings." When you are carried away with the purple of your prose, the music of your alliteration, the hilarity of your wit, the profundity of your insights, then the chances are that you are having a better time writing than the reader will have reading. No reader will forgive you, and no reader should. Just tell the story. The style will follow of itself if you just tell the story.

Where is it too long? Most of us, and even the best of us, write too long. We are so anxious to explain every nuance, cover every possible aspect of character, action, and setting that we forget the necessity of stringent selection. In fiction, and especially in the short story, we want sharpness, economy, and vivid, telling detail. More than necessary is too much. I have been helped in my own tendency to tell all by a friend who went through a copy of one of my novels, drawing a line through the last sentence of about every third paragraph. Then in the margin he wrote, again and again, "Hit it, baby, and get out." That's good advice for anyone.

Where is it undeveloped in character, imagery, theme? In any first, second, or third draft of a manuscript there are likely to be necessary passages sketched, skipped, or skeletal. What information is missing, what actions are incomplete, what motives obscure, what images inexact? Where does the action occur too abruptly so that it loses its emotional force?

*   *   *

Where is it too general? Originality, economy, and clarity can all be achieved through the judicious use of significant detail. Learn to spot general, vague, and fuzzy terms. Be suspicious of yourself anytime you see nouns like *someone* and *everything,* adjectives like *huge* and *handsome,* adverbs like *very* and *really.* Seek instead a particular thing, a particular size, an exact degree.

Although the dread of "starting over" is a real and understandable one, the chances are that the rewards of revising will startlingly outweigh the pains. Sometimes a character who is dead on the page will come to life through the addition of a few sentences or significant details. Sometimes a turgid or tedious paragraph can become sharp with a few judicious cuts. Sometimes dropping page one and putting page seven where page three used to be can provide the skeleton of an otherwise limp story. And sometimes, often, perhaps always, the difference between an amateur rough-cut and a publishable story is in the struggle at the rewriting stage.

An Example of the Revision Process

Short story writer Stephen Dunning won the 1990 "World's Best Short Story Contest" with a tight, complex, and evocative story that illustrates most of the principles discussed in this book. "Wanting to Fly" has, in two hundred and forty-five words, eight characters, a power struggle that builds and comes to a crisis, dialogue that reveals character and moves the action, a strong voice, irony, metaphor, and a pattern of change that reveals a theme.

Assuming that a story of such density was not "tossed off," I asked Dunning if he would share his revision process with other writers. What follows are four (of perhaps nine or ten) versions of the story, with Dunning's generous notes. He says:

> Mornings I often fast-write, try to hang onto my dreams. Not "free-write," but go so fast I leave censors behind, stumble and goof, hoping to trick myself into a little chunk I like. A word or an image. (Much less often, an "idea.")
>
> Very inefficient! I collect fast-writes (I do them on processor now, for speed) and when I have a stack, I search for chunks of language that interest me. I do this search with high-lighters in hand—pink, for hot items, yellow, for "maybe," green that means "Huh?" Things that puzzle me, but might be important. Obsessions, for example. I highlight words, phrases, images, "talk," mistakes. (Unproved theory of mine: write fast enough, make enough mistakes, you can track your obsessions. They leak out on you.)
>
> How much do I glean?
>
> As little as possible. I've learned, a few words per page. An occasional sentence.
>
> I type these little chunks fresh, set them up in their new environment. Then I doodle, connecting items with lines, starring something special. Now I'm ready to

"practice writing," which is what practicing writers do.

How? By answering my own questions: Why does this interest me? What else can I say about it? What does it remind me of? What would _____(Mother, my childhood sweetheart, Jesus, my mean sister, Winston Churchill—plug in someone who fits) say about this?

In a journal entry dated "somewhere around Halloween 1989," Dunning produced the "fast-write" (what I've referred to in this book as freedrafting) that provided the seeds of the story "Wanting to Fly." The fast-write passage is reproduced here exactly as it came from his word processor, "stumble and goofs" intact.

Version 1

fqast write from dreamsone is a computer dream. it's twenty two fifty eighjt st clair with the mansion full of statues, hedges. thje magraw boiys danny, oliver, the disapproving one with glasses   in the mansion games i did ook, better than the midget biully k but often last withj danny ollie. a bunch of othjer boys, the skinny lop-jawed one who spit at me in fooitball. the golden moment, facing him down. leary, he weas. hius name. stsate fair time, aboiut ten guys playing ball   leary was spitting and and tried to tackle me on the rocks, us others, us good guys, would try not to, ill fighjt you fair and square. god, i was good. the other boys waiting. leary backing down. some superboy hero! the evenings when the magraws had to go, id fly over into the mansion. crosbys'. sail from our back porch, go low over the hedges between crosbys and us, soar arouind statues, swoop along hedges. then poull up into resting places, a sectret birdself, something i swear i did, i was a bird, i flew. i restded on statues and tree limbs. i can see the hedges and statues. did the dream go bad? at some pooint i wasn't in it, but watching.   dozens of little figures, Boschian. a camera scan a huge painting made up of hundreds of little vignettes of weird, gnome like, devilish flyuers. pictogfraphs, almost, but lots of soaring and dipping. i know it was not the way it shoild be. i was watching, helpless to make everone everhything stop. the other flyers shoildn't be there. my place to fly. the night wqas purple and i love the lightness and speed of my flying. then the dream ended, I tried to identify the wonder of it. it seemed to end on Where did these wondrous things come from? They weren't the neightborhood boys. not worried///tjhere at the ened.

This first-draft-of-something-or-other clearly draws on both dreams and memory. In the second version (which Dunning says is four or five drafts/editings into a possible story) the author has achieved a gently ironic distance on the character of the boy, but it is interesting to note that he has provided a "frame" with a writer in it—something that many writers do, sometimes in an early version, sometimes in a final publication. Perhaps the introduction of an autobiographical element in the frame helps of itself to find authorial distance. By now the bird-boy of the dream has transmogrified into a human cannonball.

Version 2

Leroy slid open the bottom drawer where they kept his costumes. The white and red looked shabby; the silver looked ok. Nylon, and shiny. He thought of something he wanted to write.

"*Part four,*" he wrote. "*I always wanted to fly.*"

I was eight years old, in third, in Mrs. McKissup's third grade, when my father took me to State Fair. In the grandstand, after the horse races, sitting close to the track and the infield stage, we saw a man in silver tights and big handlebar moustache shot from a cannon. The name I remember is "The Great Zambini," but that doesn't look exactly right. Later my father gave me names like "The Flying Weenie" and "Zamboosi, the Goosey."

That same night of the State Fair I tried to paint my BVD longies with the gold paint in the tiny spray can Mother used to gild the birdcage. Right over my belly button I made a spot the size of a golden apple before the paint ran out. When my father saw it he paddled my ass with his hairbrush. That May, for my ninth birthday, Mother gave me a silver-grey t-shirt with a picture of Halley's comet flashing in red across the front.

Leroy got up from the table to get a beer. In the Lucky Lager six-pack, Carmen had set two cans of Diet Pepsi. Hint, hint, lay off the sauce. Leroy rolled his eyes and twisted out one of the beers. Well, that was like her, fairly comical.

I could fly in that shirt. Summer evenings in the eerie dusk after supper I wheeled around the neighborhood, content to fly alone. Daytimes at Duncan Frenzel's house I pumped the backyard tire swing higher than anyone and learned how to fly out from it just right before the swing reached the top of its arc. I flew out three or four feet beyond Duncan. At school in the sixth grade me and two buddies took over the primary grades' slide and slid down on our stocking feet, launching off from the lip to see who could jump farthest. Mrs. McKissup came over to tell us to let the little children use the slide. When Mrs. McKissup's back was turned, we went back to the slide, and before that day is out, of course, the three of us are in Mr. Beaver's office.

He calls us "childish" and "selfish." This happens again, he'll have to call our parents. Duncan giggles then, and gets a dirty look. When Mr. Beaver asks what would we do if we were trying to run a decent school, we both giggle. Maybe we had the same idea. Mine was to get rid of Mrs. McKissup and let our student teacher teach. She was beautiful, like a model.

My father heard about it anyway and beat me with the hairbrush until finally I cried and spit "I hate you!" in his face.

The summer between seventh and eight, Philip Callum and me made a slide from a refrigerator carton and nailed it onto the Callum's back porch roof. It hung out two feet past the edge of the roof. Mrs. Callum worked at the Police Department, and

I called her there when Philip landed wrong and broke his ankle. I didn't know the ankle was broke, just that Philip was screaming like crazy and couldn't walk. Before she got home, I tore the slide off the roof, and it wasn't until the first rain that Mr. Callum found out that his porch roof sprinkled like a watering can. After the phone call on that, Daddy beat me hard with the hairbrush. This is like ten days after.

That was my last beating. As long as I was still there, he never beat me. I think that in some serious way Mother told him not to, and he listened. I felt he could do what he wanted to her, but not to me. Later, once I'd run away and started coming home to visit, my father and I got along.

I was visiting after New Year's, home from Ice Capades, when he drowned. January fifth. Out ice-fishing with Arn Bower, he went out further than he should. He knew it was thin. He broke through and came up under the ice. I saw his face before they got him out.

I cancelled the gig I had starting mid-January. I was tired anyway.

Then I remember maybe once a day Arn would call on my mother. They'd drink a few. Arn would put his arms around her, holding her what seemed more than she wanted, but it was hard to tell. Sometimes I watched from outside, saw Mother push Arn's hands from her legs and breasts. But she didn't push hard or seem not to like it when he started again. I always made plenty of noise so Mother could get herself arranged before I come in.

Before, when I was fifteen, I saw the ad for Wallace's World Carnival coming to Anoka. I left a note for Mother, saying I was going to hitch-hike to my Aunt's, at White Bear Lake. I took the Selby-Lake streetcar the opposite direction to the end of the line, and thumbed to Anoka.

I slept that night in the back end of a truck that hauled the ferris wheel; I left the following night in the cab of that same truck. Willie Farley drove, another runaway named Annette sat in the middle, and me against the side door. I'd got hired as roustabout. I'd help put up the rides and tents, clean up after the animals. A dollar a day, food, sleep wherever I could.

He got the next-to-last beer. How long since he'd thought about Annette! Writing was terrific that way, making you remember things.

Willie was my best friend for two years. Long before Annette left to go home to Anoka, Willie got her drunk on dago red and held her head in his lap, in case she tried to get away. It was Willie's plan to help me lose my cherry. "It's time, Little Buddy, don't use it, you lose it."

"How's Annette going to like it?"

"How about you think about your own end, you let me take handle Annette here?"

Then after Willie got her so drunk she didn't know which end was up, he held her head while I pumped myself into her. I'd like myself better if I said I didn't enjoy it, but I did. Annette hardly seemed to notice.

Then Willie left us, going off to get some food. I lay alongside Annette, my right *hand under her sweatshirt on her chest. Later she threw up. I got her drinks of water and told what had happened. She already sort of knew. She cried and then we slept there restlessly. At dawn we woke up together, she said she loved me and made me do it to her again. This time was nice. I was full of the wonder of sex, thinking it would be even better if you loved the girl you were making love to, and I didn't love Annette. She never had enough in her mind.*

Willie was glad to have Annette shift over on to me. I was up to three dollars a day when Salazar, The Silver Bullet, joined our show, expanded for a two-week stay outside Memphis. In his first flight Salazar broke through his net—It was terrible rotted—and smashed his face bad. Lost half his nose, some teeth, broke his cheekbone and jaw. Willie and Old Man Wallace himself had four hours to talk me into doing the night show. "You're the right size," Old Man Wallace said. Salazar had a small barrel to his cannon. "You bail me out on this one, you're on your way to the big time." With help from Alex the Alligator Man we hauled the gun to a nearby high school football field and rigged a good net. The two of them told me what they thought was true about cannon-balling. Before that night was over, I'd found out they didn't know beans. I can say these three things. You have to push off of the plunger and you have to stretch out in flight. You have to land some way you don't break your bones. Otherwise, it's easy if you have the nerve and don't mind the jolts to your joints.

Carmen came in from her hymns. Leroy hoped she'd say something, like "What you writing there, Leroy?" Anything. But her face was shiny with the humidity and her joy. She was still in Beulah Land. "Oh, the singin was so fine, Leroy, you should of heard us sing."

"I've been writing, here," he said.

"They're raising money for a new organ," Carmen said. "Praise the Lord, we need it."

Leroy turned back to his notebook. "Annette found some silver tights . . ." he said aloud, thinking that might catch her. He wrote that down and went on.

. . . a silver bowling jacket that she took the name off, and a silver spray for my hair. By showtime, I could have flown without the cannon. It was partly knowing that Annette was there, but it was also inevitable: me being a human cannonball was what had to happen because I was me. My father's Flying Weenie. Because of all those nights and dream-times of flying, and the flight from Philip Callum's porch roof. I spelled inevitable in the fifth grade bee but sat down next-to-last on paranoid, putting in a y even though I knew better.

Polly Pineo won. I wanted her to win. I don't know exactly what I thought would happen if she won, but I know I was glad when she did.

I never saw that Salazar again. Old Man Wallace bought the cannon. Or said he did. They used me wherever the space laid out right. Willie and I fixed up Salazar's old cannon until I could fly one hundred fifty feet.

Annette went home, but there were other girls and women everywhere.

Dunning confesses that the second version puzzles him, and that it's possible "the market" was beginning to play a role. "My hunch is: I was trying to get a piece both for the PEN Syndicated Fiction Award" (which Dunning has won twice) "and for the World's Best Short Short Story Contest. Both contests have word limits—PEN's 2,500 and WBSSSC's severe 250."

Dunning also felt that both contests had "taboos, stated or inferred." Perhaps for that reason he drew back in a subsequent long version from the narrator's loss of virginity to a—stronger, in my opinion—bittersweet kissing scene. Gone also are the characters of the writer and his girlfriend Carmen, and the whole frame with its writer writing. The boy's story is sharpened and tightened, but otherwise remains substantially the same.

It's interesting that at this point Dunning began to title his versions, a clue that he had a sense of shape and theme. The progression of titles indicates a subtle shift of emphasis, from "Flying," to "I Always Wanted to Fly," to "Wanting to Fly."

By the time he came to write the penultimate version, Dunning knew he was aiming for the 250-word maximum demanded by the World's Best Short Short Story Contest. He had drastically pruned and condensed. "Note a shift to the present," he says, "a fine way to cut words." One consequence of the shortening is that characters are squashed to sketches ("Bye-bye, Annette: In longer versions she was prominent; here she's a walk-on.") Yet this distilling represents a natural process of characterization, and the richness of the earlier portraits no doubt contributes to the vividness of the later one.

This version of Dunning's story is reproduced as a facsimile of his working manuscript. He says, "Here the inked numbers in the upper right corner indicate that with my pen editings, I've cut 338 to 307. (Lord, Lord! Another 57 to go.)"

Version 3

WORLD'S BEST SHORT STORY CONTEST
991/620/551/496/418/400/369/362/338

                    I always wanted to fly.   338
                                                                31
                                                               ___
                                                               307

                                            with   *a*
    At State Fair we see a man [in silver tights and/handle-
                                        a name like
bar moustache shot from a cannon ʌ ''The Great Zambini''?
Driving home
ʌFather calls me [~~names like~~] ''Zamboosi, the Goosey'' and
                                   But
''Flying Weenie.'' ʌThat night, when I paint my BVD's
with Ma's birdcage spray, he paddles me good.)

My ninth birthday Ma gives me a silver-grey t-shirt
with Halley's comet [flashing] across the front. I can fly
in that shirt. (Arms out stiff, I tilt around the neigh-
borhood.) [~~Duncan Frenzel and I use~~ *catches Duncan and me on!*] the kindergarten
slide.] Mrs McKissup comes over: ''Now you big boys, let
the children use it.''

[We don't listen.] Before long we're in Mr. Beaver's
office.

''Childish,'' he says. ''Selfish.'' Duncan giggles,
(~~and gets a look~~.) Mr. Beaver asks what *we'd* do if we was
trying to run a decent school. We both giggle, and Father
gets the (~~old~~) call. He beats me with his hairbrush.
(~~We nail it good to Frenzel's porch roof, but~~) *nailed good to F's roof* Our refrigerator-carton slide ∧ isn't steady. Duncan lands
wrong, screaming and hollering, and I call the police,
(~~where his ma works.~~)(~~Turns out~~) the ankle was broke. When
it rains, Mr. Frenzel's (~~porch~~) roof sprinkles like a
watering can.
That was my last beating.
~~The last time Father beats me is for that.~~

Wallace's Carnival hires me to assemble rides (~~tents
and clean after animals.~~) A dollar a day, food, sleep
where I can. *Next day* We leave for Toledo ~~the next day~~, Willie Farley driving the ferris-wheel truck, [another runaway
named Annette in the middle, me against the door.]

It's Willie teaches me to fly.
[Annette knows other things.]
And I've been flying ever since. Once I'm famous, Fa-
ther and me get along fine. I'm home from Cole Brothers

when he drowns. [January fifth,] ice-fishing with Arn
Bower. [Father knows the ice is thin, but breaks through
and comes up under it] (Before they get him out,) I see his
face, mouth open and lopsided, a giant perch.

Arn Bower starts keeping Ma company, (and that's good.)
Wherever I fly there's women for me.

The final award-winning and published version of Dunning's story is so dense
that it verges on that hybrid form, the prose poem.

"At some point," he says, "there's tension between the stuff (language, content)
and the form. One effect, unfortunate, is sentences that sound more like telegrams
than art. But another effect comes from the demands of the form, inviting the writer
to 'imaginative' uses of language. Not *altogether* different from writing a haiku or a
sonnet, is it? In the third version I wrote:
We don't listen. Before long we're in Mr. Beaver's office. Trying to hang onto the
'stuff' and still honing the piece, the final version reads:
In two minutes Duncan and me're in Beaver's office.
A slender nine words instead of ten! The final version has a little more stuff and
'shows' (images) more than it 'tells.' It's more specific—'In two minutes' instead of
'Before long'—*adding* a word!; 'names' (Duncan and me), and has that lovely con-
traction (me + are into me're.)
Makes me smile even now."

Final Version

      ∞

Wanting to Fly

At State Fair a man in silver tights and handlebar moustache—some name
like The Great Zambini—blasts from a cannon. Driving home, Father calls
me "Goosey Zamboosi" and "Flying Weenie." But later, when I spray my
BVD's with Ma's birdcage paint, he paddles me good.
Again.
For my ninth birthday, Ma gives me a silver-grey t-shirt with Halley's
comet flashing across. I can fly in that shirt—arms stiff, tilting. Then Mrs.
McKissup catches us on the kindergarten slide. "You boys! Let the children
use it."

In two minutes Duncan and me're in Beaver's office.

"Childish," Mr. Beaver says. "Selfish." Duncan giggles. "What would you do, you're trying to run a decent school?" We both giggle.

Father uses the hairbrush.

Duncan and me nail a refrigerator-carton to Frenzels' porch roof. Duncan falls awful hard, grabbing his ankle. "It's broke," he hollers. I run for his ma. Next rain the Frenzels' roof sprinkles like a watering can.

My last beating ever.

Wallace's Carnival hires me to assemble rides—dollar a day, food, sleep anywhere I can. We head for Toledo, Willie Farley driving the ferris-wheel truck. It's Willie teaches me cannon-flying. I get pretty famous.

Then of course Father and me get along. I'm home from Cole Brothers when Father drowns, ice-fishing with Arn Bower. Before they hook him, I see his face—mouth open and lopsided, a giant perch.

Arn Bower starts keeping Ma company, and that's good. There's women wherever I fly.

What you have just read is the story of a story, with Dunning as hero trying to catch a little bit of a literal dream, wrestling it, messing up, sidetracked, persistent, pulled by contradictory forces (the dream, the market), learning as he goes, changing as the thing he is making changes. If you think that is a lot of trouble to go to for two hundred and fifty words, think again. That's what writing is.

I remember that in my freshman English class at the University of Arizona, Patrick McCarthy was trying to impress us with how hard we ought to work. He described his own struggle the night before, till two A.M., for a single paragraph. He was a powerful storyteller, and he made it grindingly awful. I was appalled. I put up my hand. "But doesn't it," I asked cheerfully, "get easier?"

McCarthy thought a moment. "No," he said. "It doesn't get easier. It gets better."

And that's the truth of it. There are fine professional writers who never, as a contemporary said of Shakespeare, "blot a word." (Twentieth-century translation: blip a word.) But they are precious few, and you and I are not among them. The minute we get comfortable doing something, we'll do something else; the minute we reach our standards, we'll raise them. The reward will probably not be fame or money or even an intense life replete with talk of illusion and reality, art and death. More likely the reward will be, now and then, some such thing as a "lovely contraction." It'll be enough.

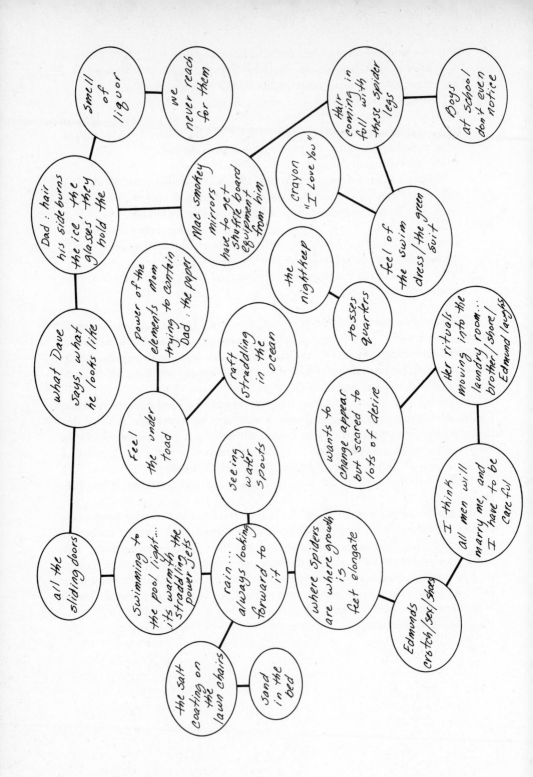

Unlike Stephen Dunning's "Wanting to Fly," the short story "From Dawn to Noon" by Heather Sellers underwent major expansion in the revision process, from about one thousand to about four thousand words. The first and final versions of the story are reproduced here, together with the author's first clustering exercise.

Version 1

⚬⚬⚬

Aliki Towers

HEATHER SELLERS

For a brief year, a long moment, we are going to be rich. My father has a temporary and mysterious job teaching professors in a Florida beach city. We close up our inland house and buy a purple parakeet and my mother makes everyone bathing suits in a burst of polka-dot energy before we head to the east coast.

Breast buds distract the clothes I wear that year in Ormond Beach. At the gas station across the street from our apartment, big as a house in the smooth white towers, my skirt blows up around my wing muscles, my dark hair shows and my brother sees.

My brother and I cannot run down the red carpeted halls of Aliki, soft as beds. We cannot race in the twin gold rocket ship elevators, or sign the brass and mirrored walls with our sweaty palm prints. There is only one child, here half the year, a sweet ghost in the catacombs of Aliki Towers, Edmund. We force him to race, run, stain, steal fake palm pieces and pretend they are antlers but, he, of course, cannot, a Richie Rich, a living peanut head, dedicated to sitting still and saving a world we do not notice.

My father moves onto the balcony. Our parakeet dies. My father joins a singles club. My mother quits sewing for me. She considers a thing called Powder Puff Auto Repair all winter.

We walk to a school on the beach. Aliki is not a family atmosphere. We do not take friends home. The rental furniture in our condo is wicker which bites and the credenza creases our shins and foreheads when we fall into it. We are not allowed onto the balcony, except to take our father the paper, because my mother thinks the building is moving, rocking in the ocean wind. She's seen this from the grocery store, Aliki swaying on its slapdash foundation.

"Give is built into these places," my father says. He starts drinking and going outside for the sunsets, moonrises, high tides, intracoastal waterway fluctuations. "Just wait for the next hurricane and you'll see what I mean about give."

Our car erodes in the salty wind. Pits and sores, and whole pieces of metal peel off like mica that has been handled by a hundred children.

During our beach year, my brother begins his career as a truant, and he teaches me what he has learned after I get out of school. I join him on the beach, leaving my school things at the back door of Aliki's smooth white coquina. The doors don't easily open because there is always a fierce wind caught in the corridors. My brother can now spot shark teeth from thirty feet and he never bends over for black shell shards, like I still do.

My breasts hurt and I float along as he stalks the beach, keeping the teeth in the side of his mouth. I like to be all under the water with just my breast nodes and nose out. It gets dark and he teaches me tricks in the pool which carries off our salt and sand each day. We find our debris by the drain, and leave pennies there. We practice holding our breath in the deep end and before dinner, later than our bedtime now, we get a whirlpool going, flinging ourselves around the edges of the pool so long and fast that soon we are carried by our own forces. I see Edmund part the curtains on floor 22 more than once when we are sweeping the water in circles with our bodies.

My brother gets huge. He directs me in shuffleboard, kites, skimboarding. His hair turns green. I can often see him falling down the beach, pulling me from geography, geometry.

My father sunburns his penis on the balcony.

I tell the Nancies at school that my mother makes all my clothes when they ask why I wear what I wear. But they find labels on my nape, at my waist. I tell more lies, and I cry and am not spoken to by girls in my classes. They pimple, I get none. My skin is burned off every day keeping up with my brother, scraping the sides of the pool, the bottom of the ocean, buried in the sand for his machinations. Hair is coming in everywhere, my body feels as if it is going from bird to lizard to sloth. I can't keep up with my green beacon of a brother.

We make trips down to the gas station late at night now that there is summer light off the ocean past ten o'clock and music eats up delicate bites of the wind.

I have a new swimdress, and I wear it all of the time, even though you are supposed to be completely covered—feet, arms, hair parts—in the Aliki lobbies at all times. No children can move into the apartments anymore. Edmund is safe his half of each year. We are the last of our Mohicans, we learn. I wear my swimdress and get Starbursts and Mambos with Max at night for our dessert.

Then, coming home with our brown bags like alcoholics, we find a new nightkeep where before there was just a camera. His name is Dave and he detains us. He has mistletoe up above the registration office, and extracts kisses from me. My brother says I have to do this in January, February, March, April. Dave leaves the mistletoe up until May, demanding kisses. He asks me all kinds of questions about my swimdress. My brother stays down there with Dave after I take the stairs home.

Dave knows all about Aliki. There is not a floor thirteen. We dash to the elevator and see that the little lights the size of gold quarters do go from twelve to fourteen. We cannot believe we didn't notice this before. The controls belong to Dave.

He steals soaps and pens and towels and pucks for us. I have interest in very little. The ocean is uninhabitable now—full of red sargasso, and slimy berries get stuck between my toes and elastic.

My father fails all of the professors in his classes and is fired. He locks himself in the master bathroom and turns on the sunlamp. My mother screams and screams. The fake red sun is breathing cancer onto all of us—it knows no boundaries like walls.

The end of that year is the beginning of my thirteenth summer. My brother won't get out of the pool where he's become a fish in a cooler. I watch him from the balcony, letting my body burst over the hot metal rail. Inside the sliding glass doors, my mother rises from deep in the center of the white circular sofa and draws the drapes.

Final Version

⌦∽◯

From Dawn to Noon

HEATHER SELLERS

For a brief year, a long moment, we are going to be rich. In August, my father receives a temporary and mysterious job teaching professors in a Florida beach city with an ugly name I keep forgetting: Ormond. We close up our inland house, buy a purple parakeet, and my mother sews everyone bathing suits during the polka-dot burst of energy before we head to the east coast, to Ormond Beach.

We live in Aliki, a tall white tower of condos on the beach, with a big black cursive "A" under the lightning rod; rhymes with sneaky. There is not a floor thirteen in Aliki. Children are not allowed, not aloud. I help haul our stuff in, brown boxes, and I keep looking for some sign of the superstitious oldsters my parents promise live in sleek white Aliki; their only trace is a fleet of dormant black Cadillacs parked under a corrugated roof.

On each trip down to the car for another load of linens or books, I write my initials, BLP, in the sandy stripes on these long hoods. I write my name, Bronwyn, in cursive in the baby dunes I find in the parking lot. It's a name that looks good in cursive. Ormond will stay hot and empty all fall, all spring, and my initials are intact at the end of the week.

My brother, Max, and I settle in and swim every afternoon. We share a bedroom—there are only two in our corner condo, both of them three times the size of rooms we're accustomed to. At night we imagine the other condos filling with dead bodies, picked bones.

He marks off the area around his bed with strips of crepe paper from my mother's ancient party supplies box. If any of my possessions contact his area, he will have to destroy them, drop them, drown them. I am left with a much smaller part of the room. We wrestle in my area, defined by what isn't his, like large clumsy, hog dogs. Max forces my head under the bed.

"Hen-child," he says to me. "You are going to get hurt." I resort to pinching and biting—I would not do these things at home, on the common ground we had there. I starting fighting like a girl in Aliki, and losing. His sweat is starting to smell like hot dogs. To get out onto the balcony, I have to walk along the wall through a trough he's allowed as wide as one of my feet. The wall is getting a little water stained—my hands sweat when I am inside, and I am always wet from swimming. At night, when he is in his bed, above the covers, feet hanging over the wicker footboard, reading, I walk the plank to watch night lap over the ocean. It doesn't look like night in paintings. My view from Aliki is monstrous. I get dizzy trying to see around the corner. Soon I see my first shooting star. It promises me wings, but instead of falling into the ocean to sleep, the star is erased by the Polynesian Room's search-lights. The hotels across the street are empty; Aliki may as well be vacant. Max locks me out, and I am forced to watch him through the sliding glass doors as he threatens my possessions, panties, a sock on the border.

The night after the shooting star, I go down alone to the beach where the sand is dark and leathery. Aliki is dark as the ocean. Our lights are the only ones lit in the whole huge building, and they are dim, lost against the flat string of cities that tangle the night-pink horizon.

Gulls line Aliki's empty balconies by day. From our astroturf wrap-around balcony on the twenty-second floor, Max and I pour juice, drop a double deck of cards. We pretend grapes are watermelons. From our balcony, we get bored racing our spit. We drop a glass glass, a stuffed gingham frog, marbles, pieces of cheese. All my brother's new ideas require being on the edge of something.

When school starts, my brother and I race each morning to the elevators in order to press little lights like peach quarters that skip from twelve to fourteen. The elevator is our focus, like a teenager's car. It is our only transportation, and we have to share it and cherish it, and make its thrill last longer than it does.

We walk to school together, through the armada of hotels and gas stations in the morning. The second day of my new sixth grade I am asked to create singlehandedly the homonym bulletin board, my forced and unfortunate alienation from the class. I tack with sweaty hands letters to make bare bear, weather whether, board bored, belle bell, sent scent, sun son, not sure how to use the words from now on without their mates. The construction paper absorbs my sweat, and the effect of the bulletin board is mumpy.

Breast buds appear under the clothes I wear that fall in Ormond Beach. When the Nancies at school ask why I wear what I wear I tell them that my mother makes all my clothes. But they find labels on my nape, at my waist. I tell more lies, and I cry and am not spoken to by girls in my classes. They pimple. I do not. My skin is burned off every day keeping up with my brother, scraping the sides of the pool, the bottom of the ocean, buried in the sand for his machinations. We have no remedies for each other.

Hair is coming in everywhere, my body feels as if it is going from bird to lizard to sloth.

Max and I walk home from school along the empty beach. I have trouble keeping up with my green beacon of a brother. Of course there are no shells left in Florida, my father says, erosion, corrosion, snowbirds. We find the birds are all sitting griping out of reach on the rails of our building. Sometimes there is a piece of wood or a shirt on the sand. We collect. Beech beach, there their, air heir.

One warm morning at the gas station across the street from our apartment, big as a house hidden in the smooth white towers of Aliki, my skirt blows up around the wing muscles on my back. My dark hair is creeping out of my skin all over, and my brother sees; his face freezes going too many places at once.

There is always a serrated wind blowing sheets of sand. We learn to look to the side.

Very soon my brother and I are not allowed to somersault—the quietest of all escapes—down the red carpeted halls of Aliki, soft and soundless as mattresses. We can no longer race in the twin gold rocket ship elevators, or sign the brass and mirrored walls with our sweaty palm prints. The elevators are always waiting at our floor, as if sent to tattle on us. Our mother comes out of their enormous white quilted room to complain about this.

"You children are keeping other residents from getting up and down. I'm afraid we are keeping them waiting." She is wrinkling up with worry, not sun, and we don't know why. There are no other residents as far as Max and I can see. The hotels are all empty. We dream of swimming down the strip in every last pool together.

Our mother is dizzy in Aliki—too high. She wants a yard to mow, cardinals, a tree. Her appetite for fish turns to nausea as my father brings home red fish, blue fish. We never see or hear her in the thick white carpet of our apartment. She tells us what we cannot do, but nothing is said about razors, wax, cream. I am asked at school what bra size she wears, how old she is. I lie now because I do not know. I can't picture her body, or cup her breasts. I don't know what she does all day.

A child arrives, one child, at Christmas, of course. Hear here, half the year, a sweet ghost in the catacombs of Aliki Towers, Edmund. Ugly name, ugly boy. We attempt to force him to do what we are not supposed to: race, run, stain, steal segments of fake palm—they unscrew—and pretend they are antlers, but, he, of course, cannot, a Richie Rich, a living peanut head, dedicated to sitting still and saving a world we do not notice.

Edmund wears a nice belt with his khaki pleats. He quotes from his grandmother, who has never gone outside since she moved to Aliki, Ormond, Florida. His shoes make his feet flap like beaver tails. I watch his pink head through his pale floss when we sit on the lounges by the pool, freezing in the grey ocean spray winter now sends.

For these meetings my brother wears nylon gym shorts with elastic waists that stretch out suddenly like chewing gum when he is running or laughing too hard—and I wear under my raincoat the new bathing dress and skinny white sneakers that barely hold these new feet of mine that have a hair apiece on the big toe. This hair is the worst sight I've ever seen, it's what I pull on at night to get to sleep. The bathing dress is a red polka dot top with a ruffle that goes to the very tops of my thighs, and a blue polka dot panty. I am not supposed to wear this anywhere but to the pool, but in it I go to the store, our lobby, other lobbies, with Edmund and Max. Max bats at the dress, lifting it up behind me when I don't wear the raincoat. In my swimdress, I feel pinched like a baby.

Edmund walks slow and waddly and we call him penguin. He follows after us spouting facts from the history of crime when we steal papers from the machines at the Sandpiper and the Ramada and we carry down to the beach loose towels, and cocktail glasses left outside rooms and Edmund shakes the sand out of his huge boaty shoes as Mas and I fling our loot into the wind. The newspapers mate noisily in the wind above us and briefly draw the dozens of pink-eyed gulls.

Edmund does not touch my hands when we fight for control of the elevators with Max. I worry he will see how hairy my underarms have become. I sweat around him, anxious he will see what I'm becoming, intriguing and disgusting as the bodies I build on the beach, decorated with pointy shell shards and black curly seaweed like spiders.

On weekends, the elevator doors open spontaneously, and Edmund is often standing there in his costume, which comes to look exactly like a bellboy's. He grows paler. We are never admitted to his grandparent's unit—they are beachside, we are streetside, and he doesn't get invited into ours.

After Edmund grows even paler, the outer doors to Aliki cease to open easily because there is always a fierce winter wind caught in the corridors. I like this. Whenever I leave or enter the building, I lean forward and then turn around and lean backwards, laying into it, trusting the blast to buoy me.

My father moves onto the balcony just after Christmas. He clears off the dining room table and the credenza, puts his papers and green graph papers and ledgers into the boxes that held our dishes and linens (saved by my mother because we will be leaving Aliki, soon now—she's counting the days with little pieces of paper in a jar). The southside catches lumps of sunlight, and he dozes there; classes are cancelled for a little while. He hasn't graded everyone's midterm. This makes me sad because it seems he is bragging about badness. I can't see him teaching, he is too to easily sidetracked. He is grow-ing sideburns. He uses his squat amber drinking glasses for ashtrays now, and these ugly nests accumulate, sour the balcony. My mother won't go within three feet of the outside walls, much less through the sliding glass doors onto the balcony, so his mess grows, his plastic chaise stretches under his weight, and soon his rear end is grazing the astroturf. Max avoids the southside—there's not a slice of windy resistance there—but I am compelled to watch my father. He fingers his sideburns, and they fork on his red face. He is a molted thing caught mid-migration out there.

My mother no longer allows us on the balcony, but all of our doors are sliding glass doors, every room has them on at least one side, and I still like to creep around Max's territory to go out on the balcony at night, after our father has gone in to sleep. I see the sea reflected in the stars on good days. Some nights my father goes out, out of Aliki. The weather does not reflect this.

I watch the men in gas stations, worried they'll meet my eye. The roads are covered with greasy colors, tracing paths to the empty Tiki Lounge, the Beachcomber where my father goes. Ormond is a dead beach; southward, Daytona stays gold all night and all day.

Our parakeet dies. Max orchestrates a sea burial from the pier, and I do not go with him. My mother doesn't like to be the only one in the apartment. My father joins a singles club for professional reasons. My mother won't get near his sideburns—she dodges his hair, and I end up feeling ugly, mannish. My mother quits sewing for me. She considers a thing called Powder Puff Auto Repair all winter. My feet grow longer, obscene. Hair hare.

My mother thinks the building is moving, rocking in the ocean wind. She's seen this from the grocery store, Aliki swaying on its cushion founda-tion.

"Give is built into these places," my father says. He starts drinking and going outside for the bare sunsets, moonrises, high tides, slight intracoastal waterway fluctuations. "Just wait for the next hurricane and you'll see what I mean about give."

Our car erodes in the salty wind. It pits and sores, and whole pieces of metal peel off like mica that has been handled by a few children.

We are not taking regular meals, baths. My brother promises he hasn't brushed his teeth once since we moved. I wear for five days without washing my polka dot bathing panty. I wear it to school as underwear and swim all afternoon. I drip dry on the velvet dining room chair, leave a print the shape of an ear, and I sleep in it every night, always a little cool and damp there.

It is during our beach year my brother hones his career as a truant, and he teaches me what he has learned after I get out of school. I join him on the beach, leaving my school things at the back door of Aliki's smooth white coquina. I don't worry they will disappear, I worry that my bathing suit will be stolen by the hands of the wind off my body as I run down to the pool. I know soon my worm white underbody will be exposed, that a negative suit where I am not tan will be revealed under the worst possible circumstances. This is all I know.

Aqua menstrual how-to manuals are passed at school, but they do not show the tan lines.

Max can now spot shark teeth from thirty feet and he never bends over for black shell shards, fakes, like I still do. My breasts hurt and I float along in the shallow water as he stalks the beach, keeping the teeth in the side of his mouth. I like to be all under the water with just my breast nodes and nose out. The current carries me down alongside him, and I walk on the bouncy sand back to Aliki, at his side, tasting the teeth by turn.

When it gets dark, he teaches me tricks in the pool that carries off our salt and sand each day. Treading in the deep end, he holds my ankles strong and straight as I flip in the air, smack the water with my back. We hit our heads on the edge, but if there is blood, it is tiny, and it disintegrates in the chlorine which heals our bites and sores like magic.

We find our debris in moraines around the drain, and we leave pennies and teeth there. We practice holding our breath in the deep end before dinner, which is served by my father hours later now than our bedtime. He always goes out to the balcony for his moon tan while we eat. "Now think about it," he says, telling us the indecipherable stories of his departure from the department.

So Max and I get a whirlpool going, flinging ourselves around the edges of the pool so long and fast that soon we are carried by our own forces. This fills our stomachs with the fear of delight. My feet are becoming flippers. More than once I see Edmund part the curtains on floor eleven—where the only lights on the beachside of Aliki eye the pool dimly—more than once when we are sweeping the water into powerful circles with our bodies.

Spring comes, and Edmund slips through our waterlogged fingers.

One evening my brother and I come home from the candy rack on the boardwalk to a nightkeep, and our idyllic days in Aliki Towers end instantly. Staggering towards Aliki with our sweaty-necked brown bags of Bit o' Honey and my new specialty, white chocolate, Max and I have been pretending we are alcoholics. Suddenly, where there was once an impotent camera at the front entrance, there is a man in a metallic striped shirt with two television screens and a buzzer to open the smokey glass door and admit the familiar.

He lets us in without any trouble, electrifying the door so that it opens, his door now.

"You're the kids," he says. His name is Dave. I don't like it that we are known, but Max starts telling him how dull it is, encouraging him.

Dave waves us in his office, a small white reception room I've never noticed. Dave looks like he has broken into a dentist's office to me. He has a patchy beard and two rings on his bird finger and long storky thigh bones. He smiles and slides across the terrazzo towards us in a chair with shiny casters.

Dave is not watching the two televisions mounted in the corners of his chamber. One shows the empty doorstep of Aliki, and one a silent ball game. Dave watches the flowers embroidered across my chest. It's as if he is watching something alive, his face is a bright otter. There's nothing available on the twenty-second floor to protect me from this.

Dave changes one of the stations to reveal the parking lot, points Max to his special MG sitting by the pool like an old hopped out grasshopper. I can't breathe in the little room. Max is very polite, his voice high and thin, his candy behind his back.

"Got any boyfriends? Got any mini-dresses?" Dave asks me all kinds of questions I can't answer. He seems to get angry when he finds out we don't have a television set. He cools when Max explains how we play Life a lot in our room together.

It's all I can do to stare at Dave's face. Since I don't talk at school or to strangers, and the only people I know are my family, I am accustomed to staring at people and though I feel uncomfortable, it is this very wormy ache I am most used to.

I wish desperately I lived alone as we ascend to our mother and father. I am frightened as we ride up to talk to Max about Dave. We won't mention him to either parent—they'll either make us take him things, to be polite, like cookies, or forbid us to see him, whichever is worse, and on this they'll disagree.

As we get out of the elevator, Max streaks his hands down the columns of numbered lights and the elevator quickly works itself into a fit, a death dance. I discover oil from the candy has leaked through the bag onto my hands. I worry Dave will come by our apartment, act as if I like him.

We give our mother her change and we go into the utility room to eat and reclaim our share of pocket change from our dad's trousers in the laundry pile. Max seems greedy as we discuss Dave.

"We can get anything we want, we can get the keys to any door," Max says, pressing the Bit o' Honey to his lips.

I can't see my body any more. I can't imagine it around me. All I can do is see Dave watching me.

He calls me Bonnie. "Bonnie, bunny, do you have a boyfriend yet?"

It is high spring and finally time to swim, but now that Dave is here, we must walk past him to get a passkey on our way to the pool, and I balk in my part of the bedroom. The seams pull out of my faded bathing dress, white tracks of thread lace my hips—what's usually pressed, folded, tucked, and hidden shows. My mother gets out my old terry cloth cover-up, and I am to wear it at all times. I am not supposed to parade around. When she says this, I realize what I have to do to get by Dave. I find things easier parading.

Only Max knows that Dave keeps mistletoe tacked above the registration office, in order to extract kisses from me. My brother says I have to do this in March, April, June, until the Fourth of July, when Dave will buy us fireworks to drop from our balcony. He gets Max talking about skateboards, surfboards, woos him with talk of the invitations the sea and cement extend to the fearless.

My brother stays down there with Dave. They share pizzas for dinner. I cannot eat around Dave, of course. I take the stairs home after our swims, which may as well be in different pools now, worried that Dave has a channel for every corner of Aliki.

Max knocks all of the water out trying to do the butterfly. He breaks the diving board jack-knifing and doesn't even care. The metallic stripes in Dave's shirt keep me short of breath in the pool, the metal ladders slip through my hands—too silver. The tile edge bites my back on my double flip, and Max makes me quit early so he can go talk to Dave—my body is acting like mercury. All this keeps me awake in my dreams, in my wicker bed next to Max's on the twenty-second floor of Aliki. I see the silver stripes, Dave's silver mustache in our dishwasher, the burnished aluminum oven. I want to live alone and never marry.

When I look at the gas stations at night from my balcony, the men look up my legs and I freeze.

The ocean is uninhabitable now—full of red sargasso, and slimy berries get stuck between my toes and the elastic around my thighs. Dave gives us shuffleboard lessons and we are to bring him beer from our candy hauls.

My brother gets huge. His hair turns green again. I can often see him falling down the beach, pulling me from Geography, Geometry. We are doing antonyms. Everyone agrees on opposites.

My father sunburns his penis on the balcony.

I make trips down to the gas station late at night now that there is summer light off the ocean past ten o'clock and music eats up delicate bites of the wind.

I have a new swimsuit, green, sleek—the Frog, my brother calls it. It dries in minutes, and I swim faster with no drag. Water rushes between my legs, and I wear the Frog all of the time, even though I am supposed to be completely covered—feet, arms, hair parts—in the Aliki lobby at all times. No special exceptions can be made for children to move into the apartments anymore. Edmund is not coming back next fall, and neither are we.

One night I sleep in the utility room to get away from the sound of the ocean, the throb of neon, the musky oyster odor of Max sweating in his dreams, all of which I believe make me grow hair, breasts.

My father fails all of the professors in his classes and is fired. He locks himself in the master bathroom and turns on the sunlamp. My mother screams and screams: the fake red sun is breathing cancer onto all of us—it knows no boundaries like walls or glass.

The end of that year is the beginning of my thirteenth summer. My brother won't get out of the pool where he's become a fish in a cooler. He has stolen money from Dave, and I don't ever go downstairs. I watch Max from the balcony, my bare feet on remnants of my father's cigarettes, letting my body burst over the hot metal rail. I sway, holding on to the balcony with both hands, and feel Aliki swaying against my rhythm. It gathers energy, and I see the pool, the towers, the glass of the city and sea in perpetual motion. Inside the sliding doors, my mother rises from deep in the center of the white circular sofa and draws the drapes.

Suggestions for Discussion

1. Why is the fuller picture of Aliki Towers in the final version important to the progress of the story?

2. Has the relationship between brother and sister been changed as well as developed in the revision?

3. How does the story shape change by having Edmund arrive after Max and Bronwyn instead of before?

4. How is the mother's character developed in the longer version, and to what effect? The father's?

5. Hair, teeth, feet, flesh, breast, sweat—an awareness of bodies reveals Bronwyn's adolescent anxiety. How does the augmentation of this imagery from the shorter version to the longer help develop the theme?

6. Perhaps the most significant expansion is in the portrait of Dave. Why is this revision important to the structure and theme of the story?

7. If you were the editor of the magazine publishing "From Dawn to Noon," what further changes would you ask the author to make?

What follows here are Bob Shacochis's notes for the short story "Squirrelly's Grouper," three versions (out of at least five drafts) of the opening few paragraphs, and then the full story. Interestingly, one version of the opening was published in Shacochis's collection *The Next New World*; the lead was then further revised for *Outer Banks Magazine*. Although Shacochis preferred this last version, and it appeared before the book, it was too late to change the book's galleys. This may seem confusing; consider it grist for future critics. Some writers have been known to tinker with work published half a century before.

Squirrelly Notes

> changeling
> some are born stupid and never change no matter how much you educate them. accent became heavier as he spoke.
> fuzzy stiff swoops of hair   veined with gristle.
> cocky, curt, hostile, authority, seclusion   motives   banish
> teeth like a field of crystal tacks   not discredited.
> People use the word sentimental as a gun to shoot you with.
> Whatever the places are where beasts live.   felicity   euphoria
> unmistakable   endowed
> None of us tried to stop it, None of us said, Hey, what's going on, none of us said or even thought of saying, Willie, goodbye. We all just thought this: There goes Squirrelly, not in style.

Shacochis's first draft of the opening paragraphs reads as follows:

> After all the boats went out, Mrs. Terbill came in the marina store on Tuesday to post a sign she had made on a little grey card: *Lost dog. Yorkshire terrier. Name: Alphonse, My Sole Companion. Reward,* and then a number to reach her at. Same reward as for the other two? I asked her. She wibbled her pumpkinself: *oh Lord yes,* she says; maybe there's tears in her sodden eyes but who would know. Five dollars, that's about right for a Yorkie, paid by the pound and measured by appeal. *You don't put no price on what my baby means to me,* she says, and that's an opinion I shared. She spent that much plus tax on a twelve-pack and trudged back out the door in her fishwive's rubber boots, going back to her trailer up behind the packing house to sit by the phone.
>
> Funny thing, the last two times the widow Terbill's dogs disappeared never to be seen again, monstrous catches were brought onto the dock. Bobby Rambles from Kinnakeet showed up with a hammerhead bigger than an Oldsmobile, that was the first—dog named *Prince Ed,* I believe—then the second, Captian Lloyd Conroy tied up the *Tarbaby* after dark and winched himself off a blue marlin made the one in the window at the Chamber of Commerce look like a perch. Dog's name was *Winchester,* I believe. Damn dogs must be

good action in the water, I figured, or it might just be a coincidence of events, so I couldn't say much to these young men who would be responsible. I like dogs, have two of my own, big bull and bitch Bay Retrievers, sweet as retard children, mother and son, momma's purblind and pursues sleep, sonny boy's always on the go, not my sole companions but I prefer their company to misfit fishermen, and neither is the size you'd mistake for bait. What's been happening to Mrs. Terbill, who lost her old man and her dope-smoking boy three Januarys ago, when they ran up off Cape May into some weather, flounder fishing I believe it was: It might not get you, but it gets me.

A second draft of the opening retained substantially the same structure but clarified characters and tightened the imagery. Then, eight pages into a third draft, Shacochis found a passage that presented itself as a better opening.

Some folks think the only style of story I'll bother to tell is a fish story, and they're mostly right because, by right of our daily bread, what nurtures me nurtures others, and those who don't care for a waterman's tales, the ones who walk away when I get started, make this mistake: A fish story is never about a fish; it's always about a man. When you get down to it, fish is just Pleasure with a capital P. Rule of thumb, bigger the fish, bigger the Pleasure, but pleasure's pleasure, hardly matters if you hook it, smoke it, sleep with it, buy it burn it, build it. What counts is what the pleasure means to the man, how he goes about getting it, and what it does to him. That's one side of the ticket, the personal side, the best, but this is Hatteras, and there's another side, and on that side size counts, wakes the sleepyheads right up, becomes everybody's business, and like the old-timers say, what's everybody's business is nobody's business.

This lead went through at least one more full draft before Shacochis came up with the version that was published in *The Next New World*.

A fish story is like any other, never about a fish but always about a man and a place. I wouldn't even mention it if I thought everybody knew. When you cut down to the bone of the matter, a fish is just Pleasure with a capital P. Rule of thumb—the bigger the fish, the bigger the pleasure. That's one side of the coin of fishing, the personal best and finest, but this is Hatteras, and there's that other side. On the Outer Banks of North Carolina, you can't pitch a rock in the air in the morning without rock-throwing becoming widespread ruthless competition by the time the sun goes down over Pamlico Sound, and that is because we go to sea for our living, and because commercial fishermen think they are God's own image of male perfection. I've seen it go on all my life here on the coast, each generation afflicted with the same desire to lord, bully, and triumph; doesn't even matter where they come from once they're here, north or south or bumbled in from Ohio and beyond like Willie Striker. So that's the other side, where size counts, wakes the sleepyheads right up, subdues the swollen-head gang, and becomes everybody's business.

We saw the boats off that morning like we always do, and near an hour later Mrs. Mitty Terbill came in the marina store to post a sign she had made, a little gray cardboard square she had scissored from the back of a cereal box. It said: LOST DOG. YORKSHIRE TERRIER. NAME—PRINCE ED, MY SOLE COMPANION. REWARD, and then a number to reach her at.

Here is Shacochis's "final" version as it appeared in *Outer Banks Magazine*.

Squirrelly's Grouper

BOB SHACOCHIS

I'll say straight out: Here on Cape Hatteras, on the Outer Banks of North Carolina, we are far off the flow of civilized currents, distant from man-made horizons and modern complications of life. It's no mystery to us that down through the wind-blown years, we have been haven to all manner of scoundrel, every stripe of ruffian, desperado, and holy terror you'd care to name. Edward Teach, whom most called Blackbeard, was one you'd know, but there were plenty others drifted over from the world to shelter from the law, murderers and smugglers, embezzlers and robbers, some who walked the beach in shiny shoes. Willie Striker had a past, too, but none would ever have known it if he hadn't gone to sea for a living and hooked his grouper, because commercial fishermen think they are God's own image of male perfection, a swollen-head gang afflicted with the desire to lord, bully, and triumph when they think they can get away with it. I'll say also that a fish story is like any other, never about a fish but always about a man and a place. I wouldn't even mention it if I thought everybody knew.

We saw the boats off that morning like we always do, and near an hour later Mrs. Mitty Terbill came in the marina store to post a sign she had made, a little gray cardboard square she had scissored from the back of a cereal box.

It said: LOST DOG. YORKSHIRE TERRIER. NAME—PRINCE ED, MY SOLE COMPANION. REWARD, and then a number to reach her at.

"What's the reward, Mitty?" I asked. It was five dollars, which is about right for a Yorkie, measured by appeal per pound. Mitty Terbill is not an upright-standing woman, but then considerable woe has befallen her and keeps her squashed into her pumpkin self, allowing for only brief religious ascension. She spent that much plus tax on a twelve-pack and trudged back out the door, foot-heavy in her fishwife's boots, going back to her empty house on the beach to sit by the phone. Well, this story's not about the widow Terbill, though plenty of stories are since she lost her old man and her dope-pirate offspring two Januarys ago when they ran into weather off Cape May, up there flounder fishing I believe it was. That's just how I remember the day settling down after the dawn rush, with Mitty coming in, some of the fellows cracking jokes about how one of the boys must have mistook Prince Ed for bait and gone out for shark, and although Mitty likes her opinions to be known and gets the last word in on most events, let me please go on.

Life is slack at a marina between the time the boats go out early and vacationers get burnt off the beach about noon and come round to browse; then in the afternoons all hell breaks when the boats return. Anyway, after Mitty stopped in, Junior left to pull crab pots; Buddy said he's driving out to Cape Point to see if the red drum are in on the shoals with the tide change; Vickilee took a biscuit breakfast over to her cousins at the firehouse; Albert went down to the Coast Guard station to ingratiate himself to uniformed men; Brainless was out at the pumps refueling his uncle's trawler so he could get back to the shrimp wars, which left just me, my manager Emory Plum, and my two sacked-out Bay Retrievers in the place when I hear what might be an emergency broadcast on the citizen's band, because it's old grouch Striker calling J.B. on channel seventeen. Willie Striker has been one to spurn the advancement of radio and the charity of fellow captains, not like the other jackers out there bounced wave to wave on the ocean. They yammer the livelong day, going on like a team of evangelical auctioneers about where the fish aren't to be found, lying about how they barely filled a hundred-pound box, complaining how there's too many boats these days on the Banks and too many Yankees on land, in a rage because the boys up in Manteo are fetching a nickel more for yellowfin, and who messed with who, and who's been reborn in Christ, and who knows that college girl's name from Rodanthe, and who's going to get theirs if they don't watch it. Willie Striker has something to say himself, but you wouldn't find him reaching out. He kept to himself and preferred to talk that way, to himself, unless he had a word for his wife, Issabell. Keeping to himself was no accident, and I'll tell you why if you just hold on.

J.B.J.B. . . . *come in, Tarbaby,* I hear, and even though an individual's voice coming through the squawk box fizzes like buggy tires on a flooded road, you know it's Willie Striker transmitting because his words had the added weight of an accent, nothing much, just a low spin or bite on some words. Like mullet, Willie Striker would say, *maul-it*.

Tarbaby Tarbaby . . . come in. That was the name of J.B.'s workboat.

I was restocking baits, ballyhoo and chum, my head bent into the freezer locker, and Emory, he was back behind the counter studying delinquent accounts. "Turn her up a bit there, Emory," I told him, "if you please."

He didn't need to look to do it, he's done it so many times. He just reached behind and spun the dial to volume nine, put a hailstorm and a fifty-knot blow between us and the boats. "Well, who's that we're listening to?" Emory yelled out. "That's not our Mr. Squirrel, is it?"

Some twenty-five years it'd been I guess that Willie Striker had lived among us, married Issabell Preddy, one of our own, came south it was said sick and tired of Dayton and a factory job, and from the day he showed his jumpy self at Old Christmas in Salvo, folks called Striker Squirrelly. If you've seen his picture in the paper, you might think you know why. Squirrelly's got a small shrewd but skittish face with darting, then locking, eyes, a chin that never grew, some skinny teeth right out in the front of his mouth, and his upper lip was short, tight, some called it a sneer. The top of his head was ball-round and bald up to the crown, then silver hair spread smooth like fur. But like any good made-up name that fits and stays, there was more to it than manner of appearance.

Way-of-life on Hatteras Island has long been settled, that's just the way it is. A couple dozen families like mine, we lived together close back to Indian times, wreckers and victims of wrecks, freebooters and lifesavers, outcasts and hermits, beachcombers and pound netters and cargo ferrymen, scoundrels and tired saintly women, until they put the bridge across Oregon Inlet not long after Willie moved down. Outsiders meant complications to us one way or another; the truth is we don't take to them very well—which used to have significance but doesn't anymore, not since the herd stampeded in the last ten years to buy up the dunes and then bulldoze the aquifer. That's the island mascot these days, the yellow bulldozer, and the Park Service rules the beach like communists. That's one thing, but the fact is Willie Striker wouldn't care and never did if a Midgett or a Burrus or a Foster ever said, "Fine day, iddn't Skipper" to him or not. He wasn't that type of man, and we weren't that type of community to look twice at anything unless it had our blood and our history, but Issabell Preddy was the type of woman inwardly endeared to signs of acceptance, which you could say was the result of having a drunkard father and a drunkard mother. Issabell and her brothers went to live with their Aunt Betty in Salvo until they finished school, but Betty had seven children of her own, a husband who wouldn't get off the water, and no time to love them all. I went to school with Issabell and have always known her to be sweet in a motionless way, and not the first on anybody's list. She had one eye floating and purblind from when her daddy socked her when she was small, wore hand-down boys' clothes or sack dresses on Sundays, her fuzzy red hair always had a chewed-on aspect about it, and her skin was such thin milk you never saw her outside all summer unless she was swaddled like an Arab. Back then something inside Issabell made her afraid of a good time, which made her the only Preddy in existence with a docile nature, and the truth is a quiet girl who is no beauty is like a ghost ship or a desert isle to the eyes of young and active men: No matter how curious you are you don't want to be stuck on it.

One by one Issabell's brothers quit school and took off, joined the Navy and the Merchant Marines, and Issabell herself moved back down the road to Hatteras, rented the apartment above the fishhouse and got employed packing trout, prospered modestly on the modest fringe, didn't hide herself exactly but wouldn't so much as sneeze in company without written invitation. The charter fleet was something new back then; there were not-un-friendly rumors that Issabell upon occasion would entertain a first mate or two during the season. These rumors were not so bad for her reputation as you might expect in a Christian village except none of us really believed them, and it would have come as no surprise if sooner or later one of our crowd got around to marrying Issabell Preddy, but the island had temporarily run out of eligible men by the time Terry Newman met Willie Striker in a Norfolk juke joint and brought him back with him for Old Christmas in Salvo. Old Christmas all the long-time families come together to feast by day, to game and make music and catch up with the facts of the year; by night we loudly take issue with one another and drink like only folks in a dry county can, and of course we fistfight—brother and cousin and father and godfather and grandfather and in-law; the whole bunch—and kid about it for three hundred sixty-five days until we can do it again. A few years back a lady from a city magazine came to write about our Old Christmas, called it culture, I told her call it what the hell you want but it's still just a bust-loose party, gal, and when the night fell and fur started to fly she jumped up on a table above the ruckus, took flashbulb pictures, and asked me afterward why Hatterasmen liked to brawl. I told her there's nothing to explain, we all think we're twelve years old, and if it was real fighting somebody'd be dead. Anyway, Terry Newman showed up that January with his twenty-four-hour buddy, Willie Striker, and it was the year that Terry's brother Bull Newman decided Terry was good-for-nothing and needed to be taught a lesson. One minute Bull had his arm across Terry's shoulder laughing, and the next he had knocked him down and out cold, continued through the room rapping heads of all he perceived to have exercised bad influence on his younger brother, including the skull of his own daddy, until he arrived at Willie, nursing a bottle of beer off by himself at a table in the corner. Bull was a huge man but dim; Willie Striker was no young buck but was given to juvenile movements the eye couldn't properly follow—twitches and shoulder jerks and sudden frightening turns—so even as he sat there holding his beer he seemed capable of attack. Bull towered over him with an unsure expression, a dog-like concern, trying to determine who this person was and if he was someone he held an identifiable grudge against or someone he was going to hit on principle alone, and when he swung Willie dodged and lunged, laid Bull's nose flat with his beer bottle without breaking the glass, threw open the window at his back, and scrambled out.

"That'll teach you to go messin' with squirrels," someone said to Bull.

No one saw Willie Striker again until a week later, raking scallops in the Sound with Issabell Preddy. The way I heard it was, Willie got to the road that night about the same time Issabell was headed back to Hatteras from her visit with her Aunt Betty, driving a fifty-dollar Ford truck she had bought off Albert James, her Christmas present to herself, and even though Willie was hitching back north, she stopped and he got in anyway and went with her south, neither of them, the story goes, exchanging a word until they passed the lighthouse and got to the village, everything shut down dark and locked up, not a soul in sight of course, and Issabell said to him, so the story goes, that he could sleep in the truck if he wanted, or if he was going to be around for the week he could come upstairs and have the couch for thirty cents a night, or if he had plans to stay longer he could give her bed a try. Willie went the whole route: truck, couch, Issabell Preddy's lonely single bed.

In those days scalloping was women's work, so it was hard to raise any sort of positive opinion about Willie. He was a mainlander, and worse, some brand of foreigner; out there wading in the Sound it appeared he had come to work, but not work seriously, not do man's work; he had moved into Issabell's apartment above the firehouse and burdened her social load with scandal; and he had clobbered Bull Newman, which was all right by itself, but he hadn't held his ground to take licks in kind. He had run away.

The following Old Christmas Willie wedded Issabell Preddy in her Aunt Betty's kitchen, though for her sake I'm ashamed to say the ceremony was not well-attended. She wanted kids, I heard, but there was talk among the wives that Willie Striker had been made unfit for planting seed due to unspecified wounds. For a few years there he went from one boat to another, close-mouthed and sore-fingered, every captain and crew's back-up boy, and Issabell scalloped and packed fish and picked crabs until they together had saved enough for a down payment on the Sea Eagle. Since that day he had bottom-fished by himself, on the reefs and sunken wrecks, at the edge of the Stream or off the shoals, got himself electric reels a couple of years ago, wouldn't drop a line until the fleet was out of sight, wouldn't share Loran numbers, hoarded whatever fell into his hands so he wouldn't have to borrow when the fish weren't there, growled to himself and was all-around gumptious, a squirrel-hearted stand-alone, forever on guard against invasion of self, and in that sense he ended up where he belonged, maybe, because nobody interfered with Willie Striker, we let him be, and as far as I know no one had the gall to look him straight in his jumpy eyes and call him Squirrelly, though he knew that's what he was called behind his back. Whatever world Willie had fallen from at mid-life, he wound up in the right place with the right woman to bury it. Maybe he had fallen from a great height, and if the plunge made him a loon, it also made him a man of uncommon independence, and so in our minds he was not fully without virtue.

Squirrelly finally connected with J.B., who bottom-fished as well, not possessing the craft or the personal etiquette—that is to say, willingness to baby the drunken or fish-crazed rich—to charter out for sport. Likewise, he was a mainlander, a West Virginian with a fancy for the rough peace of the sea, and for these reasons Willie, I suspect, was not loathe to chance his debt. They switched radio channels to twenty-two in order to gain privacy and I asked Emory to follow them over. Up at their trailer in Trent, Issabell had been listening in too; hers was the first voice we found when we transferred. She questioned Willie about what was wrong; he asked her to pipe down.

"What you need there, *Sea Eagle?*" J.B. squawked. After a moment Willie came back on; hard to tell through the greasy sizzle, but he sounded apologetic.

"*Tarbaby,*" he said, "(something . . . something) . . . require assistance. Can you . . . ?"

"What's he say was the trouble?" Emory bellowed. "I couldn't tell, could you?"

"Roger, *Sea Eagle,*" J.B. answered. "Broke down, are you, Captain?" Willie failed to respond, though J.B. assumed he did. "I didn't get that, Willie," he said. "Where the hell are you? Gimme your numbers and I'll come rescue your sorry ass."

"Negative," we heard Willie say. "Report your numbers and I come to you."

So that's how it went, Striker ignoring his Issabell's pleas to divulge the nature of his trouble, J.B. staying at location while *Sea Eagle* slowly motored through three-foot seas to find him while we sat around the marina, trying to figure out what it meant. Squirrelly had a problem, but it didn't seem to be with his boat; he needed help, but he would come to it rather than have it go to him. J.B. was about twenty miles out southeast of the shoals, tile fishing; likely Willie was farther east, sitting over one of his secret spots, a hundred fathoms at the brink of the continental shelf. We heard no further radio contact except once, more than an hour later, when Striker advised J.B. he had the *Tarbaby* in sight and would come up on his starboard side. Back at the marina the Parcel Service man lugged in eighteen cartons of merchandise and we were fairly occupied. Then past twelve J.B. called into us, jigging the news.

"Diamond Shoals Marina," J.B. crowed, "y'all come in. Dillon," he said to me, "better clean up things around there and get ready for a fuss. Squirrelly caught himself a fat bejesus."

I picked up the transmitter and asked for more information but J.B. declined, claiming he would not be responsible for spoiling the suspense. I slid over to channel twenty-two, waited for Issabell to stop badgering Willie, and asked him what was up.

"*Up?*" he spit into the microphone. "I tell you *up!* Up come victory, by God. Up come justice . . . Going to seventeen," he muttered, and I flipped channels to hear him advertise his fortune to a wider audience. "Ya-ha-ha," we all heard him cackle. "Cover your goddamn eyes, sons of bitches. Hang your heads. Age of Squirrelly has come . . ."

We had never heard him express himself at such provocative length.

The island's like one small room of gossip-starved biddys when something like this happens. People commenced telephoning the marina, took no more than five minutes for the noise to travel sixty miles, south to north to Nags Head, then jump Albemarle Sound to Manteo and the mainland. "Don't know a thing more than you," Emory told each and every caller. "Best get down here to see for yourself when he comes in around three." I took a handcart to the stockroom and loaded the coolers with Coca-Cola and beer.

Now, there are three types of beast brought in to the dock. First kind are useless except as a sight to see, tourists gather round and take snapshots, Miss Luelle brings her day-care kids down to pee their pants, old stories of similar beasts caught or seen are told once more, then when the beast gets rank somebody kicks it back into the water and that's that. I'm talking sharks or anything big, boney, red-meated, and weird. Second style of beast is your sport beast: marlins, tuna, wahoo, barracuda, etcetera, but primarily billfish, the stallions of wide-open blue water. This class of beast prompts tourists to sign up for the Stream, but Miss Luelle and her children stay home, as do the rest of the locals unless a record's shattered, because these are regular beasts on the Outer Banks, at least for a few more years until they are gone forever, and after the captain and the angler quit swaggering around thinking they're movie stars, I send Brainless out to cut down that poor dead and stinking hero-fish and tow it into the Sound for the crabs and eels, and that's that too. The third style of beast is kidnapped from the bottom of the world and is worth a ransom, and that's what Striker would have. He wouldn't bring anything in for its freak value, he was the last man on earth to recognize sport—all he did day in day out was labor for a living, like most but not all of us out here—so I figured he hooked himself a windfall beast destined for finer restaurants, he'd weigh it and set it on ice for brief display, then haul it to the fishhouse, exchange beast for cash and steer home to Issabell for supper and his bottle of beer, go to bed and rise before dawn and be down here at his slip getting rigged, then on the water before the sun was up.

First in was J.B. on the *Tarbaby,* which is a Wanchese boat and faster than most; J.B. likes to steam up a wake anyway, put spray in the air. Already the multitudes converged in the parking lot and out on the porch, elbowing in to the store. Vickilee came back across the street with her cousins from the fishhouse to start her second shift; Buddy led a caravan of four-wheelers down the beach from Cape Point. Packers and pickers and shuckers shuffled drag-ass from inside the fishhouse, gas station geniuses sauntered over from the garage. Coast Guard swabs drove up in a van, the girls from Bubba's Barbe-cue, Barris from Scales and Tales, Geegee from the video rental, Cornbread from the surf shop, Sheriff Spine, Sam and Maggie from over at the deli, the tellers from the bank, Daddy Wiss leading a pack of skeptical elders, and tourists galore drawn by the scent of photo opportunity and fish history. Be-fore three all Hatteras had closed and come down, appetites inflamed, won-dering what the devil Willie Striker was bringing in from the ocean floor that was so humongous he had to defy his own personal code and ask for help.

J.B.'s mate tossed a bowline to Brainless; took him in the face as usual because the poor boy can't catch. J.B. stepped ashore in his yellow oilskins and scale-smeared boots, saying, "I can't take credit for anything, but damn if I can't tell my grandkids I was there to lend a hand." Without further elaboration he walked directly up the steps to the store, went to the glass cooler, and purchased one of the bottles of French champagne we stock for high-rollers and unequaled luck. Paid twenty-eight dollars, and he bought a case of ice-colds too for his crew, went back out to the *Tarbaby* with it under his arm, going to clean tile fish.

"Well, come on, J.B.," the crowd begged, making way for him, "tell us what old Squirrelly yanked from the deep." But J.B. knew the game, he knew fishing by now and what it was about when it wasn't about paying rent, and kept his mouth glued shut, grinning up at the throng from the deck, all hillbilly charm, as he flung guts to the pelicans.

Someone shouted, *He just come through the inlet!* The crowd buzzed. Some-one else said, *I heard tell it's only a mako shark.* Another shouted, *I heard it was a tiger!* Then, *No sir, a great white's what I hear. Hell it is,* said another boy, *it's a dang big tuttie. Them's illegal,* says his friend, *take your butt right to jail.* One of our more God-fearing citizens maneuvered to take advantage of the gathering. I wasn't going to have that. I stepped back off the porch and switched on the public address system. *Jerry Stubbs,* I announced in the lot, *this ain't Sunday and this property you're on ain't church. I don't want to see nobody speaking in tongues and rolling on the asphalt out there,* I said. *This is a nonreligious, nondenominational event.* You have to take things in hand before they twist out of control, and I run the business on a family standard.

Here he comes now, someone hollered. We all craned our necks to look as the *Sea Eagle* rounded the buoy into harbor waters and a rebel cheer was given. Cars parked in the street, fouling traffic. The rescue squad came with lights flashing for a fainted woman. I went and got my binoculars from under the counter and muscled back out among the porch rats to the rail, focused in as Willie throttled down at the bend in the cut. I could see through the glasses that this old man without kindness or neighborly acts, who neither gave nor received, had the look of newfound leverage to the set of his jaw. You just can't tell what a prize fish is going to do to the insides of a man, the way it will turn on the bulb over his head and shape how he wants himself seen.

I went back inside to help Emory at the register. Issabell Striker was in there, arguing politely with Vickilee, who threw up her hands. Emory shot me a dirty look. Issabell was being very serious—not upset, exactly, just serious. "Mister Aldie," she declared, "you must make everyone go away."

"No problem, Mizz Striker," I said, and grabbed the microphone to the P.A. *Y'all go home now, get,* I said. I shrugged my shoulders and looked at this awkward lonesome woman, her floppy straw hat wrapped with a lime-green scarf to shade her delicate face, swoops of frosty strawberry hair poking out, her skin unpainted and pinkish, that loose eye drifting, and Issabell just not familiar enough with people to be used to making sense. "Didn't work."

Her expression was firm in innocence; she had her mind set on results but little idea how to influence an outcome. "Issabell," I said to her, "what's wrong, hon?" The thought that she might have to assert herself against the many made her weak, but finally it came out. She had spent the last hours calling television stations. When she came down to the water and saw the traffic tie-up and gobs of people, her worry was that the reporter men and cameramen wouldn't get through, and she wanted them to get through with all her sheltered heart, for Willie's sake, so he could get the recognition he deserved, which he couldn't get any other way on earth, given the nature of Hatteras and the nature of her husband.

Issabell had changed some but not much in all the years she had been paired with Squirrelly in a plain but honest life. She still held herself apart, but not as far. Not because she believed herself better; it never crossed our minds to think so. Her brothers had all turned out bad, and I believe she felt the pull of a family deficiency that would sweep her away were she not on guard.

Her hands had curled up from working at the fishhouse. Striker brought her a set of Jack Russell terriers and she began to breed them for sale, and on weekends during the season she'd have a little roadside flea market out in front of their place, and then of course there was being wife to a waterman, but what I'm saying is she had spare time and she used it for the quiet good of others, baking for the church, attending environmental meetings even though she sat in the back of the school auditorium and never spoke a word, babysitting for kids when someone died. Once I even saw her dance when Buddy's daughter got married, but it wasn't with Willie she danced because Willie went to sea or Willie stayed home, and that was that. I don't think she ever pushed him; she knew how things were. The only difference between the two of them was that she had an ever-strengthening ray of faith that convinced her that someday life would change and she'd fit in right; Willie had faith that the life he'd found in Hatteras was set in concrete. The man was providing, you know, just providing, bending his spine and risking his neck to pay bills the way he knew how, and all he asked in return was for folks to let him be. All right, I say, but if he didn't want excitement he should've reconsidered before he chose the life of a waterman and flirted with the beauty of the unknown, as we have it here.

"Mizz Striker, don't worry," I comforted the woman. Besides, a big fish is about the best advertisement a marina can have. "Any TV people come round here, I'll make it my business they get what they want."

"Every man needs a little attention now and then," she said, but her own opinion made her shy. She lowered her eyes and blushed, tender soul. "Is that not right, Dillon?" she questioned. "If he's done something to make us all proud?"

Out on the bayside window we could watch the *Sea Eagle* angling to dock, come alongside the block and tackle hoist, the mob pressing forward to gape in the stern, children riding high on their daddies' shoulders. Willie stood in the wheelhouse easing her in, his face enclosed by the bill of his cap and sunglasses, and when he shut down the engines I saw his head jerk around, a smile of satisfaction form and vanish. He pinched his nose with his left hand and batted the air with the other, surveying the army of folks, then he looked up toward me and his wife. You could read his lips saying *Phooey*.

"What in tarnation did he catch anyway?" I said, nudging Issabell.

"All he told me was 'a big one,'" she admitted.

One of the porch layabouts had clambered down dockside and back, bursting through the screen door with a report. "I only got close enough to see its tail," he hooted.

"*What in the devil is it?*" Emory said. "I'm tired of waitin' to find out."

"Warsaw grouper," said the porch rat. "Size of an Oldsmobile, I'm told."

"Record buster, is she?"

"Does a whale have tits?" said the rat. "'Scuse me, Mizz Striker."

You can't buy publicity like that for an outfit or even an entire state, and taking the record on a grouper is enough to make the angler a famous and well-thought-of man. I looked back out the bayside window. Squirrelly was above the congregation on the lid of his fishbox, J.B. next to him. Squirrelly had his arms outstretched like Preacher exhorting his flock. J.B. had whisked off the old man's cap. Willie's tongue was hanging out, lapping at a baptism of foamy champagne.

"Old Squirrel come out of his nest," Emory remarked. I fixed him with a sour look for speaking that way in front of Issabell. "Old Squirrelly's on top of the world."

Issabell's pale eyes glistened. "Squirrelly," she repeated, strangely pleased. "That's what y'all call Willie isn't it." She took for herself a deep and surprising breath of gratitude. "I just think it's so nice of y'all to give him a pet name like that."

The crowd multiplied; a state trooper came to try to clear a lane on Highway Twelve. At intervals boats from the charter fleet arrived back from the Gulf Stream, captains and crew saluting Squirrelly from the bridge. Issabell went down to be with her champion. Emory and I and Vickilee had all we could do to handle customers, sold out of camera film in nothing flat, moved thirty-eight cases of beer mostly by the can. I figured it was time I went down and congratulated Willie, verify if he had made himself newsworthy or was just being a stinker. First thing though, I placed a call to Fort Lauderdale and got educated on the state, national, and world records for said variety of beast so at least there'd be one of us on the dock knew what he was talking about.

To avoid the crowd I untied my outboard runabout over at the top of the slips and puttered down the harbor, tied up on the stern of the *Sea Eagle*, and J.B. gave me a hand aboard. For the first time I saw that awesome fish, had to hike over it in fact. Let me just say this: you live on the Outer Banks all your life and you're destined to have your run-ins with leviathans, you're bound to see things and be called on to believe things that others elsewhere wouldn't, wonders that are in a class by themselves, gruesome creatures, underwater shocks and marvels, fearsome life forms, finned shapes vicious as jaguars, quick and pretty as racehorses, sleek as guided missiles and exploding with power, and the more damn sights you see the more you never know what to expect next. Only a dead man would take what's below the surface for granted, and so when I looked upon Squirrelly's grouper I confess my legs lost strength and my eyes bugged, it was as though Preacher had taken grip on my thoughts, and I said to myself, *Monster and miracle greater than me, darkness which may be felt.*

J.B. revered the beast. "Fattest damn unprecedented jumbo specimen of Mongolian sea pig known to man," he said (he could be an eloquent fool). "St. Gompus, king of terrors, immortal till this day." He leaned into me, whispering, fairly snockered by now, which was proper for the occasion. "Dillon," he confided, "don't think I'm queer." He wanted to crawl down the beast's throat and see what it felt like inside, have his picture taken with his tootsies sticking out the maw.

"Stay out of the fish," I warned J.B. "I don't have insurance for that sort of stunt."

A big fish is naturally a source of crude and pagan inspirations. I knew what J.B. had in mind: get my marina photographer to snap his picture being swallowed and make a bundle selling copies, print the image on T-shirts and posters too. He could snuggle in there, no doubt, take his wife and three kids with him, there was room. The fish had a mouth wide as a bicycle tire, with lips as black and hard, and you could look past the rigid shovel of tongue in as far as the puckered folds of the gullet, the red spikey scythes of gills, and shudder at the notion of being suckered through that portal, wolfed down in one screaming piece into the dungeon of its gut. Don't for a minute think it hasn't happened before.

Willie wasn't in sight, I noticed. I asked J.B. where the old man had put himself, it being high time to hang the beast and weigh it, see where we stood on the record, have the photographer take pictures, let tourists view the creature so we could move traffic and give the other fishermen space to go about their daily business, lay the beast on ice while Willie planned what he wanted to do.

"He's up there in the cuddy cabin with Issabell," J.B. said, nodding side-ways. "Something's gotten into him, don't ask me what." Vacationers shouted inquiries our way; J.B. squared his shoulders to respond to an impru-dent gal in a string bikini. "Well ma'am," he bragged, "this kind of fish is a hippocampus grumpus. People round here call 'em *wads*. This one's a damn big wad, iddn't it." As I walked forward I heard her ask if she could step aboard and touch it, and there was beast worship in her voice.

I opened the door to the wheelhouse; ahead past the step-down there was Willie Striker, his scrawny behind on a five-gallon bucket, the salty bill of his cap tugged down to the radish of his pug nose, hunched elbows on thread-bare knees, with a pint of mint schnapps clutched in his hands. If you've seen a man who's been skunked seven days running and towed back to port by his worst enemy, you know how Willie looked when I found him in there. Issabell was scooched on the gallery bench, her hands in front of her on the chart. She was baffled and cheerless, casting glances at Willie but maybe afraid to confront him, at least in front of me, and she played nervously with her hair where it stuck out under her hat, twisting it back and forth with her crooked fingers.

I tried to lighten the atmosphere of domestic strife. "You Strikers're going to have to hold down the celebration," I teased. "People been calling up about you two disturbing the peace."

"He don't want credit, Dillon," Issabell said in guilty exasperation. "A cloud's passed over the man's golden moment in the sun."

Here was a change of heart for which I was not prepared. "Willie," I began, but stopped. You have to allow a man's differences and I was about to tell him he was acting backwards. He cocked his chin to look up at me from under his cap, had his sunglasses off and the skin around his eyes was branded with a raccoon's mask of whiteness, and I'm telling you there was such a blast of ardent if not furious pride in his expression right then, and the chill of so much bitterness trapped in his mouth, it was something new and profound for me, to be in the presence of a fellow so deeply filled with hate for his life, and I saw there was no truth guiding his nature, I saw there was only will.

His face contorted and hardened with pitiless humor; he understood my revelation and mocked my concern, made an ogreish laugh in his throat and nodded like, *All right, my friend, so now you are in the presence of my secret, but since you're dumb as a jar of dirt, what does it matter,* and he passed his bottle of bohunk lightning to me. Say I was confused. Then he mooned over to Issabell and eased off, he took back the pint, rinsed the taste of undeserved years of hardship from his mouth with peppermint, and jerked his thumb aft.

"Where I come from," Willie said, rubbing the silvery stubble on his cheek, "we let them go when they are like that one." His face cracked into a net of shallow lines; he let a smile rise just so far and then refused it. "Too small." (*Smull* is how he said it.) "Not worth so much troubles."

I thought what the hell, let him be what he is, reached over and clapped him on the back, feeling the spareness of his frame underneath my palm. "Step on out of here now, Captain," I said. "Time for that beast to be strung up and made official."

"Willie," coaxed Issabell with a surge of hope, "folks want to shake your hand." He was unmoved by this thought. "It might mean nothing to you," she said, "but it makes a difference to me."

Striker didn't budge except to relight his meerschaum pipe and bite down stubbornly on its stem between packed front teeth. On the insides of his hands were welts and fresh slices where nylon line had cut, scars and streaks of old burns, calluses like globs of old varnish, boil-like infections from slime poison.

"What's the matter, honey?" Issabell persisted. "Tell me, Willie, because it hurts to know you can't look your own happiness in the face. We've both been like that far too long." She tried to smile but only made herself look desperate. "I wish," she said, "I wish . . ." Issabell faltered but then went on. "You know what I wish, Willie, I wish I knew you when you were young."

Issabell jumped up, brushed by me, and out back into the sunshine and the crowd. Willie just said he was staying put for a while, that he had a cramp in his leg and an old man's backache. He had let the fish exhilarate and transform him out alone on the water, and for that one brief moment when J.B. poured the victor's juice on his head, but the pleasure was gone, killed, in my opinion, by distaste for society, such as we were.

"Now she will despise me," Willie said suddenly, and I turned to leave.

*   *   *

J.B., me, and Brainless rigged the block and tackle and hoisted the beast to the scales. The crowd saw first the mouth rising over the gunnel like upturned jaws on a steam shovel, fixed to sink into sky. People roared when they saw the grisly, bulging eyeball, dead as glass but still gleaming with black wild mysteries. Its gill plates, the size of trash-can lids, were gashed with white scars, its pectoral fins like elephant ears, its back protected by a hedge of wicked spikes, and it smelled to me in my imagination like the inside of a castle in a cold and rainy land. You could hear all the camera shutters clicking, like a bushel of live crabs. When I started fidgeting with the counterweights, the whole place hushed, and out of the corner of my eye I could see Striker come to stand in his wheelhouse window looking on, the lines in his face all turned to the clenched pipe. He was in there percolating with vinegar and stubbornness and desire, you know, and I thought, What is it, you old bastard, is it the fish, or have you decided Issabell is worth the gamble? The grouper balanced. I wiped sweat from my brow and double-checked the numbers. Squirrelly had it all right, broke the state mark by more than two hundred pounds, the world by twenty-six pounds seven ounces. I looked over at him there in the wheelhouse, and brother he knew.

I made the announcement, people covered their ears while the fleet blasted air horns. A group of college boys mistook J.B. for the angler and attempted to raise him to their shoulders. A tape recorder was poked in his face; I saw Issabell push it away. Willie stepped out of the wheelhouse then and came ashore to assume command.

You might reasonably suspect that it was a matter of honor, that Willie was obliged to make us acknowledge that after twenty-five years on the Outer Banks his dues were paid, and furthermore obliged to let his wife, Issabell, share the blessing of public affections so the poor woman might for once experience the joy of popularity, just as she was quick to jump at the misery of leading a hidden life, so ready to identify with the isolation of the unwanted that night of Old Christmas all those years ago. Willie knew who he was but maybe he didn't know Issabell so well after all, didn't see she was still not at home in her life the way he was, and now she was asking him to take a step forward into the light, then one step over so she could squeeze next to him. You just can't figure bottom dwellers.

Anyway, I swear no man I am familiar with has ever been more vain about achievement, or mishandled the trickier rewards of success, than Willie after he climbed off the *Sea Eagle*. The crowd and the sun and the glamor went straight to his head and resulted in a boom of self-importance until we were all fed up with him. He came without a word to stand beside the fish as if it were a private place. At first he was wary and grave, then annoyingly humble as more and more glory fell his way, then a bit coy I'd say, and then Bull Newman plowed through the crowd, stooped down as if to tackle Willie but instead wrapped his arms around Willie's knees and lifted him up above our heads so that together like that they matched the length of the fish. The applause rallied from dockside to highway.

"I make all you no-goodniks famous today," Willie proclaimed, crooking his wiry arms like a body builder, showing off. Bull lowered him back down.

"Looks like you ran into some luck there, Squirrelly," Bull conceded.

"You will call me Mister Squirrel."

"Purty fish, Mister Squirrel."

"You are jealous."

"Naw," Bull drawled, "I've had my share of the big ones."

"So tell me, how many world records you have."

Bull's nostrils flared. "Records are made to be broken, *Mister* Squirrel," he said, grinding molars.

"Yah, yah." Willie's accent became heavier and clipped as he spoke. "Und so is noses."

Bull's wife pulled him out of there by the back of his pants. Willie strutted on bow legs and posed for picture takers. His old adversaries came forward to offer praise—Ootsie Pickering, Dave Johnson, Milford Lee, all the old alcoholic captains who in years gone by had worked Willie like a slave. They proposed to buy him a beer, come aboard their vessels for a toast of whiskey, come round the house for a game of cards, and Willie had his most fun yet acting like he couldn't quite recall their names, asking if they were from around here or Johnny-come-latelys, and I changed my mind about Willie hating himself so much since it was clear it was us he hated more. Leonard Purse, the owner of the fishhouse, was unable to approach closer than three-deep to Willie; he waved and yessirred until he caught Squirrelly's eye and an impossible negotiation ensued. Both spoke merrily enough but with an icy twinkle in their eyes.

"Purty fish, Willie. How much that monster weigh?"

"Eight dollars," Willie said, a forthright suggestion of an outrageous price per pound.

"Money like that would ruin your white-trash life. Give you a dollar ten as she hangs."

"Nine dollars," Willie said, crazy, elated.

"Dollar fifteen."

"You are a schwine."

"Meat's likely to be veined with gristle on a beast that size."

"I will kill you in your schleep."

"Heh-heh-heh. Must have made you sick to ask J.B. for help."

"Ha-ha! Too bad you are chicken of der wadder, or maybe I could ask you."

Vickilee fought her way out of the store to inform me that the phone had been ringing off the hook. TV people from New Bern and Raleigh, Greenville and Norfolk were scheduled by her one after the other for the morning.

Newspaper people had already arrived from up the coast; she and Emory had talked to them and they were waiting for the crowd to loosen up before they tried to push through to us, and one of them had phoned a syndicate, so the news had gone out on the wire, which meant big-city coverage from up north, and of course all the sport magazines said they'd try to send somebody down, and make sure the fish stayed intact. Also, scientists were coming from the marine research center in Wilmington, and professors from Duke hoped they could drive out tomorrow if we would promise to keep the fish in one piece until they got here. The beer trucks were going to make special deliveries in the morning, the snack man too. Charters were filling up for weeks in advance.

So you see Squirrelly and his grouper were instant industry. The event took on a dimension of its own and Willie embraced his role, knew he was at last scot-free to say what he pleased without limit and play the admiral without making us complain. He sponged up energy off the crowd and let it make him boastful and abrupt, a real nautical character, and folks not from around here loved his arrogance and thought we were all little squirrelly devils. Issabell seemed anxious too, this was not quite how she had envisioned Willie behaving, him telling reporters he was the only man on Hatteras who knew where the big fish were, but she beamed naively and chattered with the other wives and seemed to enjoy herself, even her goofed eye shined with excitement. It was a thrill, maybe her first one of magnitude, and she wasn't going to darken it for herself by being embarrassed.

Willie left the fish suspended until after sun went down, when I finally got him to agree to put it back on the boat and layer it with ice. Its scales had stiffened and dried, its brown- and brownish-green-marbled colors turned flat and chalky. Both he and Issabell remained on the boat that night, receiving a stream of visitors until well past midnight, whooping it up and having a grand time, playing country music on the radio so loud I could hear it word for word in my apartment above the store. I looked out the window once and saw Willie waltzing his wife under one of the security lightpoles, a dog and some kids standing there watching as they carefully spun in circles. I said to myself, That's the ticket, old Squirrel.

Life in Hatteras is generally calm, but Tuesday was carnival day from start to finish. Willie was up at his customary time before dawn, fiddling around the *Sea Eagle* as if it were his intention to go to work. When the fleet started out the harbor though, he and Issabell promenaded across the road for breakfast at the café, and when he got back I helped him winch the fish into the air and like magic we had ourselves a crowd again, families driving down from Nags Head, families who took the ferry from Ocracoke, Willie signing autographs for children, full of coastal authority and lore for the adults, cocky as hell to any fisherman who wandered over. A camera crew pulled up in a van around ten, the rest arrived soon after. What's it feel like to catch a fish so big? they asked. For a second he was hostile, glaring at the microphone, the camera lens, the interviewer with his necktie loosened in the heat. Then he grinned impishly and said, I won't tell you. You broke the world's record, is that right? Maybe, he allowed indifferently and winked over the TV person's shoulder at me and Issabell. When the next crew set up, he more or less hinted he was God Almighty and predicted his record would never be broken. After two more crews finished with him the sun was high; I made him take the fish down, throw a blanket of ice on it. Every few minutes Emory was on the P.A., informing Squirrelly he had a phone call. Vickilee came out and handed Willie a telegram from the governor, commending him for the "catch of the century." I guess the biggest treat for most of us was when the seaplane landed outside the cut, though nobody around here particularly cared for the fellows crammed in there, Fish and Game boys over to authenticate the grouper, so we pulled the fish back out of the boat and secured it to the scales. Hour later Willie took it down again to stick in ice, but not ten minutes after that a truck came by with a load of National Park Rangers wanting to have individual pictures taken with Squirrelly and the grouper, so he hung it back up, then a new wave of sightseers came by mid-afternoon, another wave when the fleet came in at five, so he just let it dangle there on the arm of the hoist, beginning to sag from the amount of euphoric handling and heat, until it was too dark for cameras and that's when he relented to lower it down and we muscled it back to the boat, he took her down past the slips to the fishhouse, to finally sell the beast to Leonard I thought, but no, he collected a fresh half ton of ice. Willie wanted to play with the grouper for still another day.

That's almost all there is to tell if it wasn't for Squirrelly's unsolved past, the youth that Issabell regretted she had missed. On Wednesday he strung the fish up and dropped it down I'd say about a dozen times, the flow of onlookers and congratulators and hangarounds had decreased, Issabell was as animated as a real-estate agent and as girlish as we'd ever seen, but by midday the glow was off. She had been accidentally bumped into the harbor by a fan, was pulled out muddy and slicked with diesel oil, yet still she had discovered the uninhibiting powers of fame and swore that she had been endowed by the presence of the fish with clearer social vision.

By the time Squirrelly did get his grouper over to the fishhouse and they knifed it open, it was all mush inside, not worth a penny. He shipped the skin, the head, and the fins away to a taxidermist in Florida, and I suppose the pieces are all still there, sitting in a box like junk.

Now if you didn't already know, this story winds up with a punch so far out in left field there's just no way you could see it coming, but I can't apologize for that, no more than I could take responsibility for a hurricane. About a week after everything got back to normal down here, and Squirrelly seemed content with memories and retreated back to his habits of seclusion, Brainless came crashing through the screen door, arms and legs flapping, his tongue too twisted with what he was dying to say for us to make any sense of his message.

Emory looked up from his books. I was on the phone to a man wanting a half-day charter to the Stream, arguing with him that there was no such thing as a half-day charter that went out that far. "When's that boy gonna grow up," Emory clucked. He told Brainless to slow down and concentrate on speaking right.

"They're takin' Squirrelly away," Brainless said. He pointed back out the door.

I told the fellow on the line I might call him back if I had something and hung up, went around the counter and outside on the porch, Emory too, everybody came in fact, Vickilee and Buddy and Junior and Albert and two customers in the store. It was a foggy, drizzly morning, the security lamps casting soupy yellow columns of light down to the dock; most of the boats hadn't left yet but their engines were warming up. I don't think the sun had come up yet but you couldn't be sure. The boy was right, a group of men in mackintoshes were putting handcuffs on Squirrelly and taking him off the *Sea Eagle*. The other captains and crews stood around in the mist, watching it happen. The men had on street shoes and looked official, you know, as you'd expect, and they led Willie to a dark sedan with government license plates. One of them opened the rear door for Willie, who kept his head bowed, and sort of helped him, pushed him, into the car. None of us tried to stop it, not one of us spoke up and said, Hey, what's going on? He was still an outsider to us and his life was none of our business. None of us said or even thought of saying, Willie, good-bye. We all just thought: There goes Willie, not in high style. The sedan pulled out of the lot and turned north.

"He's a goddamn natsy!" squealed Brainless, shaking us out of our spell.

"I told you not to cuss around here," Emory said. That was all anybody said.

Squirrelly's true name, the papers told us, was Wilhelm Strechenberger, and they took him back somewhere to Europe or Russia, I believe it was, to stand trial for things he supposedly did during the war. The TV said Squirrelly had been a young guard for the Germans in one of their camps. He had been "long sought" by "authorities," who thought he was living in Ohio. One of his victims who survived said something like Squirrelly was the cruelest individual he had ever met in his entire life.

Boy, oh boy—that's all we could say. Did we believe it? Hell no. Then, little by little, yes, though it seemed far beyond our abilities to know and to understand.

Issabell says it's a case of mistaken identity, although she won't mention

Willie when she comes out in public, and if you ask me I'd say she blames us for her loss of him, as if what he had been all those years ago as well as what he became when he caught the fish—as if that behavior were somehow our fault.

Mitty Terbill was convinced it was Willie who grabbed her Prince Ed for some unspeakable purpose. She's entitled to her opinion, of course, but she shouldn't have expressed it in front of Issabell, who forfeited her reputation as the last and only docile Preddy by stamping the widow Terbill on her foot and breaking one of the old lady's toes. She filed assault charges against Issabell, saying Issabell and Willie were two of a kind. Like Mitty, you might think that Willie Striker being a war criminal explains a lot, you might even think it explains everything, but I have to tell you I don't.

Now that we know the story, or at least think we do, of Willie's past, we still differ about why Willie came off the boat that day to expose himself, to be electronically reproduced all over the land—was it for Issabell or the fish?—and I say I don't know if Willie actually liked fishing, I expect he didn't unless he craved punishing work, and I don't know what he felt about Issabell besides safe, but I do know this: Like many people around here, Willie liked being envied. The Willie we knew was a lot like us, that's why he lasted here when others from the outside didn't, and that's what we saw for ourselves from the time he conked Bull Newman on the nose to the way he abused what he gained when he brought in that beast from the deep and hung it up for all to admire. He was, in his manner, much like us.

We still talk about the grouper all right, but when we do we automatically disconnect that prize fish from Willie—whether that's right or wrong is not for me to say—and we talk about it hanging in the air off the scale reeking a powerful smell of creation, Day One, so to speak, and it sounds like it appeared among us like . . . well, like an immaculate moment in sport. We've been outside things for a long time here on the very edge of the continent, so what I'm saying, maybe, is that we, like Issabell, we're only just discovering what it's like to be part of the world.

Suggestions for Discussion

1. Identify first-draft language—awkward, unclear, or clogged—that Shacochis has taken care of by the final version.

2. How is the tone of the story altered by beginning with a generalization that introduces the narrator, rather than an immediate scene?

3. Which of the published openings do you think most effective, and why?

4. How does the narrator's voice characterize both himself and the community of Cape Hatteras? Is he in any way in conflict with his background?

5. How do dialogue, metaphor, scene, and detail contribute to the theme of "Squirrelly's Grouper"? Is there a phrase in the story that you think sums up the theme?

6. This is "a fish story." How is that label ironic?

RETROSPECT

Pick any story in this book that dissatisfied you. Imagine that you are the editor of a magazine that is going to publish it. What suggestions for revision would you make to the author?

WRITING ASSIGNMENTS

1. If you did assignment 4 or 8 in chapter 2 (the 100-word or page-long short story), rewrite your story, making it at least three times as long, so that the development enriches the action and the characters.

2. Choose any other story you wrote this term; rewrite it, improving it any way you can, but also cutting its original length by at least one quarter.

3. Pick a passage from your journal and use Stephen Dunning's method (page 339) of highlighting "words, phrases, images, 'talk,' mistakes." Cluster and/or freedraft a passage from some of these highlightings. Rewrite the passage. Put it away for a few days. Is it a story? Rewrite it. Put it away. Rewrite it.

4. A class project: Spend about a half-hour in class writing a scene that involves a conflict between two characters. Make a copy of what you write. Take one copy home and rewrite it. Send the other copy home with another class member for him or her to make critical comments and suggestions. Compare your impulses with those of your reader. On the following day, *forgive* your reader. On the day after that, rewrite the passage once more, incorporating any of the reader's suggestions that prove useful.

APPENDIX A

NARRATIVE TECHNIQUES
Workshop Symbol Code

Format

Manuscripts should be double-spaced, with generous margins, on one side of 8½-by 11-inch white paper. If you use a typewriter, it should have a new black ribbon and well-cleaned keys; if a computer, make sure your printout is easily legible. Title and author's name and address (or class identification) should appear on a cover page. Most editors and teachers now accept copies from a copy machine; make sure they're clear. Always keep a copy of your work.

The symbols listed here are a suggested shorthand for identifying common errors in usage and style. A few of the marks are standard copyediting and proofreading symbols.

Usage

sp.   Misspelling.

gram.   Grammar at fault. Consult Strunk's *Elements of Style*, Fowler's *Modern English Usage*, or any good grammar text.

¶   Paragraph. Begin a new one here.

↪   No new paragraph needed.

⌢	Comma needed. Insert one here.
⌿	No comma needed.
p/c	You have used a possessive for a contraction or vice versa. *Its*, *their*, and *your* are possessives. *It's*, *they're*, and *you're* are contractions of *it is*, *they are*, and *you are*. *They're going to take their toll if you're not sure of your usage.*
p/p	Participial phrase at the beginning of a sentence must refer to the grammatical subject. "*Failing to understand this, your prose will read awkwardly,*" means that your prose fails to understand.
s/i	Split infinitives *tend to always read* awkwardly. Try *to immediately correct* it and *to never do* it again.
T	A pointless change of tense. It leaves the reader not knowing *when* he is.
n/s	Not a sentence. Technique okay if effective, otherwise not. Here, not.
tr.	Transpose. This can refer to letters, words, phrases, sentences, whole paragraphs.
#	Insert a space here (between words, paragraphs, etc.).

Style

V	This is definitely vague. Or, you have used a generalization or an abstraction where you need a concrete detail. Specify. See pages 61–68.
A	Use the active voice. If "she was happy" or "she felt happy," she was not nearly as happy as if she laughed, grinned, jumped, or threw her arms around a tree. See pages 68–70.
un.	Unnecessary. Delete.
↕	Compress this passage to half the words for twice the strength. You're writing *long*.

?   Either you are confusing or the reader is confused or both. What do you *really* mean?

awk.   Awkward. This sentence is related to the auk, a thickbodied, short-necked bird without grace. Restyle.

R   Repetition to unintended or undesirable effect.

⌒   Cliché.

m/m   Mixed metaphor. See page 276.

o/w
o/s   Overwritten, overstated, overinsistent. You're straining. Lower
o/i   the key to raise the effect.

conv.   In the exceedingly likely and, one might say, almost inevitable event, in view of your enrollment in this class, that you are not Henry James, the use of convoluted language is considerably less than certain to contribute to the augmenting of your intended effect. Simplify.

coy
pomp.   Coy, pompous, precious, pretentious—all meaning that you are
prec.   enjoying yourself more than the reader is. No reader will forgive
pret.   you.

chron.   Chronology unnecessarily violated. "She sat down after having crossed to the couch." Except for very special effects, let the reader's mind follow events in their order.

d/t   Unnecessary dialogue tag. "'Shut your stupid mouth!' he said angrily." We do not need to be told that he said this angrily. If he said it sweetly, then we would probably need to be told. See pages 135–136.

dial.   Dialect is overwritten. You are probably misspelling too much, so that your character sounds stupid rather than regional. Let the syntax do the work; keep misspellings and grammatical mistakes to a minimum. See pages 134–135.

int.   Author intrusion. You are explaining, judging, or interpreting too much. Show us, and let us understand and judge.

p.v.   You have violated point of view, bouncing from one mind to another in a way the reader is not prepared for. See page 208.

APPENDIX B

SUGGESTIONS
FOR FURTHER READING

Most of the following books (an incomplete list, to be sure) are written by writers for writers; all can be useful to the practicing storyteller.

Aristotle, *The Poetics*. The first extant work of literary criticism, and the essay from which all later criticism derives. There are numerous good translations, of which one of the best (particularly for its full and helpful comments by O. B. Hardison, Jr.), is that by Leon Golden, *Aristotle's Poetics*, Prentice-Hall, 1968.

Atchity, Kenneth. *A Writer's Time*. Norton, 1986. Atchity focuses on the problem every writer complains about most, and offers startling perceptions and helpful directions for finding and apportioning time.

Bernays, Ann, and Pamela Painter. *What if? Writing Exercises for Fiction Writers*. HarperCollins, 1990. Bernays and Painter identify more than seventy-five situations that a writer may face and provide exercises for each; included are student examples and clear descriptions of objectives. Useful and provocative.

Bly, Carol. *The Passionate, Accurate Story*. Milkweed Editions, 1990. A genuine original, this book makes a thoughtful plea for value in writing and writing from your values. It combines the insights of literary technique, therapy, and ethics. Since it is written in the form of interlocking stories, it reads quickly and entertainingly.

Booth, Wayne C. *The Rhetoric of Fiction*. University of Chicago Press, 1961. This is a thorough, brilliant, and difficult discussion of point of view, which well repays the effort of its reading.

Braine, John. *Writing a Novel.* McGraw-Hill, 1975. Braine gives writerly advice very much from the perspective of his own experience, which will not be useful to everyone. But *Writing a Novel* is anecdotal, interesting, and readable.

Brande, Dorothea. *Becoming a Writer.* J. P. Tarcher, 1981. For those who are overmeticulous, or who have a hard time getting to the typewriter, Brande's mind-freeing exercises may be enormously helpful.

Dillard, Annie. *The Writing Life.* Harper and Row, 1989. This stunningly written account of "your day's triviality" touches drudgery itself with luminous significance. Every writer should read it. Also recommended is Dillard's *Living by Fiction.* Harper, 1982.

Edwards, Betty. *Drawing on the Right Side of the Brain.* J. P. Tarcher, 1979. Although it is aimed at the artist rather than the writer, this book offers invaluable help for writers as well, in the ability to think spacially and vividly.

Elbow, Peter. *Writing Without Teachers.* Oxford, 1973. A young classic of creative writing. Elbow is excellent on how to keep going, growing, and cooking when you haven't the goads of teacher and deadline.

Forster, E. M. *Aspects of the Novel.* Harcourt, Brace, Jovanovich, 1956. Forster delivered these Clark Lectures at Trinity College, Cambridge, England, in 1927. They are talkative, informal, and informative; still the best analysis of literature from a writer's point of view. A must.

Gardner, John. *The Art of Fiction: Notes on Craft for Young Writers.* Alfred A. Knopf, 1984. A new classic among books on writing. Gardner's advice is based on his experience as a teacher of creative writing and is addressed to "the serious beginning writer." The book is clear, practical, and a delight to read. Also recommended is Gardner's *Becoming a Novelist.* Harper and Row, 1983.

Gibson, Walker. *Seeing and Writing.* David McKay, 1974. This is a book of exercises in perception, aimed primarily at the writer of essays rather than fiction. But it is nonetheless provocative, fresh, even startling in its suggestions for observing and capturing sense detail—and therefore useful to the fiction writer as well.

Goldberg, Natalie. *Writing Down the Bones.* Shambala, 1986; and *Wild Mind.* Bantam, 1990. Goldberg is the guru of can-do, encouraging the writer with short, pithy, personal, and cheerful cheerings-on.

Guthrie, A. B., Jr. *A Field Guide to Writing Fiction.* HarperCollins, 1991. Advice full of pith and punch from a writer who has made his living at it for forty years.

Hills, Rust. *Writing in General and the Short Story in Particular.* Bantam, 1979. A former literary editor of *Esquire Magazine,* Hills has written a breezy, enjoyable guide to fictional technique with good advice on every page.

Hughes, Elaine Farris. *Writing from the Inner Self.* HarperCollins, 1990. This book imaginatively makes connections between writing and meditation, leading you through exercises that involve awareness of the body, feelings, observations, and memories in order to enrich the imagination.

Knott, William C. *The Craft of Fiction.* Reston (Prentice-Hall), 1973. An excellent practical text with useful exercises.

Madden, David. *Revising Fiction: A Handbook for Fiction Writers.* New American Library, 1988. Although it is too weighty to operate as a handbook, this volume, uniquely devoted to the art of revising, shows the process convincingly and in full. Also useful as a reference tool is Madden's *A Primer of the Novel for Readers and Writers.* Scarecrow Press, 1980.

May, Rollo. *The Courage to Create.* Bantam 1976. A philosophic classic on the subject.

Minot, Stephen. *Three Genres,* 4th ed. Prentice-Hall, 1988. This text covers the writing of poetry, fiction, and drama, so that each is necessarily treated briefly. Nevertheless, Minot is direct and insightful, well worth reading.

Nelson, Victoria. *Writer's Block and How to Use It.* Writer's Digest Books, 1985. Among the new breed of writers' books that use the insights of psychology and therapy, this is exceptionally helpful. Nelson is sensible as well as sensitive. Her suggestions work.

Rico, Gabriele Lusser. *Writing the Natural Way.* J. P. Tarcher, 1983. Describes in full the technique of clustering and offers useful techniques for freeing the imagination.

Sloane, William. *The Craft of Writing,* edited by Julia Sloane. W. W. Norton, 1979. This book was culled posthumously from the notes of one of the great teachers of fiction writing. The advice he gives is solid and memorable, and the reader's only regret is that there isn't more.

Stafford, William. *You Must Revise Your Life.* University of Michigan, 1986. An inspiriting potpourri of poems, essays, and interviews on writing.

Stern, Jerome. *Making Shapely Fiction.* Norton, 1991. A witty, useful guide. Stern illustrates various possible shapes for stories; he includes a cogent list of don't's and discusses the elements of good writing in dictionary form so you can use the book as a handy reference.

Strunk, William C., and E. B. White. *The Elements of Style,* 3rd ed. Macmillan, 1979. Strunk provides the rules for correct usage and vigorous writing in this briefest and most useful of handbooks.

Ziegler, Alan. *The Writing Workshop* (in two volumes). Teachers and Writers Collaborative, 1981 and 1984. The author calls these useful books a "survey course" in writing. They are mainly intended for teachers of writing but can be adapted to use as a self-teaching tool; they're full of interesting practical advice.

Marketing

Of the guides and services offered to writers, three of the most helpful follow.

Associated Writing Programs (Old Dominion University, Norfolk, VA 23508). Those enrolled in the creative writing program of a college or university that is a member of AWP are automatically members. Others can join for a reasonable fee. AWP's services include a magazine, *The AWP Chronicle,* a catalog of writing programs, a placement service, an annual meeting, and a number of awards and publications. The organization is probably the nearest thing to a "network" of writers in the nation, and can provide contact with other writers, as well as valuable information on prizes, programs, presses, and the ideas current in the teaching of writing.

Poets & Writers, Inc. (72 Spring St., New York, NY 10012). Poets & Writers issues a bimonthly magazine that has articles of high quality and interest to writers, and provides information on contests and on magazines and publishers soliciting manuscripts. The organization also has a number of useful publications that are periodically revised: the *Directory of American Poets and Fiction Writers, Literary Agents: A Writer's Guide,* and *Author and Audience: A Readings and Workshops Guide;* and an annual listing called *Writers' Conferences.* Their Information Center keeps track of more than 6,000 writers and provides a telephone service to answer questions relating to writers' practical needs.

Writer's Market, Writer's Digest Books (Cincinnati). A new edition comes out each year with practical advice on how to sell manuscripts as well as lists of book and magazine publishers, agents, foreign markets, and other services for writers.

ACKNOWLEDGMENTS

INDEX